AVID

READER

PRESS

THE
ROAD
THAT
MADE
AMERICA

A MODERN PILGRIM'S JOURNEY
ON THE GREAT WAGON ROAD

JAMES DODSON

AVID READER PRESS

NEW YORK   AMSTERDAM/ANTWERP   LONDON
TORONTO   SYDNEY/MELBOURNE   NEW DELHI

AVID READER PRESS
An Imprint of Simon & Schuster, LLC
1230 Avenue of the Americas
New York, NY 10020

First Avid Reader Press hardcover edition July 2025

AVID READER PRESS and colophon are trademarks of Simon & Schuster, LLC

Interior design by Ruth Lee-Mui

Manufactured in the United States of America

1   3   5   7   9   10   8   6   4   2

Library of Congress Control Number: 2025936160

ISBN 978-1-4767-4674-6
ISBN 978-1-4767-4677-7 (ebook)

To the many descendants of the Great Wagon Road

History will always find you, and wrap you in its thousand arms.
—Joy Harjo, Poet Laureate of the United States

Every tourist should become a pilgrim.
—Rupert Sheldrake

For where the beginning is, there will the end be.
—The Gospel of Thomas

CONTENTS

PROLOGUE

THE LOST MILL

NOT LONG AFTER DAWN ON A FOGGY NEW YEAR'S MORNING, MY WIFE, WENDY, and I picked our way through a tangle of thorns and swamp alders to the base of an eight-lane interstate bridge spanning the Haw River, one of North Carolina's most historic waterways.

We were in search of something I'd lost.

Or, more accurately, hoped to find again: the remains of my double-great-grandfather's gristmill and furniture shop.

I'd seen it only once, stony remnants in the river's ice-jointed waters on a late-December afternoon in 1966 when my older brother, Dick, and I accompanied our father to gather bittersweet and shoot mistletoe out of the ancient white oak forest that grew around his grandparents' long-abandoned homeplace on Buckhorn Road, not far from the colonial-era town of Hillsborough, North Carolina.

Until that winter afternoon, save for a general understanding that our family had deep roots in the red clay of the upper Carolina Piedmont reaching back to pre-revolutionary times, Dick and I knew few details of our ancestral origins in the Old North State. We knew that our grandfather was a skilled cabinetmaker like his grandfather, and that our people were rural farmers, craftsmen, and preachers living along Buckhorn Road near Dodsons Crossroads for many generations, but that was pretty much the extent of it. The story of where our people originated and how they got to

North Carolina in the first place curiously remained an untold tale in a family full of Southern storytellers.

That gap began to narrow significantly that afternoon, however, when our father, whose enthusiasm for outdoor life was rivaled only by his passion for American history, decided to act upon one of his favorite expressions, which Dick and I heard often: "How can you possibly know where you're going, boys, if you never learn where you came from?"

My brother was fifteen. I was two years younger. At a minimum, we knew where we'd *been*.

We were sons of a veteran newspaperman who'd hauled his young family to outposts across the Deep South during some of the most turbulent years of the early Civil Rights Movement, before returning us home to Greensboro midway through my second year of grammar school; seasoned explorers of historic towns and battlefields, Indian burial mounds, state and federal parks, anyplace where "nature and history are calling," as our wise old man liked to say. Family vacations and camping trips had always involved some form of investigation of local history or folklore—hikes through historic forests, guided ghost walks, overnighting in drafty hotels where George Washington or Robert E. Lee allegedly once billeted, dining in places where history left its indelible mark in the form of a suspicious hole above the fireplace mantel, possibly from a stray Yankee Minié ball. Even hokey roadside tourist traps—*especially* hokey roadside tourist traps—plentiful across the sleepy American South of the 1950s and '60s, had to have, at a minimum, some shred of connection to "real history" to merit a stop. The purchase of a "genuine" coonskin cap (made in Taiwan) or replica Confederate forage cap inevitably inspired lengthy ruminations on the rigors of pioneer life or the tragic consequences of the South's doomed Lost Cause.

In time, as girls and cars seized custody of our teenaged brains, my brother and I affectionately took to calling our quirky, quote-loving, history-mad old man "Opti the Mystic" owing to his unassailable belief in the importance of knowing "America's story—the good, the bad, all the gritty and inconvenient details"—to say nothing of his embarrassing habit of quoting long-dead poets and Roman philosophers to our impressionable dates when they least expected it.

Perhaps the best example of Opti's newsman's nose for history, in fact, occurred days after we arrived home to Greensboro following an odyssey through the Deep South in early January 1960. Without warning, he turned up at our new elementary school on the pretense of returning library books we'd acquired only days before at the ornate redbrick downtown public library. In reality, it was a jailbreak.

Experience told us a new field adventure was afoot, perhaps another hike through nearby Guilford Courthouse National Military Park, where we'd recently learned how General Nathanael Greene's ragtag Continentals and local militias mortally wounded Lord Cornwallis's redcoat army in a forest of beech and oak, not three miles from our new backyard. Instead, a short time later, we wound up in a milling crowd of agitated white onlookers near the "colored" entrance to the Center Movie Theater on Greensboro's main drag, North Elm Street, watching as four brave African American students from nearby North Carolina A&T University (now State University) attempted to nonviolently integrate the "Whites Only" lunch counter at the Woolworth's just across the street. This important day, February 2, 1960, day two of the historic peaceful sit-in protest that would become broadly cited as a defining moment in the birth of the nonviolent Civil Rights Movement in America, was my seventh birthday.

"Fellas," Opti was moved to say as we looked on, "you're witnessing important history here. This moment isn't just going to change Greensboro or the South. It's going to change America."

The old man was right, of course, though Greensboro would be merely one small signal fire in a social revolution that was beginning to send up sparks (and sadly remains incomplete more than half a century after the fact). Still, looking back through the palimpsest of years, that moment brought home to both my brother and me the complexity of America's ever-evolving story, the contradictions as well as the conventional narratives, the importance of learning the unassailable facts behind events, *especially* the gritty and inconvenient details.

Six years later, on Buckhorn Road, that feeling emerged again as we followed an overgrown road through a forest of white oaks to my great-grandfather's homeplace half a mile off Buckhorn Road, a silvered ruin missing doors and windows, long abandoned, with dark birds nesting in its eaves and saplings sprouting through its collapsed porch.

"That's where Uncle Jimmy and Aunt Emma lived, your grandfather's birthplace," Opti explained as we stood staring at the house. One end of the front porch had been swallowed whole by a Gordian knot of wisteria vines thick as a grown man's arm. Seeing the place after so many years, I noticed, visibly stirred something in our father. "I spent some of the happiest summers of my life right here," he said, noting how "Uncle Jimmy," his grandfather, would allow him at age ten to lead the horses up from the lower pasture to the barn in the evening and Aunt Emma often took him along when she gathered native plants for her wildflower remedies and healing balms. "She was a genuine healer and a remarkable woman, beloved by everyone along Buckhorn Road."

For good reason, it seemed: Mary Emma Tate Dodson, we learned, was the closest thing Dodsons Crossroads had for a doctor between Chapel Hill and the county seat of Hillsborough, a woman completely in her element in the surrounding forest and meadows of her farm. She was the middle child of a prominent Orange County citizen named George Washington Tate, who owned the most important gristmill in the region and his grandfather's furniture shop on the banks of the Haw River.

The Tates, Opti explained, were socially prominent people of Scottish heritage who called the nearby town of Mebane home, probably not entirely pleased that their middle female child had chosen to marry a poor but charming horse farmer named Jimmy Dodson. "Uncle Jimmy was a real character, a land-rich, dollar-poor horse breeder who loved to play his fiddle at country dances. Quite the rural dandy. You've seen his picture."

Indeed, I was fascinated by the photo that had long sat on a shelf at home in Greensboro, a hand-tinted daguerreotype of a thin but dapper fellow dressed in a cheap Sunday suit of blue serge, sporting a bristling white mustache and fedora hat tilted at a jaunty angle, a rogue twinkle in his eye. (To this day, Uncle Jimmy's fiddle sits on my own fireplace mantel. That same photograph hangs on a nearby wall.)

But if Aunt Emma meant so much to the people of Buckhorn Road and Dodsons Crossroads, I wondered, why were there also no photographs of *her* on our family wall?

"Fair question. Don't recall ever seeing a photograph of Aunt Emma,"

Opti admitted. "Quite possibly because of what happened to her. There are unanswered questions."

With that, he fell silent. Dick and I exchanged looks, wondering what the old man *wasn't* telling us. After a few moments, however, he continued.

Clearing his throat, he explained that Aunt Mary Emma Dodson had taken her own life by hanging herself from a crossbeam of the porch where sparrows now wintered. "That was the summer of 1928. Her four sons and two daughters were all grown and gone by then." He looked at me. "I was your age that summer, Bo. Suicide was an unspeakable tragedy back then, a black mark on any proud country family. No one spoke of Emma's death for decades. Her death became our family's biggest tragedy. And our greatest mystery."

I asked why she would kill herself.

"Another good question. I always felt, as did others in the family, that she was a woman living with a foot in two very different worlds."

Not long after her death, he added, unable to make sense of what happened, Uncle Jimmy abandoned their farm and lived with relatives till the end of his days. Jimmy and Aunt Emma were buried side by side over in the Chestnut Ridge Methodist churchyard not far from where we stood. Nature soon reclaimed the Dodson homeplace.

And then we just kept walking. As was his way, however, Opti had casually passed along something important that took me the rest of our time in the woods that afternoon to process. As we headed back to the car, loaded with mistletoe and bittersweet, I asked what he meant by "a woman with a foot in two very different worlds." His answer was a big surprise.

"There's a strong possibility, though no one knows for sure, that your great-grandmother was Native American, a full-blooded Cherokee or possibly Catawba Indian lady, adopted when she was an infant by old George Tate during one of his trips to the Blue Ridge hills to help establish Methodist churches out west. Someone called them 'gospel rides,'" he said. "In my mind this would explain a lot about my grandmother—her strong connection to nature and intimacy with the land, her powerful sense of place and medicinal knowledge of plants, even the choice of husband. Uncle Jimmy was the black sheep of the Dodson clan—in his own way."

Orange County Courthouse records only compounded the mystery around Aunt Emma's death, he continued. Unlike with other Tate family members, records conflicted about her date of birth as March 6 of either 1860 or 1857, with no mention of the location of the event. "That was a particularly unsettled time in America, especially in this state's western counties. Debates over secession were growing violent and President Andrew Jackson's removal of the Cherokee to Oklahoma still reverberated two decades after the fact. A lot of courthouses were burned, and records were either destroyed or altered in the chaos of the war and Reconstruction. No one ever said it out loud, but my brothers and sister certainly believed that our grandmother was an Indian orphan. So did my father and his cousins, Josie and Ida. You can ask them about it when we see them."

Josie and Ida Dodson were our father's elderly second cousins, a pair of independent spinster ladies well into their eighties who lived a mile or so farther down Buckhorn Road in a log house their father built after the Civil War. They were proud country women still happily residing in the nineteenth century, heating their modest log dwelling by a lone woodstove and lighting it by oil lamps and a single electric kitchen light bulb. They were locally known for their bounteous vegetable garden that fed neighbors as well as themselves and for raising and butchering their own chickens and pigs. Beyond their antique style of dress—floral high-neck dresses, laced-up ankle-high boots, and wool sweaters that Ida knitted—to my mind the most exotic things about them were their impressive wall of books and their separate outhouses. Josie was the serious reader of the two, with a collection of religious titles and histories that included several biographies of her hero Daniel Boone, the famous frontiersman who spent his teenage years in the nearby Yadkin Valley, a direct ancestor of whom had supposedly been a childhood friend of Josie's as a young girl. Their separate outhouses were the real showstoppers, however. Ida's featured an elaborate carved moon on its applewood door; Josie's an elegant five-pointed shooting star. Dad affectionately called his spinster cousins the "Moon and Star Girls." Every Christmas and Easter we took them Whitman's Samplers, new yarn, Pond's cold cream, and back issues of *Reader's Digest* and *Life* magazine.

When we took them these items plus a sugar-cured ham for the New

Year, Josie—the cheerful "talker" of the two—gave me a slim biography of Boone (that I still own) and a reproduction of Ben Franklin's *Poor Richard's Almanack*, pointing out that Franklin was a newspaperman "like your smart daddy." And more important to me at that moment, she also confirmed the intriguing story of Aunt Emma's unexplained origins and death. "Her passing, child, was such a grievous thing for us all," she remembered, shaking her head. "It broke all our hearts, especially Uncle Jimmy's. He was never the same after that, a ruined fella."

"Was she really an Indian?" I blurted out.

Cousin Josie's dark eyes suddenly shone. "Oh, *yes*, dear. Very much so! A real Indian princess, a true healer. She taught all of us young ones about living in God's majestic natural world."

As she said this, I was still thinking about what transpired on the drive home from Aunt Emma's homeplace weeks before, when Opti showed us something incredible.

As a newly finished interstate bridge approached, he suddenly veered to the shoulder of the highway and switched off the engine, hopping out.

"Since we're on the subject, fellas, there's something you need to see."

We followed him down a steeply graded slope thick with weeds and brambles to the edge of the darkly swirling Haw River. He pointed to something in the water, near the pylons of the new bridge.

"It doesn't look like much now but *that's* the remains of George Washington Tate's gristmill. Aunt Emma's daddy. I used to stop and fish here when I had my first car and newspaper job in Durham."

It took us a moment to see what he saw, but then there it was: an arrangement of submerged stones that, indeed, appeared to be the foundation of something carved into the west bank of the river. "In its day, this was the most important mill in this part of the state because it was the primary ford of the Great Trading Path that came this way from Virginia to the Great Wagon Road in the west, which is how our people got here before the Revolutionary War."

"What's the Great Wagon Road?" The name sparked like flint in my head.

That was the name, he explained, of the primary road of frontier America used by thousands of European settlers from Pennsylvania to reach the colonial backcountry of Maryland, Virginia, and the Carolinas in the eighteenth century, a mass migration route that brought all three wings of our family to the western frontier—our Scottish and English ancestors who settled in the Piedmont region of North Carolina and our mother's German ancestors who came down the road to western Maryland sometime before the Revolutionary War. "Up North it was called the Great Philadelphia Wagon Road," he added, "because that was where most of them arrived on American shores. Down this way it had other names like the Carolina Road or simply the Great Road. It had not only opened the Southern frontier and wilderness east of the Appalachian Mountains to America's first settlers but served as the gateway for the exploration of the American West."

This was pure catnip to my eighth-grade brain, to think our people originated someplace in the heart of faraway Europe and traveled over an ocean and crossed an uncharted wilderness simply to reach the place where we were standing at that moment by the River Haw, hundreds of years later.

"Is it still here?"

I remember how Opti the Mystic glanced over at the submerged stones in the water. As usual, well ahead of my thoughts.

"No question about it. But civilization has a way of covering up the past, leaving nature to reclaim whatever is no longer of use. I'm sure you could find traces of that old road if you knew where to look and took the time to seek it."

As we climbed back up the bank, I asked if we could someday do that—go searching for the Great Wagon Road.

My father smiled. "How about this, sport. Someday I'll give you the keys to the Roadmaster and *you* can go find it yourself."

To this day, I have no idea whether Opti was joking or planting a seed in my head.

Whichever it was, I never forgot.

Now, after more than half a century, no mill stones were visible in the swirling Haw that cold New Year's morning Wendy and I went in search of George Tate's mill—just debris from recent winter flooding and pieces of garbage flung from vehicles hurtling over the recently expanded interstate bridge.

Even so, I knelt on its bank, sipping my cold coffee as I tried to picture what the spot must have looked like when creaking wagons carefully crossed the fording spot below the gristmill, heading east to Hillsborough bearing weary settlers from faraway Scotland, England, or Germany. Family ground, someone said, is sacred ground.

As she is prone to do, my plucky wife wandered off to explore a bit on her own.

How long I squatted there in my private fog bank, I simply cannot say. The Franciscan theologian Richard Rohr talks about the power of liminal space—the *thin* space that exists between what is familiar and the holy unknown, where one world touches another for a few precious moments and everything suddenly becomes clear. This is where I was at that instant, a spiritual kid of thirteen briefly kneeling between worlds, suddenly thinking about Opti, Aunt Emma, and the wintry sight of her vanishing homeplace, hearing the altar call of a lost frontier road I'd probably traveled most of my life without knowing it.

A short while later, I heard Wendy's quiet voice from a deep tangle of thorny overgrowth near the base of the bridge.

"Hey, babe. Come have a look at this."

I picked my way through a wall of briars and found her standing halfway along a narrow metal maintenance footbridge running above the base of the bridge. She was looking down at an even larger mass of matted vegetation. As I joined her, she smiled and pointed.

"There."

It took me a moment to see what she saw. But suddenly, I saw it too—a deep cut in the earth, a narrow channel lined with perfectly smooth stones, unmistakably a water source of some sort made by long-forgotten men, perhaps the millrace or a feeder stream leading to the mill's waterwheel, buried by a century's worth of mud and overgrowth.

"How about that," I said.

Blessed with the intuitive wisdom of her own immigrant Irish grandmother, who found her way to rural Ohio in the early nineteenth century, my Yankee wife, familiar with a boyhood notion that had gripped my inner eighth grader for at least half a century, knew exactly the right words to say.

"I do believe I hear that old wagon road calling your name."

I simply nodded. Not for the first time, I heard it too.

PART ONE

BEGINNINGS

ONE

GOD AND GOOD BEER

IF THERE'S ANY TRUTH TO THE ANCIENT IDEA THAT A GOOD JOURNEY BEGINS with a single step—even one delayed many decades—perhaps it's only fitting that a journey I've dreamed of making since I was knee high to a historic road marker begins with an excellent colonial beer and a surprise wedding toast.

Four fine colonial-era-inspired beers sit at my fingertips on a late-August evening, a sampling board of brews that includes Alexander Hamilton's Federalist Ale, Thomas Jefferson Tavern Ale, George Washington's full-bodied porter, plus a spruce beer called Poor Richard's, made from Ben Franklin's own house recipe. While I await delivery of my period-correct supper, savoring the thought of the long and unknown road ahead, I nibble delicious cinnamon-and-pecan biscuits from Tom Jefferson's own Monticello recipe book and polish off all four mini-glasses of beer, promptly ordering a full pint of Franklin's best.

Three hours after my arrival in Philadelphia, I am a party of one but hardly alone in the noisy, candlelit second-floor dining room of historic City Tavern, a place that claims to be the birthplace of American cuisine.

A few feet from where I sit, awaiting delivery of their own suppers, is a table with three young couples who seem to be having a lively celebration of friendship and matrimony, offering rowdy toasts to a blushing couple while a ginger-haired woman struggles to keep their trivia game on the rails.

"Where and what year," she calls out over her boisterous tablemates, reading from a game card, "were the Articles of Confederation, the nation's first constitution, created?"

My ear rises to the question like a trout to a mayfly. Nobody but me, however, is paying the slightest attention.

"Earth to *people*," the frustrated moderator declares, "are we playing pub trivia or *not*?"

The big fellow seated next to her at the table, his Penn State ball cap reversed, makes a comment that produces a burst of laughter and touched pewter mugs. She glances my way and shrugs.

"Sorry for the noise," she apologizes. "We're celebrating a surprise engagement. You probably can't even enjoy your book because of us." She nods toward the paperback resting at my elbow.

I assure her that reading by eighteenth-century candlelight isn't my thing.

"Tony and Elise—they're the two cuties at the end of the table— surprised us this afternoon with news of their engagement."

She adds that they are the last of her college crowd to marry, having met on trivia night at a bar at Penn State thirteen years ago. "The boys played club lacrosse together. We do this every few years in the cities where we now live." They've convened from Nashville to San Francisco. This year it's Philadelphia, so American history and the birth of democracy is their chosen topic. My new friend sips her white wine and gently slurs her words. "Every time we get together, I'm afraid, we seem less interested in trivia and more interested in just being silly tourists."

For an instant, I'm tempted to make a plea for more silliness in a world that seems to be fracturing by the minute. But there's a response more relevant. "I believe it's York, Pennsylvania. November 1777. By the way, the Articles of Confederation contained the first use of the phrase 'United States of America.'"

She checks her game card and her freckled face lights up, evidently pleased that the lonely old dude in the dark corner of the room knows the answer off the top of his graying head.

"*Correct!* How'd you know *that*?"

"Because it happened on the Great Wagon Road."

Her eyebrows arch. She scooches her chair closer to mine and tilts forward, so we don't have to shout as her mates launch into some sort of fraternal fight song. "So, what is the Great Wagon Road?"

She is far from alone in asking. The Great Wagon Road is probably the least known historic road in America. So, I give her the brief elevator speech I've prepared for just such moments: "It's the eighteenth century's backcountry road that tens of thousands of European settlers traveled to find their place in the wilderness of North America, our original immigrant highway."

She gulps her chardonnay, surprised and grinning. "Seriously? That is *so* cool!" A firm hand comes at me in the candlelight. Gina Sparrow, I learn, hails from Grand Rapids.

"As it happens," I add, taking her hand, "I'm setting off tomorrow to travel it."

She wonders how long the trip will take. I admit that I have no clue. The road stretches more than eight hundred miles, beginning on Market Street in Philadelphia and ending in Augusta, Georgia, crossing six contiguous states and some of the most historic and hallowed landscapes, battlefields, and burying grounds of eastern America, not to mention village squares where democracy first took root and bloomed. During its peak years of use in the 1750s, I explain, a determined traveler on horseback could sometimes make it from Philly to Virginia or the Carolinas in a matter of weeks, though most traveled by wagon and in groups for safety and often took two or three months to arrive (provided decent weather and no unexpected problems like flooded river fords, wrong turns, sudden illness, or hostile encounters with man or beast). Many travelers stopped along the way to rest and resupply for lengthy periods of time, sometimes taking years to reach their final destinations. My hope is to split the difference and complete the road in just three or four weeks, I tell Gina, though in truth I have no idea if this time frame is reasonable or a romantic pipe dream.

"In that case," she says with a laugh, "I sure hope you have a good horse and wagon!"

"As a matter of fact, I do. My wagon has three hundred and fifty horses."

She gives a charming goose honk when I explain that I'm traveling in a vintage 1994 Buick Roadmaster Estate station wagon with a 350-horsepower V-8 engine, acquired ten years ago from an elderly retiree in North Carolina with this very trip in mind. The Pearl, as I call it, is like many things in America: a symbol of a bygone era, one of the last true iconic station wagons that rolled off the line before General Motors switched to building SUVs.

"Is that the one with, like, the seat facing backward and fake wood paneling and stuff?" she asks.

"That's it."

"Oh, wow! We had one like that when I was little. My younger brother and I fought to the death over that third seat every time we went on a vacation."

Just then a pair of waiters in colonial livery and brass-buckled shoes swoops down on us holding six suppers on large trays for Gina's table. Quickly but carefully, they place steaming dishes in front of each member of her party.

"Well," she says, "I guess I should get back to my friends. Sorry to interrupt your reading. What's your book about, if I may ask? The Great Wagon Road, I suppose?"

"Indirectly." I show her Susan Cheever's addictively readable *Drinking in America: Our Secret History*, one of several histories, biographies, and works of favorite poets I've packed for the road.

Gina tilts forward and asks if I can give her a "juicy tidbit" about drinking for the group's next trivia night, since drinking now seems to be their favorite group activity.

I mention that the Pilgrims were probably legally drunk when they landed at Plymouth Harbor in 1620, missing their target area of Virginia by hundreds of miles, and only put to Cape Cod Bay's cold November shore because they'd run out of beer.

She looks surprised. "I thought the Pilgrims were *religious*!"

"Very much so. But theirs is a story of God and good beer."

Ignoring her supper, she asks to hear more. I briefly mention that fermentation made beer safe to drink from the Middle Ages to the Age of Enlightenment, even suitable for small children. As a result, according to Cheever, every man, woman, child, and ship's mate on the *Mayflower* was provisioned a full gallon of beer per day for their grueling ocean crossing.

The big fellow next to Gina suddenly leans our way, tuning in as I mention that after three terrible months at sea, one of the first things the pious

Pilgrims did was construct a brewhouse for making fresh beer, followed by a tavern and a house of worship, a pattern of settlement that established itself across New England and the rest of colonial America.

"That's why Ben Franklin said beer is proof that God loves us, hon," he contributes with a mouth full of something.

"This is Jerry. My husband," Gina says, stopping just shy of a wifely eye roll. "We got married in April. I don't think Ben Franklin really said that, Jerry. You just saw it on a T-shirt at Penn's Landing."

Jerry grins. "True, babe. But everyone knows Ben Franklin really said it."

"He's going down the Great Wagon Road," Gina declares matter-of-factly, nodding at me. "All the way to Georgia."

Jerry, chewing slowly, considers this news. "Never heard of it."

Gina shakes her head. "It's *only* the most historic road in America, Jerry."

He nods. "Yeah? So why you doin' *that*?"

The simplest explanation is that I am finally yielding to my inner eighth grader, hoping to find the flame tenders of a forgotten American highway before time runs out, though I don't feel the slightest inclination to share this with Jerry, or anyone else for that matter. Six months ago, two weeks before my planned starting date, a mysterious pain in my side sent me to see Doc Morris for a checkup that led to a surprise double surgery to remove both a dodgy gallbladder and a carrot-sized tumor from my lower intestines, the first serious medical crisis of my life. Time waits for no man. All that matters now, following several months of slow recovery, is that I've been cleared by Doc Morris to hit the road, and not a minute too soon.

Fortunately, Jerry's plucky bride rises to my rescue.

"Because, *Jerry*, his people came down the Wagon Road and family history is totally freaking hot right now. Even you should know *that* much."

In truth, Jerry is far more interested in his platter of ale-braised sausage, garlic mash, and seasoned German sauerkraut. And who can blame him? His supper smells divine. I ordered the same dish, as it happens, with a side of chestnut fritters and corn-fried oysters from Martha Washington's personal cookbook.

Gina gives me a second firm handshake. "Well, golly, it's been so much fun to talk with you. I hope you find lots of cool things on the Great Wagon Road."

I thank her for the kind words and wish she and her merry band of trivial pursuers a long and prosperous journey of their own.

My choice of City Tavern as a starting point is no accident.

Not only does it sit just two short blocks from the original Great Philadelphia Wagon Road, but it opened for business in January 1773, just past the peak years of the Wagon Road's use. At the time, Philadelphia was the second-largest and most prosperous town in North America, the third largest in all of the British empire, and the center of colonial art, culture, and commerce, boasting twenty thousand citizens, brick streets illuminated by whale oil lamps, a college, three libraries, and the first hospital in the New World. Twenty ships a week arrived at its busy ports on the Delaware River, releasing hundreds of European immigrants into Philly's bustling streets, where wagons teeming with produce cultivated by German immigrant farmers south and west of the city arrived daily through the summer months.

Funded by fifty-three prominent Philadelphians who paid twenty-five pounds sterling to be chartered members and investors, among them a future governor of Pennsylvania and several future signers of the Declaration of Independence, the tavern was considered the finest dining experience in the British colonies. Its grand opening was accompanied by glowing notice by the ambitious publisher of the *Pennsylvania Gazette*, a sociable polymath named Benjamin Franklin, who noted that the five-story brick building featured the best equipped kitchen in the city, a well-stocked bar, two coffee rooms ideal for private conversations, three dining rooms, and the second-largest ballroom in the New World. There were also five lodging rooms and a servants' quarters for hire.

It became a weekly gathering spot for foreign dignitaries and members of the First and Second Continental Congresses. Regulars included Franklin, Thomas Jefferson, Sam Adams, Dr. Benjamin Rush, George Washington, and Patrick Henry. It was here, as talk of revolution crackled in the steamy summer air of 1776, that George Washington supposedly met John Adams for the first time, following Adams's wearying ride down the King's Highway from Boston. Adams was particularly impressed with City Tavern's quality of fare. ("A fresh welcome," he committed to his diary afterward. "As elegant as was ever laid upon a table.") And even after the British army took possession of the city in 1777 and the Congress fled town, it remained the place to be for Philadelphia's elites. Its popularity lasted well into the early nineteenth century, declining only after the surrounding neighborhood fell into disrepute, causing the once proud establishment to eventually shut its doors. The building was used as a mercantile exchange until fire gutted the structure in 1834, only to sit as a vacant hulk until the building was razed twenty years later.

Its seeds of rebirth were sown in 1948 when the Truman administration authorized the US Department of the Interior to create an Independence National Historical Park, which would include several original structures in the oldest part of the city. Following twenty-five years of painstaking research and urban archaeology, City Tavern was reproduced brick-for-brick in time to celebrate the nation's bicentennial in 1976, becoming a popular tourist stop for almost two decades until it closed doors for a second time in 1992.

Two years later, it was resurrected again by an enterprising German immigrant named Walter Staib, an award-winning chef who hailed from a family of celebrated cooks and bakers. With an exclusive contract to serve as the sole proprietor of historic City Tavern, Staib researched and developed a revolutionary culinary concept based on the authenticity of colonial-era cooking. An award-winning cooking show on PBS called *A Taste of History* soon followed.

"You had two irresistible subjects—cooking and American history," Chef Staib told me over the phone. "No nation on earth can match the cultural diversity of America, a fact beautifully reflected in the astonishing diversity of our early American cuisine. We talk about farm to table today— ha! Everything then was fresh, local, and far more creative than people of today can even imagine. The more I traveled and researched, the more I became convinced that we had the opportunity to tell the story of America through colonial cooking, a melting pot of blended traditions and tastes from everywhere beyond our shores. That's what made City Tavern the first great restaurant in America."

Trooping downstairs for a nightcap in the tavern bar, I find myself thinking about Staib's mission, and how it mirrors my own. I, too, had come to this odyssey through researching frontier American life. The source that rekindled my long-dormant fantasy of finding and traveling the Wagon Road of my ancestors had been a folksy, dog-eared, long-out-of-print gem from 1973 called *The Great Wagon Road: From Philadelphia to the South* by the late Williamsburg historian Parke Rouse, Jr. that I'd found in a used bookshop in Roanoke in 2006 while serving as writer-in-residence at Hollins University. Packed with information and a schematic drawing that showed the approximate path of the road from Philadelphia to Georgia, it quickly became my inspiration, and my bible.

Owing to poor or nonexistent early recordkeeping, historians have never fully settled on the precise numbers of America's first mass migration movement. But most generally agree that well north of one hundred thousand immigrant travelers made the arduous trek down the Great Wagon Road between the close of the seventeenth century and the start of the American Revolution—hearty dreamers who arrived from all corners of western Europe in successive waves large and small: German Lutherans, English Quakers, Saxony Moravians, and Swiss Mennonites; Scots-Irish Presbyterians and Wesley Methodists; French Huguenots and Dutch adventurers, foundational generations of the world's first immigrant nation.

Not unlike refugees from our own time, the road's original travelers were life-hardened souls willing to brave a perilous ocean crossing to escape a continent ravaged by a thirty-year religious war. Fleeing their fractured native lands, some arrived hoping to build a New Jerusalem in the southern American wilderness. Others came in search of a mythic land of milk and honey they'd heard awaited in the untamed vastness of the North American backcountry.

Many sold everything they owned to fund the journey, or traveled as indentured servants committed to work their way into a New World life, most arriving on the busy docks of Philadelphia or nearby Delaware shore fueled by blind faith and a willingness to endure whatever hardships of disease or danger they might encounter for the chance of a fresh start. Others left behind hard-earned lives as prosperous farmers and skilled artisans, answering an ageless call to seek greater prosperity in a place they'd only heard wondrous tales about.

Undeterred by uncertainty, they claimed land and carved out farms, planted crops, formed communities and militias, built taverns and raised churches, created log schools and trading posts that grew into crossroad settlements as southbound traffic increased across the turbulent decades of the eighteenth century. Many put down roots while others moved on, restless to find even more land, fewer people, more freedom, and better soil. In time, a dozen towns populated the great fertile valleys that lay between the Blue Ridge and the Allegheny Mountains, an Appalachian wilderness stretching from Western Pennsylvania to Georgia, seeding a fledgling nation's first tender shoots of commerce, politics, religion, education, and industry—providing both a gateway and a staging ground for an even broader opening of the lands beyond the Appalachian range, into the Golden West itself.

A longtime friend named Tom Sears, an expert on Southern colonial architecture and furniture, once described the Great Wagon Road to me as "America's first technology highway and Fertile Crescent of American democracy—essentially the road that made America." Everything from the Conestoga wagon to early computer processing was developed along it. As the nation grew, villages and towns and cities of the Wagon Road became, in effect, the first incubators of America's early industrial age.

By my rough count, more than a dozen colleges and universities had their beginnings on or near the Great Wagon Road, simple affairs typically begun by Presbyterian preachers who maintained that Christian education was next to godliness. Equally important to the evolving culture, technology, and commerce was the flood of German artisans and farmers who brought refined farming techniques and Old World craftsmanship to the beating heart of a wild frontier, resulting in revolutionary agriculture and some of the world's finest furniture, decorative arts, and metal craftsmanship. Along with their advanced farming skills, Wagon Road Germans also imported their love of communal sacred hymns and the music of Haydn and Bach, while their feisty independent Scots-Irish counterparts brought Old World balladry and narrative folk song, dance, and poetry, and a God-given skill for fighting and making excellent corn whiskey.

In time, their soulful fiddle music took permanent root in the shaded hollers of Appalachia, blending with African slave songs to give birth to the original American musical forms of Southern gospel, bluegrass, and country music; Johnny Cash's and June Carter's ancestors were travelers of the

Great Wagon Road. So were the forebears of Bill Monroe, the Father of Bluegrass, and Nashville songbirds Patsy Cline, Dolly Parton, Willie Nelson, and a thousand other sons and daughters of today's country music scene.

And they were not the only ones: Joe Wilson, America's leading roots-music historian, observed that "a quarter of Americans today have an ancestor who traveled the Great Wagon Road. You can still see traces of it, a track across high ridges, a trough through piney woods, guarded by wild turkey and chipmunks, a road that was in use for a century—the most important road in American history."

Given the road's strategic importance on the edge of the contested western frontier, it's no mystery why three major North American wars happened on or near it, including the early days of the bloody French and Indian conflict and pivotal Revolutionary War encounters at Camden, Kings Mountain, Cowpens, and Guilford Courthouse.

Eighty years on, the Confederacy's doomed Valley of Virginia campaigns followed the road north to the pivotal bloodbaths of Antietam and Gettysburg, bold strikes meant to force an end to the war in the South's favor; instead, they became killing fields that turned the tide in favor of the Union. In November 1863, Abraham Lincoln—whose grandfather settled on a homestead just off the Wagon Road north of Harrisonburg, Virginia—gave his Gettysburg Address from the Soldiers' National Cemetery overlooking an early branch of the Great Wagon Road.

Half a dozen of America's presidents, in fact, grew up on or near it, including a young George Washington, who began his military service as an Indian scout along the road and later lost—then won—his first elected office in the settlement of Winchester. Thomas Jefferson, whose daddy, Peter Jefferson, helped William & Mary mathematician Joshua Fry survey and officially name the "Great Waggon Road" on a map from Philadelphia to North Carolina's Yadkin River in 1753, traveled the road extensively throughout his life, and even owned the spectacular Natural Bridge that the Great Wagon Road traversed.

Fellow Virginian James Madison, Andrew Jackson, James Polk, and Woodrow Wilson each had birthright connections, while Zachary Taylor and Andrew Johnson traveled it extensively throughout their early careers in service to war and government.

Equally important to the evolving narrative of a young nation were legendary folk figures like Daniel Boone, who at age sixteen followed the Wagon Road with his family to North Carolina's fertile Yadkin Valley, and later took the road back to Big Lick (today's Roanoke) before blazing the Wilderness Road through the Cumberland Gap to the unsettled territories of Kentucky and Ohio; likewise, icons Meriwether Lewis, David Crockett, Molly Pitcher, Susanna Wright, General Daniel Morgan, General Nathanael Greene, Francis Marion, Sam Houston, Thomas "Stonewall" Jackson, "Light-Horse" Harry Lee, and his son Robert E. Lee were part of the romantic saga of the Great Wagon Road.

From the outset of my adventure, the leading question—echoing the one I put to my father by the Haw River in 1966—was whether the original path of the road of my ancestors could somehow be determined after the Great Road effectively accomplished its own vanishing act with the coming of the railroads and ever-expanding towns that created new and improved highways for a nation on the move.

During the early days of my physical recovery, this question was answered by a pair of sources from my own backyard.

The first was an old friend and distinguished Southern historian and expert on North Carolina's historic backcountry roads named Charles Rodenbough, who invited me to lunch after hearing from a mutual friend about my planned Wagon Road odyssey.

It was Charlie who pointed out that interest in the Great Wagon Road had grown dramatically in recent years thanks to the work of a small army of colonial historians, state archaeologists, Southern genealogists, state and local historical associations, preservationists, museum curators, and even everyday history nuts like me. "As a result," said he, "the original path of the road has been pretty well determined and you can follow it. It's probably the most important—but least known—old road in America, one that shaped the values and culture of this country. There are people along the road today who are keeping its stories alive. How exciting that you plan to find them and listen to those stories."

But he had one caveat: "Keep in mind that the Great Wagon Road didn't travel in a straight line. It also had several branches, which might be confusing. Don't be surprised if you get lost just like many of the road's original travelers undoubtedly did. That will probably be half the fun."

It was Charlie who also showed me a copy of the 1753 Frye-Jefferson map that delineated the original path of the road to upper North Carolina, and explained that if I started my "pilgrimage"—his word—by venturing up Sandy Ridge Road just west of Greensboro to the Virginia line, I would eventually come to a small meadow by the South Mayo River where, as he put it, "you will see the spot where your Scottish ancestors crossed into North Carolina."

A few days later, as winter slipped into spring, on a cold afternoon threatening snow, my dog Mulligan and I drove up Sandy Ridge Road to the Virginia state line and found the spot Charlie had described. Ice glittered in the South Mayo River's shallows. Wading ahead of me across a slippery shelf of submerged rock, Mully, my aging flat-haired retriever, dropped her nose and charged up the far bank, while I found myself staring at a wide gully ascending the bare winter woods, clearly the sunken remains of a forgotten road. A shiver ran through me that had little to do with the cold of the afternoon. In my imagination, I almost heard the creaking hinges and grinding complaints of farm wagons inching across the shallow fording spot.

I followed Mully a quarter of a mile up that darkened leaf-strewn gully before turning back in a sudden downpour of sleet, feeling the road's gravitational pull like never before.

Several weeks later, my colleague on the staff of O.Henry magazine, senior editor Nancy Oakley, walked into my office and placed an item from the magazine's events calendar on my desk. "Talk about the hand of providence," she said with a grin.

It was an announcement from the Museum of Early Southern Decorative Arts (MESDA) in Old Salem of an upcoming one-day seminar on the furniture and decorative arts of the Great Wagon Road.

Nancy promptly put me in touch with her friend Robert Leath, MESDA's director of collections, who graciously invited me to sit in on the seminar with a half dozen experts on Southern furniture and decorative arts, several of whom proved to be incomparable sources up and down the Wagon Road, including Alexandra Kirtley of the Philadelphia Museum of Art, who gave me her card and invited me to come see her when I arrived in Philly to start my journey down the road.

Without a doubt, these generous folks, who appeared serendipitously during my summer-long recovery, fired up my imagination and set me on the road of my ancestors with high expectations.

TWO

SIX HUNDRED MILES NEARER THE SUN

THE MORNING AFTER MY NIGHT AT CITY TAVERN, I SET OFF IN THE HEAVY Philadelphia mist to visit Penn's Landing and Penn Treaty Park on the waterfront, places where, according to lore, province founder William Penn made his famous peace treaty with the Delaware Indians in 1683.

Without William Penn, after all, the "Forgotten Founding Father" as he's been called by historians of his era, there would be no Philadelphia Great Wagon Road, not to mention Philly cheesesteaks, Hall & Oates, and possibly American democracy as we know it today.

While boning up on Penn's life and legacy, a man Thomas Jefferson hailed as "the world's most important lawgiver," I came across a portrait of the colony's lord proprietor by muralist Violet Oakley that hangs in the commonwealth's state capitol in Harrisburg. Oakley was the first female artist in America to be granted a commission to produce a mural for a public building. Her soulful *Penn's First Sight of the Shores of Pennsylvania* depicts the moment young William Penn, the new owner of the infant colony of Pennsylvania, stands at the rail of the good ship *Welcome*, chin resting reflectively in hand, all silk ruffles and velvet cape, soberly contemplating the heavily forested shore and monumental task before him.

Penn's haunting stare at his new domain was understandable. Behind him stretched a decade of intense struggle as he—a rebellious Oxford dropout with basic legal training—defended fellow Quakers from being persecuted by the English Crown for their unorthodox religious beliefs, including George Fox, the pacifist founder of the Society of Friends. These actions, underscored by an early rejection of his family's powerful connection to the ruling Anglican Church and startling conversion (via ecstatic awakening at age twenty-three) to the "inner light" of Quaker doctrine, placed the young idealist directly at odds with his own father, a celebrated admiral who had helped Charles II, the so-called Merry Monarch, return to the throne from exile in France by loaning the monarch considerable sums of his own fortune.

These conflicts led to the younger Penn being jailed for alleged treasonous advocacy and briefly tossed into the Tower of London. There he developed a skillful pen and an audacious plan to create a permanent Quaker settlement in the wilds of North America, a scheme he called his "Holy Vision" of a New Jerusalem. It would be open to religious dissenters of every kind.

Like many New World dreamers, however, the only thing the young Quaker firebrand lacked was sufficient funding for his plan. To that end, not long after his father's passing, Penn boldly approached Charles II with the idea of settling his lordship's debt of sixteen thousand pounds to the family Penn by granting him extensive land holdings in North America. In March 1681, to the astonishment of the king's advisers (and even Penn's own family), the young man—then just thirty-five years old—was granted a royal charter to vast holdings of land wedged between the colonies of Maryland, New Jersey, and New York, roughly forty-five thousand square miles, that made Penn, for one shining moment, the largest private landowner in the British Empire. The only condition King Charles included was that the new colony bear "Penn" in its formal name, a tribute to the family's late patriarch. For reasons unknown, young William had initially hoped to call his North American creation "New Wales," but settled on "Sylvania," Latin for "forest land," and was persuaded to add the family name. Thus "Penn-Sylvania" was born. As he wrote to an Irish cloth merchant and close friend named Robert Turner sometime later, he hoped God would make Pennsylvania the "seed of a nation."

Key to establishing the first Quaker colony in North America was a governing set of principles called the Concessions and Agreements. This early document guaranteed freedom of speech and impartial justice for every citizen under British law, but more important, granted Penn sweeping powers to create a basic legal framework upon which the basic principles of American democracy would, in time, take root and grow. Among the new ideas he advanced was a scheme to welcome people of all nationalities and faiths to his new colony, as well as the promise of self-government and religious freedom.

In a letter to Quakers already residing in Pennsylvania, Penn assured his future fellow citizens, "You shall be governed by laws of your own making," and offered a newly enhanced document called a Frame of Government that established a representative form of government highlighted by a council and general assembly, including upper and lower houses of delegates to be elected annually. "Given his own personal austerity," writes Andrew Murphy in his splendid, comprehensive 2019 biography *William Penn: A Life*, "Penn also insisted that Pennsylvania was to have no taverns or alehouses, 'nor any playhouses, nor Morris dances, nor games of dice, cards, board tables, lotteries, bowling greens, horse races, bear baitings, bull baitings, and such like sports, which only tend to idleness and looseness.'"

(Given that by the end of Penn's lifetime there were probably as many taverns as there were churches in cosmopolitan Philadelphia, as Murphy makes clear, much of the groundbreaking Frame of Government was more theoretical than practical. But a century later, it would become, at least in part, inspiration for the writing of the Constitution of the newly created United States of America.)

According to his own diary, Penn placed feet to soil of his new colony on the morning of October 28, 1682, four days after his thirty-eighth birthday. Upon his arrival, he took possession of the village of New Castle and its surrounding territory before heading upriver to the village of Upland, where he disembarked a second time to meet settlers and members of the local Lenape tribe, officially renaming the village Chester.

A short time later, he made an even more significant visit to the Lenape village of tribal chief Shackamaxon to sign the Great Treaty. Pennsylvania lore holds that he also met Turtle Clan chief Tamanend beneath an ancient

elm at river's edge, unarmed and in accord with Quaker custom, reportedly declaring, in the Algonquin language he'd taken pains to learn: "We
meet on the broad pathway of good faith and good-will; no advantage will
be taken on either side, but all shall be openness and love. We are one flesh
and one blood," to which the chief famously replied: "We will live in love
with William Penn and his children as long as the creeks and rivers run, and
while the sun, moon and stars endure." Remarkably, given the European
penchant for violent colonization, the treaty the two men made by mere
handshake would survive for the next seventy years—"The only [American]
treaty sworn to and never broken," as Voltaire dryly pointed out.

By this time, work crews had already started to bring together Penn's
plans for the idealized city he imagined years before laying eyes on the
forested shore of Pennsylvania. His forward-thinking design called for a
buffer zone stretching one-quarter of a mile inland from the waterfront
(thereby avoiding rats and diseases that often accompanied arriving ships)
highlighted by a pair of wide, tree-lined streets, one called High, the other
named Broad, with a large park at their intersection to promote healthy
living and open spaces. This stood in stark contrast to the narrow, congested lanes of most English towns and villages, where disease, vermin, and
sickness flourished in confined spaces, not to mention elevated dangers of
fire and crime. Planned around these main arteries was a grid of smaller
streets with well-spaced houses situated in the center of designated lots.
Every quarter of his visionary city featured its own park or garden area, laid
out over the remaining mile and a half between the banks of the Delaware
and Schuylkill Rivers. "For gardens or orchards, or fields," Penn recorded
in his diary, "that it may be a great green country town which will never
be burned, and [its] spirit always be wholesome." For a name, he chose
Philadelphia, which is Greek for "brotherly love," a message he intended to
profitably send out to the world.

For at the end of the day, though his soul may have shone with the inner
light of Quaker benevolence, William Penn's pragmatic mind was all about
the business of colonization—i.e., finding the right mix of European refugees and immigrants who could make him wealthy. During his earlier travels over the Low Countries of Europe promoting Quaker doctrine among

dissenting Protestant separatist groups, Penn had flooded Holland, Germany, and France with pamphlets written in their native languages, extolling life and unbounded opportunity awaiting in his new American paradise.

Arguably the New World's first great real estate marketer, initially identifying the location of his welcoming new colony as "Six Hundred Miles Nearer the Sun than England," Penn followed with a florid exegesis titled *A Brief Account of the Province of Pennsylvania*, which promoted the superiority of everything from the fine quality of Delaware River fish to the "unrivaled fertility" of Pennsylvania farmland. A confirmed abstainer from alcohol, Penn also rhapsodized about "virtuous" grape vines and grains that were better suited for making wine and beer than any found in Europe; bounteous midsummer hay that rivaled that of England's midlands; glorious fruit trees and abundant game meats all winter. "Mighty Whales roll upon the Coast," he evangelized, "near the mouth of the Bay of Deleware [*sic*] . . . " and on it went.

He even helpfully advised potential colonists on what to bring for the long journey over the salt and suggested the most favorable times to depart—either late winter or early autumn months to avoid the worst of Atlantic storms—helpfully prescribing natural remedies to bring along to prevent seasickness, scurvy, and "foul smells."

"All in all," he modestly summed up, "as we read over this scheme of colonization, it appears to our hearts and better natures as the wisest as well as most generous that has ever appeared among men. Plato's Republic, and Sir Thomas More's Utopia, present nothing with all their wealth of ideal beneficence more striking than this practical, everyday humanitarianism of William Penn."

His most promising clients were prosperous German farmers who were weary of decades of religious-fueled violence, persecution, and social instability resulting from three decades of warfare that wiped out an estimated seven million Europeans, believing they would jump at the chance to pull up stakes and make a fresh start in North America.

To potential settlers, he offered to provide new farm tools and seed free of charge for their first-year harvests, along with a sliding scale for land purchase beginning at fifteen pounds per acre, with "easy terms upon which payment may be made by various plans." Underscoring his sales pitch, he

promised fine weather, productive soil, abundant rain, and excellent relations with local native populations, all of it governed by an enlightened municipality whose laws were shaped by "Brotherly Love."

All this history feels at once very close and very distant as I walk around
misty Penn Treaty Park, where the inveterate tree hugger in me holds out
the impossible hope of finding traces of the famous Treaty Elm beneath
which William Penn met and befriended the Delaware Indians.

Unfortunately, the elm was already 155 years old when Penn and Chief
Tamanend met beneath it in 1683, and became such an attraction it's unlikely that it survived much longer. Benjamin West's painting of the mythical encounter was so significant and well-known across Europe that John
Graves Simcoe, the ruthless commander of the Queen's Rangers, allegedly
posted guards to protect the aging elm during the British occupation of the
city in 1777. The Treaty Elm also made a cameo in some of the paintings
in Edward Hicks's famous *Peaceable Kingdom* series, which depicts Penn
and his new friends making peace beneath its arching limbs in the golden-
lit distance. On my walk through the swirling morning mist to the park, I
manage to learn from my brand-new smartphone that the great elm finally
toppled over in 1810 at the ripe old age of 283, but lived on in the form of
commemorative boxes made from surviving pieces of its wood. One such
box reportedly graced the desk of Abraham Lincoln. Seedlings from shoots
of the Treaty Elm were propagated and distributed across Pennsylvania and
the commonwealth.

"You lost, buddy?"

As rain begins falling, I glance up through misted eyeglasses to find
a grizzled fisherman standing in front of me with a small brown beagle
leashed at his sodden sneakered feet. We appear to be the only idiots out
before official hours in Penn Treaty Park. Beneath his yellow slicker and a
gray hoodie, my questioner wears a vintage Phillies ball cap and unshaven
grin, and he's holding a small spinning rod and can of Yuengling beer.

I explain that I'm looking for the exact spot where the Great Treaty Elm
once stood—or, at a minimum, where one of the tree's great-grandchildren
might be today.

"Can't be sure, but I think we might be standing near the spot," he says,
glancing around. "Or maybe it was over there near that monument." He

nods toward the river where a gray stone rises in the foreground. In the background, a grimy tug is churning past the slate-gray Jersey shore, pushing a barge loaded with garbage toward the Ben Franklin Bridge. The lights of the bridge shine through the gloomy morning like a gilded necklace.

"How's the fishing?" I ask, rather pointlessly, bending to scratch his dog's soggy head, feeling a predictable pang for Mully.

He sips his beer. "Evidently you can't fish here now, but you could when I was a kid. Or at least I remember it that way." He explains that he'd come here to fish off the park's rocks one summer morning with his late grandfather, a foreman with the city water department who told him that shad from the Delaware fed the Founding Fathers.

"Mostly, I think he just wanted to show off the view of the bridge and city. He thought Philly was Emerald City."

With that, the fisherman frees up a hand and introduces himself as Fred Boone from Tennessee. He and his daughter, Emily, are staying at his cousin's place across the street in Fishtown. They're making a late-summer tour of colleges in eastern Pennsylvania, scheduled to visit Swarthmore this noon before heading out to see Lehigh and Moravian University in Bethlehem tomorrow.

"As in Dan'l?"

Fred Boone smiles. "Could be. Most of my family came from North Carolina originally, and some of them claim there's a connection. I don't discourage the impression with my students, even if I have my doubts. There's only a couple thousand Boones in that neck of the woods."

I learn that Fred teaches eighth-grade social studies and driver's ed back home.

"How about you? Chasing the ghost of William Penn?"

I give him my second Wagon Road elevator speech of the trip, casually mentioning that I also hail from the Old North State, as the pace of the rain picks up.

"Fantastic," says Fred. "Maybe you can come talk to my social studies class when you finish your trip. My kids think American history began with the invention of MTV." He tells me about a recent study by the Institute for Citizens & Scholars that found only one in three Americans could pass a citizenship test today. Seventy-two percent couldn't name the original thirteen colonies. Only a quarter could name something Benjamin Franklin invented. "Forty percent believed it was the light bulb."

I share his concerns about the nation's declining knowledge of its own history, adding I'm making this road trip to shore up my own understanding of America's formative years at a moment when our democracy is tearing itself apart from the inside out.

Fred nods in agreement, reaching into his slicker to offer me a lukewarm Yuengling as a tiny consolation prize for the heavy rain and no Treaty Elm. "It's a little early for beer," he says with an embarrassed grin, "but this is all my cousin had for breakfast beverages."

I accept his gift, pop it open, and ask about his grandfather, the proud Philly waterman.

"He took me to my first major league ball game, Phillies versus the Reds. He even bought me a beer. I was fifteen. Can you believe that?"

"Yes, I can."

Since we're swapping crazy uncle stories in the rain, I tell him about my uncle Carson Jewell from Baltimore who took me to my first Orioles game at Memorial Stadium when I was eleven. A mountainous Irishman and leather-lunged Kelly Tires factory foreman who spent the entire pregame warm-ups yelling obscenities at the visiting Yankees, in particular Roger Maris and Mickey Mantle, he bought me a cup of National Bohemian beer and promised to introduce me to Brooks Robinson so I could get my new fielder's glove autographed on condition that I not mention anything about our day at the ballpark to his wife, my sainted Aunt Leona.

"He was as good as his word. I still have the glove."

"Only in America," agrees Fred Boone. We touch cans in tribute to baseball, long-gone grandfathers, and leather-lunged uncles. "Good luck on the Wagon Road. I'm serious, come over to Tennessee and talk to my kids when you finish. I'll take you to my favorite trout stream."

Being a fly fisherman myself, I promise to do that and bid him and Emily good college hunting, recalling a similar journey I made with my own daughter, Maggie, just ten minutes ago, or so it seems.

With a warm beer in hand, I head for Penn's Landing in the steady rain, thinking about the Treaty Elm and this virgin land, how wild and possibly forbidding it must have looked and felt to Penn and his followers as they stepped off the good ship *Welcome*. The teeming modern city I see now as I approach Penn's Landing would have been beyond imaginable to the new arrivals, a trickle of hopeful settlers that would soon become a flood.

It started when French monarch Louis XIV revoked the Edict of Nantes in 1685, a treaty that assured freedom of religion to France's sizable Huguenot population, prompting half a million French and Swiss Huguenots to flee their native lands for sanctuary in England, Northern Ireland, and ultimately the American colonies.

Thirteen German families settled on the outskirts of Philadelphia proper under the care of one Francis Daniel Pistorius, a broad-minded writer and poet who had purchased fifteen thousand acres from William Penn and founded a prosperous settlement called Germantown. It became the prime welcoming spot for various religious sects of German settlers—Lutherans, Mennonites, Moravians, Anabaptists, Amish people, and Dunkers—before they set off to claim farmland that Penn's agents made available in the fertile country south and west of Philadelphia. Among other things, Pistorius became an early outspoken opponent of human slavery and passionate voice for religious freedom, not to mention the first public servant elected to Penn's visionary general assembly.

Even more German immigrants reached Philadelphia's docks in three major phases from 1683 to 1709; 1709 to 1714; and 1717 to 1760. By the outbreak of the American Revolution, when immigration briefly slowed for the duration of hostilities, an estimated forty thousand German immigrants had successfully made the trip. One early historian places their numbers at well over fifty thousand German settlers by the end of the century.

With such growth came a thorny problem: Where to put them? By culture and temperament German immigrants were remarkably stable people, tending to travel in groups and form close-knit communities in order to preserve their faith and culture in every aspect of daily life. Many were fairly well-off, while others traveled as indentured servants determined to pay off their passage before pushing on to find farms of their own. As these newcomers poured into Philadelphia and adjacent Delaware ports, many English Quakers began to question the cultural and political impacts of this mass migration on the unsettled frontier.

Hoping to find more space to accommodate the influx of well-behaved German families, Penn persuaded Charles II's brother the Duke of York (soon to be crowned James II) to grant him title to three counties on the Delaware coast lying south of Penn's original grant, lands that would provide a direct outlet to the sea. The duke allowed the transfer to Pennsylvania's lord proprietor, but the counties had originally belonged to England's flinty Lord Baltimore, and he soon made a claim in the high courts of England to restore them to his own fledgling colony of Maryland. The legal wrangling would drag on miserably for decades, draining William Penn of time, fortune, health, and, ultimately, family holdings in Pennsylvania.

By 1717, according to Great Wagon Road historian Parke Rouse Jr., so many Germans had arrived in the colony of Pennsylvania that authorities began requiring them to formally register before seeking work as indentured laborers or moving on to purchase farmland. Though they brought essential skills to the new colony as mechanics, gunsmiths, shoemakers, blacksmiths, and ironmongers, poorer and less skilled German immigrants raised the ire of Philadelphia's Quaker elite. In 1727, William Penn's loyal secretary, Scotsman James Logan, complained to Penn's son John of having "many thousands of foreigners, most Palatines . . . of whom 1500 came last summer; many of them are a surly people, divers Papists among them, and ye men generally well arm'd."

Even the normally measured Benjamin Franklin complained via *Poor Richard's Almanack*: "Why should the Palatine boors be suffered to swarm into our settlement, and by herding together, establish their language and manners, to the exclusion of ours? Why should Pennsylvania, funded by the English, become a colony of aliens, who will shortly be so numerous as to Germanize us, instead of us Anglifying them, and will never adopt our language or customs any more than they can acquire our complexion?"

Waves of German settlers, however, were only half the story of America's first great immigrant boom. An even larger and more influential mass migration was already underway.

The saga of the Great Migration of the Scots-Irish (sometimes called "Scotch Irish" or simply "Ulster Scots") began when hundreds of highly educated Presbyterian ministers led a mass exodus out of Ulster for the new promised land of America, sons of Calvinism wooed by William Penn's Holy

Experiment: the promising freedom of worship, good land, and representative government. After decades of discrimination and violent persecution by the English Crown and Anglican Church, the first Presbyterian ministers showed up in America a decade after William Penn began laying out the city of Philadelphia. By 1706, they had organized the first American Presbytery, officially establishing the church's North American synod just one decade later.

Successive years of punishing drought and crop failures in Ulster contributed to a flow estimated at five to ten thousand settlers a year and growing. By the summer of 1718, there were reports of a dozen ships a month arriving in Philadelphia from Belfast and other Northern Ireland ports. In 1729, Secretary James Logan lamented in a letter to Penn, "It looks as if Ireland is to send all its inhabitants hither, for last week no less than six ships arrived, and every day, two or three arrive also." Logan presciently added, "The Indian themselves are alarmed at the swarms of strangers, and we are afraid of a breech between them—for the Irish are very rough to them."

A third wave came during the infamous Irish famine of 1740–41, prompting Penn's government to push them beyond the outer edges of Philadelphia into the wilderness that lay past the first (future) inland village of Lancaster. Enticements from Lord Baltimore's Maryland and favorable reports of cheap land available in the largely unexplored Valley of Virginia and the Carolinas also compelled many late-coming Germans and Scots-Irish to continue their migration west toward the Southern wilderness.

With their legacy of unyielding disregard for any ruling authority and insatiable hunger for personal freedom, the Scots-Irish would become the Great Wagon Road's greatest—and most restless—travelers, the vanguard of a fledgling nation's frontier exploration, not only defining the backbone of American democracy as they pushed across the continent, but in time producing more than a dozen presidents and a majority of America's citizen warriors and top military leaders who would fight the nation's wars for the next two and a half centuries.

In rain-swept Penn's Landing, I come upon a moving tribute to Irish tenacity and immigrant spirit in the form of a memorial statue.

Dedicated in October 2003, standing twelve feet high and thirty feet long, the extraordinary Irish memorial titled *An Gorta Mor*, by artist Glenna Goodacre, best known for her tribute on the Washington Mall to women who served in Vietnam, graphically depicts thirty-five life-sized figures who tell a sweeping story of suffering and hope. The lower end of the statue, aimed due east, memorializes the potato famine and Great Hunger of 1845–1850, during which a million men, women, and children perished in their homeland, while the statue's opposite end, directed to the west, depicts figures anxiously disembarking from a ship carrying infants and their meager possessions, faces lit by hope and anticipation.

A few minutes later, in an adjoining vest-pocket park, I discover a smaller but no less impressive monument to Scottish immigration by Philadelphia sculptor Terry Jones, dedicated in 2011, depicting a proud Scottish family (and their dog!) on the march into the American backcountry. A standing stone near the memorial marks the site of Tun Tavern, the historic waterfront tavern where the St. Andrews Society of Philadelphia was born, in part to help waves of poor but proud Scottish emigrants who began disembarking at Philadelphia's docks around 1707. Tilting up the last of my lukewarm Yuengling, I decide that Tun Tavern was where my own weary arriving Scottish ancestors, the brothers George and William Tate, must have hoisted their first brews in the land of the free.

As a descendant of these Scottish travelers (not to mention a member of the Royal and Ancient Golf Club of St. Andrews), I feel obliged to jot down a few lines from the memorial's plaque:

> The Scots adapted quickly to the American way of life and were soon accepted as an asset to the United States. They left an enduring mark on their new homes. As educators and writers, they influenced the founding constitutional documents of the USA and established many schools and some of America's most prestigious universities. . . . They were much to the fore as hardy pioneers, Ulster Scots in particular migrating to the lands of the west . . . never among the largest immigrant groups in the USA but the evidence leaves little doubt that they punched well above their weight in the history of our nation.

And what of the man whose extraordinary holy vision created this mass birthing of an immigrant nation—a promised land of unlimited milk and honey that lay, as he evangelized, "Six hundred miles nearer the sun"?

In October 1682, Penn began construction of his family estate, Pennsbury Manor, twenty miles up the Delaware River, anticipating the planned arrival of his wife and family in the future. Family lore holds that the lord proprietor quickly learned to fluently speak the Lenape language in order to converse directly with tribal leaders and took great pleasure, corroborated by his own diary, in participating in their sporting games, earning the affectionate nickname of "Onus" from his Indian friends. Penn's respect and fair dealings with the Delaware people established a baseline for friendship that averted the disaster of an Indian war in Pennsylvania for more than half a century.

He also opened the first provincial court in New Castle and gaveled a representative assembly into session, passing laws that, according to Penn's biographers, "embodied the humanitarian and tolerant spirit of Penn and his fellow Quakers," even granting protection to unpopular Christian sects that had escaped their Old World oppressors.

By late summer of 1684, however, the dispute with Lord Baltimore over his claim on the southern counties had escalated to the King and the Privy Council, and Penn reluctantly returned to England hoping to peaceably resolve the matter.

As he prepared to leave Pennsylvania for the first time, Penn gave instructions to his gardener Ralph Smyth to begin laying out the gardens around Pennsbury Manor and build a gravel road with steps at the water's edge for the impending arrival of Penn's wife and family. He departed fully expecting to return within months.

But William Penn did not return to his Holy Experiment for more than fifteen years.

During this time, his primary benefactor, the Duke of York, became James II and ran afoul of Parliament and the Church of England and fled to France, allowing William and Mary to assume the throne. Under suspicion of treason for supporting his family friend, Penn was forced to live in hiding for six years in England until he was captured and—once more—tossed into prison. Moreover, in 1694, his wife Gulielma died, leaving him with three children and a mountain of debts. Two years later, his name finally cleared of treason, he married Hannah Callowhill, an attractive Quaker lady twenty-five years his junior.

Finally, in December 1699, William Penn returned to his beloved colony accompanied by wife Hannah and a daughter from his first marriage, Letitia. He was, according to his own writings, delighted to find Philadelphia a thriving city that was now second in size only to Boston in North America. During the visit, he successfully negotiated a deed with the powerful Iroquois leaders of the Five Nations for additional lands adjoining the Susquehanna River, promising never to cross to the mountains beyond. This expanded the footprint of his colony through a series of peace treaties that survived for decades.

Briefly, Penn enjoyed an interlude of domestic tranquility at Pennsbury, and it was during this relatively peaceful time that he achieved his most enduring legacy by promoting a revised charter for the city of Philadelphia that broadened municipal authority. He proposed expansion of the rights for landowners and also legislation that regulated the colony's judiciary by providing for fairer treatment of prisoners—a cause close to Penn's heart and another "first" in all of the world.

This new Charter of Privileges, as it was known, sometimes also called the Charter of Liberties, was enacted into law on October 28, 1701, a major step toward legitimate self-government that lasted until the outbreak of the American Revolution. Shaped by the Age of Enlightenment and Penn's own Quaker beliefs, the charter would become one of the foundation stones of America's constitutional democracy, a "document [that] guaranteed religious freedom, strengthened the separation of church and state, granted popularly-elected officials the ability to enact laws, and balanced the powers between the offices of the governor, legislature and judiciary," as commonwealth historian Linda Ries summarizes.

Just weeks after the passing of this groundbreaking document, however, news reached Penn that his enemies in the British government had introduced legislation designed to strip him of his ownership of the colony and place its governance directly under control of the Crown. He set off with Hannah to appear before England's Privy Council not only to defend his property but also to address old claims by a former secretary named

Ford that Penn owed more than eleven thousand pounds for unpaid services.

England's latest outbreak of war with France only complicated matters. Penn correctly calculated that Europe's rising hostilities might spill across the salt to his fragile colony, which prompted him, before leaving Philly, to authorize his Scots-Irish secretary, James Logan, to run his personal affairs and keep a firm eye on Pennsylvania's evolving interests and political intrigues in his absence.

Though Logan artfully enriched himself from private deals struck with fur traders and Indian groups in the western portions of the colony, he was a generally faithful steward of Pennsylvania's legal affairs and kept his aging boss more or less apprised of changing political and social developments. Unfortunately, the balance of Penn's life in England soon devolved into a protracted struggle against mounting debt and renewed religious persecution.

One Sunday in 1708, during services at the Quaker church he and Hannah attended, bailiffs acting on behalf of his aggrieved former secretary's family burst through the doors and arrested the sixty-year-old Penn, tossing him into debtor's prison. Outraged, nine of his Quaker friends petitioned the high court demanding to examine the accusing secretary's books. The court agreed, and an investigation determined that Ford—recently deceased—had, in fact, spent years swindling his former employer. Queen Anne ultimately dismissed the claims of the Ford family and Penn's friends paid off his arbitrated debt of 7,600 pounds. Penn showed his gratitude by granting them generous mortgages on much of his remaining Pennsylvania property.

After years of disappointment and upheaval, with the help of friends and James Logan's management of revenues from holdings in Pennsylvania, the old Quaker and his family found a large house in a wooded vale in the village of Ruscombe, halfway between London and Oxford. For a brief and hopeful time, Penn began negotiating with the British government to sell his remaining interests in Pennsylvania for twenty thousand pounds, a sum that would have finally cleared his debts and provided the family a means to live life in relative peace and comfort. To his many friends and admirers, it appeared that William Penn's troubles had finally reached their end.

During a visit to Hannah's family in Bristol on October 4, 1712, Penn suffered a stroke that left him partially paralyzed while writing a letter to James Logan. Though he briefly rallied, he was never able to resume work and suffered a second stroke that affected his focus and memory. As a result of this infirmity, his negotiated deal with the Crown was suspended and never brought to fruition, allowing the Penn family to keep its ownership of Pennsbury Manor and a few other significant holdings in Pennsylvania. As her husband's health and mental faculties failed, Hannah Penn took over governing the colony in her husband's name.

Ironically, the man whose holy vision of a nation where newcomers would feel welcome and protected by fair-minded laws mentally drifted away from a troubled world he had dreamed of improving, reportedly in good spirits even as all memory ebbed and even his ability to speak finally vanished.

William Penn died peacefully on July 30, 1718, at home in Ruscombe, and was buried in the graveyard adjacent to a Friends meetinghouse in Buckinghamshire, beside his first wife and several of his children.

In his will, he granted Hannah Callowhill Penn full control of his remaining lands in the colony of Pennsylvania and surviving financial assets. Despite a legal effort by Penn's first son, William, a dissolute youth who failed in his subsequent attempt to claim his father's legacy and estate, Hannah Penn remained in charge of the colony until her death at age fifty-five at her son Thomas's house in London, in 1726.

As rain comes off the river in billowy gusts, I cross the footbridge over I-95's gridlocked morning traffic to lower Chestnut Street, pausing to read a historic marker that displays all 272 words of Lincoln's Gettysburg Address. Then I move on hoping to be among the first to visit the recently opened Museum of the American Revolution.

Unfortunately, a long line of folks already waits in the rain outside the museum for the ten o'clock opening, now only moments away.

"We were fortunate to get our tickets two months ago online," a pretty young woman holding a pink umbrella informs me at the end of the line.

"My wife is a serial planner," the young man standing beside her says with a beaming smile. "She's got our whole vacation planned out down to the minute."

"We only have three days. There's so much to see," she points out.

Their names are Selie and Hector, recent graduates from a small college in Maryland. Selie already has a bank job waiting in suburban Washington, DC, and Hector is scheduled to enter graduate school in Baltimore. They hail from South Africa. Both have green cards and hope to eventually become US citizens.

I'm tempted to ask their views on America's eternally raging immigration crisis, but why spoil their brief summer getaway. Instead, I inquire about their favorite things to do in America's solitary World Heritage site.

"The Liberty Bell and jolly big statue of Benjamin Franklin at the institute were my favorites," Selie provides. "The parks and buildings are also quite lovely. I'd like to someday move here, I think. Next visit, it will be a full day in the Museum of Art for me."

Hector laughs. "The food! I've had the famous Philly cheesesteak . . . twice!"

"Gracious *noooo*, love," Selie corrects him, taking her husband's arm, "you've had at least *five* famous Philadelphia cheesesteaks in just three days!"

As the line begins to move forward, I wish them Godspeed and good luck in their quest to become American citizens, hoping that somewhere six hundred miles nearer the sun, even William Penn might be smiling upon them through the gloom.

THREE

AMERICA'S ORIGINAL MAN

THAT SAME AFTERNOON, BENEATH A RETURNING BUT FIERCE AUGUST SUN, I limp into the quiet courtyard of historic Christ Church to find none other than Benjamin Franklin sitting on a wooden bench. He's just removed a buckled shoe to massage a foot.

"This gout," he cheerfully grumbles, looking up. "Murder on the feet."

"I know what you mean. Mine are barking too."

Franklin pats the bench. "In that case, sir, I am happy to share some hardwood relief while I wait for my wife to come and collect me."

So I take a seat, casually remarking, "I hoped I might bump into you. Been chasing you all over town today."

He looks amused, mischievous gray eyes twinkling beneath the bifocals he supposedly invented.

"Indeed? And here I am, before your very eyes, caught at last. If I may inquire, where exactly has this exciting pursuit taken you?"

I give him a brief summary of the chase.

Following my rainy walk through Penn Treaty Park and Penn's Landing, I'd made a beeline for Ben Franklin's house and his museum on Market Street, where young Franklin, a seventeen-year-old Boston runaway, arrived on a Sunday morning in 1723 while most of Philadelphia was at church. The choice of location was no accident. So many European arrivals passed that spot on their way from the bustling docks of the city to the American heartland that Market Street eventually earned the first designation of being "the most historic road in America," the beginning, as it were, of the Philadelphia Great Wagon Road.

I was the first visitor through the door at Franklin's museum, and a thoughtful National Park docent named Gibson Reynolds had been kind enough to give me a personal walking tour of the Founding Father's diverse life as a printer, scientist, inventor, writer, businessman, gossip columnist, social gadfly, public relations man, patriot, and foreign ambassador. It was a revelatory visit. I knew Franklin started America's first hospital and fire company and organized the country's first lending library, invented bifocals, and tried to harness electricity. But I'd had no idea that he was also a failed bricklayer and sawyer, and invented a soup bowl that would never spill, the first swimming flippers, and a para-anchor for steadying ships at sea.

"In essence, he was America's answer to Leonardo da Vinci," docent Reynolds told me as we walked. "He was also among the first to champion the use of the microscope, saying it would open a world unknown to the ancients. He was right about that. He also introduced the idea of daylight savings time and loved to play chess by candlelight late at night."

Following this deep dive into one of the Wagon Road's most important travelers, I hoofed on to Logan Square to view the original display copies of *Poor Richard's Almanack* (in honor of late Cousin Josie) at the Franklin Institute, standing in a throng of schoolkids taking selfies in front of sculptor James Earle Fraser's thirty-ton Franklin sitting like a bemused American Buddha in his classical rotunda. Then it was on to lunch with a leading Franklin scholar and historian named Page Talbott, who served as the primary consultant for the Franklin Museum's spectacular renovation and chief curator of the acclaimed Franklin touring exhibit in 2006, which celebrated the tercentenary of Franklin's birth. After traveling to eleven American cities and making a mandatory stop in Paris, France, where Franklin is said to be held in higher esteem than any other American, living or dead, Talbott's Franklin exhibit was redesigned as a panel show that traveled to forty libraries across the US and served as the narrative framework for Philly's reimagined Franklin Museum, which opened in time to celebrate the US National Park Service's centennial in 2016.

Over a chef salad and glass of Sonoma County chardonnay, Talbott had shared something else unique about Franklin. "He probably traveled your Great Wagon Road more than any of the other Founding Fathers in his capacity as the country's first postmaster general. He also negotiated numerous treaties that helped establish civil order along the expanding frontier and developed a network of powerful friends on the road who proved useful in coming conflicts. The Continental Congress used the road to flee Philadelphia in 1777, for example, traveling to Lancaster and York, where they worked on the Articles of Confederation, our first constitution. One could argue that the America we know today wouldn't be the same without Ben Franklin and the Great Wagon Road."

Talbott smiled when I asked if she could think of anyone in contemporary America who rivals the scope of Franklin's originality.

"Funny you should ask that. The short answer is no. Ben Franklin is more popular today than any other Founding Father, especially with young people. There's a perfectly reasonable explanation for this. Apart from the important institutions he helped create and the many inventions and innovations credited to him, Franklin was a humanly endearing figure, so approachable and full of life and curiosity, he seems to transcend time. First and last, he was a product of the Age of Enlightenment, embracing many of our national aspirations and values—our Original Man, if you like, America's first true renaissance figure. Equally important, he possessed the gift of making friends wherever he went in life. More than two centuries later, he's still doing just that."

She then mentioned a fascinating thought experiment that confirmed her own hunches about the man's enduring appeal. "After we finished work on the touring exhibition, I invited our team of Franklin scholars who'd worked on the project and the museum restoration for many years to try and imagine a version of Ben Franklin in today's world, a figure of comparable vision and achievements. We came up with absolutely . . . *nobody*. Lots of names were tossed out from Albert Einstein to Bill Gates. But every possible candidate was so narrow in their scope of genius, nobody came close to Franklin. That's why he's still very much alive and with us. Just google him," she wryly added, sipping her wine, "and you will see what I mean."

So I did just that. During my walk to Christ Church in the steamy afternoon heat, I discovered that there are twenty-four counties and forty-nine municipalities in America named in honor of America's Original Man, not to mention eight colleges and universities worldwide, fifty-one American public schools, six major urban streets, a vintage brand of automobile, Philly's most impressive bridge, three major parkways, a defunct chain of five-and-dime stores, an international investment firm, more than a dozen municipal parks, a major city zoo, a shopping mall, two plumbing companies, an electrical firm, three mountain ranges, a popular recreational lake out West, a US Navy aircraft carrier, a nuclear submarine armed with ballistic missiles, a rare species of tree growing in Bartram's Garden, and the football field at the University of Pennsylvania. Dear old Ben's instantly recognizable mug not only graces the hundred-dollar bill but appears on the sides of buildings and nearly every city-owned bus in greater Philadelphia. There's even a crater on the moon named for him.

Upon his death in April 1790, twenty thousand Philadelphians reportedly followed Franklin's funeral cortege to the burial ground at Christ Church. The bells of the statehouse (Independence Hall) were swaddled in muslin cloth, and lengthy eulogies were offered in the US Congress and across the nation, not to mention in the French National Assembly in Paris.

Fittingly, my final stop before Christ Church was the walled burying ground on North 5th Street where Franklin and his common-law wife, Deborah, rest beneath a large engraved slab of stone, a secular shrine where tourists daily leave coins and personal messages.

"My good gracious," remarks my fellow sore-footed companion on the bench after I give him these highlights of my Franklin-filled day. "You should be *quite* exhausted by all of that. I certainly am, just listening to you. Do hope you weren't disappointed by what you learned."

"Not in the least," I say. "But I do have a few questions."

His real name is Rick Bravo, one of maybe half a dozen Ben Franklin "interpreters" I've heard about from Philadelphia friends—the very one, in fact, I'd hoped I might bump into. Word on the street has it that Bravo, seventy, is perhaps the most convincing of those who work the turf around historic Christ Church, where the original was a member in good standing. Though Bravo is admittedly a dead ringer for America's Original Man, I am not fully convinced this Franklin is *actually* Rick Bravo until he formally presents his embossed business card: "Benjamin Franklin, Esq. a/k/a Rick Bravo, 55 Cricket Lane, Turnersville, New Jersey."

I can't help but smile, for I harbor deep affection for people who are obsessed enough to portray famous or historic persons, living or dead (especially dead), out of their simple love of history or human eccentricity. According to my sources along the frontier highway, historic interpreters and dedicated reenactors abound along the route of the Great Wagon Road, news that gladdens my eighth grader's heart.

Putting on his shoe, Bravo smiles again. "Happy to entertain any question you have. For Ben Franklin or Rick Bravo, sir."

"Let's start with Rick Bravo. How long have you been Ben Franklin?"

"That's easy. I was born to be Benjamin Franklin."

Bravo grew up just across the Delaware in North Camden, the son of a railroad fireman. From an early age he was fascinated by history and electricity and was eventually drawn to acting in community theater. "During my senior year in high school, on something of a lark, I tried out for a part in the school musical and got it. That's how you met girls in those days, by the way . . . being an actor. It's how I met my wife, Eleanor. I went off to Rutgers to study electrical engineering and we got married after my sophomore year. After college I went to work for a large public utility and got seriously involved in local theater in South Jersey." His early roles for the Washington Township Stage Scripteasers and other theater groups included Fagin in *Oliver!* and King Arthur in *Camelot*.

"You will concede," he says, "I had the perfect name for the stage."

Then along came Ben. During the bicentennial year of the signing of the US Constitution in 1989, his former director from high school invited him to play Franklin in a special production. "Growing up near Philly, I already knew a great deal about my preferred forefather, probably because we shared a thing for electricity. But when I take on any role, I study it in as much depth and detail as possible. Pretty soon I wasn't just copying how Franklin behaved, but how he lived day to day and what he thought about in life. In a sense, he came to possess me. I loved the guy from day one. He's a historian's dream because his life was full of extraordinary achievements and fascinating contradictions."

Take for instance, Bravo explains, Franklin hastily organized a citizen army during the winter of 1763 to face down a murderous mob of Scots-Irish thugs from Northern Lancaster County who threatened to torch Philadelphia. "There was actually concern expressed by the governors of neighboring colonies that Franklin could easily have taken control of Pennsylvania and maybe much more if he'd so desired. But that thought never entered his head. In gratitude for saving the city, they made him honorary colonel of the militia. The point is, he was a man of true decency and principles—not a power-hungry politician. How rare, eh?"

He gives another example. When British Major General Edward Braddock came to Philadelphia desperately seeking wagons and horses for his ill-fated campaign against the French out West in 1754, it was Franklin who persuaded hundreds of German farmers along the Wagon Road to loan their horses and durable farm wagons to the cause, offering to personally compensate any losses. "He produced a broadside in Lancaster and York that was distributed among German farmers and got more than a hundred wagons and teams within two weeks."

Bravo Ben pauses and thinks for a moment.

"I am, however, equally if not more fascinated by Franklin's dark side. Everyone has one, you know, including great men and women. *Especially* great men and women. Here's something you probably don't know. After his father's death, Thomas Penn became the colony's proprietor with his brothers, and called me—Franklin, that is—the 'most dangerous man in America.' This was during the difficult years Franklin spent in England attempting to persuade the king to have Pennsylvania's proprietary government replaced by a royal government that would guarantee broader rights and safety to all citizens. Their dispute became quite bitter. With the old Quaker founder gone, the greedy Penn boys betrayed just about every principle their late father stood for. Along with James Logan, Thomas Penn engineered a shameful con called the Walking Treaty that basically cheated the region's Native Americans out of lands granted to them in perpetuity by their father, and thus turned native tribes against the colony, sending them straight into the arms of the French. Among other things, Thomas—a converted Anglican—attempted to dispose of Quaker rule in a shameless attempt to prevent Catholicism from taking root in America. Fortunately, the Quaker assembly overrode his craven efforts. In essence, Thomas wanted to be a feudal lord, an autocrat. Thanks to Franklin and others, however, he failed and many of the higher principles of William Penn survive to this day. As an opponent, Ben Franklin could, if need be, be quite ruthless. We owe him greatly for that."

Since we're exploring the man's complexity, I ask about his unconventional spirituality.

"Glad you asked. Ben was a practicing member of Christ Church—inside the church you can sit in his pew—but also a deist like Jefferson and a few other of the broader-thinking founders. But even that doesn't fully explain the breadth of Franklin's spiritual reach. In essence, he believed that any religion that advocates being kind and helpful to your fellow human beings is a very good thing. He was basically your early American humanist liberal, open to any idea or concept that expands one's understanding of a compassionate universe. He wrote with feeling about his admiration for the messages of Jesus. His personal motto, if there was one, was simply 'Be good and do good'—echoes of which you may hear in John Wesley's famous motto. He genuinely believed that was the way to a fulfilling life. I would add to that—and having fun doing it. Franklin loved to have fun. He enjoyed every inch of his long and productive life, even the seeming contradictions."

He also mentions Franklin's curiously intimate relationship with George Whitefield, the gifted English pulpiteer who toured the colonies in 1740 preaching a fiery brand of charismatic Gospel-based fundamentalism and redemption that fertilized the grassroots of America's first Great Awakening along the emerging backcountry of the Wagon Road. After attending one of Whitefield's Philadelphia revivals that drew thousands of faithful and curious, a deeply impressed Franklin agreed to publish the preacher's sermons and meditations, which became bestsellers across the colonies for decades, "Making a liberal-minded universalist tradesman printer named Benjamin Franklin a small fortune in the process."

This notoriously inspired a generation of "New Side" evangelical preachers who fanned out along the Wagon Road to preach the power of the Gospels (i.e., the dangers of hellfire and damnation) to an untamed wilderness rapidly filling with settlers from many lands, sowing the seeds of America's first great religious fervor. The charity school Franklin helped Whitefield establish in Philadelphia a short time after he arrived eventually became the Academy of Philadelphia and later a college of the same name, which would become the University of Pennsylvania. (To this day, a statue of George Whitefield stands in the heart of the university's campus.)

Thinking of Page Talbott's description of the Original Man's enduring popularity, I wonder aloud to Bravo what message Franklin sends to us at a moment when intense political partisanship and social division threaten the fragile fabric of America's experiment with democracy.

Ben Franklin Bravo shakes his head. "A very relevant question. Franklin speaks quite urgently to us today, I think, asking us to restore our faith in the power of compromise and honest listening, to avoid quick judgment and the kind of poisonous name-calling and fractured debate that is dividing us at this moment. He was, at heart, a natural compromiser who saw the advantage of keeping his mouth shut until he had a full grasp of the facts, knowing when to stand firm on principle—as he did with the nasty Penn children, resulting in more representative government—and when to yield the debate. Not unimportantly, he saw great value in allowing each side of the issue to feel invested in a reasonable outcome. You see this pattern across his life and career, especially in the debates around the creation of our bicameral government and Constitution. We can all take comfort and wisdom from his commonsense approach to the common good and hopefully learn from him."

Before I can pose a final question, Bravo adds with a flourish: "In other words, he kept an open mind and changed his views as he grew older. That seems to me another cherished American quality, rarely exhibited these days in the public arena, a willingness to see reason and change your views. He supported slavery at the beginning of his public life, for example, yet became a staunch and early abolitionist during the second half of his life—once again ahead of his time. Franklin never stopped growing, and we shouldn't either."

I let his perspective wash over me. Truthfully, I could sit at the elbow of the man who became Benjamin Franklin for at least another hour in Philly's murderous August heat.

But his wife, Eleanor, is due any moment and I need to duck my head into the church before I set off to see an expert on the Wagon Road's frontier craftsmanship at the Philadelphia Museum of Art before heading on down the road. So I ask if we might continue our conversation when I return to have dinner with Chef Staib at City Tavern.

"I would enjoy that immeasurably," he replies as we rise on rested feet. "Mr. Franklin never turned down a fine free meal—especially there. I was an original investor, you know. Hopefully you shall return before I am summoned to higher account."

With the gentlest of smiles, he reveals that he is scheduled to undergo major heart surgery within days.

I offer him my hand and best wishes for a speedy recovery. "One more question before I go?"

"God willing not your last question nor my last answer."

"What's it like to *be* Ben Franklin?" Rick Bravo may not be America's Original Man, but he is a true American original in other endearing ways.

He glances off into the shaded courtyard, where a mom and three small children are chattering like magpies as they eat dripping ice cream cones. My eyes trail his. He speaks with quiet emotion.

"Let me tell you. It's simply . . . *wonderful*. Next to my wife and children, being Ben Franklin is the most meaningful thing in my life. Speaking of children, I've done a one-man show called *The Life and Times of Benjamin Franklin* for decades all over this city. The kids love it. The show never fails to give me hope about the future. Ben Franklin is such a lovable and fun-loving soul, not a trace of pretention in the man. It never fails to get young scholars laughing when I urge them at the end of the presentation to 'fart proudly,' as Franklin took such delight in saying. Both he and we know that life is hard, short, and woefully unpredictable. Yet honest laughter can cure anything that ails you."

I'm about to let him go, when I realize there's something else I need to know.

"A *second* one more thing, sir, if I may . . . Did you, in fact, say that beer is proof that God loves us?"

Once again, Ben Franklin's gray eyes hover mirthfully behind his bifocals.

"That's what they say. Who am I to ruin such an excellent story?"

Christ Church historian Neil Ronk stands in Betsy Ross's Sunday spot, pew box number 12, giving a talk to a handful of tourists clustered into pews 56 to 58, the presidential pews where George Washington and John Adams sat when attending Sunday worship services.

I quietly seat myself behind them in pew 70, which I'm pleased to discover was Ben Franklin's own private pew, making me wonder if sitting here was where his grand ideas about a compassionate universe came from.

Christ Church is a magnificent Georgian structure designed by a student of Christopher Wren's, completed in 1744, boasting a soaring steeple that was financed by a lottery organized by the old gentleman waiting for his wife outside. For the next fifty-six years it remained the tallest structure in the British colonies, home to a congregation that had more signers of the Declaration of Independence buried on its property than anyplace in America, a tally of five signers.

As I entered, Ronk was telling his audience the pyrrhic tale of Rev. Jacob Duché, the Christ Church minister who gave the prayer to open the First Continental Congress and daringly removed the name of King George from the church's "prayers of the people," an act at least as perilous as placing his name on the Declaration of Independence itself, having given his sacred pledge to support king and country. Though he was jailed when the British occupied the city in September 1777 for sympathizing with the patriot cause, Duché became disillusioned with the mayhem and mob violence unleashed by the revolution. Hoping to stem the tide of civic violence engulfing the city streets, he penned an infamous letter to George Washington, who was encamped at Valley Forge, urging him to negotiate peace terms with the British, which earned him the label of traitor from the same Congress he'd served as chaplain. When his house was confiscated, Duché was forced to flee to England with his family, where he served as the chaplain of an orphans' asylum for the next decade.

"But as with most things in America, that wasn't the end of the story," Ronk tells his audience. "In truth, George Washington artfully exploited Duché's letter, misrepresenting his intent, which was simply to stop the violence and bring a peaceful resolution to the conflict. For this sin, seeking peace, Duché was labeled the Benedict Arnold of American clergy. But there's an interesting twist to the end of his story. After the war and ratification of the Constitution, Duché returned to Philadelphia in 1792 only to be embraced by the public that once scorned him—celebrated as a man of conscience who took a moral stand against mob violence. He became, in effect, an unsung hero of the American Revolution."

His audience shows their approval by lightly applauding, and I join in, having never heard this amazing story.

A few minutes later, as we sit together in the empty church, the historian explains the purpose of telling Duché's story.

"I use it to illustrate the fact that few stories in American history are as black and white as typically portrayed. There were good and moral people on both sides of the revolution," he says, reminding visitors that we are only nine or ten generations away from America's revolutionary summer. "Ten generations in the scope of human history is a mere blink of an eye. And in a nation made up almost entirely of immigrants, as I like to point out, we are still struggling to make our young democracy work for everyone. You see it every day in the news."

While I digest this sad reality, he asks me what brought me to historic Christ Church late on a hot Friday afternoon in August. When I tell him that I am about to set off down the Great Wagon Road to Georgia, he smiles. Turns out, he has a strong ancestral connection to it.

"In another nine years, my family will have been in Pennsylvania for three hundred years," he explains. "German immigrants who put down roots in 1727 near the township of Ronks, just off the Wagon Road in the heart of Amish country outside the city of Lancaster." Several generations later, his great-grandfather moved his wing of the family to Chester and later Delaware County, where Neil grew up. His grandmother's German ancestors, the Hottensteins, settled around the town of Reading, connected to the oldest stone house in that part of the state.

"I've driven Route 30—which is also the old Lincoln Highway that follows the original Wagon Road west—for most of my life. I don't believe there's a more historic road anywhere. It's how the nation went west."

Never having traveled the Lincoln Highway from Philly to York, Pennsylvania, I mention my excitement at the prospect of seeing Amish country for the first time and allow that a golf pal from Lancaster has even arranged for me to visit with an Amish family that has been on their land since the days of William Penn.

Ronk nods approvingly. "They're amazing people, among America's finest farmers. The Old Order Amish brought ingenuity and intelligent land stewardship to this country. George Washington praised them for the care they took with their livestock, the cleanliness of their rock barns, and the unrivaled fertility of their lands.

"Unfortunately," he adds, "it may not be that way for long. The Old Order Amish are leaving this part of the world in droves."

Rampant commercial development and urbanization, he tells me, have nearly rendered once-bucolic Lancaster County a suburb of Philadelphia, causing large-scale relocation to places like southern Ohio (which now holds the largest number of Amish people in the nation) and the middle South, including parts of western Virginia and North Carolina, in order to maintain their history and way of life.

He lets that sink in, then adds, "Farmland is disappearing at a frightening clip. Amish children are the real victims because they can no longer afford to inherit the land their ancestors cultivated before America was even a nation. Shopping centers and subdivisions are swallowing up their cornfields. Theme parks, factory stores, and subdivisions are everywhere. If something doesn't change soon, the fertile land those German farmers turned into the Breadbasket of the Revolution will just be a memory."

He pauses again and gazes up at one of the Christ Church's clear tall windows.

"My big fear is that Amish culture that flourished along the Great Wagon Road will be a lost lifestyle, like artifacts displayed in a museum. This is something *every* American ought to be concerned about. That's why the Amish are moving out in such numbers.

"But that's not my only concern along the Wagon Road these days," he says.

I ask what else worries him.

"Statues."

Grimacing, he mentions the national debate of recent years over whether Confederate memorials and statues should be removed from public spaces. There's even a report of a grassroots campaign by civil rights activists aimed at removing all Confederate statues from the National Military Park at Gettysburg. Some are calling it the "Second Battle of Gettysburg."

Naturally, I ask how he feels about the issue (one, in truth, I wrestle with myself). He answers with a fascinating personal story.

"Some years ago, I dropped my girlfriend off for her reunion at Gettysburg College and was driving back to Philadelphia when I suddenly remembered something my father told me as a boy. 'Don't ever forget about those rebel Ronks,' he said—almost out of the blue, no pun intended. It was a surprising comment that wedged itself in my head. Ronks in the *Confederacy*? It didn't make sense. So, I called my sister, who is the keeper of our family records."

A week later, his sister called back with news that in a book titled *Their Tattered Flags*, she had discovered a list of names from every regiment involved in George Pickett's disastrous charge at the Battle of Gettysburg—including a Confederate soldier named Ronk.

"There he was, in the Virginia Twenty-Eighth Regiment, Company K, of the Bedford Grays, a thirty-one-year-old wagon builder named Samuel Ronk. It was the same spelling as ours—a branch of the family, we subsequently learned, that took the Great Philadelphia Wagon Road out to the Shenandoah Valley with thousands of other German settlers to make a life on the western frontier."

My host cracks a thin smile, glancing at a trio of heat-flushed tourists who've just begun trickling in for his final scheduled talk of the day.

"Turns out, like untold numbers of Americans, I have ancestors who served on *both* sides of that disastrous war, including a regimental surgeon named Hottenstein who served in the Pennsylvania 121st Regiment, which also saw action at Gettysburg. It's strange and moving to think about this fact, truly brother against brother, which makes you step back and wonder where we are headed today. That's what I mean when I tell our visitors to the church how *incredibly* near we are to our own past, in many cases haunted by it, a complicated and fragile bond. There are no real winners in a war, but lots of losers in every family tree."

"Did your rebel ancestor survive Pickett's Charge?"

"As a matter of fact, he made it through and died in 1909. His brother David served in the 22nd from Virginia under George Patton's grandfather; the Patton family later moved on to California to get away from his terrible memories of the war."

Docent Ronk glances up at the church's tall windows for a second time. The afternoon light falls like a benediction upon Christ Church's empty pews. The tourist cameras are already clicking.

"We're still not over that trauma, I fear," he muses. "This debate over Confederate monuments being taken down is merely a symptom of a long-overdue reckoning. But if we only study fragments of our history," he adds, "choosing only what we find most compatible with our culturally embedded beliefs, we lose the full impact of our country's evolution, including its past failings."

"So, I gather you think the Confederates should go."

He gives a gentle snort. "On the contrary! I actually believe we should be putting up *more* statues instead of tearing them down. That way, we're telling a much deeper and more authentic story. Otherwise, we'll never learn where we came from and how—or if—we have any hope of healing the past!"

It's a beautiful meditation, and a solution I've honestly never considered. Ronk stares at me with calm, deep-set eyes, as if awaiting my opinion on the subject.

As a son of the Civil Rights–era South who grew up hearing elders at family reunions quietly refer to a "lost Confederate" in a family tree composed of Methodists largely opposed to the war, I don't yet know how I feel about the statue debate. I admit to him that I'm still trying to work out where I come down on the subject, something I hope this journey might clarify.

Walking me out to the churchyard, Ronk pauses and points to an ancient-looking structure in the narthex.

"By the way, that was William Penn's baptismal font."

The font, I suddenly remember, was the prime reason I'd stepped inside Christ Church. But I am grateful that Neil Ronk's masterful storytelling and concerns about the Amish and statues at Gettysburg completely stole the show, perhaps a glimpse of things to come.

As we walk over to the old Quaker's font, I ask this wise, deep-eyed historian what he thinks the founder of Pennsylvania would make of the state of America at that moment, a dozen or so generations after his Holy Experiment of democracy began.

"I'm not sure he'd be terribly happy," Ronk replies. "Only time will tell. At best, I'm hoping we're still a work in progress."

• • •

It's almost closing time when I reach Lenfest Hall at the Philadelphia Museum of Art, my last stop before heading off on the Wagon Road.

Alexandra Kirtley, the museum's curator of American Decorative Arts, has generously offered to show me a few important items before she zips off to join her family for a final summer weekend on the Delaware coast.

"The decorative arts and furniture of colonial North America make an excellent road map for your trip," she explains as we rise to the museum's fourth-floor galleries in a freight elevator. "They tell the story of brave and resolute immigrants on the move, determined to preserve and import their language, culture, religion, and traditions to the American wilderness. This goal resulted in family treasures passed down for generations because they connected people to their places of origin. They also give us a vivid picture of these newcomers to North America, including their daily lives and dreams. The Great Wagon Road was essential to creating that American story for those British, Irish, and European immigrants."

So, this was *her* elevator speech. I could hear echoes of a delightful talk I'd heard Kirtley give months before at the Museum of Early Southern Decorative Arts in Old Salem, North Carolina, as part of a special symposium on the Furniture of the Great Wagon Road. It had been informative and engaging, but now the journey was mine.

"I'm sorry this has to be such a rushed tour," she apologizes. "But I want to show you some important pieces to keep in mind as you travel the road."

As we rise in the elevator, she asks if I have colonial ancestors who traveled the road to Carolina, prompting me to give her an abbreviated version of my own origin story. Two Scottish ancestors, a pair of brothers named Tate, George and William, who arrived in Philadelphia from Aberdeen, Scotland, sometime in the mid 1750s and made a beeline for Hawfields in Piedmont, North Carolina, where their fifth-great-grandson, one George Washington Tate, owned his great-grandfather's gristmill and furniture shop on the Haw River.

I also mention a lone German lad from the Palatinate region who arrived in Philly a decade before the Revolutionary War, most likely an indentured servant who eventually married and took his own sweet time arriving in western Maryland, later settling in eastern West Virginia. There he became the patriarch of a large German family of coal miners and farmers named Kessell, my mother's people. Finally, there were the English Dodsons, rather bland and boring Methodists whose family records suggest they probably landed in eastern Virginia just after the Revolutionary War and moved west to the Blue Ridge mountains before filtering down to North Carolina in the early 1800s.

"I find it inspiring how so many Americans are researching their family origins these days," Kirtley remarks as our elevator bumps to a stop. "By the way, I've heard of George Washington Tate. I believe some of his pieces are in museums in Williamsburg and Old Salem."

She is correct. I mention a beautiful walnut cupboard made by G.W. Tate that has been passed down to my father's first cousin Roger Dodson. It's stood in his dining room for decades, signed by the artisan who made it.

My tour guide smiles. "Lucky Cousin Roger! In that case, I have the perfect place to begin."

She briskly walks me to a gallery that houses a detailed restoration of an immigrant German family's early eighteenth-century kitchen. The cabinetry is as finely crafted as anything found in a luxury furniture showroom. "Cabinetmaking was one of America's first true industries, created by people who brought little with them save for their artistry, tools, and ambitions. The forests of Britain were largely depleted of trees by the eighteenth century, but North America was full of gorgeous hardwoods—chestnut, hickory, walnut, maples, and oaks galore. You'll find this pattern all through colonial America. Sons following in their fathers' trades as skilled carvers and joiners migrated down the Wagon Road."

She explains that furniture was used not only to mark a family's passage through the wilderness but to celebrate important events in a family's life—like weddings, anniversaries, engagements, births, and deaths. "Owning fine furniture was an indication of a family's wealth. In Philadelphia, the finest pieces were typically made of imported Caribbean mahogany, whereas almost everything the German cabinetmakers made—and the Scottish-Irish as well—was from walnut, a fine and hard cabinetmaking wood that was locally available." Land traditionally passed down to male family members, she explains, but finer objects like furniture, decorative arts, and valuable household goods typically transferred through male and female lines. "Colonial women were the keepers of the family history and we have them to thank for what we know of those early European Americans today."

Because they wished to preserve their culture through folksways, German artists and farmers decorated everything from family blanket chests to their distinctive rock barns with images from nature and biblical references from their spiritual homelands, aiming to deepen the bonds of community while preserving their cultural heritage.

As it happens, Kirtley is of the powerful Rittenhouse bloodline, Dutch and Swiss, and explains that her historical research at that moment is focused on combing through colonial wills and probate documents to truly understand who owned what and determine the provenance of furniture and other works of art. "It's tedious work," she admits, "but deeply rewarding and very important."

As we stand together in the middle of the actual kitchen of one George Miller and family from Millbach in Lebanon County, circa 1752, my host explains that there was a definite hierarchy in America's early commercial woodworking culture. "To begin with, these creators were never called craftsmen. They called themselves either mechanics or artisans. Cabinetmakers were definitely at the top of the pecking order, based on European guild systems. They were prolific and versatile," she adds, pointing out how the walnut panels of the Miller kitchen perfectly match the exquisitely carved staircase and other furnishings in the room.

"And here's the most important point. You'll find that the people who came to America then—fleeing troubles back home or just seeking new opportunities—created a stream of immigration that has never really ceased, renewing and enriching this country with talented artisans, joiners, clock makers, mechanics, silversmiths, tinsmiths, chest makers, painters, and artists of every sort. They absorbed so much from their new physical surroundings (flora and fauna), from the enslaved and free Africans who worked in artisanal shops, and from trade with Native Americans. What they left in their wake was a rich tapestry of our living history—the extended story of who they were and the lives they led. That's why people passed beautiful furniture and household possessions down through generations. What you choose to leave behind says a great deal about who you were—and are."

Over the next half hour—fifteen minutes beyond closing time—she walks me through several stunning galleries of early Pennsylvania workmanship: stately tall walnut clocks with painted faces, ornately carved benches, intricately decorated cradles and blanket chests, carved spice boxes, handsome high chests, even toys that display extraordinary visual wit and mechanical ingenuity. The biggest surprise is discovering that I possess an unexpected attraction to Fraktur, the soulful German art form of personalizing everything from dowager chests to ordinary painted plates and platters with elaborate images and designs drawn from Scripture and nature—tulips and pomegranates, vines reaching to heaven, angels hovering on birth certificates—typically displaying folk wisdom, snippets of biblical verse, even frisky jokes about sex and marriage, all in the German language and meant to preserve Old World culture in a dangerous outland.

"Fraktur animated their lives, simultaneously documenting themselves and explaining why they were here. That's why these pieces show such a range of human emotion—love, grief, humor, compassion, everything we feel in our world today." Kirtley smiles. "In other words, they were just like us."

As we trek back to the freight elevator, she steers me past a particularly good version of one of the Quaker sign painter Edward Hicks's most famous *Peaceable Kingdom* paintings, a small, framed print of which my own German-heritage mother kept in her curio cabinet of painted porcelain figures and exquisitely carved birds. Seeing the Hicks original, however, stops me in my tracks, bringing a rush of emotions and thoughts about my late mom, the youngest of her eleven siblings, a former Miss Western Maryland, a true Wagon Road babe.

"Do you still have that print?" she asks.

I do indeed, along with two of the carved birds and a small oval sideboard made by Amish craftsmen in western Maryland sometime in the early 1800s. The sideboard is now a reading table in my home office.

My host smiles again. "See what I mean? Those pieces are your direct link to the past—your own family's immigrant story, and your mother."

As the elevator carries us down, we talk more about my coming trip. "I envy your trip down the Great Wagon Road. I think anyone who likes history and furniture should do it. For that matter, so should every American!"

The marble foyer is empty save for a lone security guard, who stares at us as we approach the locked exit doors, ready to shut us out.

"What's your next stop?" Kirtley asks.

I pause and laugh, frozen by a realization. Because my first day on the Great Wagon Road has been such a jam-packed affair, I haven't given a passing thought to where I might stay for the night. But like my Scottish and German forebears, I'll simply place myself in the hands of Providence and see what the road ahead provides.

Kirtley likes this idea, offering a slim hand.

"Your Scottish ancestors would be proud. But this is the height of summer tourist travel, not to mention Philadelphia's infamous Friday rush hour! Everyone is desperate to get out of town. You may be lucky to make Bryn Mawr by sunset!"

FOUR

REMEMBER PAOLI

A **FUNNY THING—OR MAYBE NOT—HAPPENS ON MY WAY TO FIND A BED FOR** the night at the General Warren inn, one of the few surviving original inns on the most traveled road of colonial America.

As I exit Philly's heavy westbound traffic from US 30 in Malvern, following the charming BBC voice I call Daphne Dewhurst on my smartphone's GPS app, I nearly jump out of my skin when an arctic-white BMW zooms around me on the insanely narrow exit ramp, sending me into the guardrail. Before I can regain my wits and catch up to this maniac at the top of the ramp, the devil in white is long gone and my heart is still in my mouth. An old dude driving an old station wagon, I suppose, makes an irresistible target to the young and speedy who have somewhere vitally important to be.

By the time I reach the General Warren inn my blood pressure is back to normal thanks to a serenely handsome structure surrounded by lush summer gardens and mature hardwoods, heralded by a pale blue oval sign on the side of the building that reads "Historic General Warren, 1754."

The parking lot is full.

Thanks to Parke Rouse Jr.'s folksy history of the Wagon Road, I know a good bit about the Warren's place in GWR lore, including the fact that it and its close neighbor the Paoli Inn were perhaps the two most popular stops on the entire Wagon Road, along with the White Horse Tavern a few miles farther west. A quick check of Google Maps indicates that the White

Horse Tavern might also still be in business, but there's nothing about the Paoli Inn.

The Warren was a particular favorite of Ben Franklin's during his journeys to the western frontier, and was even used as a recruiting station by agents of George Washington during the French and Indian conflict. According to Rouse, its predecessor, then called the *Admiral* Warren, was cruder and smaller, standing directly across Old Lancaster Road from its current location. In 1786, it was purchased, along with 335 acres, from the Penn family by a plump, enterprising German innkeeper named Casper Fahnestock, who ran it as a family affair that prohibited the sale or consumption of alcohol on Sundays. His wife, Maria, and her mother handled cooking and cleaning duties, while his son Charles poured drinks in the bar and two daughters, Esther and Catherine, served food.

About the time the brothers Tate of Aberdeen passed this way in the mid-1750s, a weary traveler could get a bed at the Admiral (that he might have to share with two or three strangers) with reasonably clean straw plus a ration of rough beer or new Madeira wine along with a stew made from local game for about eight shillings, reportedly a bit higher in quality—and price—than at the competing Paoli Inn.

By the outbreak of the Revolutionary War several competing inns and taverns were in operation, serving every kind of traveler between Philadelphia and Lancaster, a popular starting point where many travelers acquired their wagons to begin the journey west. Early records of drovers hauling goods and produce before the revolution note that a typical trip with a team of oxen or six mules pulling a fully loaded half-ton Conestoga wagon averaged three to four miles per hour in good weather, requiring two full days of travel between Philly and Lancaster that included an overnight stop at one of the inns or taverns that sprung up as commerce increased and road conditions improved between the towns.

"A sign at the door with a simple name indicated the class of clientele to which it catered," relates Pennsylvania historian Beth Arnold. "The first class inns, which were stage stops, bore such names as 'King George' and the 'Crown.' These quickly became the 'General Washington' and 'The Eagle' after the war. Second class establishments were the wagon stands and bore such names as 'The Wagon' and 'The White Horse.' The third type of inn . . . provided numerous pens for various types of livestock being moved along the road to market. Droves of turkeys, for example, were not uncommon. The last class was the tap stand, like the corner bar of today. Many sold only beer and cider and were known by such names as 'The Jolly Pot' and the 'Cat and Fiddle.'"

In addition to providing food and modest overnight accommodation, most of these taverns and inns saw dual service as local post offices, court-rooms, regular coaching stops, auction houses, even military recruiting cen-ters and polling stations—equal to churches, Arnold writes, "in importance as centers of commercial, economic, political, and social life in the early days of the township." In the 1750s, the years during which tens of thou-sands of arriving European settlers set off for Maryland, Virginia, and the Carolinas, Pennsylvania passed a law prohibiting tavern keepers from dis-pensing "strong liquors" at auctions and polling places, though the English tradition of providing plentiful alcohol to voters on Election Day remained a common practice throughout most of Pennsylvania's sister colonies of the day.

Tonight, unfortunately, there is no room at the beautiful General War-ren due to a large wedding party that has the place booked for the weekend. The courteous young woman on the front desk, however, provides me with a brochure for future reference and invites me to have a look around the property. She helpfully points me to a parlor bar, where the barman is chat-ting with an older gentleman in a navy blazer and fancy French-blue bowtie.

I take a seat two stools away from him and order a Sam Adams, pictur-ing Ben Franklin kicking back with a cold one after a daylong dusty ride from Philadelphia.

My elegant bar mate smiles. He's having something clear on ice with a twist.

"You here for the wedding too?"

As I pour my beer, I mention that I'm just passing through but drawn to historic taverns, especially ones that may have survived on the Great Wagon Road. The name drop is to see if he's ever heard it. To my pleasant surprise, he has.

"Very nice. In that case, have you seen the battleground? It's almost directly on the Wagon Road."

I wonder if he means Valley Forge, which lies less than ten miles away.

"No. I'm talking about the Paoli Battlefield Park. That's just south of downtown Malvern, a couple miles from here. Most visitors go straight to Valley Forge and completely miss the Paoli Battlefield. That's too bad."

I sip my beer and invite him to tell me more.

His name is Paul. The Battle of Paoli, he explains, is probably the "Rev War's"—his words—best kept secret. It is every bit as important as Valley Forge in the struggle for American independence, and yet most Americans have never heard its name. He suddenly has my undivided attention.

Paul, by way of a preamble, explains that he knows so much about the subject because an old college chum from Temple serves on a committee of local history lovers that recently submitted a proposal to the US Department of the Interior to have the Paoli Battlefield Park and its parade ground designated as a National Historic Landmark. "It's a long-overdue honor that has grated on local history buffs forever," he says. The campaign is funded by donations from local civic organizations and individuals plus a grant from the American Battlefield Protection Program, which is a grass-roots movement aimed at preserving America's important—if woefully neglected—battlefields from commercial development.

"If you'll pardon the pun, they've been fighting a losing battle for decades, to hear my friends around here tell it. The massacre that happened at Paoli Battlefield shaped the outcome of the war and produced a famous battle cry. By the way, Malvern also holds the oldest memorial parade in the nation and has the second-oldest battlefield monument, too, after Lexington. You just missed the parade. It's quite a patriotic show."

He sips his clear-through. I ask about the battle cry.

"*Remember Paoli!*"

"But no one does . . . "

"Not enough who matter. The story is pretty incredible."

I open my notebook, hoping I've stumbled onto my first hidden Great Road gem.

Paul smiles. "You a reporter?"

"Once upon a time. Now I'm just an old guy following an even older road." I admit that I might write about my travels for people who dig lost American roads.

"Happy to tell you what I know," says Paul. "But please don't use my whole name."

"Gotcha. Witness protection program?"

He smiles, rattling his ice. "Worse. My granddaughter grew up here and is a bridesmaid in the wedding tomorrow. She's upstairs getting dressed for the rehearsal dinner tonight." He lowers his voice to a conspiratorial whisper. "I'm on a serious heart medication, see, and not supposed to consume alcohol. My daughter, her mother, has spies everywhere in Malvern." He winks. "Like the British in 1777."

I suggest calling him Paul Revere, my friendly tavern spy. The barkeep glides our way.

"That has a nice revolutionary ring to it."

So as Paul narrates, I order a second Sam Adams and begin to scribble. Paul is right; it turns out to be one fine story.

Before the Rev War, the Admiral Warren was a well-known roadhouse friendly to the area's Royalists and Tory sympathizers. The proprietor in those days, one Peter Mather, was long suspected of providing British troops with confidential info on Washington's troop movements in the area, including the precise location of a large American encampment led by American General Anthony Wayne of Paoli.

On a rainy September night in 1777, nine days after George Washington's defeat at the Battle of Brandywine, two thousand seasoned British troops commanded by Major General Charles "No Flint" Grey launched a sneak attack on a brigade of Pennsylvania Continentals that had been deployed by Washington under Anthony Wayne's command to protect the western flank of Philadelphia. By removing flints from their muskets, the British force (including fearsome Scottish Highlanders) caused panic and mayhem by attacking with only swords and fixed bayonets, killing fifty-three Americans and wounding or capturing two hundred and twenty more. The attack was widely reported as a "massacre" due to the savagery of the British troops. By comparison, only four British troops were killed and eleven were wounded.

Days after the attack at Paoli, the Second Continental Congress fled on the Wagon Road to Lancaster and, one day later, moved on to York Town as the city of Philadelphia fell to the British army. Hoping to tactically regroup his scattered forces, Washington withdrew to nearby Valley Forge to reorganize his twelve thousand haggard troops for the winter, a safe haven where he could keep an eye on the large, well-fed, and superbly trained British army just across the Schuylkill River.

Before long, word spread beyond the army. "Outrage over the atrocities helped fuel citizen anger and boosted recruitment for the Continental Army," Paul explains, "and led to the famous battle cry 'Remember Paoli!' Some historians believe that to be the war's first true battle cry." The phrase was also used, he adds, as the secret password Anthony Wayne employed when his troops launched their own bayonets-only revenge attack on the British fort at Stony Point in New York two years later, capturing hundreds of British troops, marking one of the first turning points of the war. General Wayne and his men were awarded special commendations by the Continental Congress for their compassionate conduct there, a model of honorable wartime behavior in battle that changed how prisoners and wounded combatants were treated going forward.

He clears up one commonly misunderstood detail.

"The attack wasn't entirely a surprise to General Wayne, as typically reported. He heard from a local farmer at the Paoli Inn—which was near his home—that redcoat troops had been snatching locals off the Wagon Road to use as hostages and were preparing an assault on the encamped Americans, a tip that provided Wayne just enough time to post extra pickets and begin a measured, tactical retreat from the area. The massacre could have been much worse than it was."

A young woman with coiling blond hair suddenly appears beside us, smiling broadly. "There you are, I should have known! They're starting, Poppy."

Poppy gives me a wry glance. "No worry. She's no tavern spy. We're best of buddies."

I thank him for the story as he takes my notebook to jot down the name of the man who heads up the Paoli Battlefield Preservation Fund. He suggests that I give him a call to get an update on the campaign and provides me with directions to the Paoli Battlefield Park.

"Here's another interesting tidbit for your Wagon Road journal," he says, sliding a ten-dollar tip under his empty glass. "After the war, the owners of the Paoli Tavern embedded copper pennies into the inn's foyer floor spelling out the words 'Remember Paoli!'"

"I'd love to see that. Is the tavern still around?"

"Unfortunately, it was torn down decades ago. I think it's where Paoli's main post office stands today."

With a hot summer day sliding into a cooler twilight, I pay my tab and make haste for the battlefield, following Paul's excellent directions through downtown Malvern until I come upon a pastoral meadow framed by mature hardwood trees, stone walls, and split rails. A lot of folks are still out walking the park's winding pathways around the battlefield in the fragrant summer dusk, many with leashed dogs, while a group of kids play Frisbee football in the fading light.

A large unleashed black Lab bounds past me chasing his own Frisbee, reminding me of my missing travel mate, as I hike toward the second-oldest battlefield monument in America.

A weathered brass plaque on a stone obelisk reads:

> *Here repose the remains of fifty three American soldiers who were the victims of cold blooded cruelty in the well-known MASSACRE AT PAOLI while under the command of Genl. Anthony Wayne | An officer whose military conduct, BRAVERY AND HUMANITY were equally conspicuous throughout THE REVOLUTIONARY WAR.*

Just then my cell phone rings, yanking me back from the mid-eighteenth century.

"So, where are you? Mully wants to know what she's missing."

"I was just thinking about her—and you."

Wendy laughs. "Nice recovery. Good first day on the old Wagon Road?"

"Very full. Quite encouraging." I provide a brief field report on meeting Ben Franklin and friends, my stop at the museum, and the historic General Warren inn, where I may have stumbled on the best kept secret of the entire Rev War.

"That's a pretty good first day," she agrees. "But where do you plan to lay your weary head tonight? It's getting late."

Long familiar with my tendency to get lost in whatever story I'm chasing and forget such details, Dame Wendy has already taken the task in hand and scoped out a nearby Hampton Inn and the Sheraton at Valley Forge, both of which are nearly full for the night. (*When in doubt, book a room* is her motto, as a savvy traveler who belongs to half a dozen hotel membership programs. Long ago I decided the woman could organize a convention of anarchists.)

The historic White Horse Tavern is supposedly somewhere in the vicinity, I offer as an alternative. It's another of the celebrated inns on the original road to Lancaster, rumored to be among the first places where the Declaration of Independence was publicly read aloud after its signing in July 1776. The "Sign of the White Horse" was a phrase known far and wide and up and down the Wagon Road. Dating from the 1720s, the tavern also served as a courthouse and polling station and General Washington's headquarters during the Battle of Brandywine and aborted Battle of the Clouds before his strategic retreat to nearby Valley Forge.

Before I've even finished the thought, I hear her fingertips clicking on a keyboard.

"The good news is the White Horse is a wine bar. Let me check something else . . . "

More furious clicks. In the interim, I snap a photo of the Paoli monument and start back toward the Frisbee football match, now in full dusk with scattered fireflies. "No worries, babe," I remark with a yawn, suddenly feeling the effects of the beer and a long but productive first day. "I can always just curl up in the back of the Pearl somewhere. That's probably what my frugal Scottish ancestors did on their first night on the Wagon Road—"

"Ah, I just snagged their last room!" she says triumphantly, cutting me off.

"Where's that?"

"The Sheraton Great Valley Hotel *is* the White Horse Tavern. Seven miles from where you're standing. Looks very nice."

It suddenly hits me that, thanks to my fancy new smartphone, which Dame Wendy thoughtfully programmed, she knows exactly where I stand at this moment. This is either comforting or frightening. It's almost impossible to get lost anywhere in modern America. Someone can *always* find you.

"Frankly, I'd rather sleep in the back of a wagon. That's much more in tune with the spirit of my journey."

"Yeah, well, Dan'l Boone, this isn't the eighteenth century. Your bed at the Sheraton awaits. That way *both* of us can get a good night's sleep."

As I approach the entrance ramp to get back on Route 30 west, the rush-hour traffic has remarkably thinned out. I've stopped at a traffic signal near the entrance ramp to Lincoln Highway, and as I wait for the light to change, an arctic-white BMW with dark-tinted windows eases up beside me. I can't believe my eyes. The Beemer's driver's-side window glides down and a cute young woman with blond hair grins at me. She looks to be about my daughter Maggie's age. I put down my passenger-side window, wondering what the hell she has to say.

"Listen, I'm *so* sorry about what happened earlier. I realized that I almost made you crash. But I was twenty minutes late for closing on a house my husband and I are buying. It's our first house and I was just losing my mind. It was foolish driving. Can you forgive me? I really am *sorry* . . . "

"Did you get the house?"

She beams. "We sure did! We plan to move in in five weeks!"

I ask her name. It's Trisha.

"Congratulations, Trisha. All's well that ends well. I'll just stay out of your way."

"Not necessary. But thank you! Oh, if you don't mind me saying so, that's a really cool car. My grandfather had one just like it. You look like Clark Griswold driving it."

It takes me a senior moment to realize she means Chevy Chase in the epic cinematic achievement *National Lampoon's Vacation*.

Before I can find the words, she grins and adds playfully, "Hey, Clark, want to race me to Wally World?"

I smile, picturing Dame Wendy's face as she gets a call from the Malvern Police to inform her that her elderly husband has been arrested for drag racing a blond in a BMW.

"Better not. Thanks, though."

The light changes and she zooms ahead toward the highway's east-bound ramp.

Just for fun, I gun the Pearl's 350-horsepower Corvette engine and almost catch up to her in the left lane as she merges to the right up the ramp toward Philly. She toots her horn several times and even fist pumps out her window.

"Remember Paoli!" Clark Griswold shouts back.

FIVE

YOUNG DANIELS

BY THE TIME I ARRIVE AT THE DANIEL BOONE HOMESTEAD, THERE ARE ONLY two cars left in the parking lot. Next to them, a woman wearing a flowered smock and sunglasses chats with a young dark-haired man dressed in colonial garb who looks like a young Daniel Boone.

"I'm sorry," the woman says firmly as I approach. "We're closing for the day but will reopen tomorrow morning at ten."

I apologize for arriving late, explaining that I missed a turn from Valley Forge and took myself on an unplanned tour of the local countryside.

"I've never been lost," I joke, "though I have been confused for several weeks."

Her blank expression tells me she's unfamiliar with one of Daniel Boone's most famous quotes. But at least young Daniel smiles.

Up till now, it's been a day of fine surprises. A helpful checkout clerk at the Sheraton had mentioned that the original White Horse Tavern—now a private home—lay just a mile or so farther up Route 202 toward Valley Forge National Historical Park, providing all the encouragement I needed to take a look at the house before proceeding on to the nearby park, where I took myself on a two-hour self-guided walking tour. In the park gift shop, I found a history of the Battle of Paoli, which I speed-read over lunch, corroborating everything Paul Revere told me at the General Warren. With the number he gave me, I also phoned for Jim Christ, the president of the Paoli

Battlefield Preservation Fund, and left a voicemail explaining my desire for an update on the Paoli Battlefield campaign for federal recognition.

The clerk in the gift shop also mentioned that Daniel Boone's birthplace lay just half an hour away in Birdsboro, which prompted me to head that way, because few traveled the Great Wagon Road more diligently than young Boone, or better symbolized its importance to America's westward expansion. A brief side trip off the Wagon Road to see where his life began seemed absolutely in order.

As I was halfway there, following Daphne Dewhurst's somewhat confusing directions, Jim Christ returned my phone call and filled me in on his group's recent progress to secure federal historic recognition for Paoli Battlefield. The conversation was so engrossing I drove straight past a key turnoff onto PA state road 23 and wound up in the heart of remote and beautiful French Creek State Park and the Birdsboro Preserve. With no cell service available, Daphne Dewhurst was useless, so I navigated the old-fashioned way by asking a country store clerk who kindly drew me a map on a paper bag involving several back-road turns that got me to the Boone Homestead with five whole minutes to spare.

I reach the end of my sad lost-dog story, but the Homestead Boss Lady appears unmoved. So, I try one last thing: my cousin Josie Dodson sympathy card.

"May I just take a quick walk around the house? I had an elderly third cousin who knew some of Boone's family out in the Yadkin Valley of North Carolina. Daniel Boone was her hero. She gave me his biography when I was a kid . . . " I plead, seemingly to a brick wall. And then:

"I'm in no rush," young Daniel casually interrupts. "I can show him around before I go."

His name, I learn, really *is* Daniel.

Daniel Levitsky is a twenty-one-year-old summer intern and homestead guide studying historic preservation at nearby Kutztown University.

He walks me around the rugged Pennsylvania bluestone house to its cellar entrance explaining that this is the only surviving part of the original log house Squire Boone constructed for his family in 1730. Son Daniel was born here in November 1734, the sixth of Sarah Boone's eleven children.

After the Boones departed for North Carolina on the Great Wagon Road in 1750, an Englishman named William Maugridge purchased the house and lived in it until his death in 1766, whereupon a German farmer named John DeTurk purchased the property and eventually replaced the log walls with locally quarried stone.

As we duck into the cool, damp root cellar, where meat and other perishables were kept in natural refrigeration provided by an open spring, Daniel reminds me that Boone's father, Squire Boone, was an English Quaker born in Devonshire who answered William Penn's call to America accompanied by his sister Sarah and brother George. After marrying Sarah Morgan on the thirtieth day of the sixth month in 1720—Quakers avoided using pagan-named months—he purchased 250 acres in the Oley Valley and started building his family home. Among their closest neighbors was another immigrant family named Lincoln, which intermarried with the Boones and eventually produced a grandson born in Kentucky named Abraham.

Owing to my fellow Carolinian Robert Morgan's superb 2008 biography of Boone, I know the Boone saga almost chapter and verse. Yet it's delightful to hear about the iconic frontiersman's beginnings from the mouth of a bright young fellow who clearly seems to dig American history.

Squire Boone, Daniel continues, was your basic backcountry polymath: a gifted blacksmith, farmer, and weaver who owned a gristmill and a sizable herd of cattle, a man of smallish physical stature known for his patience and common sense who battled an inner restlessness and powerful streak of independence, traits his son Dan'l would inherit. Young Boone's closest relationship, however, was with his mother, a tall, raven-haired beauty with dark Welsh eyes and a cheerful disposition. "From the very beginning," Morgan writes, "the family sensed Daniel was different from the other children. Lively, apparently tireless, curious, when very young he helped out in the family trades of blacksmithing, milling, and farming. But the family lore has it that from the very first Young Daniel liked to roam the woods."

Beginning around age ten, young Daniel helped his mother look after sheep and cattle pastured on twenty-five acres of land five miles from the Boone homestead, sharing a rough cabin together there from spring to autumn. Sarah Boone, as Morgan beautifully relates, countenanced her son's "tendency to slip away into the forest for hours, for whole days. The bond between mother and son was intense, affectionate, and inspiring. It seems she put her fondest hopes in this independent, somewhat wayward boy driven by enthusiasms for the wild places and world beyond the farm, beyond the river.

"For the rest of his life Boone would look back on those summers as an idyllic time," adds Morgan. "For Daniel, the forest was his mother's world, a place of shadows and mystery, infinite pleasures and diversions . . . He would always be closer to the mother's world than the father's world. His deepest affinity was with the forest and the streams."

Boone was thirteen when his father gave his son his first firearm, "a short rifle gun" made by Squire Boone that allowed Daniel to hunt for days in the nearby Neversink Mountain and Oley Hills. Like William Penn, the family enjoyed peaceful relations with native tribes of the area—Delawares, Nanticokes, and Tuscaroras—encounters that fascinated young Boone and drew him even closer to the forest. One nearby Indian village he frequented was called Manangy's Town; it would eventually become the town of Reading.

In 1750, Squire's restlessness got the better of him. Most Boone biographers—by my count there are at least a dozen over the past two centuries—attribute the family's decision to pack up and follow the Great Wagon Road to the wilds of North Carolina's Yadkin Valley to the patriarch's innate desire to keep moving west, a theme that permeates the lore and literature of the Wagon Road. Some also insist that, as the Great Awakening was rapidly spreading fear of damnation and hellfire through the frontier, a falling-out with their local Quaker meeting over the marriage of Squire Boone's eldest daughter, Sarah, to a non-Quaker was perhaps the motivation. In 1750, whatever the cause, they joined the Great Migration, an entourage that included seven other unmarried children ages four to eighteen; married daughter Sarah and her husband, John Wilcoxson; plus sons Israel and Samuel and their wives. A farmhand and Daniel's best friend, Henry Miller, also joined the traveling party. That same autumn, Daniel Boone turned sixteen.

They followed an old Indian trail to Harris's Ferry on the Susquehanna River, "following the line of the Appalachian Mountains by what was called either the Virginia Road or the Great Wagon Road," writes Morgan.

According to a report made to the Board of Trade in London in 1751, the road was 435 miles from Philadelphia to the Yadkin Valley.

Following a lengthy stop in western Virginia during the summer of 1752, the family resumed the pilgrimage and settled on the banks of the Yadkin River in western Piedmont, North Carolina, where Daniel Boone would soon begin his own journey into the mythology of the American frontier.

In the meantime, I'm curious what drew *this* young Daniel to the life and times of Daniel Boone.

"I've always been interested to see where famous individuals start out before anyone knew about them," Levitsky explains as he walks me through the silent rooms of the Boone House, today named for the DeTurk family that eventually took over and expanded the property. "I think someone's life before fame or accomplishment can tell us a great deal about how they became the person they did."

He tells me about growing up in Reading—a town settled by German immigrants—where he fell in love with history early in life, the reason he is studying German history in America at Kutztown University and hoping to someday land a job in historic preservation. In the meantime, one of his primary passions is Revolutionary War reenacting as one of the youngest members of the Pennsylvania First Continental Regiment of Foot, which annually travels to reenactments from Quebec to Savannah, Georgia. "My favorite reenacting event is our traditional appearance at Independence Hall every Fourth of July," he tells me. "The uniform of our regiment is very special. We're a crowd favorite." The First Continental's dress includes traditional breeches, wool stockings, a linen waistcoat, buckled shoes, and a hunter-green frock.

"I guess I love reenacting because I get to meet people from all over the country and even the world," Levitsky adds. "Also, it's a great way to get others interested in history and learn cool things they've never heard before. We drill using Von Steuben's famous handbook that shaped up Washington's army at Valley Forge, for instance, and was used by the American military from 1778 onward—still in use by the military today."

As it happens, I had learned about Baron Frederick Von Steuben's indispensable manual just that morning back at Valley Forge. Von Steuben, introduced to George Washington by the ubiquitous Benjamin Franklin, was a decorated Prussian commander who spoke no English but employed his formidable bearing and brilliant organizational skills to impose a strict rule of order and discipline on Washington's ragtag army of twelve thousand starving troops gathered from eleven different colonies, one in four of whom was either barefoot or unfit for service due to outbreaks of smallpox, pneumonia, and dysentery. Somehow Von Steuben transformed them into a disciplined fighting force that would eventually turn the tide of the war.

Daniel Levitsky gives me a few extra details about the Prussian and his famous manual. Originally drafted in French, translated into English by Alexander Hamilton and Nathanael Greene, Von Steuben's *Regulations for the Order and Discipline of the Troops of the United States*—sometimes called the Blue Book—became the standard training manual for American troops for the next two centuries. Along with Washington's daring gambit to inoculate his troops against smallpox—believed to be the first mass immunization program in history—Von Steuben's restoration of the Continental Army gradually began to shift the balance of power in America's favor. On Washington's recommendation, Von Steuben went on to become the army's inspector general, serving as a division commander at the Siege of Yorktown in 1781, where the British finally surrendered.

As he walks me to my car, Daniel Levitsky tells me the story of how the Boone Homestead sat abandoned and forgotten for decades until a local minister from Birdsboro and a history-loving gentleman from East Orange, New Jersey, purchased the property in 1926, determined to preserve the homestead. A decade later, President Franklin Roosevelt tapped Pennsylvania's Gifford Pinchot to help form an organization known as the Daniel Boone Memorial in Berks County. Two years later, in 1937, by act of the Pennsylvania legislature, the commonwealth acquired the Daniel Boone Homestead for the "purposes of preserving it as a historic place and park for the benefit of the people of the Commonwealth."

A year later, during a ceremony attended by Boy Scouts and Reading High School students, the property was officially dedicated to "the American Boy." Today, the 579-acre site includes the Boone House, various restored outbuildings, a Visitor Center, miles of hiking trails, camping facilities, and a lodge used for educational programs and organized youth groups.

Speaking as a former Boy Scout and American boy myself, I thank Daniel

Levitsky for using his after-hours time to show me around the property and share his stories of Von Steuben and Boone's beginnings.

"No problem. Happy to do it. I'm not meeting my friends for beer for another hour, anyway."

I offer to buy their first round and wonder what beer he prefers.

"That's okay. You've probably never heard of it. It's called Ben Franklin's Spruce Beer."

He laughs when I explain that it's my new favorite too. What a small colonial world this is.

Somewhere in the backwoods of eternity, I hope Cousin Josie and her hero Daniel Boone may both be pleased by how this serendipitous day of wandering just off the Great Wagon Road has turned out so splendidly.

PART TWO

HEROES AND VILLAINS

SIX

THE LAST CONESTOGA

A **LARGE BREAKFAST CROWD FILLS THE CONESTOGA WAGON RESTAURANT ON** a bright Sunday morning, buzzing with neighborly conversation.

I grab the only empty seat at the crowded horseshoe counter between a burly fellow wearing a faded yellow Salt Life T-shirt and a snowy-haired couple telling the frazzled waitress about their recent two-week trip to Myrtle Beach.

First item on my day's agenda is to find authentic Pennsylvania scrapple, a Keystone breakfast staple that's been around since the days of Ben Franklin, reportedly brought to America by the Swiss and German Anabaptists who first settled Lancaster County in the early 1700s. My late mom's German clan, the colorful Kessells of western Maryland, absolutely lived off the stuff, which is reportedly made from leftover meat scraps, nonspecific pig parts, rotten garden vegetables, minced week-old daily newspapers, and enough garlic to turn a good family to blows. Truthfully, I have no idea what's actually in it—possibly colonial America's answer to English blood pudding or Scotland's famously repulsive national dish, haggis, which I also have an unaccountable late-in-life fancy for.

In any case, my mission is fueled by a fond memory of the first time I tasted the dish at my Uncle Russell Goodfellow's rustic "camp" on the south branch of the Potomac River, just off the Wagon Road in West Virginia, sometime in the early 1960s. It required a slug of his daily breakfast

Natty Boh to clear my nine-year-old head. Five decades later, on a trip to cover the US Open at Philadelphia, I tried Keystone scrapple again and—go figure—discovered that I actually liked the stuff and maybe even loved it.

Of more relevant purpose on this sweet Sabbath morning, I hope to pick up an extra detail or two about the development of the Conestoga wagon in the village where, legend holds, the iconic vehicle was invented by German "mechanics" in the early 1700s.

(Another version credits wily James Logan, William Penn's enterprising secretary, with developing the revolutionary freight wagon—probably spread by Logan himself—but a docent at the Conestoga Area Historical Society had assured me that the wagon's true provenance was a trio of clever German Mennonite mechanics, though their names are lost to history.) Whichever story turns out to be the correct one, I am here in part thanks to a beautifully restored Conestoga wagon that sits in a rear gallery of my hometown history museum in Greensboro, one that transported a German family from Pennsylvania to Guilford County in the late 1750s. Not only did it confirm my father's story about our family's connection to the Great Wagon Road, but it familiarized me with the basic characteristics of this engineering marvel of transport.

The uniquely nautical-looking Conestoga's distinguishing features include a solid oak construction buttressed by steel-reinforced ribs and rails that are naturally curved to cause the wagon's contents to shift toward the center of the wagon when traveling over rough or uneven ground. Its high bed clearance, revolutionary independent braking system, and wheel-locking chains were other major engineering innovations, providing strength and safety on unstable surfaces. Benjamin Rush, the Philadelphia physician who signed the Declaration of Independence, called Conestoga wagons "Ships of Inland Commerce," emphasizing their vital role in saving Washington's skin at Valley Forge and helping America achieve independence and growth on the frontier. "These wagons," echoes transportation historian Arthur Reist, "helped to establish new towns, cities, and a line of communication from east to west opening up new frontiers before railroads would eventually replace them."

A large Conestoga with a standard team of four oxen or mules could carry anywhere from three to five thousand pounds with ease and featured removeable panels that made loading and unloading a breeze, explaining why the Conestoga became the workhorse of colonial freight hauling, constructed with design principles still used in modern trucking.

During a visit to the Conestoga Area Historical Society the afternoon before, I'd picked up a few additional lovely bits of lore surrounding the pioneering wagon, including the fact that it was named for the winding river and peaceful Indian tribe that inhabited the area, and that most Conestoga teamsters—as the wagon's drivers were commonly called—walked on the left side of the wagon beside their draft horses, mules, or teams of oxen, though under the wagon bed was a stout oak "lazy board" that could be pulled out for a weary teamster to stand or sit on. (Transportation historians also believe that the tradition of a steering wheel on the left side of modern automobiles had its origin with the Conestoga wagon.)

Before and during the Revolutionary War, fleets of commercial Conestoga wagons were often distinguished by their vermillion undercarriages and bright blue beds, with hoop coverings made from white homespun cloth, a combination believed to have inspired America's choice of patriotic colors—red, white, and blue. In a pinch, a teamster whose wagon was disabled could pay for assistance or repairs with a rack of bells from his own teams of horses, giving rise to a phrase to departing teamsters: "Please return with your bells on!"

My third reason for dropping by the Conestoga Wagon Restaurant on this pretty Sabbath morning relates to the historic treaty that failed to protect the Conestoga Indians, resulting in a massacre that appears in few histories of colonial America, an atrocity that effectively obliterated whatever remained of William Penn's lofty Holy Experiment.

During the winter of 1763, the last of the Conestoga Indians (remnants of the once-mighty Susquehannock tribe, decimated by disease and a ruinous war with the powerful Iroquois) resided on a five-hundred-acre tract of land called Conestoga Indian Town, a few miles east of Lancaster City, land that colony founder William Penn had personally set aside for them by signed treaty in April 1701. The Quaker founder believed that the pledge of protection would strengthen trade and improve relations between settlers and Native Americans as the colony grew, supporting his vision of a "Peaceable Kingdom" where all could live in harmony.

Just after dawn on a snowy February morning, not long after the signing of the Treaty of Paris brought the brutal French and Indian War to a close and granted the British Crown governance of Canada and all lands from the Atlantic to the Mississippi River, Penn's hopes were dashed by a group of fifty self-styled Scots-Irish militiamen from northern Lancaster County who called themselves the Paxton Rangers. Allegedly fed up with Indian raids by less-peaceful tribes on frontier settlements, and fueled by lingering anger at Pontiac's Rebellion in the Great Lakes region, the horde thundered into the sleeping village of Conestoga Indian Town and brutally murdered Conestoga Indians in their sleep, hacking or shooting them to death and torching their houses.

Most of the town's other twenty residents were away at the time, delayed by heavy snowfall after taking their homemade baskets and earthenware to sell at the public marketplace in Lancaster. As historian Jack Brubaker recounts in *Massacre of the Conestogas*, "The Rangers went about their business in a rush. They dismounted and fired their flintlocks at the Indian huts. They rushed inside and tomahawked the survivors. They scalped everyone. Then they looted the huts, lashed the booty to their saddles, and set the buildings on fire. The entire operation must have consumed only minutes."

Three men, two women, and one child were murdered, including the elderly chief who negotiated the original peace treaty with Penn. Only a seventh young boy survived, the story goes, by fleeing into the woods. Ironically, among the few charred remains found one day after the massacre was the original treaty parchment that established the creation of Conestoga Indian Town—the only surviving peace treaty formally signed by William Penn.

Within days, an outraged Benjamin Franklin published his own account in the newspaper of the shocking incident under the headline "Narrative of the Late Massacres, in Lancaster County, of a Number of Indians."

Fifty-seven Men, from some of our Frontier Townships, who had projected the destruction of this little Common-wealth, came, all well-mounted, and armed with Firelocks, Hangers and Hatchets, having traveled through the County in the Night, to Conestoga Manor. There they surrounded the small

Village of Indian Huts, and just at Break of Day broke into them all at once. Only three Men, two Women, and a young Boy were found at home, the rest being out among the neighboring White People, some to sell the Baskets, Brooms and Bowls they manufactured, and others on other occasions. These poor defenseless creatures were immediately fired upon, stabbed and hatcheted to Death! The good Shehaes, among the rest, cut to pieces in his bed. All of them were scalped, and otherwise horribly mangled. Then their Huts were set on Fire, and most of them burnt down. When the troop, pleased with their own Conduct and Bravery, but enraged that any of the poor Indians had escaped the Massacre, rode off, and in small parties, by different Roads, went home.

Despite the fact that Lancaster magistrates reportedly knew the names of several key participants of the mass murder, notably the Presbyterian elders who may have instigated the attack, an official coroner's inquest determined that the slaughter had been committed "by a person or persons to this Inquest unknown." Meanwhile, the tribe's Mennonite neighbors sheltered surviving tribe members until county magistrates ordered them all to be taken into "protective custody" and housed at a newly opened workhouse in Lancaster.

On Sunday afternoon, December 27, fourteen days after the massacre, as church services were ending across the Lancaster Town, between one hundred and one hundred and fifty Paxton riders stormed into the courtyard of the workhouse, bludgeoning and reportedly scalping the fourteen "protected" Conestoga Indians, as the sheriff and county coroner stood aside. According to a local justice of the peace, the massacre lasted no more than twelve minutes. The killers departed the bloody scene firing their guns and "whooping and hollering."

As Brubaker recounts, no perpetrators were ever brought to justice—or even charged. Many Lancaster residents, in fact, tacitly supported the atrocity, citing growing concerns of Indian raids on frontier settlements. "Before leaving Lancaster," he writes, "the Paxton Rangers had informed bystanders that they had not yet finished with Pennsylvania's protected Indians. They claimed they would move on to Philadelphia and there attack the 125 Moravian Indians who had settled on an island in the Delaware."

By late January, reports filtered along the Wagon Road that those fears had prompted some German and English residents of Lancaster County to join a growing army of fifteen hundred vigilantes, now calling themselves the Paxton Boys and threatening to sack the city of Philadelphia itself. "The largest city in the colonies—ten times the size of Lancaster—was a tempting target," writes Brubaker. "Philadelphia's twenty thousand residents included most of the colonies' movers and shakers." The pacifist Quaker city had no standing militia.

On the eve of the insurrection, Robert Fulton Sr., a Lancaster Presbyterian and father of the future inventor of the steamboat, who happened to be sympathetic to the cause of the killers, reported that the Paxton Boys had swelled to an angry mob of five thousand strong, hoping to spark a sweeping reaction of retribution across the colonies.

When he caught word of the approaching horde, Ben Franklin convinced Philadelphia's governing authorities to put aside their pacifist Quaker principles and pick up firearms for their own good, rallying five hundred armed citizens to meet the arrival of the vigilantes. The colony's general assembly also hastily passed a rioting act that targeted any "group of twelve or more turbulent and evil-minded persons" that conspired to disrupt civic order.

The two sides faced off in Market Square on February 6. The city's church bells tolled to raise the alarm, and a warning cannon shot was fired from Franklin's citizen militia. Residents and businesses lit tapers in their windows to show support for the home guard.

Surprised by the resolve of the citizens prepared to face them, the Paxton Boys decided to momentarily stand down and negotiate on the city's outskirts. The next day, Philadelphia's mayor and attorney general as well as Franklin himself met with the leaders of the vigilantes in Germantown.

Two deals were reportedly struck. In one, the Paxton Boys agreed to return to their homes if their grievances were officially heard by the colony's general assembly. When they were given the opportunity to speak, chief among their complaints was a familiar gripe that the citizens of Philadelphia, Bucks, and Chester Counties enjoyed better representation in the Pennsylvania assembly than Lancaster and other frontier counties, and that government taxes were funding the protection of hostile Indian tribes attacking settlers across the colony.

The Pennsylvania assembly officially considered these concerns on the condition that the Paxton Boys agree to return home. They did withdraw, but on their way out of town the mob's leaders held a private meeting with Governor John Penn, fueling rumors of a secret deal that absolved the Paxton Boys of their alleged crimes in exchange for a pledge never to take up arms against the colony again. (Weeks after the crisis, in fact, Ben Franklin bitterly complained that John Penn had abandoned his grandfather's principles by refusing to arrest and prosecute the killers of the Conestoga Indians, setting a dangerous precedent.)

"The Paxton Boys returned to their farms and went about their business without disturbance from any authority," Jack Brubaker sums up. "By spring, the men who'd brutally slaughtered twenty Indians in their huts at Conestoga and in the workhouse yard at Lancaster realized they had escaped punishment."

The extermination of the Conestogas would quickly be covered up and officially forgotten, warranting only the briefest of mentions—if at all—in most histories of the American frontier. Even more troubling, six months after the massacre, the commonwealth agreed to promote frontier settlement by essentially doubling bounties paid to soldiers and local militias for killing "troublesome" Indians—a scheme that amounted to open season on native peoples. As the Paxton mob had hoped, the consequences of this horrific episode—and its staggering absence of justice—had a profound ripple effect across the colonies, unleashing government-sanctioned genocide into the bloodstream of a new America, opening the doors to frontier violence on an unprecedented scale.

"The result was wave after wave of violence on the frontier," Kevin Kenny writes in his outstanding book *Peaceable Kingdom Lost*, "culminating in total war against Indians during the American Revolution. The Paxton Boys' brutality was anomalous as late as 1763, in Pennsylvania at least; by the time of the American Revolution, it had become commonplace."

"So, what kind of mileage does that monster get?"

The question comes from Salt Life man, who is gazing over my shoulder at the Pearl through the café's front window directly behind me.

I am silently enjoying my scrapple breakfast and deep in thought about the last of the Conestogas, momentarily forgetting about the famous wagon named for them, thinking how history may not repeat itself but certainly seems to rhyme, as historian Jon Meacham likes to say.

I look at Salt Life man wondering if he's somehow reading my deep and troubling thoughts until I realize that he's simply asking about my vintage Buick's gas mileage.

"Not great, I'm afraid. Twenty miles per gallon on the highway, half that around town."

He nods, stabbing his pancakes. "Nice ride, though."

"Like seeing America in your living room."

He tells me his name is Tim. He asks where I'm from. I tell him North Carolina, traveling the Great Wagon Road in my version of a gas-guzzling Conestoga wagon.

"I've heard of it," he says. "So what do you think of when I say 'stogie'?"

I tell him about Aubrey Apple, a crusty golf pro I worked for one summer who always sported a smoldering butt of the world's foulest cigar in his mouth, a rancid *stogie*. Good old Aubrey was in the North Carolina Golf Hall of Fame, I add, for profanity.

Tim chuckles. "That's pretty funny. The word 'stogie' actually originated here."

He explains that just over the hill and down the block are a couple of ramshackle buildings that once housed the Conestoga Tobacco Company, which made the finest cigars of early America out of Lancaster County tobacco.

"This is where Conestoga wagons were also built," he adds. "The drivers took Conestoga cigars with them. Those cigars identified them. Someone out west—Pittsburgh, I think—started calling them 'stogies.' The name stuck. Not many people around here even know that story."

He finishes his pancakes and waves the waitress over for more coffee, explaining that his fifth-great-grandfather worked on the original Conestoga wagons.

"So you grew up around here?"

"I did. Always took this part of the world for granted, though. Couldn't wait to leave—like the folks in Conestoga wagons."

He goes on to say he lived in Alaska for twenty-nine years, but after the death of his wife, his brother convinced him that it was time for him to come home to Lancaster County.

I ask if home feels different now.

"In some ways. People are still friendly around here. But in other ways it's changed, way too built-up. All the tourists."

"We're *all* friendly at the Conestoga Wagon Restaurant, hon," the waitress chimes in, topping up my coffee along with his. Her name is Brenda. Pausing, she asks how I like the scrapple. I inform her that it is about the best I've ever tasted. No cleansing slug of Natty Boh needed.

She grins. "Only *about*?"

"You need to go to Myrtle Beach," pipes up the elderly woman two stools down. "People are really friendly down there. Must be a Southern thing. You from down there?"

"No, ma'am. North Carolina," I repeat. "Big difference." I resist the temptation to explain that South Carolina, which was settled by wealthy plantation Brits and ornery, dirt-poor Wagon Road Scots-Irish, started a Civil War and had nothing like decent scrapple.

"You should check out the Hans Herr House over on Willow Street," adds a gentleman just getting up to pay his bill. He's wearing a green tweed sports coat and striped tie, as if he's headed off to church. "It's the oldest house in the area. Not to be missed. Built in 1719."

He smiles when I mention that I checked it out yesterday afternoon.

"There's so much history here," offers another lady from across the horseshoe. "If you go down the hill to the arboretum at Safe Harbor, you can see the remnants of the big ironworks where they made steel for the Pennsylvania railroads and cannons for the Union Army. There was a whole town there long ago, too, lots of rowdy taverns and such, the Vegas strip of colonial America. All vanished now."

Since I have their attention, it seems like an opportune moment to ask about the elephant in the dining room.

"Any of you know about the Conestoga Indians who died here in a massacre in 1763?"

I might as well have belched the national anthem. Heads dip; nobody replies.

"It's an old story," Tim finally allows with an uneasy shrug, checking his bill. "Some say it never even happened. I think it probably did. But it was so long ago, you know? Nobody wants to talk about that stuff nowadays."

Safe Harbor is a beautiful place, with groomed ballfields, hiking trails, and a lovely public park of old shade trees stretching peacefully along the winding Conestoga River. During a walk to digest my big breakfast, I spot a road sign that reads "Safe Harbor Village" and hoof up a steep paved road hoping to find remnants of the lost Vegas strip of colonial America.

Instead, I come upon a collection of strikingly ornate brick residential buildings with slate roofs surrounded by a beautiful forest that is silent save for the sound of mourning doves. The only living soul I see is a woman lifting a grocery bag from the trunk of her car. She greets me and we chat a bit. Sue Fisher, just back from the grocery store in Lancaster, explains to me that Safe Harbor got its name from the Conestoga Indians who used the area as a gathering spot near the confluence of the Conestoga and Susquehanna Rivers, producing a small protected "harbor" where there existed a plentiful supply of fish and game that sustained local tribes for centuries.

"Because of the ironworks, this was once quite the lively place. The ironworks were where the tennis courts are today. If you take the hiking trail behind them you can even see ruins of a Masonic lodge, the Catholic church, and a cemetery. The ironmaster's house is still there too. There were lots of bars for the workers. It was pretty rowdy, they say. The bridge down there is a remnant of an old canal lock, probably from colonial times. But the flood of 1916 changed everything. After that, the town slipped into ruin. They eventually tore down the houses and nature reclaimed the site of the vanished company town."

"Sounds like a story from the Old Testament—or a Hollywood script."

She smiles. "Doesn't it? It's our lovely secret place in the woods now."

I ask about the collection of handsome brick residences, which, I think, resembles a peaceful college campus.

The buildings were constructed, she tells me, between 1929 and 1931 to house workers for the Depression-era hydroelectric dam that was built at Safe Harbor as part of the federal government's national public electrification project. In the 1970s the power company sold them off to a private consortium that maintained them as apartment dwellings. Most of the complex's buildings are private residences now; a few are apartments with lengthy waiting lists. I can understand why. The setting is like a peaceful forest glen from a Yeats poem. She catches me looking at them. "Beautiful, aren't they? They're classic art deco, like the dam. They once had copper flashing and downspouts. There was real pride in their workmanship. It was a different time."

As we chat—she still holds her bag of groceries—a male cardinal lands on a limb not five feet away.

"The birds love it too." She smiles at the bird, which sits and watches us for several moments.

I learn that Sue is a former employee of FEMA, and a retired architectural historian for the state of Indiana. Her true passion is architectural history and her connection to the area is deep: her people were Mennonites and Scots-Irish from Massachusetts and New Jersey, respectively, some of whom may have traveled the Wagon Road to South Carolina.

We spend another twenty minutes chatting about the Wagon Road and her growing concerns about global warming. Finally, I ask if she happens to know the location of the monument that commemorates the massacre of the Conestogas.

She nods. "It's called the memorial stone. Actually, it's not far."

She directs me across the bridge and up Safe Harbor Road to the intersection with Indian Marker Road, a short but lovely drive past tidy well-kept farms with oceanic fields of head-high late-summer corn, a pastoral tableau that confirms George Washington's reference to Lancaster County's rich limestone farmland as the "breadbasket of the Revolution."

In his 2002 book *Garden Spot: Lancaster County, the Old Order Amish, and the Selling of Rural America*, native son David Walbert points out that the first white settlers to Lancaster County called themselves Mennonites, after Menno Simons, the founder of their Anabaptist movement, the so-called Plain People welcomed by William Penn and his fellow Quakers who shared their refusal to participate in military service and lived simply in harmony with God and nature. "By [eighteenth] mid-century," he writes, "their numbers included several settlements of Amish, a sect that had split with the Mennonites in the late seventeenth century."

As Walbert notes, no place in early America was as fertile or productive as the limestone farmlands of Lancaster County. And no farmers in our history were more successful—or innovative (the first to rotate crops and plant fallow fields with soil-enriching red clover)—than Old Order Amish and Mennonite farm families, producing more food than anywhere in the country for the next two hundred years, feeding the growing cities of the Northeast and revolutionizing American farming in the process. The nickname "Garden Spot of America" was coined during colonial times, prompting Thomas Jefferson to call Lancaster's farmers the "Chosen people of the Earth."

William Penn's invitation to these industrious German sects, famous for their well-cared-for livestock and beautiful stone "bank" barns, was a pragmatic strategy designed to showcase the value of Pennsylvania settlement and increase sale prices of the colony's land. The founder's simultaneous welcome of the Scots-Irish was also pragmatic, though in a very different way—believing that their highly independent nature and combative disregard for authority would make them the ideal buffers against both the neighboring French and hostile Indian tribes on the frontier. As the massacre of the Conestogas proved, this was a strategy destined to lead to disaster and end any hope of a truly peaceful coexistence.

The drive is so pleasant I almost miss the modest memorial, which is set off in a small cutout of woods at the T-junction of Safe Harbor and Indian Marker Road: a large conical-shaped boulder mounted with an oxidizing brass plaque. A limp American flag on a short pole stands next to the stone. I park by a cornfield and walk across the road to have a closer look. I'm half tempted to knock on the door of the small stone farmhouse adjacent to the site to ask a few questions, but suddenly remember that it is 11:28 on a quiet Sunday morning. Church hours, as my Lutheran mother would have firmly reminded. The only sound I can hear is birds calling in the woods and the rustle of starlings in the cornfield across the road.

According to Jack Brubaker, the large memorial stone was hauled out of the same ravine that the murderous Paxton Rangers used to mount their dawn assault on the sleeping Conestogas. The 1924 ceremony to mark its installation was reportedly attended by a thousand citizens of Lancaster and a chief from the Ojibwa tribe of northern Wisconsin who claimed to be a direct blood relative of the Conestogas. The plaque describes the Conestogas as "largely the survivors of the defeated ancient Susquehannas of Iroquoian stock who inhabited various villages in lands granted to them by the treaty made with William Penn, who visited in 1701."

The last line simply reads: "The tribe was exterminated by the Paxton Boys in 1763."

When I contacted him later, Brubaker, a son of Lancaster County and veteran newspaper columnist who lives not far from the memorial stone, provided an updated perspective on the tragic story's painful evolution.

"Like a lot of Lancaster natives, I grew up hearing about the Conestoga murders off and on, but the story always seemed to change, to shift the blame." The confusion stemmed, he explained, from an account by a local Presbyterian clergyman in 1843 that was told from the perspective of the men who committed the crime, a sympathetic retelling that "resulted in a lot of distortion, misinformation, and outright lies about what really happened. Even during the many years that I occasionally wrote about the massacre in my [Scribbler] column for the Lancaster newspaper, the story kept changing. That's why I decided I needed to find out the truth."

Brubaker's comprehensive research involved state archaeologists, local historians, Native American experts, area residents, and even descendants of both the Conestogas and the Paxton Boys, and took four years to complete, resulting in the most detailed and accurate picture to date of the massacre—almost two and a half centuries after it happened. "Even then, I'm not sure I even got to the bottom of it," he admits, "though I think I got close."

Published in 2010, Brubaker's testament helped fuel a groundswell of public reconciliation among Lancaster County's disparate communities that has helped to bring the tragedy of the Conestogas into clearer focus, particularly among the Mennonite and Amish communities. In October 2010, as part of the celebration of the tercentennial of the first Lancaster County Mennonite settlement, for example, the Lancaster Mennonite Historical Society sponsored a program to expand a theme of reconciliation. A series of similar sessions have continued across the county ever since involving Mennonite, Quaker, and Presbyterian churches.

"The Mennonites and Amish in particular have fully embraced the tragedy," Brubaker sums up. "I've seen people crying at these sessions—on both

sides. They feel guilty because their ancestors were the Europeans who settled here and may have profited in some way from the tragedy. But I think
by coming much closer to what really happened—and why—we've finally
addressed the darkest chapter of this county's history. Nothing can change
what happened here. We can only learn from it."

Two days later, my quest for the Conestoga wagon and the fate of the
peaceful people for whom it was named leads me to a lunch table by the
front window of the Press Room Restaurant on West King Street in downtown Lancaster, the original path of the Wagon Road—and starting point
for many travelers—that passes through the heart of this beautiful old city.

The restaurant is housed in the historic Steinman Hardware Building,
formerly the site of America's oldest hardware store, and features a handsome stained-glass window depicting a Conestoga wagon over its entry
doors, emblematic of the establishment's vital role in servicing and repairing Conestoga wagons as they passed through Lancaster on their way to
the Susquehanna. For many travelers of the GWR, Lancaster was the actual
starting point where they acquired their wagons or signed on with others
making the long journey.

In anticipation of my stop here, I've been reading the Lancaster newspapers online for weeks, boning up on a modern city of forty thousand that
has many "firsts," including two major historical storylines of particular interest to me, both directly related to the Wagon Road.

One is the massacre of the Conestogas; the other is the pyrrhic presidency of James Buchanan, the nation's fifteenth president, who rose to the
highest office in the land only to lead the nation to the brink of civil war.

My lunch companion this noon is Mitch Sommers, a Franklin & Mar-
shall graduate and local family lawyer and writer who grew up in the Red
Rose City and regularly contributes op-ed columns to the Sunday paper.
Sommers drew my interest because he is completing work on a novel based
on the massacre of the Conestogas that explores the event from three different perspectives, that of a Paxton Boy participant, a local magistrate who
investigated the crime, and the wife of one of the murdered Indian leaders.

He sees an interesting link between the massacre and the failed presidency of James Buchanan, both of which fueled the kind of bitter partisanship that plagues American politics to this day.

"I don't perceive a more divided time in our history since the days of Buchanan's presidency," Sommers says. "In my mind, the neo-Nazis and other fringe militia groups of today are the spiritual descendants of the Paxton Boys of two hundred and fifty years ago."

He tells me that it is important to remember that Lancaster in 1763 was the edge of the American frontier. "If you went beyond the Susquehanna River into York County it was 'Here Be Dragons,' essentially lawless and ungoverned. I think that was one reason local authorities and even the governor of the colony colluded with the Paxton Boys to cover up their atrocities—fear of frontier justice and further mob rule. As a result, the perpetrators escaped justice and there was never a reckoning of any kind until this century."

Like Jack Brubaker, Sommers's optimism resides in the periodic Mennonite peace and justice services that are finally bringing awareness and healing to many Lancaster Countians. "They've helped a lot of folks begin to face up to the tragedy and heal the city's oldest wounds. If that doesn't amount to perfect justice at last," he adds, "at least it's a good beginning. Hearing the true story has changed hearts and minds."

"Any final thoughts on James Buchanan?" I ask, reaching for the lunch check. "I'm starting on him first thing tomorrow."

Mitch Sommers laughs. "Oh, a totally wonderful character, a true villain. Our greatest failed president. What a disaster. Have fun! But please don't forget dear old Thad Stevens. He's also a son of the Wagon Road—a true hero and a vastly better symbol of what Lancaster is today."

SEVEN

THE MOST IMPORTANT MAN IN AMERICA

TURNED OUT IN AN ELEGANT BLACK MORNING COAT, LOOKING EVERY BIT THE nineteenth-century gentleman of leisure, Wheatland tour guide Bob Thee greets us with a slight bow at the kitchen door of James Buchanan's stately Lancaster mansion.

There are only three of us for the first tour of the day of the house and the grounds on North President Avenue it shares with LancasterHistory, the Red Rose City's historical society. My tour companions are a cheerful apple-cheeked couple from Minneapolis in town for their oldest grandchild's soccer tournament. Unlike me, something of a presidential geek, neither Heidi Thurman nor her husband, Ralph, are particularly keen on the homes of dead presidents and confess little desire to learn about arguably America's most inept president.

"To tell the truth, dear, we just needed a break from teenage soccer drama and too much fast food," Heidi confides with a cheery Minnesota whisper as Bob Thee waits solemnly by the kitchen door for any last-minute arrivals. "Also, we love antiques. My daughter, Lucy, told us that Wheatlands has loads of really nice ones. After this we're checking out the big farmer's market downtown. Ralph wants some genuine Amish bologna. How 'bout you, dear?"

I also dig genuine Amish bologna and plan to make my own stop at

Lancaster's historic Central Market, which sits just off the Wagon Road. But first on my agenda is to learn about the private life of maybe the most peculiar peacock to ever occupy the White House.

For decades, Lancaster's most famous citizen, James Buchanan, the nation's fifteenth president, has held the dubious distinction of being ranked as the worst president in American history by leading presidential scholars and historians. Having read two of his biographers myself and finding little to praise about his chaotic administration, my job this sunny morning (ever the optimist) is to see if I can find anything to like (or simply not dislike) about Old Buck—especially since he stands in such stark contrast to his fellow Lancastrian Thaddeus Stevens, a social reformer whose progressive ideas were decades ahead of his time, inspiring his own nickname: the Great Commoner.

"It's hard to think of two figures—both sons of the Great Wagon Road, by the way—who better embody the bitter political divisions that tore apart America in the nineteenth century than our own James Buchanan and Thaddeus Stevens," LancasterHistory's president and CEO, Tom Ryan, told me the previous afternoon when I dropped by the society's fine museum to get a general overview of the city's history and Old Buck Buchanan in particular.

"One can make a convincing argument, in fact, that many of the powerful divisions they represented are still with us today, bitterly dividing Americans and shaping our current polarized climate of politics," Ryan added.

If the average American knows anything about the life and times of James Buchanan, it's probably the fact that he entered the job as one of the most experienced public servants to achieve the presidency, and was our only bachelor president, employing his comely niece, Harriet Lane, to serve as a stand-in First Lady during his four-year term. On paper, at least from the outset, Buchanan appeared to be a promising commander in chief, a fellow many hoped could steer an increasingly fraught nation through its most perilous days since the American Revolution, but soon proved to be one of our most chaotic.

Bob Thee clears his throat.

"Greetings, gentle lady and gentlemen," he says with an air of presidential formality. "I would like to welcome you to the home of James Buchanan,

America's fifteenth president. It is a pleasure to tell the story of this most interesting man's home life."

Over the next forty-five minutes, Thee leads us on an engaging walk through Wheatland's three main floors and several of the mansion's twenty-three rooms, briefly touching on the notable highs and numerous lows of Buchanan's professional career and peculiar home life, focusing largely on details about the handsome period furnishings and the social life Wheat-lands provided him, all maintained and orchestrated by his longtime house-keeper, Miss Hetty Parker, and niece Harriet Lane. (The antiques of Old Buck's homeplace—all from the period of his lifetime, a few even original to the property—exceed Heidi Thurman's highest expectations.)

Buchanan was born in 1791, the second child of an immigrant also named James Buchanan who owned a trading post in Pennsylvania's south-western Franklin County. According to his most notable biographer, Jean H. Baker, it was a point of pride to Buchanan that he was almost as old as the nation he wound up leading. His father was part of the Scots-Irish migration that resumed after the American Revolution, and became pros-perous enough from commerce along the Wagon Road to send son James, just sixteen, to Dickinson College. Despite being booted out for a time for drunkenness and rowdy behavior, and reinstated only through the efforts of a local Presbyterian minister, the young man graduated and made a beeline for Lancaster to pursue a degree in law.

As a tight-fisted general-practice lawyer specializing in wills and busi-ness contracts, Buchanan quickly ingratiated himself with the city's social elite and made powerful political connections that led to several terms as a Federalist representative in the Pennsylvania House of Representatives. About that time, already eyeing higher office, he began a romance with a twenty-three-year-old beauty named Ann Coleman, the daughter of a man reputed to be Pennsylvania's wealthiest citizen. By the summer of 1819, the pair was engaged to be married, but the arrangement collapsed when Cole-man abruptly broke things off citing Buchanan's "inattention" and rumors that he was mostly interested in her money and social connections. She took swift flight to visit her sister in Philadelphia and mysteriously died days later of what her physician vaguely termed "hysterical convulsion," though an overdose of laudanum or chloral hydrate—either accidental or intentional—was suspected. Whichever it was, the scandal enthralled Lancaster's social set for more than a year, underscored by the elder Coleman's refusal to allow Buchanan to attend his daughter's funeral or even walk behind her cortege to the cemetery in Lancaster.

Though he later cultivated a reputation for being a shameless flirt in the social swirl of Washington, DC, especially among the married wives of Southern lawmakers, Old Buck never took a wife and dodged whispers about his sexual preference by claiming, to anyone who dared to inquire, "my heart is in the grave."

It wasn't necessarily an odd stance to take. "Before the Civil War," notes Baker, "only three of every one hundred American men stayed single—typically a career killer for most aspiring to high office. Buchanan propagated the myth that he maintained his single status as a measure of devotion 'to the only earthly object of my affections,'" attributing his lack of a spouse to an outside devotion to his work. A frugal bachelor lifestyle, not to mention the A-list of legal clients and astute business investments, quickly made him one of Lancaster's wealthiest citizens.

After five terms in the Pennsylvania legislature, artfully swapping constitutional Federalism for Democratic populism, he courted and won a post under populist president Andrew Jackson, who, considering him a rising rival, dispatched Old Buck to Russia as foreign minister in 1832. There, Buchanan negotiated the first trade deal between the two nations. Two years later, he was appointed to the US Senate (in those days, senators were chosen by state legislatures rather than elected by voters). During that time, Buchanan let it be known to the press that he intended to "soon wed," but to no one's surprise, no marriage materialized.

Over his subsequent two terms in the US Senate, it did not go unnoticed by opponents and reporters that Buchanan strongly gravitated toward Southern lawmakers in general and one in particular—a fellow bachelor senator named William King, a handsome, charming Alabaman considered by old-line Washington and most of his constituents to be something of a political dandy. The pair roomed together at a Washington boardinghouse on F Street for a time, exchanging intimate notes (which their families later strived to destroy), prompting unsubtle wags to refer to the pair as "Old Buck and his wife." (Editorial cartoonists, in fact, often depicted Buchanan as a fussy old maid and nicknamed him "the Old Functionary" and "Dough-face," a slang term for Southern sympathizers.) Yet onward he soldiered, visibly undeterred, with sallow gray eyes fixed on the prize of a presidency he publicly claimed he had no interest in pursuing—until he did.

In 1845, President James K. Polk, also a son of the Wagon Road, tapped Buchanan for secretary of state, a job Old Buck initially considered turning down for a potential seat on the Supreme Court, but then reconsidered and accepted. It was a good decision. Instead, between 1845 and 1849, Buchanan became the enthusiastic point man for the largest land acquisition in American history, the defining moment of so-called Manifest Destiny during which the American government gained roughly 1.2 million square miles of North American land that, in time, comprised twenty-two separate American states, including Oregon, parts of California, Arizona, and New Mexico.

Aiming to gild his self-lauded reputation as a "nation builder," Buchanan initially supported extension of the Missouri Compromise, which prohibited slavery north of Missouri's southern boundary all the way to the Pacific Coast (and mollified some Northern abolitionists) but maintained that the unresolved "question" of slavery in the South should be left to the respective states—or as he put it, ever the populist voice, "decided by the people." It was precisely this brand of political ambiguity over the era's most highly charged issue that would, in time, doom his political legacy.

In 1848, following a second failed reach for the presidency—the election that swept Whigs Zachary Taylor and Millard Fillmore into office—Buchanan came home to Lancaster and purchased Wheatlands for $6,750, a twenty-two-acre estate set on a hill above lush grain fields that included a large three-story brick house, a carriage house, and extensive gardens.

It was a lot for one wealthy bachelor to keep up with. Owing to the deaths of several of his brothers and sisters, Buchanan had by then become the legal guardian of thirteen orphaned nieces and nephews, several of which eventually wound up in government patronage jobs. Upon settling into his new digs, purportedly to begin working on his memoirs, Buchanan dispatched Harriet Lane, his favorite sister's youngest daughter—whom he'd put through the finest boarding school in America—to buy heavy walnut furniture for the house, including a large desk where he smoked

cigars, composed letters, and issued policy statements to political cronies while sipping rye whiskey for several hours each afternoon. He also
routinely took evening carriage rides through the expanding suburbs of
Lancaster, adopting the role of the landed gentryman, frequently stopping
off at his favorite tavern, called the Grape, to rub elbows with "the ordinary people." In letters to the outside world, Old Buck informed friends
that he was having "a cozy time in the country," though most thought he
was utterly bored of "retirement" and restless to get back into the moil
of public life.

In time, they were proven right. Upon Zachary Taylor's unexpected
death in 1850, Millard Fillmore ascended to the presidency but lost his party's nomination two years later to Mexican War hero Winfield Scott. The
Democrats meanwhile elevated moderate New Hampshire Senator Franklin Pierce, who ultimately carried twenty-one of thirty-seven states in the
election with Buchanan's former F-Street roommate William King as his
running mate, cinching the support of slave-owning states. King died of tu-
berculosis after just forty-five days in office.

Six months later, Pierce lured Buchanan out of retirement by offering
him the post of envoy to England's Court of St. James's, something of a
demotion from being secretary of state but a job Old Buck was happy to
take on and—by most accounts—relished for the next three years. Harriet
Lane accompanied her uncle to his new post, where she performed ably as
his hostess at diplomatic functions and was befriended by Queen Victoria.
Emboldened by his past expansionist successes, Buchanan initiated a plan
during this time to purchase Cuba from Spain for thirty million dollars, or
take it by force, if necessary, under the doctrine of Manifest Destiny.

Back home in America, slave-owning Southerners applauded the proposal, which came to be known as the infamous Ostend Manifesto (so
named for the Belgian town where it was created by the hand of Buchanan),
because they envisioned Cuba and neighboring islands of the Caribbean to
be friendly havens for greater slave-owning commerce. Abolitionist Northerners, on the other hand, viewed the manifesto as a naked effort to expand
the wretched institution's footprint at a moment when the territory of Kansas was erupting into open warfare between pro and antislavery factions, in
the wake of the Kansas-Nebraska Act, which had been signed by Franklin

Pierce in 1854 and allowed the new territories to determine their own status on slavery by popular sovereignty rather than congressional fiat.

The resulting land war, known as Bleeding Kansas, between free-soil northerners and pro-slavery forces spilled over the border into Missouri and threatened to further spread into neighboring states. As his term approached its end and the issue of slavery intensified, an exhausted Franklin Pierce allowed the Ostend Manifesto to die a quiet death, even as the growing furor over slavery began to tear America apart from the inside out.

Old Buck went home to Wheatlands for a second time in 1856, advising friends that his public life was truly over. They knew better, of course. With the presidential election looming that year, he began cranking out policy papers and flooding newspapers below the Mason-Dixon Line with a biography that emphasized his extensive government experience and core beliefs in states' rights that, in his mind, specifically protected the constitutional rights of slave owners. (Tellingly, the sympathetic campaign materials that were generated from his Wheatlands redoubt were accompanied by a lithograph of his handsome antebellum Lancaster estate, which to many sympathetic eyes resembled the homes of wealthy Southern lawmakers.)

"As a result, Buchanan was deemed the favorite to capture the Democratic nomination," Bob Thee explains to us as we huddle in the chilly west parlor of the mansion, "but made only two campaign speeches in the fall of 1856—both from the front porch of Wheatlands." The ensuing election was an unusually heated affair between the nation's first Republican candidate, famed explorer and former Senator John C. Frémont from California—the newest state—running on an antislavery platform, and the pro-slavery Democrats, who chose James Buchanan on their seventeenth ballot in Cincinnati. A third party calling itself the American Party—aka the Know-Nothings—was also in the mix, putting up weary former president Millard Fillmore.

"If elected," Thee added, "Mr. Buchanan promised to serve only a single term in order to unify America. He was sixty-five years old."

On election day 1856, Old Buck Buchanan swept the South, carrying every slave state but Maryland, while splitting the Northern vote with his running mate, John Breckinridge of Tennessee. Ultimately he captured the fifteenth presidency with just 45 percent of the vote.

"No man in history had ever taken so long to get to the White House," notes another fine Buchanan biographer, Garry Boulard, "more than four decades in public office at almost every level of government, four decades of dreaming for an office that always eluded him, four decades of maneuvering that, up to now, had fallen well short of its goal. But now he had the job. He was the most important man in America."

In his combative victory address, Old Buck denounced Republicans as "dangerous" and repeated his obsessive view that Congress should have no role in determining the fate of slavery in states and territories, music to Southern ears but fighting words to growing numbers of Northern ones, including many back home in Lancaster.

Now in office, Buchanan also affirmed his support of popular sovereignty by recommending a new federal slave statute that would protect the rights of all existing slave owners. But, paradoxically, he also stated that a major objective of his presidency was to end the nation's bitter sectarian politics and finally lay to rest the divisive issue of slavery by essentially preserving the status quo until the institution could somehow "go away on its own."

On the one hand, Old Buck argued, the nation's Constitution did not expressly forbid slavery and prevented states from legally seceding from the Union, while on the other, the federal government was essentially helpless to do anything about the matter if states did indeed pursue secession. It was a fence-straddling strategy that was doomed to fail on a catastrophic scale.

Two days after Buchanan took the oath of office, the nation's widening rift was made further evident when the Supreme Court handed down a verdict in the incendiary Dred Scott case, declaring that enslaved individuals were not US citizens and thus had no legal right under the Constitution to sue owners for their freedom. Chief Justice Roger Taney—who had administered the oath of office to Buchanan and was rumored to be unduly influenced by him—ruled that the Missouri Compromise itself was unconstitutional, meaning that the federal government had no right to prohibit slaveholding in states and new territories. The Northern antislavery movement exploded with rage.

In an effort to stem the violence in Bleeding Kansas, Buchanan appointed a new territorial governor to oversee the creation of a constitution that would allow Kansas to finally achieve statehood, resulting in a protracted battle in Congress between pro-slavery and antislavery factions that consumed his entire presidency.

On a different battle front, an overheated stock market crashed, taking down fourteen hundred banks and five thousand businesses nationwide. Unemployment in Northern cities soared. True to his parsimonious ways and Jacksonian impulses, however, Buchanan refused additional relief to the victims of the Panic of 1857. Recovery took years. In the meantime, millions needlessly suffered. Owing to the invention of the telegraph, the panic became the first economic crisis to be broadcast around the world in real time, affecting America's global standing.

Days before he left office in late January 1861, Buchanan finally signed the bill making Kansas the nation's thirty-fourth state. In the conflagration to come, the free state of Kansas would commit two-thirds of its men of military age to the Union Army, resulting in nearly 8,500 dead or wounded, the highest casualty rate (proportionate to population) of any state in the Union.

As the 1858 midterms approached, criticism of Buchanan increased. During that year's famous debates, a taciturn backwoods lawyer named Abraham Lincoln frequently attacked the president as a man whose inaction only deepened divisions between Americans, placing his political opponent, Democrat Stephen Douglas, in the uncomfortable position of having to defend a party rival he detested. Douglas won the election but Lincoln's eloquence gained national prominence for himself and his rising Republican cohorts; that fall, Democrats lost an epic twenty-six seats in the US House, including eleven new seats in President Buchanan's own Pennsylvania. In a letter to a worried friend back home in Lancaster, Old Buck assured him that William Seward, not smooth-talking Abe Lincoln, would be the Republican candidate for 1860, confidently predicting that the Democrats would easily retain the presidency, the first of many faulty predictions.

The next problem arose after John Brown's failed seizure of the federal arsenal at Harpers Ferry, Virginia, in October 1859. During his third annual address to Congress, Buchanan attempted to place blame for the insurrection directly on Republicans and their "incurable disease . . . open war by the North to abolish slavery in the South." He labeled Republicans the "Party of

Treason" and confidently told cronies that the failed slave rebellion would doom Republicans in the coming presidential election. He also survived a scandal over alleged bribery and fraud stemming from his 1856 presidential campaign, charges he dismissed as character assassination.

As he complained to friends back home in Lancaster, the final year of his presidency turned out to be the worst year of his life.

Facing Republican dark horse Abraham Lincoln in the general election of 1860, the Democratic Party split over the question of states' rights and expansion of slavery, selecting Stephen Douglas as its candidate for president, while a splintered wing of the party—renamed the Southern Democrats—put up Kentuckian John Breckinridge, Buchanan's beleaguered vice president. A fourth party called the Constitutional Union—taking no position on slavery or states' rights, instead simply promising to somehow defend the Constitution and Union from breaking apart—offered Tennessee slaveholder John Bell and former Harvard President Edward Everett.

Lincoln captured the presidency with a landslide of 180 electoral votes, six more than Buchanan won in 1856, despite claiming less than 40 percent of the popular vote. He won the entire North but failed to carry a single Southern state, the reverse of his predecessor, a majority of which went to Breckinridge. Thus marked the official birth of the Republican Party and began a period of domination of the White House that lasted for the next twenty-four years, until the election of Grover Cleveland in 1884.

When news of Lincoln's victory reached the muddy streets of Washington, angry mobs of Buchanan's followers rioted, claiming election fraud, smashing windows and attacking any business or person that visibly supported the new Republican president. The current chief executive, meanwhile, remained utterly silent and squirreled out of sight in the White House, increasingly detached from the responsibility of governing.

Spending his final days in complete isolation, Old Buck gave up his habit of taking afternoon walks and some days had to be helped from his bed. According to reports, he suffered fits of cursing and trembling, even weeping. Biographer Baker compares his black moods and moral inertia to Nixon's final days and Woodrow Wilson's mental breakdown during debates over the League of Nations. According to historian Samuel Eliot Morison, "[Buchanan] prayed and frittered and did nothing." "In his betrayal of the national trust," concludes Jean Baker, "Buchanan came closer to committing treason than any other president in American history."

And yet, during his final address to Congress that December, he rose from his gloomy state to demand funding to either purchase or take Cuba by force of arms—one of his golden-oldie hits from his high-flying Manifest Destiny days—and additionally advocated invading Mexico to carve out a protective buffer zone for Texas. (Neither proposal reached the floor of Congress.)

Then, maybe most damning of all, when multiple advisers urged him to fortify Southern military posts against the gathering threat of national insurrection, especially around the stewing city of Charleston, Old Buck dithered and declined to move for weeks on end, finally reversing himself and sending Federal troops to South Carolina that had little effect on stemming the contagion of rebellion. As the day of Lincoln's inauguration neared, he even refused to order extra troops to guarantee the peaceful transfer of power within the city of Washington, fearing it might upset his Southern followers.

In his historic inauguration speech on the steps of the unfinished Capitol building, with the threat of war hanging in the frosty air, Lincoln extended an olive branch to the South by promising not to interfere with the institution of slavery where it already existed—a stance, incidentally, not terribly different from Buchanan's own—but made clear his intention to prevent Southern secession and seizure of Federal property at all costs.

"We are not enemies, but friends. We must not be enemies," he famously reminded Southern ears. "Though passions may have strained, it must not break our bonds of affection. The mystic chords of memory, stretching from every battlefield and patriot grave to every living heart and hearthstone, all over this broad land, will yet swell the chorus of the Union, when again touched, as surely they will be, by the better angels of our nature."

During the carriage ride back to the White House after the ceremony, Old Buck turned to his eloquent successor and dryly remarked, "If you are as happy entering the White House as I shall feel returning to Wheatland, you are indeed a happy man."

In May 1868, after more than four hundred home visits by his Lancaster physician, James Buchanan developed pneumonia—a disease sometimes called "the old man's friend"—and died on the first morning of June. He was seventy-seven years old.

The next day, the *Chicago Tribune* reported: "The desolate old man has gone to his grave. No son or daughter is doomed to acknowledge an ancestry from him."

"So, you might ask, where do most historians rank James Buchanan among our former presidents?" our gracious Wheatlands host rhetorically asks as the three of us reach Old Buck's private study at the end of the tour.

I stay mum. Why steal an excellent tour guide's big finale?

"This is a man, after all, who gave forty-two years of service to his city, state, and nation. He believed the Union was indivisible. Unfortunately, he proved to be terribly mistaken, and James Buchanan today is generally ranked near or at the bottom of our presidents. Why do you suppose that is?"

"He probably just needed a good wife to tell him what to do," pipes up Heidi Thurman right on cue.

Bob Thee cracks a wintry smile. "You're probably right about that, madam. Fortunately, he had Harriet Lane, a highly polished young woman who filled the White House with flowers and her natural talents as a hostess. The Washington press adored her. The term 'First Lady' was regularly used to describe her—the first usage of the term."

Thee clears his throat.

"At the end of the day, I believe James Buchanan's greatest failure was simply his inability to keep the Union from breaking apart. That dark legacy is how history chooses to remember him."

As we stand by the walnut desk where Buchanan spent the balance of his days scratching out his defiant memoirs and letters to cronies, I notice a bottle of red wine with an unbroken seal and faded label sitting among his Bible and law books.

"Against all of that," our host adds, "the question we must ask ourselves today is, could *anyone* at that time have accomplished the task of saving the Union under such circumstances?"

"What do *you* think?" a newly engaged Heidi is eager to know.

Thee shrugs. "Actually, I think not. I compare him to Herbert Hoover, a decent man who tried to do something good for his country but failed, only to be followed by a strong and popular president."

A statue of James Buchanan, he points out—ironically dedicated *by* Herbert Hoover in 1930—stands today in Washington, DC's Meridian Hill Park, bearing the equally ironic inscription "An Incorruptible Statesman and a Faithful Public Servant."

Our host thanks us for coming and wonders aloud if there are any final questions.

"So, who inherited the house?" Heidi asks, now fully into the sad presidential saga, clearly animated by the funky "hat" bathtub that sits in Buchanan's upstairs bedchamber, Harriet Lane's Chickering grand piano in the main salon, and the fact that there are no closets anywhere in the mansion because coat hangers hadn't been invented yet.

Harriet Lane, Thee explains, inherited Wheatland following her uncle's passing, then valued at about twelve thousand dollars. Over the next few years, she made extensive updates and home improvements that included steam heat, a functioning doorbell, and an expanded kitchen with gas stoves and a dumbwaiter. The house's furnishings were eventually divided between her and Buchanan's longtime housekeeper, Miss Hetty Parker. America's original First Lady then went on to marry a Baltimore banker and create a vast collection of European works of art that she bequeathed to the US government upon her death in 1903. She also endowed an outstanding pediatric facility at Johns Hopkins Hospital that bears her name to this day.

Bob Thee glances at me as if he expects a serious question.

A little one comes to mind. "Is the wine original?"

This makes him smile. "As a matter of fact, it is. An 1827 red Madeira that personally belonged to President Buchanan."

"Maybe we should open it. Just to see if it fared better than his presidency."

Thee sighs.

"I'm afraid you're not the first visitor to Wheatland to suggest that."

EIGHT

THE GREAT COMMONER

IN 1709, NOT LONG AFTER WILLIAM PENN SIGNED A TREATY WITH THE Conestoga Indians, a Swiss Mennonite preacher named Hans Herr was granted his own swath of land along Conestoga Creek. Within a year, other Mennonite refugees along with French Huguenots, English Quakers, and Reformed Germans began settling in the area. Two decades later, a Susquehanna River ferry operator named John Wright was appointed to survey the boundaries of a fourth county to be carved out of sprawling Chester County. Wright named it Lancaster after his birthplace in Lancashire, England, and adopted the heraldic red rose of the house of Lancashire.

About that same time, a lawyer from Philadelphia named Andrew Hamilton purchased five hundred acres in the geographical center of the new county that included a tavern beside a large hickory tree—thought to have stood just east of Penn Square in today's downtown Lancaster. Residents began calling the settlement "Hickory Town." In June 1744, an important event occurred there when several hundred Native Americans from the powerful Six Nations of the Iroquois Confederacy assembled on the outskirts of Lancaster to make a historic peace agreement with colonial leaders from Pennsylvania, Maryland, and Virginia.

The Great Treaty of 1744, signed at Lancaster's first courthouse, secured native lands for English settlement highlighted by a pledge from tribal chiefs not to join with the French in a brewing border war in exchange for blankets, rum, gunpowder, Jew's harps, and articles of clothing. During the celebration that followed, fearing the English were no match for the military prowess of rival New France, the respected chief of the Onondaga Nation, Canassatego, proposed to his new colonial friends that they adopt a form of government like that of the Iroquois Confederacy, highlighted by a mutual defense pact among its six member tribes. His words were soon published and read by leaders across the colonies, including by one Benjamin Franklin, who appropriated the idea during the writing of the US Constitution forty years later.

For the most part, the Great Treaty of 1744 protected Pennsylvania's settlers from Indian raids for the next decade, up to the beginning of the French and Indian War (1754–1763), a peace deal that essentially ended with the massacre of the Conestoga Indians. For his part in the historic treaty, Chief Canassatego was presented a scarlet coat by the Virginians. (He was assassinated by the French six years later.)

By the mid-nineteenth century, the area had become home to a network of safe houses and communities where free and runaway slaves lived in relative peace and safety, a prime destination of the Underground Railroad. One year after Congress passed the controversial second Fugitive Slave Act of 1850, however—a law that permitted Southern slave owners to legally seek fugitive slaves in free states—armed conflicts between abolitionists and slave owners erupted across the region.

Some historians point to the largely forgotten Christiana Riot of 1851 as the American Civil War's first blood to be spilled. The incident began when a wealthy Maryland slave owner named Edward Gorsuch led a posse of slave catchers and federal marshals to the quiet Lancaster County community of Christiana in hopes of apprehending four of his former slaves who were sheltering on the farm of a free slave named William Parker. In the ensuing fight, Gorsuch was killed and his son wounded. The marshals retreated and returned with a detachment of US Marines. By then, however, Parker and his wife had safely fled to Canada with the assistance of Frederick Douglass and other abolitionists, but thirty-eight men were arrested and charged with treason by a grand jury for "intending to levy war against the United States," including four white Quakers. In all, 117 indictments were handed down, making it the largest treason trial in the history of the United States at that time.

The defense was led by Thaddeus Stevens, Lancaster's representative in the US House, a short, pugnacious, poorly bewigged legislator with a silver tongue who made ending human bondage the work of his life.

The first defendant to be tried, a Quaker miller named Castner Hanway, was acquitted after just ten minutes of deliberation by a jury of twelve local men. All the other defendants were subsequently found not guilty and released, an outcome widely portrayed as a victory for the growing abolitionist cause in the antebellum North that unleashed fury below the Mason-Dixon Line.

Born in Danville, Vermont, during the administration of George Washington, and just months before the birth of James Buchanan, Stevens grew up hobbled by a congenital foot deformity and extreme poverty. His father, a failed farmer, abandoned his wife and four sons to run off and join the army. He died in the War of 1812.

A hardworking mother and excellent grades, however, propelled young Thad Stevens through the University of Vermont and Dartmouth College. After graduation, he taught public school in York, Pennsylvania, before settling in Gettysburg, where he was accepted to the bar. The small farming community lay just miles from the border with Maryland and was a well-known stop on the Great Wagon Road and the Underground Railroad, which shaped Stevens's evolving views of politics. Among his first clients were former slaves, whom he often represented without charge, even as he was dabbling in local political affairs. In 1833, he was elected to the state legislature, quickly gaining renown for his savage wit and public abhorrence of slavery. At age fifty-one, in 1842, he moved to the city of Lancaster, where he began to make his mark as a gifted orator and tireless voice of abolition politics.

Elected to the US House as an antislavery Whig in 1848, Stevens fought tenaciously against the Fugitive Slave Act of 1850 and defended the men in the Christiana Riot, which brought him national attention but probably cost him a third term in the House in 1852, at which point he became a leader of the newly formed Republican Party. His return to Congress came in 1859 as the leading voice of the radical abolitionist cause, heading up the powerful

Ways and Means Committee that controlled the Buchanan administration's purse strings. As a supporter of Abe Lincoln—albeit an honest but critical one—Stevens became something of a thorn in the new president's heel because he believed Lincoln was moving much too slowly on Black suffrage. Lincoln respectfully referred to his frenemy as "the sagacious Pennsylvania politician," though Stevens himself preferred to be known as "The Great Commoner." Others—on both sides—had their own nicknames for the savage-tongued powerbroker.

Following Lincoln's assassination in April 1865, President Andrew Johnson became Stevens's favorite target. The fiery abolitionist found the new leader to be a corrupt and paranoidal son of the South, and was accused, along with other radical Republicans, of plotting Johnson's own assassination in 1866, even as Stevens was helping to draft the Reconstruction Act of 1867, which outlined heavy conditions for Southern readmission to the Union. The Great Commoner also had a hand in writing the groundbreaking Fourteenth Amendment, passed one year later, that provided due process to every citizen, often described as the Constitution's most consequential amendment, cited in scores of landmark Supreme Court decisions ranging from the nullification of the Dred Scott case to *Brown v. Board of Education* (1954) to *Roe v. Wade* (1973). Not surprisingly, Old Thad Stevens finished his distinguished career by leading the prosecution of Andrew Johnson's impeachment trial in 1868, the first in American history. In May 1868, the Senate voted 35–19 in favor of conviction, one vote shy of the necessary two-thirds required to remove Johnson from office.

By that point, Thad Stevens's own health was rapidly deteriorating. He briefly returned home to Lancaster, to the house at 45 South Queen Street that he shared with his housekeeper, a mixed-race woman named Lydia Hamilton Smith, long rumored to be his mistress. He passed away at midnight on August 11 of that same year.

"Before we go anywhere else," says Rick Gray, "you need to see this. It's only a couple blocks away."

I've called on Gray, a popular former mayor of Lancaster who is credited with leading a cultural renaissance during his consecutive terms in office, to get a modern perspective on a city I find both surprising and appealing.

Its clean redbrick streets appear to thrive with art galleries, upscale shops, and fine restaurants.

He walks me to Thad Stevens's headstone in historic Shreiner-Concord Cemetery, two blocks north of the Old Lincoln Highway/Great Wagon Road, and invites me to read its inscription.

I repose in this quiet and secluded spot, not from any natural preference for solitude; but finding other cemeteries limited as to race, by charter rules, I have chosen this that I might illustrate in my death the principle which I advocated through a long life, equality of man before the Creator.

"This was the only cemetery in the city that was integrated," Gray explains. "A city, I might add, that was founded by immigrants and today boasts one of the most diverse populations in America. Stevens was incredible, a man largely written out of American history due to an inconvenient truth for the South. He speaks louder than ever to us today. We had a dark history that Thad Stevens helped transform into a culture of tolerance."

This heritage of tolerance, in part, prompted Gray, a Dickinson School of Law grad and former legal services lawyer in Pittsburgh, and his wife, Gail, a successful artist from Cleveland, to settle in downtown Lancaster in 1972. They paid eighteen thousand dollars for their attractive town house on Prince Street—now part of the city's fashionable Gallery Row—that is a gallery in its own right, filled with works by local artists, Gail's contemporary art, and an eye-popping collection of midcentury American commercial ceramics.

"When first we came here, like a lot of old industrial cities of the Northeast," Gray recalls as we set off toward the historic Fulton Theatre, "Lancaster was at a tipping point. There were still four longtime department stores downtown—also companies like Bulova watches and Armstrong Flooring that employed thousands—and the streets were still full of people on Friday nights and shoppers on weekends. But that would soon change."

Indeed, by the end of the decade, rising crime drove residents to safer communities in the county, taking restaurants and downtown services with them. "For a time," says Gray, "the city became a ghost town after five o'clock and on weekends. Fortunately, this city had one major asset that never left during our most difficult days—its artists.

"I describe myself as a Democratic capitalist," he quips as we settle into rear seats at the spectacularly restored Fulton Theatre, where a stage crew is working on sets for a production of *Peter Pan*. "I think it's the job of government to level the playing field, mow the grass and get the hell out of the way. In truth, a lot of people had a hand in Lancaster's revival. Our local government, community activists, neighborhood leaders, artists, and historians were all crucial. In some ways, the city has come full circle. It's thriving and more diverse than ever." In the next breath, Gray mentions plans for a new $22 million museum and center for democracy and history to be built at the former home and office of The Great Commoner. "When I look at our history," he adds, "I can think of only one other figure in our history who matches Ben Franklin's living legacy—Thaddeus Stevens."

First elected mayor in 2005, Gray put together a coalition of progressive city leaders and arts activists who transformed empty buildings into art galleries and affordable residences and unique small business spaces, fueling a downtown renaissance by focusing on the city's surviving architecture and historical landmarks like its historic Central Market, America's longest-running public farmer's market, and Fulton theater, both of which underwent major renovations and became symbols of Lancaster's cultural revival, along with a new $170 million convention center and hotel. Freshly retired from three terms in office and twelve years on the job, Gray was honored with numerous state and national awards for presiding over Lancaster City's dramatic revival, including a special governor's award from the State of Pennsylvania citing both Rick and Gail Gray for their contributions to the arts in the region.

Since we sit in a theater named for native son Robert Fulton, the Lancaster County engineer and inventor who made steamboating a commercial success, I wonder if the mayor has any thoughts about the Paxton Boys who terrorized the town on a cold winter morning in 1755. It was Fulton's father, after all, a sympathetic Scots-Irish immigrant, who warned that a vast Presbyterian militia of Paxton Boys was poised to overthrow the Quaker government of Pennsylvania. What a different turn history might have taken.

Gray smiles. "Fortunately, thanks to Ben Franklin and the citizens of

Philadelphia, that did not happen. The rebellion fizzled out. In some ways, however, the murder of the Conestogas and the fact that no one was held accountable still haunts this country, a social disease Thad Stevens dedicated his life to eradicating.

"On that note," Mayor Gray sudden says, hopping up, "let me show you something before we move along."

He leads me outside to the back of the theater and points to a historical marker on the wall. It reads: "Site of Conestoga Indian Massacre, December 27, 1763."

"This is where the old jail stood when the surviving fourteen members of the tribe in protective custody were hacked to death two days after Christmas."

He lets this sink in, falling silent. I actually place my hand to the marker, imagining the horrific scene in my head.

"Smart people don't forget the lessons of their history," he continues. "There are so many good things about Lancaster County and this city in particular that people here are justly proud of. During the first century of this country's life, this was the breadbasket of the nation, the place where religious and cultural tolerance first took root in America, where German farmers revolutionized farming, and the nation's first industrial town, that produced everything from the Conestoga wagon to Bulova watches."

He looks at me and smiles. "For untold thousands of immigrants who traveled the Great Wagon Road to find a new life and opportunity on the frontier, this was the starting place. They carried that spirit with them across young America."

As we head back to Prince Street, ever the charming ambassador, Mr. Mayor wonders if I've seen the city's historic Central Market yet, "the nation's oldest farmer's market, in operation since 1730."

"My next stop," I provide. "I hear the sweet German bologna is not to be missed."

He laughs. "All true. You'll see the abundance of Lancaster County. We put a brand-new slate roof on the building not long ago. It's the pride of the city."

And he isn't wrong. The market, my final stop in the Red Rose City, is architecturally stunning. I spend more than ninety minutes just strolling its bustling aisles in a hungry afternoon swoon, admiring ranks of gorgeous produce and lush late-summer vegetables; mountains of fragrant cheese, breads, and smoked meats; extraordinary relishes and mustards; and pastries galore, sampling and pausing to chat with Amish farmers and other vendors.

On my way out, I purchase a pound of sweet Lancaster bologna from S. Clyde Weaver. Unable to stop myself, I also buy four different kinds of cheese, none of which I'd ever heard of, plus a Bible-sized cookbook containing five hundred classic Amish recipes for my wife.

A woman selling lovely handmade birdhouses also catches my eye. The houses are painted with German Fraktur symbols of love and nature that I now admire.

"Did you know," she says, "birdhouses were brought to America by German farmers? The first ones were probably sold in this market."

I am not in the least surprised to learn this. Another Lancaster first. I purchase one for the bluebirds back home.

NINE

FAITH & MEADOW TEA

N THE MORNING, I DRIVE TO LITITZ, A PRIM LITTLE TOWN NAMED FOR THE Bohemian village where, five hundred years ago, Jan Hus and his followers—calling themselves the Unitas Fratrum—formed the Moravian Church, the world's oldest Protestant denomination.

Lititz was established by Count Nikolaus Ludwig von Zinzendorf, patron of the church in North America, who visited Lancaster County in 1756 and gave such a rousing speech about Christian brotherhood that a German farmer named George Klein was inspired to offer his entire five-hundred-acre farm to the Moravians for the establishment of a town. About that same time, a dozen Moravian brothers from Bethlehem in the Lehigh Valley—where Zinzendorf had established the first Moravian mission on Christmas Eve in 1741—set off down the GWR to the wilderness of western North Carolina (which Zinzendorf had already explored) in order to establish Moravian communities in the foothills of the Blue Ridge mountains, notably the farming community of Bethabara and the village of Old Salem that soon followed.

Owing to school trips to see artists, craftsmen, and bakers at work in the manner of their industrious forebears, not to mention my Lutheran mother's love of Moravian traditions at Christmas and Easter, Old Salem became a significant influence early in my life. The annual Christmas Love-feast service, which celebrated the birth of Jesus with exquisite stringed music, Scripture readings, fragrant beeswax candles, sweet buns, and paper-thin Moravian cookies, was a cultural staple of the Piedmont Triad and one of my family's holiday traditions, as was Old Salem's annual Easter sunrise service held in God's Acre, a beautiful rolling cemetery where centuries of departed Moravians rest beneath flat stones in segregated rows called "Choirs." Today sunrise Easter services—meant to symbolize the new light of Christ's resurrection—are fixtures across the Christian world. But the first one is believed to have originated with the Moravians of Old Salem.

For this reason, forty years after my last sunrise service at God's Acre, I'm eager to see one of the birthplaces of American Moravian life. At the Congregational Store on Lititz's charming main drag, I pick up a history of the town and chat with a man from the local business council who points out that they have yet again been named one of the five "Coolest Small Towns in America" by a national travel publication. Perhaps this explains why its upscale gift shops and smart galleries are teeming with shoppers as the final hours of summer vacation slip away.

On my way to the Lititz Moravian Church, I poke my head into the Julius Sturgis Pretzel Bakery, reported to be the first pretzel firm in America. At that moment the shop is beseiged with giddy teenagers on a school trip taking selfies as they wait in line to have a hands-on lesson in pretzel-making. In their marvelous book *Life Is Meals*, James and Kay Salter point out that the pretzel is believed to have been providentially invented fourteen hundred years ago by a frugal monk in Southern France who twisted leftover dough into a shape that resembled folded arms in prayer, with three openings that represented the Holy Trinity. The name evolved from "brachiola"—meaning "little arms"—into "bretzel" and ultimately "pretzel" by the time German and Austrian bakers perfected the delicacy.

Mildly curious to see how these pretzels are made, I stand in line for twenty minutes, waiting for the next tour, among the chattering magpies and teenage gigglers before I bail out and make a beeline for the silence of the Moravian church across the street. There, I spend the better part of the morning looking at artifacts and documents in the church's museum and archives, including an impressive collection of ancient brass and stringed instruments—the first viola made in the American colonies, for example, circa 1764—all of which reminds me of what prodigious music makers Moravians have always been.

Not only were the early communities at Bethlehem, Lititz, and Old Salem home to some of the most influential craftsmen in early America, ranging from brickmakers to gunsmiths, bakers to ironmongers; they were also steeped in the storied musical traditions of their Germanic homeland, among the first places in colonial America where someone could hear a live Bach cantata or Brahms violin concerto played by a skilled orchestra long before concert halls were a feature of American towns and cities. As I drift into a separate gallery, my inner eighth grader is thrilled to find a hulking Feurer Spritzer from 1792, believed to be the oldest surviving fire truck in America.

Once I've seen the physical legacy of these gifted people, I sit for a while in the deep silence of the main sanctuary, wondering if the past is ever really past our attempts to make peace with it. The physical similarity to Old Salem's home church is striking, and pulls me back to a chilly Easter night in 1970 when my girlfriend Kristin Cress and I stayed out all night with a bottle of Mateus Rosé hoping to get a good spot among the large crowds at Old Salem's Easter sunrise service. As we stood shivering in the predawn April cold, an elderly gentleman in the crowd offered Kristin his tweed jacket. He turned out to be a retired history professor from Salem College just two blocks away, and as we waited for the hymns to begin, we chatted about Moravian history and I was pleased to learn that the Moravians arrived in the area via the Great Wagon Road in 1753, the first time I'd heard the road's name spoken since my father mentioned it in 1966. The professor even mentioned that the place where Daniel Boone and his family crossed the Yadkin River was just a dozen or so miles southwest of Winston-Salem at the Shallow Ford crossing near Lewisville. "In late summer when the river is low," he told us, "it's shallow enough to walk across the river in the footsteps of Boone and thousands of settlers who crossed at that very point on their way west. My late wife and I often went there for picnics. That's where I proposed to her."

"Be warned, Pook, if we ever go to the Shallow Ford for a picnic," Kristin teased me on the way home that morning, "I will expect a marriage proposal."

She was eighteen that spring, about to graduate high school and head to Lenoir-Rhyne College in the mountains to study theater, music, and social work. I was one year younger, scheduled to start my first job as an intern at our hometown newspaper. Though we'd often talked about someday getting married, we reluctantly agreed to put our romance on hold until we were better settled.

Four years later, as she was about to graduate early from college, I surprised Kristin by showing up on her doorstep in the mountain town where she had been working with poor African American families by day and part-time as a hostess at a local steakhouse on weeknights. She'd also recently been offered the chance to work as an understudy in London's theater district upon graduation. Over three spectacular October weekends in a row, we hatched a plan for me to finish my English degree and follow her to England in the spring. I even promised that, if necessary, I would take her on a picnic to the Shallow Ford on the Yadkin and make a proposal worthy of Daniel Boone, or at least the history professor who loaned her his tweed jacket.

We parted that final Sunday afternoon just days after her twenty-second birthday, and I drove five hours back to school thinking I'd never felt more alive and excited about the future we were going to share. She would act and I would write, possibly as a stringer for the *International Herald Tribune*. In my spare time, I'd practice my short-game golf skills on Hampstead Heath or London's Battersea Park and someday take the Flying Scotsman to play the Old Course at St. Andrews the way my father had done during the war.

A couple hours after I hit the road for home, a trio of teenagers held up the steakhouse and placed a .38 to the pretty hostess's head.

The gun went off.

I'd never gone back to Salem's God's Acre. Though I sat with Kristin's parents at their daughter's funeral service at the Lutheran church where we grew up together in Greensboro, I couldn't abide attending her graveside service, unable to watch the beautiful girl I'd loved since I was fifteen be committed to the earth. At least I wrote her mother, Alice, a letter explaining my absence.

"So, what do you think of our sanctuary?" A woman's pleasant voice interrupts my thoughts as she sits down beside me in a pew. Gray-haired, with a kind face and a faint perfume I can almost name, she's the volunteer docent who invited me to have a look around the church—Barbara is her name, I think, though my mind and emotions are suddenly stuck in the past.

I reply that Lititz's beautiful sanctuary reminds me of the home church at Old Salem, built by the early Moravians who came down the Great Wagon Road to Carolina.

"I've heard about that road. I believe some of my early family members traveled it."

She tells me about a colonial ancestor, a widow with three children, who supposedly made the journey with her kids from Lititz to Old Salem in the late 1750s. She has never been to Old Salem and wonders how these two Moravian towns compare.

Three centuries after their respective founding, I reply, connected by Wagon Road commerce and their powerful spiritual heritage, both places appear to be thriving.

"You should come back at Christmas for our Lovefeast. The town really gets into the spirit," says Barbara. "And our sunrise service at Easter is incredibly moving. I suppose you've attended the one at Old Salem."

"Just once. Long time ago."

"Maybe you should come back."

"You're probably right."

Fifteen minutes away, a short drive along pretty Meadow Valley Road, lies another of Lancaster County's important early Wagon Road religious communities—one that flowered and faded but left an outsized legacy all its own.

I first read about the Ephrata Cloister and the restless German mystic named Conrad Beissel who created it during a religious studies class at university. Like most of the German religious leaders who arrived in Philadelphia as the eighteenth century dawned and eventually settled "thickly" around Lancaster County, Beissel was a product of Martin Luther's Reformation fever and a radical pietist who rejected organized religion of any sort in favor of personal spiritual awakening.

When this son of a drunken baker caught wind of William Penn's Holy Experiment, he launched himself to America in 1720, working briefly in Germantown as a weaver before moving on to Conestoga, where he joined the

Anabaptist sect known as Dunkers, owing to their belief in full-immersion baptism. A gifted pulpiteer who claimed to have holy visions, Beissel quickly became the community's spiritual center until 1732, when, disillusioned by the ungodliness of everyday colonial life, he resigned his post and headed for a hermit's retreat deep in a forest local Native Americans called the "Den of Snakes," to seek solitude and contemplation. He named his woodland Ilium the Camp of the Solitary. Others soon followed.

Beissel's two big spiritual ideas were that Saturday was the true Sabbath and earthly marriage—which involved intimate social congress between the sexes—was a barrier to achieving Paradise. Not exactly a formula, one might conclude, for building a robust spiritual flock, and yet, by 1750 eighty celibate brothers and sisters came to reside and labor at Ephrata Cloister, a thriving 250-acre complex that took its name from a village near the ancient town of Bethlehem, mentioned in the book of Genesis as the place where King David spent his youth and first learned about the ark of the covenant. At its peak, the cloister was supported by a couple hundred local benefactors that Beissel—who took on the name Father Friedsam (German for "peaceful")—called Householders, married members of his congregation who provided goods and services and financial support to the cloister.

Celibate brothers and sisters were distinguished by the long white monastic robes they wore, garments that served a dual purpose of reminding them of Jesus's purity while keeping their own human bodies—"that humiliating image revealed by sin," declared Father Friedsam—safely hidden from curious eyes and straying temptation. Theirs was a life of rigid self-denial and austere plainness guided by an absolute belief in Jesus Christ's impending return; a rigorous daily routine that included meager diets of water, greens, and fresh baked bread; minimal rest followed by long hours of work; strict discipline; daily prayer; and midnight watch services, practices aimed at preparing the cloister's most committed members to enter Paradise.

As it was at the cloister, a defining feature of America's early religious development at large was end-time prophesy, which had spread like wildfire throughout frontier America since the time of the Puritans ("Englishmen who accepted the Reformation without the Renaissance," quipped Samuel Eliot Morison) and was promulgated a century later by the silver tongues of free-range Protestant evangelists like George Whitefield and generations of "new light" Methodist, Baptist, and Presbyterian preachers who fanned out into the wilderness to slay Satan and promote the coming Kingdom of Heaven.

As they waited for Paradise to arrive, Ephrata's sisters and brothers slept in segregated quarters on hard wooden benches with wood blocks for pillows, in austere wooden dormitories of Germanic design with narrow hallways meant to suggest the "straight and narrow pathway to Heaven" along with low doorways aimed at teaching one to bow with humility. More than six hours of sleep, Father Friedsam declared, was an irresistible invitation to the devil.

Outside of its ultra-strict daily practices, the cloister became known for its commitment to helping newcomers outside the faith construct their houses and tending the sick and elderly regardless of their beliefs. Members also operated a public school for village children and offered food and shelter free of charge to travelers (who got feather beds and regular pillows). Like their Moravian neighbors, cloister members were outstanding weavers, craftsmen, and artists, particularly adept at choral singing and a cappella music composition. More than a thousand four-part harmony compositions were written by Father Friedsam himself.

The cloister's Frakturschrift, a calligraphic German folk-art form, was considered the first of its kind in America, used to illustrate hundreds of religious books and pamphlets the cloister published at its busy printing house. A mammoth fifteen-hundred-page work for the Mennonites called *Martyrs Mirror*, which told the story of their journey (along with the Old Order Amish) to Lancaster County, was the largest book ever printed in colonial America. The first Bible printed in German, along with Beissel's meditation *Mysterion Anomias*, a defense of the Christian observance of the Jewish Sabbath, had a major influence in the spreading of evangelical Christianity through the colonies, along with a stream of hymnals and religious tracts for other Christian sects. Beissel also penned the earliest known American treatise on music, refining a system of simple four-part harmonic singing that is believed to be the first of its kind anywhere. As a result, the Ephrata mystic gained the admiration of religious authorities throughout the colonies. Even in faraway France, a godless Voltaire commented admiringly on the artistic reach of Beissel and his cloistered singers.

In the meantime, a Who's Who of colonial dignitaries—including the sons of William Penn, governors from neighboring colonies, and religious leaders of every stripe—made pilgrimage to the cloister to see the operational efficiency of the place for themselves. During the historic Indian Conference of 1744, for example, leaders from Maryland and Virginia were so taken with the bread supplied by Ephrata's monks, they dropped by to see how it was made and load up with more.

Historian Eugene E. Doll points out that perhaps the cloister's most far-reaching achievement was the impact of various kinds of mills the brotherhood established and operated that "helped open up the surrounding country for settlement and served as the basis for industrial enterprises still active today." Much of the early paper and ink used in colonial printing came directly from Ephrata's paper mill.

I pick up these interesting tidbits during a ninety-minute walking tour of the Ephrata grounds using my smartphone and a nifty guided narration app. After a busy summer of visitors and special events, I've managed to show up on a day when no live tours are scheduled and most of the compound's half a dozen structures are closed to the public for maintenance, but after paying a modest entry fee to walk the grounds, I manage to poke my head inside many of the humble wooden buildings, including the cloister's iconic half-timbered log-and-stone Sisters' House (1743) with its steep roofline and many narrow-gabled ends—a rare survival of medieval German architecture.

As a bonus, I have the place entirely to myself on a pleasant late-summer afternoon, save for a friendly gray cat that escorts me around the property as I check out the cloister's famous bakery, printing office, and otherworldly Sisters' House, as well as Father Friedsam's own humble cottage on the grounds. It even follows me through the cloister's own God's Acre where Beissel and other members of the sect have rested in marked and unmarked graves for three hundred years.

As I look at the grounds, from a modern perspective, it's easy to dismiss Ephrata's faithful as early American crackpots or misguided religious zealots for whom Paradise never materialized. In the end, like with ten thousand one-man theocracies that took root in the fertile soil of the American wilderness, the death of Ephrata's charismatic leader in 1768 marked the start of the cloister's rapid decline and demise (though during the pivotal winter of 1777 to 1778 the compound served as a vital military hospital that reportedly cared for 260 colonial soldiers following the Battle of Brandy-wine and Paoli Massacre, sixty patriots of whom died and were buried in a mass grave at the cloister).

Within thirty years, following the death of its last celibate member, surviving Householders formed a new entity called the German Seventh Day Baptist Church, worshipping on the grounds until 1934. By that point, many of the cloister's stately structures were either falling apart or already returned to dust, prompting the State of Pennsylvania to step in and commence an extensive restoration of the historic site, today one of the twenty-six stops on the Keystone State's popular Trails of History program. With or without feline accompaniment, I decide, it's an eerily beautiful place to visit.

On my way out, I step into the museum shop housed in the property's former stables to check out an end-of-summer sale of locally made crafts, including wooden kitchen utensils, red Pennsylvania pottery, handwoven blankets, and scarves. It's probably too much to hope there might be a com-memorative Father Friedsam cloister coffee mug for sale, but I do find a CD of his ethereal choral compositions for the road, as well as a pair of hand-some wooden spoons for my baker wife. ·

The shop's lone clerk, a trim brown-haired woman reading a romantic novel whose lurid cover depicts a bosomy young woman glancing nervously over her shoulder at a darkened mansion, keeps a discreet eye on me as I poke around her shop, touching this and that as I check out Germanic sten-ciling and finger pottery and the fabric of handmade linen tea towels and pot holders, like a five-year-old off his nanny's leash. Nary a word passes between us. But as I'm paying for the spoons and CD, I notice a simple block of wood perched on the shelf directly behind her.

"How much for the pillow?" I ask as she takes my credit card. "I could use a really firm one."

"The blocks aren't for sale," she says without looking up. Probably hav-ing heard this weary joke a hundred times too many.

My tour of Lancaster's spiritual landscapes concludes at the handsome farm of Mervin and Kathryn Lapp on the Gordonsville Road, an Amish farm family whose roots date from the days of William Penn. My friend Jim High, who grew up on an adjacent property, assures me that I will find not only a congenial welcome and valuable insights from a visit with the Lapps but a few unexpected surprises as well. He refuses to say any more than that.

The Old Order Amish and Mennonites comprise only about 8 percent of Lancaster County's population today, yet of all the Wagon Road's early pietist sects, the Plain People of the Old Order stand out most for the visible simplicity of their lifestyles and strict adherence to religious traditions that have shaped their lives for centuries. Though some of their original European communities have died out, the Amish in America have steadily increased their numbers and even become known in American culture for the superior quality of their workmanship and products ranging from food to furniture.

As I drive out the Old Philadelphia Pike (America's first fully paved highway, which parallels the Lincoln Highway/Great Wagon Road a few miles to the north) toward Mervin and Kathryn Lapp's place, I think of my historian friend Neil Ronk's concerns that members of the Old Order are slowly being driven from their family lands by rampant commercial development and escalating land prices.

As David Walbert points out in *Garden Spot*, his critique of the decline of Amish culture in Lancaster County, the Old Order became an irresistible symbol of America's vanishing rurality following the Second World War and the birth of the nuclear age, when many Americans embraced nostalgia for the nation's simpler past. Unlike many of their Mennonite brethren who adopted modern practices and evolving technology, the Old Order continue using horses and buggies for farming and transportation instead of tractors and automobiles; they wear no buttons on their clothes and rely on oil lamps to light their homes instead of electricity. On the cusp of a booming consumer age, the plain ways of the Old Order proved irresistible to suburban Americans who viewed their closeness with the earth as an echo of our vanished agrarian past. As a result, a seven-figure tourism industry was born.

Indeed, between Bird in Hand and Intercourse, one runs a gauntlet of Amish-themed motels, quilt shops, buggy rides, restaurants, candy stores, antique parlors, Christmas shops, furniture outlets, hex dealers, art galleries, and guesthouses; a commercial jamboree of all things Amish that reminds me of the Wagon Road town of Mount Airy back home in western North Carolina, the birthplace of TV sheriff Andy Griffith, where everything in town trades off a mythical Mayberry (the reason native son Griffith actually avoided his hometown for most of his life).

With half an hour to kill before I meet the Lapps, I pull in to check out something called the Amish Experience, a large entertainment complex that offers free rides in Amish buggies and van tours of surrounding Amish farms, along with a large gift shop and a film called *Jacob's Choice* playing at the Amish Experience Theater.

A pleasant young woman in a plain blue dress and matching bonnet greets me warmly as I walk in and explains that tickets for the next showing of *Jacob's Choice* are $8.95 or a special combo rate of $14.95 if accompanied by a child of twelve or under. Unfortunately, the last showing of the day is already in progress, but a ninety-minute van tour of local Amish farms is still available for $30.95 (half that if I can rustle up a child). Alternatively, she says, I could return the next day for a deluxe tour that includes the film and a visit to a real Amish schoolhouse plus three different Amish farms where I can meet "actual working Amish families," priced at $61.

I pass on the opportunity but pick up the film's flyer for future reference—"More than any other Amish attraction, *Jacob's Choice* will leave you with an understanding of what it means to be Amish, and the ties that continue to bind the community together through the centuries . . . " I also poke around the shop's displays of handsome handmade bonnets and straw hats and other articles of plain and simple Amish dress that remind me of another Lapp family.

I'm referring to the Lapps of Australian Peter Weir's 1985 hit film *Witness*, which won an Oscar for Best Original Screenplay and was filmed in the area. Starring Harrison Ford and Kelly McGillis, it follows a pair of star-crossed lovers who discover worldly passion when a badly wounded Philly detective named John Book attempts to protect Amish widow Rachel Lapp's son, who has witnessed a brutal murder during a visit to the poorly nicknamed City of Brotherly Love.

Over the course of his recovery, Book adopts Amish plain dress, learns carpentry, helps raise a barn, and falls hard for Rachel, a local beauty he happens upon while she is bathing—a scene straight out of the book of Samuel, chapter two, where young King David spies Bathsheba at her evening bath and promptly dispatches her husband, Uriah the Hittite, to die in battle. Subsequently, Bathsheba gives birth to King Solomon but the Lord punishes David by giving him another son who starts a civil war that devastates the kingdom of Israel. John Book enjoys a much kinder fate, however, catching the killer and almost getting the girl in the process.

American filmgoers adored the movie. I remember reading in *People* magazine that it inspired an invasion of Lancaster County from thousands of movie fans eager to see if the *real* Amish were anything like those in the movie.

Moments after I pull up to his stately white farmhouse, Mervin Lapp comes tooling home on—of all things—a battery-operated scooter like the ones you find on almost any urban street in America these days. As my friend Jim High promised, this is the first of several rewarding surprises.

"Hello, hello!" Mervin cheerfully calls out. "So good of you to come! What a beautiful afternoon, eh?"

He scooters to a stop, and we vigorously shake hands just as the screen door opens and his wife, Kathryn, emerges with a pitcher of "meadow tea"—a traditional Amish recipe made from boiling fresh mint gathered from surrounding fields. We take a seat beside lush Concord grapevines bursting with late-summer ripeness, in the shade of the lawn's beautiful hardwood trees, and are soon talking about their three grown sons, all of whom work in the family's highly successful masonry business, and how devotion to God, family, and the pleasure of doing good work with one's hands are the pillars of a rewarding life.

I learn that Mervin inherited the sixty-acre farm and herd of dairy cattle upon his father's passing more than a decade ago but found the dairy business difficult to sustain in the face of rising land and labor costs. And so he sold off his forty Holstein dairy cows and turned to stone masonry. He and his sons have created a thriving word-of-mouth business building spectacular stone buildings and barns across the region.

"Do you travel to job sites on a scooter?" I ask, as Kathryn refills my glass with meadow tea, just about the most refreshing thing I've ever tasted.

Mervin chuckles. "Oh, no. That has only about a three-mile range. I use it mostly for small errands and going to the bank and a supply store in Centerville."

His oldest son, Ivan, he explains, has left the church and is able to drive their work truck to job sites. His younger sons, Mervin Jr. and Stephen, also work in the business but are rapidly approaching the age—eighteen—when Amish youth must decide whether to embrace their spiritual heritage or seek the outside world. The Lapps also have two daughters.

The next surprise comes when we walk over to look at Mervin's beautiful stone barn, refilled glasses of meadow tea in hand. Ivan, he continues, and seven of his friends are currently on a weeklong junket to the Carolinas, playing several of their favorite golf courses from the Outer Banks to Myrtle Beach, the sun-splashed Sodom of the South.

"Ivan's a pretty good golfer, I must say," he explains as we sit down in the welcome coolness of his immaculate barn. "He probably gets his love of it from me. Kathryn would tell you I'm pretty much a secret sports nut."

Not long after he sold off the family herd, the Lapps took a vacation to the Poconos to be with his younger brother Lee and his family. "It was Lee who suggested that I get some clubs and take up golf. He said it was good for stress. I told him I was probably too old for golf. Also, I'm left-handed. In the local classifieds, however, I read that a set of ladies' left-handed golf clubs were for sale, like new, only used once. I bought the set for fifty dollars."

"How'd they work?"

"Pretty nicely. So, Lee and me go out to play golf and I'm on just the second hole and putting for a birdie! That's all it took. I was hooked! I still have the women's wedge," he explains. "It's always treated me very well. What's your best score?"

He laughs when I mention that my best score ever—a sixty-nine—was made using a set of Patty Berg golf clubs borrowed from a friend's wife.

"Mysterious game," Mervin agrees, sipping his tea. "My father loved golf too." He explains how Levi, his father, loved to hit balls with Jim High's father, Leon, in their adjoining pastures. "You'd see them out there hitting golf balls in the pastures, talking about farm prices and goodness knows what else!" The picture this conjures in my head is both amusing and wonderfully touching, and before I can ask more, Mervin adds that he and Ivan sometimes play another local farmer and his son in matches at a public course over in New Holland, and—since the Lapps do not own a TV set—annually watch the Masters, Ryder Cup, and other major championships at the neighboring High farm. "It's one of our family traditions," he says with a laugh. "But that's not even my favorite sport," he adds. "You like baseball?"

I do indeed. Grew up playing it, I reply. Lifelong Orioles fan due to a longshoreman uncle with a leather lung.

Mervin nods. "My team is the Dodgers. I grew up listening to their games on the radio or seeing them occasionally on someone's TV set. From an early age I was a Dodger-blue die-hard, first and last. Davey Lopes. Ron Cey. Steve Garvey. Those were my guys."

"Football?"

"Now and then. I like the Eagles. But I wouldn't go too far out of my way to watch a football game through someone's window."

We laugh, sip our tea. The deep and reverent quiet of the barn and Mervin's ease and warmth of spirit liberates me to ask about the notion that the Old Order Amish might be leaving Lancaster County. A few feet away from us sits a traditional black buggy like those one still sees traveling the back roads and shoulders of highways across Lancaster County.

"Some are doing that, sure. You can't blame them. My land would sell for a couple million dollars these days. What son could possibly afford that? What bank would even consider loaning a young person who wants to farm that kind of money to buy it?"

Mervin's father paid his grandfather Henry Lapp $185,000 for the family's sixty-two acres in the 1960s but passed away when Mervin was just thirty-five. "My mother nearly lost the farm in the 1980s, when rates jumped up to twenty percent. She remarried and passed it on to me because none of my brothers wanted it. So I inherited the farm and tried dairy farming for six or seven years, never quite as successfully as I hoped it would be. My heart just wasn't in it. Fortunately, I had good skills as a stone mason and God gave Kathryn and me three strong sons."

On the other hand, he adds, "many have stayed and found ways to adapt the way we have, building businesses that are extremely successful. It's a different world from the one my father and grandfather and ancestors knew."

We talk about building stuff for a while. I tell him about building my own house in a birch forest near the coast of Maine, with my own hands (never again), including the task of rebuilding ancient stone walls around the property, an enterprise that took almost ten years. I wonder if he thinks stones can "speak" because I frequently spoke to mine, not always kindly.

Mervin chuckles. "Oh, yes. They *do* speak. When you work with stone, your hands learn where they want to be. They speak their own language."

What a lovely image, I think.

I sense another opening and pose a slightly more personal question: How can he use an electric scooter to get around? Isn't use of electricity frowned on in Old Amish culture?

"Traditionally it is. But I got the idea of the scooter from young men who work for the local volunteer fire departments who started riding scooters to fires. In the old days, you see, they would have ridden a horse to the fire. But a scooter that's fully charged up—our charger is in the barn, where we actually *have* electricity—can take you twelve miles pretty quickly on a single charge. Every family makes their own decision about such matters."

He tells me about belonging to one of the oldest Amish congregations in the county, one that dates to the days of Penn. "I'm probably not as conservative as some of our brothers and sisters in the congregation," he admits. "But that's okay. You mind what's on your plate and I'll mind what's on mine. We're still brothers, even though I hold a little different from you."

It is a nice way of looking at life—this life of faith, work, family, a little golf on the side pasture, and Dodger blue on a neighbor's TV set—but it clearly requires the kind of devotion and dedication I suspect few Americans could achieve unless it's in their ancestral DNA. In the best sense of the phrase, these *are* the chosen people of the earth because they still choose to honor it.

A pleasant hour and interesting day have come and gone much too soon, like a scene from the Old Testament. The sun has slipped below the horizon and the evening is rapidly cooling off. Kathryn steps out to say goodbye and gives me a hug along with her recipe for meadow tea. Mervin pumps my hand and hopes I will stop again when I'm passing their farm.

"Bring your wife and golf clubs," he says with a big smile.

I thank them and promise to do just that, making a mental note to send Merv a dozen brand-new Titleist Pro V1 golf balls as soon as I get home.

TEN

TIME & A RIVER

A LIVELY LATE-SUMMER ARTS FESTIVAL IS GOING ON IN COLUMBIA, THE small Susquehanna River town of ten thousand souls that played an important role in the development of colonial America.

It was here that an enterprising English Quaker minister and linen draper named John Wright opened the first commercial ferry service in 1730, creating a frontier settlement that would soon take his name—Wright's Ferry—and open the way west to generations of Wagon Road travelers.

I've dropped in hoping to find out about Susanna Wright, his daughter, also known as the Susquehanna Muse, a gifted poet, scientist, and feisty Quaker lady who owned the first great house built at the edge of the American wilderness. But before anything else, it's nice to be in the middle of a busy arts festival in a famous old river town.

As I stand by his fair booth just outside the crowded courtyard of St. Paul Episcopal Church, where members are busy selling hot dogs to festivalgoers as fast as they can commit them to buns, Dave Haneman presses home the point that "lots of important things happened in Columbia that Americans have never heard about, true amazing untold stories."

I'm all ears. Dave, I discover, is a retired Mars candy employee and graphic artist from the neighboring town of Marietta just a few miles upriver, part of a local coalition of community leaders whose mission it is to promote the unique history, culture, and current business opportunities of

Columbia and its neighbors Marietta and Wrightsville, which lies one mile across the Susquehanna.

"Did you know, for instance, that Columbia came within a single vote in Congress of becoming America's national capital? It's true. Just imagine what this place would look like today if *that* had happened," he says with a laugh. "Crime and gridlock traffic."

As it happens, I know this curious fact about Columbia. But Dave is on a roll, and far be it from me to stop a fellow singing the praise of his hometown. "We also built the longest wooden bridge in the world, which unfortunately the citizens of Columbia were forced to set fire to a few days before the Battle of Gettysburg in order to prevent the Confederate Army from entering Pennsylvania. You won't read about that in most histories of the Civil War," he says. "But people here regard them as heroes. Their brave act may have saved the Union."

With this, he hands me *The Burning of the Columbia-Wrightsville Bridge*, which turns out to be a graphic coloring book designed to inspire and inform kids (and aging history nuts) about Columbia's largely unknown role in the Civil War. Dave has a theory about why these remarkable facts are so little known or simply ignored by most historians.

"We sit on a historic river that was once the edge of the American wilderness, situated between two of America's first great inland towns, Lancaster and York. Both became known for their rich agriculture and important industries. These small river towns of the Susquehanna, on the other hand, depended solely on whatever came up or went down the river for their livelihoods. As a result, we've had big ups and downs over the past centuries as types of transportation changed from river to rail and major highways, producing periods of boom and bust."

He sounds like an armchair historian, my kind of guy. So, I urge him on, jotting notes with a pen in one hand, Episcopal hot dog in the other. Fortunately, after many decades of economic decline and stagnation, he continues, the Susquehanna National Heritage Area, as the region is now officially called, is finally on an upswing thanks to recent development and aggressive marketing along both sides of the river. Most notably, the Columbia Crossing River Trails Center, which serves as the trailhead for a fourteen-mile river walk, has made both Columbia and Wrightsville popular destinations for day hikers and river kayakers, nature lovers and river explorers. Artists are also gravitating to the area due to its affordable rent spaces and superb river vistas.

"In a way," Dave sums up, "things are finally beginning to come full circle here in Columbia. That's how closely our history is tied to time and the river. That real story begins with Wright's Ferry, of course."

Exactly what I'm hoping to hear. I explain to Dave that a friend from the national historic preservation movement, upon learning of my Wagon Road odyssey, urged me to check out the historic Wright's Ferry Mansion and even sent me a copy of a new book for young adults by Teri Kanefield called *The Extraordinary Suzy Wright*, with a note pointing out that Wright's restored home is one of the national historic preservation movement's major success stories of the past half century.

"See what I mean?" Dave comes back. "You can learn a lot from children's books."

Like a true-blue evangelist of local tourism, he advises me not to miss an evening hike along the river walk; a visit to the Columbia Historic Preservation Society, housed in the historic English Evangelical Lutheran Church; and the National Watch and Clock Museum over on Poplar Street. "But *only* if you have the time!"

I thank Dave for his good humor and great advice, and he refuses to take my five bucks for his coloring book. "Wright's Ferry Mansion is the place to start," he says. "Susanna Wright's story is amazing. But like many things around here, both she and her house were almost lost to history."

Susanna Wright was twenty-one when she sailed unaccompanied across the Atlantic in 1718 to join her mother, Patience; father, John Wright; and three younger siblings on two hundred acres of family-owned land in Chester County, Pennsylvania. John, an ordained Quaker minister, and his brothers had been prosperous linen drapers who, like William Penn before them, suffered years of abuse for their faith at the hands of the English Crown, compelling them to pull up stakes in 1714 and make haste for Penn's Holy Experiment. Raised in a Quaker tradition that held girls should be as well educated as boys, Suzy, as she was called, stayed behind in Lancaster, England, to complete her education before setting off to join the family.

By the time she arrived, her father was the local justice of the peace and a member of the Pennsylvania Assembly, and the Wright home in Chester County had become a gathering spot for Philadelphia's cultural elites—the likes of Isaac Norris, Dr. Benjamin Rush, James Logan, and even Ben Franklin and his wife, Deborah.

Fluent in French and well-versed in Latin and Italian, a voracious reader and budding writer of essays and poetry, Suzy had a keen mind and tireless curiosity about everything from science to faith, quickly making her a protégé of Logan, Penn's longtime secretary. Isaac Norris, the powerful Quaker scholar and assemblyman who proposed the inscription on the Liberty Bell, was also taken with the sharpness of her intellect and inquisitive charm, frequently lending her books from his own library and sharing ideas about government and society. Through their influence, Wright came into the sphere of Ben Franklin, who initiated a lively exchange of letters and visits that went on with Suzy for most of her adult life.

In 1724, John Wright ventured out to an Indian settlement called Shawanatown on the Susquehanna River, fifty miles upriver from the Chesapeake Bay, where he constructed a cabin and lived for a time preaching the Gospel and befriending remnants of the area's original Susquehannock Indians. He also scouted strategic land for Logan, who proposed a Quaker settlement on the edge of the frontier (from the French word *frontière*, meaning "borderland") that would bolster Pennsylvania's claim to own all lands east of the Susquehanna.

Two years after the death of his wife, John Wright returned to the area with his children and a pair of wealthy Quaker partners named Samuel Blunston and Robert Barber to begin laying out a "second settlement" intended to serve as a natural bulwark against the colony of Maryland's intensifying claims on both sides of the river—not to mention the French who were steadily encroaching from the west with the help of hostile tribes that feared losing their traditional hunting lands to English expansion.

Blunston, a surveyor eight years Suzy's senior, reportedly fell in love with her and proposed marriage but was turned down due to her devotion to her faith, which held that all souls were equal under God's eyes. She disdained the traditional English colonial law mandating that a married woman was legally her husband's property, and couldn't understand a union based on such a principle. "A single woman, on the other hand," Teri Kanefield points out, "could own her own property and do many things a man could do, such as enter legal agreements, appear in court on her own behalf, and decide what she wanted written in her will."

Understanding the importance of that fact and outlook, she cautioned younger women not to fall for the "soft, soothing flattery" of men that would invariably lead to "wearing the chain."

In late summer 1726, Suzy Wright became the first woman to purchase land at the frontier's edge, 100 acres on the east bank of the Susquehanna River where the calmer rocky shallows made the mile-and-a-half-wide crossing somewhat easier to navigate. She was twenty-eight years old. Two weeks later, John Wright purchased 150 acres adjoining his daughter's land, and by that time, Suzy had assumed the task of "raising" her siblings. The entire family initially lived in a small log house John Wright built near the water's edge.

Three years later, John Wright, Samuel Blunston, and others petitioned the colony's general assembly to request that a new county be formed. When the request was approved, Wright was appointed the justice of the peace and named the new county after his birthplace in England—Lancaster County. Hickory Town, fifteen miles away, adopted the same name.

A year later, after the Wagon Road was improved from Lancaster to the new settlement, Wright secured a patent from Thomas Penn's government to open the first commercial ferry service on the Susquehanna, operating from Suzy's property. Though competing ferries would spring up in the coming years, including a highly successful one upriver at Harrisburg, due to its prime location on the road leading west, no other operation would be nearly as profitable or important as Wright's Ferry.

The family's first ferries were little more than hollowed-out hardwood trees, canoe-like pontoons that were large enough to transport people and small wagons and horses across the river, pulled by roped oxen or horses from one side to the other. Suzy's brother John built a tavern for travelers on the west bank of the river, while her younger brother, James, managed the ferry service from the east side.

As the volume of traffic along the road increased, however, much more stable rafts and flatboats replaced the early precarious models, capable of handling the weight of a fully loaded Conestoga wagon and its team. During the peak years of Wagon Road travel, customers awaiting their turn to cross the river at Wright's Ferry often backed up for days, their lead wheels chalked with numbers. Competing ordinaries, inns, and taverns sprang up along the road expressly to serve thirsty drovers and travelers, including one operated by John Wright himself near the ferry entrance. By 1754 the toll for a six-horse team pulling a commercial wagon was about ninety dollars in today's world; for horses and riders just twelve. From the start of the operation, preachers bound for the wilderness to spread the Gospel crossed the river for free.

Travelers took to calling busy Wright's Ferry the "Gateway to the West," and despite a period of violence perpetuated by a Maryland scofflaw named Thomas Cresap, who started a "war" aimed at driving out the Pennsylvanians and Indians who lived peacefully on the east side of the river, the enterprise prospered enough for the Wrights to build a handsome two-story stone house on Suzy's land sometime around 1738. She and her brother James would live there for the balance of their lives.

The house was a simple Georgian affair with design elements of traditional English and Germanic architecture, meant to gather cool river breezes in summer and stay warm from multiple fireplaces and a full cellar in winter, wrought from Pennsylvania limestone and timbers cut from the abundant hardwood forests of the area. Suzy amassed a library with several hundred books—in multiple languages—on science, medicine, philosophy, and classical literature, and reflecting her growing interest in agriculture and natural healing, she also cultivated a large medicinal garden from which she made and distributed homemade medicines to neighbors and local Indians for free. She also planted an apple orchard and, according to one account from a Philadelphia traveler, a lane of cherry trees running down to the entrance of the ferry. Her lively correspondence with intellectual friends in Philadelphia and a circle of literary male and female friends scattered across the coastal mid-Atlantic often contained her original faith-inspired poetry with a distinct feminist edge, such as the closing lines of a letter she sent to Isaac Norris's daughter Eliza:

He only rules those who of choice obey
When strip'd of power & plac'd in equal light
Angels shall judge who had the better right.
All you can do is but let him see
That woman still shall sure his equal be.
By your example shake his ancient law
And shine yourself, the finish'd piece you draw.

Dealing with themes of life, death, justice, family, friendship, marriage, God, and time, Suzy's works were not written with hopes of fame or profit. They were never formally published, principally circulated through letters to contemporaries that led to her being referred to as the Susquehanna Muse. Only three dozen of her short poems survive.

In 1744, Samuel Blunston's wife died and Suzy and he rekindled their romance until his death. "The romance," Kanefield writes, "in the words of Elizabeth Heistad [a descendant] 'brightened and softened' Samuel's final years." (Among other surprises, Blunston left Suzy a sizable portion of his estate and use of his lands, fueling rumors that they had been lovers all along.)

By this point in her life, highly independent Suzy Wright—who has been called frontier America's first true feminist—was a one-woman force to be reckoned with throughout the region, serving as de facto court clerk and legal adviser representing the interests of her family and many others, settling disputes among quarreling neighbors, even campaigning aggressively for her preferred candidates in the Pennsylvania Assembly. Decades later, at the start of the French and Indian War, when her friend Ben Franklin was attempting to recruit wagons, horses, and provisions to outfit British General Braddock's campaign against the French at Fort Duquesne in Western Pennsylvania, it was Suzy who helped Franklin convince German and Quaker farmers of Lancaster and York Counties to join the cause. Years later, she was among the first to warn the Pennsylvania government about a lawless band of Scots-Irish hooligans who were terrorizing the local Indian populations and raising tensions along the frontier. They called themselves the Paxton Boys.

• • •

In 1814, the same year Columbia was officially incorporated as a town, the world's largest covered bridge was built across the Susquehanna to Wrightsville, an engineering marvel constructed of oak and pine harvested from local forests that dramatically boosted commercial and personal travel along the Wagon Road. It was 5,690 feet long and 30 feet wide, constructed over thirty-four stone piers, and turned a tidy profit for its Columbia investors until it was destroyed by a fierce winter storm in 1832. Within two years, local businessmen financed a replacement covered bridge (at a cost of $157,000) that included tracks for the Pennsylvania Railroad. The new bridge was moved closer to the original landing of Wright's Ferry and retained its distinction as the longest bridge in the world.

Not long after the new bridge opened, a race riot erupted in Columbia when white workers revolted against working alongside Black freedmen, testing the town's proud reputation as an abolitionist haven. For decades, along with much of Lancaster County, it had been a prime destination for escaped slaves on the Underground Railroad. Slave bounty hunters were known to regularly watch the bridge's entrance on the Wrightsville side of the river for runaway slaves being secreted to freedom by sympathetic York businessmen and supporters. By 1852, heavy railroad traffic between Philadelphia, Harrisburg, and Baltimore was further enhanced by a canal built on the west side of the river. That expedited river traffic to the Chesapeake Bay, making Columbia the prime transportation hub of the region—one of the busiest ports in America.

In late June 1863, a week before the bloodbath at Gettysburg, Confederate troops under the command of General John B. Gordon occupying the town of York as part of Robert E. Lee's second attempt to invade Pennsylvania and capture either Harrisburg or even Philadelphia—a strategy aimed at compelling Lincoln to negotiate an end to the war in the South's favor—moved on the bridge, preparing to cross.

On a rainy Sunday night, June 28, Columbia's undermanned Union militia officers sent four local civilian volunteers under the guidance of a railroad engineer named Robert Crane and an elderly Black man named Jacob Miller to blow up a western section of the bridge, hoping to knock out only a two-hundred-foot span so repairs could be quickly made once the invasion threat passed. The explosion, however, merely blew out walls of the covered bridge section, leaving the bridge fully intact. The four volunteers hurried back to the spot with barrels filled with coal oil and kerosene in order to set fire to that section of the bridge. Local lore holds that Jacob Miller lit the flames with his own cigar.

Despite the rain, the entire bridge was quickly engulfed in flames, creeping eastward as terrified citizens of Columbia gathered belongings and fled for Lancaster City. As far away as Harrisburg, the governor and state officials anxiously watched the glowing night sky to the southeast, receiving telegraph dispatches every few minutes that described the ensuing panic in Columbia. Fifteen miles away, Lancaster citizens could also see the lurid red skies south of the city, including a seemingly unconcerned former president named James Buchanan from his Wheatland estate. It was later learned that part of the Confederate invasion strategy was to capture Buchanan and ransom him for favorable terms.

By first light, the world's largest bridge was a smoldering ruin. Only its thirty-four stone piers remained, visible to this day, and are now part of an annual reenactment put on by Rivertownes PA USA to commemorate the burning of the Columbia-Wrightsville Bridge, also memorialized by a delightful coloring book by my new friend, artist Dave Haneman.

In the aftermath of the burning, critics argued that the small Union militia that guarded the bridge and Columbia would likely have been sufficient to repel the rebel invasion. The decision to burn the bridge remained a lively debate among local officials for years, and though the federal government promised to fund construction of a new bridge, it never fulfilled its obligation.

As distinguished Civil War historian and York resident Scott L. Mingus points out in *Flames Beyond Gettysburg*, his outstanding book on a facet of Lee's ambitious Gettysburg campaign that remains largely ignored by historians, many Pennsylvanians doubted whether Lee's advance could have been stopped without the destruction of the bridge. Seven days after the torching of the bridge, the Battle at Gettysburg ended the Confederate threat to invade the North. Lee retreated south and "Pennsylvanians took stock in what they had accomplished," writes Mingus. "Neither John Gordon nor any other rebels (except prisoners and a few deserters) had crossed the Susquehanna river. The U.S. flag still flew proudly over the state capital."

News of the burning of the Columbia-Wrightsville Bridge also inspired a recruitment bonanza for the Union Army that bolstered the defenses of Harrisburg, Lancaster, and Philadelphia.

Thanks to a second rebuilt bridge, in the remaining years of the nineteenth century, Columbia flourished as a major hub for railroad, canal, and road transportation, becoming a major warehouse and shipping point for lumber, coal, pig iron, and grain. It also supported a major industrial complex of anthracite furnaces that made Columbia, Marietta, and Wrightsville leaders in production of industrial iron, fueling the growth of other local industries like wagon building, tobacco processing, woodstoves, flour production, clock making, and boatbuilding. Between 1830 and 1900 the town's population rose to 12,300 residents, an estimated growth of 50 percent.

The twentieth century, on the other hand, starkly reversed Columbia's fortunes, as local iron ore played out, blast furnaces closed, and iron production moved to Pittsburgh. Dwindling forests dealt the local lumber business a similar blow, and on top of that the Pennsylvania Railroad relocated its home base to Harrisburg. The Great Depression only accelerated Columbia's economic woes. Construction of a new Veterans Memorial Bridge in 1930—built directly beside the stone pillars of the original wooden bridge—increased the flow of traffic through the center of town, but the cost of the toll to cross the river in challenging economic times proved problematic, even lethal to some locals. During the coldest winter months, when the river froze solid, daring motorists who couldn't or wouldn't pay the toll sometimes attempted to cross the frozen river in their cars. Some were swept away.

By the 1960s, Columbia's population had shrunk back to its 1900 level. The opening of a new Wrights Ferry Bridge in 1972 didn't help matters, offering a convenient bypass for busy travelers on Route 30/Lincoln Highway and thus depriving the town of revenue from tourists and business travelers.

I learn much of this from a full afternoon at the splendidly resourced Columbia Historic Preservation Society, housed in the gorgeous old English Evangelical Lutheran Church on North 2nd Street, including details of something called the Albatwitch, Columbia's own version of Bigfoot, a fleet, red-eyed humanoid creature that has allegedly stalked Susquehanna forests since Indian times. One of the town's most popular festivals—with

Albatwitch reportedly in attendance—takes place annually in River Park, raising funds for the historical society. More relevant to my quest, I also learn that the first white grapes grown in America were planted in Columbia by a Frenchman named Lefau Bennett in 1796, who cultivated his vines at Third and Union streets; they eventually spread westward via travelers of the road.

I wait until late afternoon to visit Suzy Wright's house, also on 2nd Street. I've timed it hoping to have the place to myself. When I arrive, a young docent puts down her novel and gives me a guided walk through the mansion, pointing out unique details of its traditional English entry hall, like a wide "passageway" facing the river, which features a pair of massive split-pine doors directly across from each other. The most outstanding feature, though, is a handsome staircase with banisters made of finely milled black cherry harvested from the property's original forests, and the unique her-ringbone brick floor, scarred by centuries of booted visitors, which speaks eloquently of the house's design functionality. As the docent explains, the identities of the house's actual builders—probably the leading joiners and carpenters of the day brought from Philadelphia or Lancaster—remain unknown, but their extraordinary handwork lives on thanks to a visionary couple named Richard Von Hess and his wife, Louise. History lovers with a keen interest in early American architecture, interiors, and landscape, they acquired Wright's Ferry Mansion in 1976 from a local man named Emmett Rasbridge, who'd purchased it from the last Wright owners in 1922, princi-pally to save the property from a planned demolition to make way for a coal yard. He'd reportedly lacked the funds to properly restore the classic Geor-gian house with its distinctive oversized windows, gable ends, pent eaves, gorgeous hand-carved interiors, and strong blend of German and English influences, but he clearly appreciated the importance enough to keep up the historic property until the right owner could be found.

Once it was in their hands, the Von Hesses formed a foundation to oversee a comprehensive restoration of the property, choosing one of the nation's foremost architects and preservation experts, Pennsylvanian G. Edwin Brumbaugh, to oversee the project.

"We recognized the opportunity not only to restore a virtually un-touched house of this early period," Richard Von Hess later wrote, "but also to furnish it exclusively to its time. This we knew would fulfill a great need in the field of decorative arts: to show an early Pennsylvania house furnished exclusively to the first half of the eighteenth century. Our task was now before us: to capture the spirit of her [Suzy Wright's] soul in the house and its contents."

As curator and art historian Elizabeth Meg Schaefer explains in the preface to her lavishly illustrated and detailed account of the restoration, published in 2005, very little was known about Susanna Wright and the house from the outset of the project. But years of Schaefer's scholarly research produced a wealth of detail about not only one of colonial America's first great homes but also its remarkable unmarried and ferociously independent mistress—a gifted poet, homegrown scientist, wise counselor, prodigious correspondent, and compassionate natural healer.

Later in life, after raising her brother James's six children and numerous grandchildren, she developed an innovative system that allowed silkworms to spin silk in paper cones, producing enough of the fabric to create some of the first stockings made in America, which were given to a British commander of forces during the French and Indian War. She later made a silk court dress that was formally presented to England's Queen Charlotte by Ben Franklin in 1770.

When Suzy died on December 1, 1784, *The Pennsylvania Gazette* reported her passing with eloquent economy:

> Possessed of an elevated understanding, improved by acquired knowledge to an eminent degree, she was distinguished by her superior benevolence evinced by a multitude of pious and charitable offices done in the course of her long life, toward those within her beneficent sphere.

Four years later, in the spring of 1788, Samuel Wright, Suzy's nephew, officially surveyed and laid out the town of Columbia, named for Christopher Columbus, with high hopes of influencing Congress's pending deliberations to select a permanent national capital. George Washington himself supported Columbia's bid, reportedly expressing admiration for its new name and its strategic location near the Chesapeake Bay.

When the official vote in Congress was tallied in 1790, however, Columbia came up one vote shy of the prize, losing out to a swampy bottomland located in a bend of the Potomac River between Maryland and Virginia that was prone to seasonal fog and malarial fevers. The new capital took the first president's name but paid homage to the runner-up—or so the story goes—by naming the area the District of Columbia.

As I sit on the front steps of Suzy Wright's house, which faces the river, enjoying the late-afternoon breeze and reading Elizabeth Meg Schaefer's lovely book on the mansion's restoration, I can't help but think how fortunate it is that the vote failed to make Columbia the new capital. Dave Haneman was right. This beautiful old river town would be nothing like it is today, a place reborn and celebrating its remarkable journey through time.

"We have a saying around here, *Tempus vitam regit*—Time rules life," James Campbell says as we stand together in the elegant foyer of the National Watch and Clock Museum on Poplar Street, one hour before official opening time.

It's my last stop before crossing the river to York County. Given the way I've been hopscotching between centuries as I travel America's immigrant highway, it seems only fitting to spend a little time with people who officially keep it.

An institution was started in 1947 by a Columbia resident whose house and garage were so full of clocks and watches he decided (or maybe his wife did for him) to open a small museum in order to display his growing collection to the public, the National Watch and Clock Museum has evolved into a school and service center equipped with the largest horological library on earth.

Campbell, acting curator and chief horologist of the museum, is in charge of it all, serving collectors and museums worldwide.

Following his service in the Marine Corps, Campbell earned a degree in technology science, taught himself how to repair watches and clocks, and found his way to the museum as an associate teacher and researcher fifteen years ago.

"I guess you could say clockwork is in both my bloodstream and my heritage," he says as we set off into the museum's first gallery, a room devoted to man's earliest efforts at establishing time via the sundial and an impressive re-creation of Stonehenge. His great-grandfather, one John Erb, was a clock maker from a town near Strasburg, Germany, who came to America as an indentured servant at age fifteen. Campbell grew up in Lancaster County and knew all about the Great Wagon Road at an early age because he believes his grandfather and other ancestors probably traveled it. Also, his mother was a schoolteacher with a passion for American history.

"Many people don't realize this fact, but the Wagon Road played a major role in spreading time westward in America. I'll show you tall case clocks made by eighteenth-century clock makers that would have traveled the road as the frontier expanded. The craftsmanship is superb. I'll even show you a case clock that Charles Mason and Jeremiah Dixon took with them on their trip to establish the dividing line between the slave-owning Southern states and Northern free states, which finally settled the dispute between Pennsylvania and Maryland once and for all."

An hour passes much too quickly as we set off on a delightful walk from prehistoric sundials to modern atomic clocks, Stonehenge to the digital age, an evolutionary flow of devices large and small, the odd and the spectacular, monumental and intimate, that helped human beings capture and shape time.

My favorites include the Mason-Dixon clock and a hall full of exquisitely detailed tall clocks that would have traveled the Wagon Road, "a true symbol of affluence in colonial America," Campbell explains, "by a craftsman who would probably also make your coffin," along with an early Renaissance clock that was strapped to its owner's arm—the world's first wristwatch—which inspired the creation of a wristwatch made by Luther Goddard, America's first watchmaker, in the early nineteenth century, producing a watch boom in America. But I am also particularly drawn to the museum's huge collection of elegantly carved "railroad grade" pocket watches, timepieces prized for their fine workmanship and reliability by railroad engineers and conductors from the nineteenth century to today, reminding me of the one my late grandfather Walter Dodson carried most of his life. Several of these valuable vintage timepieces, I learn, were made by the Hamilton Watch Company of Lancaster, including Campbell's own prized Hamilton 950 railroad pocket model. Woodrow Wilson, he points out, was wearing a Hamilton watch on the day World War I began.

As we walk, Campbell shows me everything from an extraordinary monument clock called the "Eighth Wonder of the World" that toured county fairs and exhibitions across America following the Civil War, to a display memorializing the Radium Girls who were poisoned from painting watch dials with leaded luminous paint. I see the first Mickey Mouse watch along with zany 1950s theme clocks, classic car clocks, and half a dozen wristwatches worn by the stars of the James Bond films; I learn about the birth of the chronometer and see wristwatches worn by American fighter pilots serving in the two World Wars. Ditto the first electric and digital watches; the internal workings of a giant tower clock; a guitar made with a clock built into its body celebrating the Martin Guitar company's two-millionth guitar; a replica of the first atomic clock; even the Doomsday Clock, whose minute hand sits frighteningly close to midnight.

"The sad thing is," observes my host, "watches and clock makers are a disappearing breed from the world. Very few people are going into the trade of making and repairing traditional clocks and watches these days, a dying art even though making watches is a very green industry—good for the planet."

As we complete the tour, Campbell provides the example of the famous Elgin Watch Company, a legendary Illinois firm that made outstanding timepieces from 1863 to 1968. "After sixty million watches made over the company's entire life, the oil they needed for making timepieces would barely fill a single five-gallon bucket. Talk about efficient use of natural resources."

Outside, the first tourist van of the day has arrived and is off-loading a group of senior citizens, reminding me that not only does time rule life, but also how far there is yet to go.

"How much farther do you have?" asks my generous host at the door.

Six hundred miles, give or take, I reply, pointing out that my original projected time frame for traveling the Wagon Road has been tossed to the winds.

"Too much history. Not enough time," I joke, explaining that I must head home to my life as a busy full-time editor of three thriving arts-and-culture magazines in North Carolina. In the interest of serving past and present, I've revised my plan to do the road in unrushed segments, however long it takes to reach its end, taking my own sweet time to travel the road in the manner of many Wagon Road forebears.

"Like a pilgrim on God's time," suggests Campbell as we shake hands.

"I couldn't put it better."

ELEVEN

HISTORY NIGHT IN YORK

"THIS SHOULD BE AN INTERESTING EVENING," JIM McCLURE SAYS WITH A laugh. "Tonight's topic is Weird York. An overflow crowd is expected."

I've found the longtime editor of the *York Daily Record-Sunday News* and author of several excellent books on York County history sitting at his office desk ninety minutes before the start of York History Night, the latest in a popular series of community gatherings created by McClure and others to promote public interest in the area's rich cultural heritage and historical importance. The group is now called the York County History Storytellers.

The idea came out of his online newspaper blog, *York Town Square*, a forum in which McClure and local history buffs regularly post items about the county's unique history and cultural lore, averaging more than thirty-five thousand dedicated reader visits per month, including yours truly.

His book *Nine Months in York Town: American Revolutionaries Labor on Pennsylvania's Frontier* told me everything I ever wanted to know about the creation of the Articles of Confederation—a fledgling Congress's first stab at creating a formal constitution and unifying document, the first to be contemplated and adopted by representatives of all thirteen colonies at the York County Courthouse in November 1777.

At a moment when local newspapers everywhere are barely clinging to life, why every one of them hasn't adopted McClure's clever approach to make local history relevant strikes me as a lost opportunity. Without dedicated flame keepers like McClure and his league of citizen history nuts, as I've begun to learn on my journey, our understanding of our national story will become an increasingly impoverished affair.

I ask him why he thinks the citizens of York County are so keen on their history.

"Probably because there is so much of it. But that once wasn't the case."

He explains that, not long before the 2002 publication of *Nine Months*, a poll published by the Polk-Lepson Research Group indicated that nearly half of York County's residents had little or no knowledge of the county's intimate connection to the American Revolution—one of the most important moments in the nation's history.

"Less than ten percent of the respondents, in fact, even mentioned the Articles of Confederation," he remembers. "We clearly had some work to do."

As we walk out together, headed for DreamWrights Center for Community Arts on Carlisle Avenue in York's West End, I ask him what role the Great Wagon Road played in his city's development.

"Absolutely essential," he insists. "York was the first town settled west of the Susquehanna River, as you know, on the edge of the frontier. Beginning with immigrants from the Palatinate region of Germany, the Wagon Road subsequently brought waves of settlers from all over Europe here throughout the eighteenth and nineteenth centuries."

He notes that the county was carved out of Lancaster County and named for the Duke of York in 1749, eight years after a pair of German surveyors employed by the Penn family laid out a rudimentary settlement on Codorus Creek. "But as time went along, it was York's unique location on the Wagon Road that played an even larger role in shaping its destiny and even the character of America itself."

York County sits astride more than sixty-five miles of the Mason-Dixon Line: "A border county on steroids, if you will, literally the hinge point between the industrial North and agrarian South as America grew, a cultural crossroads shaped by travelers of the Wagon Road, the Susquehanna River, and the Northern Central Railroad. As a result, York became one of the nation's first major transportation hubs, a place where lots of different nationalities in addition to the Germans and Scots-Irish flowed through town year after year, many of whom chose to settle down and make the county their home. Probably half the residents here can trace their roots to those early settlers. Generations ago, it wasn't unusual to find German primarily spoken in many York households.

"From the start," he continues, clearly relishing the chance to speak on the subject, "York was—and remains—a true melting pot, one of the nation's most diverse places, a representative snapshot of what America would become as the frontier expanded. Folks here today embrace this idea, keeping family traditions and stories they brought here alive over many generations. We just sort of tapped into that with the *Town Square* blog and History Night, encouraging folks to discover where they and their neighbors came from. Whatever else may be true, Yorkers possess a strong sense of community and uncommon interest in their personal heritage. I like to say that, regardless of where they came from, Yorkers speak a language all their own. You'll see what I mean tonight."

With that and a quick wave, he's off to prepare for his hosting duties, and I set off, too, hoping to find a quick bite to eat at the historic Golden Plough Tavern, which sits directly on the original Wagon Road at 157 West Market Street in the oldest part of York City—the place where Adams, Hancock, and their revolutionary colleagues bent their elbows and debated the language of the Articles of Confederation.

It's almost impossible to explain how excited the eternal eighth grader in me is to be back on the hunt of American history at a place where the nation's founders gathered to hammer out the document that officially established the United States of America.

My disappointment comes a short time later when I discover that the historic Golden Plough is no longer a functioning tavern, simply part of a major museum complex that includes the historic General Horatio Gates House (circa 1751) and a reproduction of the original York County Courthouse where the Articles were adopted; the only soul visible on York's deserted main drag, in fact, is a bronze statue of Gates, the so-called Hero of Saratoga, standing by the curb in front of his tall brick house and the adjacent tavern, his arm extended in a toast to George Washington.

I've read that the handsome medieval half-timbered tavern structure is one of the best-preserved early eighteenth-century structures in America, built by a man named Martin Eichelberger who came to America in 1741 from the Black Forest region of Germany. The building features medieval German and French design elements echoing Eichelberger's Palatinate origins. According to Daphne Dewhurst, the Golden Plough remained a popular dining spot for locals and travelers for more than one hundred years, which means I've missed supper and a flagon of local beer by only a hundred and fifty, give or take.

By the time I arrive at the arts center on Carlisle Avenue, the house lights are being dimmed in a hall packed to the rafters with History Night fans.

The only vacant seat I can find is high up in a rear section of the auditorium, which I reach by apologetically stepping over seated folks, finally plunking down between two older couples just as Jim McClure takes the stage to welcome folks and introduce the evening's guest speakers. They include local resident Scott Mingus Sr., the award-winning Civil War historian; June Lloyd, York County History Center's librarian emerita; and a county park geology expert, Jeri Jones.

"We're also very pleased to have Lee Woodmansee and his wife, Barbara, with us tonight," McClure announces, scanning the audience. "As many of you know, Lee is the author of several popular books on York County including the classic *You Can Tell You're a Yorker If* . . . Where's Lee? Oh . . . there he is *way* up in back!" Heads swivel, the audience vigorously applauds, and the author rises.

I am seated directly beside him.

A charming evening of storytelling ensues in which I learn a quilt sampler of delightfully weird things about historic York County, including the fact that the Susquehanna River is estimated to be 340 million years old and has actually reversed directions several times during its lifetime (a river after the modern politician's heart); also that a swampy area of Northern York County produced a fossilized footprint believed to be from a giant crocodile estimated to be 200 million years old. There are numerous tales about Wally, the huggable alligator, and the famous Shrewsbury meteorite of 1907 that is now in the Smithsonian Museum. A popular one, too, about the headless horseman of East York from colonial times who could stop the flow of blood merely by placing his hand on an injured person's wound. There are colorful accounts of Abe Lincoln's two visits to York and a remembrance of the year Teddy Roosevelt showed up to open the famous York State Fair, as well as historic ghosts, peculiar landforms, the famous Hex Hollow witchcraft murder of 1928, and beloved county landmarks that are no more.

My favorite stories of the evening, though, include mention of Native American artifacts that delayed the construction of Three Mile Island nuclear energy plant in 1967 (which sits just a dozen miles due north of York's Continental Square) and Scott Mingus's amusing tale about how, during the Civil War, members of a church in the Dover area of the county protected their homemade whiskey during the rebel occupation of 1863 by placing it in whitewashed barrels labeled "Holy Water."

Once the program is over and the lights go up, having learned why I'm in attendance, Lee Woodmansee turns and hands me a copy of *You Can Tell You're a Yorker If* . . . inviting me to have a chat after he and Mingus finish signing a few copies of their books in the theater lobby.

As folks pull on winter jackets and scarves before stepping out into a cold and starry October night, the lobby buzzes with friendly voices and neighbors catching up. I join a lengthy queue browsing Woodmansee's book, eager to learn how to identify a real Yorker.

- You belong to a golf or bowling league sponsored by your Sunday school.
- You leave your lawn chairs along the Halloween Parade route two days in advance—and they are never stolen.
- All your ancestors came from one province in Germany in the 1740s.
- You put gravy on top of cake.
- You trim the grass along your sidewalks with scissors.
- You spend more on fertilizer and lime each year than you do on your wife's birthday, Christmas, and anniversary gifts.
- You golf in January . . . and you aren't on vacation.
- At least one of your grandparents didn't speak English until first grade . . . and she was a seventh-generation American.
- You seldom "cross over" the Susquehanna River to Lancaster County.

At which point, someone taps me on the shoulder.

"Excuse me, dear. By any chance, are you from Baltimore?"

The elegant gray-haired woman standing just behind me in line is wearing a smart Harris Tweed jacket and festive green scarf with a blue lapel button that reads: "My Cat Is a Democrat." Beside her stands a rangy string bean of a fellow with a deeply weather-creased face, wearing a faded denim barn jacket and a MAGA ball cap.

"No ma'am. North Carolina."

She blushes and pats my arm. "So *sorry*, hon. I was sure you were my cousin Maureen's oldest boy, Eddie. Haven't seen Eddie for years. But you could be his twin. Eddie runs a big plumbing outfit in Baltimore."

I tell her no apology necessary, offering that I spent several memorable boyhood summers visiting a trio of colorful German aunts and uncles who lived in Baltimore row houses, including a crazy-fun uncle who introduced me to Brooks Robinson, my first sports hero. Baltimore will forever own a piece of my preteen heart.

"Did you know," pipes up Make America Great Again Man, "he's from here."

I look at him, wondering if he means Donald Trump or my late Uncle Carson, the designated Orioles heckler.

"York is where Brooks Robinson started his career," he clarifies. "He played ninety-five games for the York White Roses before being called up to the bigs. I saw him play here. Helluva player. Our ballpark is on Brooks Robinson Way. He's now part owner of the Revolution."

I am delighted—and not a little embarrassed—to learn these details about my baseball hero, the so-called Human Vacuum Cleaner, whose career stats I can quote like Bible verses (sixteen Gold Gloves, MVP and Hickok Belt winner, the greatest third baseman of all time, *Amen*). A few years back, a distinguished event called the McKenzie Cup honored me for my many golf books and arranged for a surprise guest to sit with me at the dinner—Brooks Robinson himself. He turned out to be the most charming of dinner companions and even claimed to remember my infamous leather-lunged Uncle Carson. One of the greatest nights of my life.

I ask MAGA Man to tell me more.

He explains that Robinson played second base for the old Piedmont

League's White Roses, which later became the Revolution of the Atlantic League but still remains bitter rivals of the Lancaster Stormers, formerly known as the Lancaster Red Roses. Their sporting rivalry stretches back more than a century, he adds, thanks to their references to England's most famous feuding families, the powerful Yorks and Lancasters. The ancient grudge, I divine, still animates everything from middle school athletics to local professional sports for both cities. "The only good reason someone from York crosses the river," he adds with a wry smile, taking a page right from Woodmansee's funny book, "is to watch our boys whip the Stormers and play the annual War of the Roses football game."

I flip open my reporter's notebook to jot a few notes, and discover that my pen is out of ink. MAGA Man frowns. "You are a reporter?"

"Back when I carried a pen that worked."

"Here, hon. I've got one!"

The fashionably tweedy woman hands me an ink pen with a logo that reads "Pioneer Life."

Her name, I learn, is Doris. His name, Leo. They've been married fifty-four years, and their surname turns out to be one of those impossibly long German names that resist a lazy Southern tongue and is ten miles beyond spellable by me. The closest I can come up with in my notebook is "Splech-kinstocher," but I am too embarrassed to ask them to spell it. I do learn, however, that Doris is a retired school librarian, Leo a retired county ag agent from Maryland. They live in the southern part of York County, near Hanover.

Leo wonders what's brought me to town. I skip the weary joke—a wagon with three hundred horses—and give him the brief elevator speech, assuming they've never heard of the Great Wagon Road. Silly me.

"Know all about it," Leo grunts matter-of-factly. "It runs through Hanover."

He is correct about this. Some old road experts believe the earliest path of the Great Wagon Road passed from York through Hanover toward Frederick, Maryland, before veering west to Harpers Ferry, then over the hills to Hagerstown and Winchester, Virginia. But as my historian pal Charlie Rodenbough once advised, there were, in fact, many alternate branches off the original Wagon Road after York that developed for a variety of pragmatic reasons—more direct route, better road conditions, nicer towns, friendlier people, fewer hostiles—providing an endless source of debate among modern old-road enthusiasts. Perhaps the most popular and improved iteration of the Wagon Road passed from York to Gettysburg then on to Chambersburg, where it turned southwest and joined today's historic US Highway 11 through the Cumberland Hills and the entire Valley of Virginia. I explain that this is the route I've chosen to follow on my way South.

Leo nods his head and informs me that the main public library in Hanover once had an exhibit on the Great Wagon Road. "Shame to miss Hanover, though."

In truth, though Doris's lapel button seems at odds with Leo's ball cap, there is something I find endearing about these two lovely long-married souls out here on an old road of forgotten America that gives me a welcome dose of optimism. I remark that they seem comfortable with each other's views at a time when some American families refuse to speak to each other over the Thanksgiving table.

"That's America," says Leo. "You have a God-given right to believe what you want. You've just got to be decent about it."

Doris smiles and nods. "In truth, we disagree on very little. My late German grandfather liked to say that in a good marriage you never go to bed with cross words. Leo and I have always followed that rule."

"We also share a love of gardening and history," Leo puts in. "Can't argue about history on the page. It is what it is. And working in a garden makes you too tired to argue about anything except who turns out the light."

He winks at his wife. She pats his hand. God bless 'em, I think.

Around us, a small Greek chorus of their fellow Yorkers who've been listening to this exchange feel compelled to offer their suggestions of things I need to see and do in their weird and wonderful city.

A big fellow wearing a black Stetson cowboy hat says not to miss the Harley-Davidson assembly plant, noting that York was called the "Detroit of the East" thanks to thousands of automobiles once manufactured here.

Another gentleman in a gray business suit and striped necktie points out that the Agricultural and Industrial Museum is where I can learn about the historic York Plan, a landmark building program that became the model for America during the Second World War, when the county's firms pooled resources and technology to expedite wartime production.

"We were the center of that program, making everything from bombs to bandages, baseball cards to the first computer processor," he says, adding that his grandfather worked for the York company that pioneered early air-conditioning during the city's heyday in the postwar boom of the 1950s, when York manufacturing firms like the AMF corporation, Caterpillar, and many others employed tens of thousands of Yorkers. "We were the top industrial town in the world back then. Unfortunately, thanks to offshore tax breaks, many of those companies left town, leaving their workers high and dry, taking a lot of good-paying jobs with them."

"But you can still see their impact in York," chips in a striking red-haired woman standing beside him. "Blocks of mansions built in York's golden age." She explains that the city's Historic District features more than forty different architectural styles and downtown's Continental Square is undergoing a fifty-million-dollar redevelopment project that includes a redo of the historic Yorktowne Hotel. "People here have always been resourceful. We find ways to reinvent ourselves and get things done." I learn that she is a member of the York County History Center downtown.

Over the next few minutes, as our line approaches the busy authors, I learn that York was "America's first official national capital," the most important stop on the Underground Railroad, the birthplace of the coal-fired locomotive, and the home to the Weightlifting Hall of Fame. Ditto the famous York apple (America's first commercial apple, taken west by Wagon Road travelers), animal crackers, and the famous Peppermint Pattie ("Unfortunately which," someone points out, "is now made over in Harrisburg").

The hits keep coming.

"Ever heard of the Del McCoury Band? They're from York. They've won more bluegrass awards than anyone else in Grand Ole Opry history!"

"We have the oldest continuously operating county fair in the country and major antiques expo that happens twice a year! Collectors come to York from all over the world, including the major auction houses."

"Ever had Fasnachts? A guy at the Central Market sells the best you'll ever eat!"

I dare to ask what Fasnachts are, clueless how to spell it.

"Fried potato dough," he explains with a chortle. "A cross between a doughnut and bowling ball. The joke in York is that at least you can eat the bowling ball if you must."

With the authors mere steps away, I thank these proud flame keepers of America's second-oldest frontier town, managing to jot down at least a few first names—Oliver, Darcy, Debbie, Nate, Peter, and Art.

"One more question," I say to them collectively. "Is it true that York held the first Thanksgiving celebration?"

The Greek chorus offers a resounding yes.

"Had enough York history yet?" an amused Lee Woodmansee asks as we slip off to chat in a corner of the thinning-out lobby. "As you can tell, Yorkers are *very* proud of their history and culture. They're also great people—totally unique."

Woodmansee, I quickly discover, is not a Yorker. He and wife Barbara moved here from Wilkes-Barre in 1981 so Lee could take the job as township manager for West Manchester, a prosperous York suburb.

"When we moved here, it felt like people spoke an entirely different language. They had peculiar phrases and idioms unlike anywhere else in Pennsylvania or Maryland. They called scrapple 'panhas,' for instance, and this was probably the only place in the world people liked gravy on cake. I discovered this was a culture that has not changed all that much since the first German settlers came down the Wagon Road and pushed out the Scots-Irish to try and keep their own language and ways of doing things. I knew a man whose mother grew up attending public schools here and never spoke anything but German. She wasn't unusual. I call it a culture nailed down."

Woodmansee was so taken with York's unique phrases and amusing habits, he began writing them down, resulting in highly entertaining *You Can Tell You're a Yorker If . . .* His first York book was written under the playful pseudonym Curvin Diffenderfer ("a very Yorkish name"), followed by a second edition under "Curvin Diffenderfer and Friends."

"That's because, after the first book came out in 1996, I got flooded with terrific material from Yorkers themselves—so many wonderful anecdotes and odd sayings, social habits, local names, and surprising tastes, I just had to make a second book. Where else do people eat *dippy eggs* for breakfast?"

For all the etymological fun, Woodmansee's study of local census records turned out to be much more impactful, revealing why the past is never fully past in York County, Pennsylvania.

"I found that more than fifty percent of York residents over age twenty-five did not have college degrees. That's because, from its very beginning, this is a place where people used their wits and hands—artisans, craftsmen, ironworkers, inventors, builders of all kinds—and thrived in the traditions of their German ancestors, a strong self-reliance that comes from the county's relative isolation and deep rural past. That's what eventually made York an industrial dynamo, and though the county has lost big manufacturing industries like Caterpillar, the AMF corporation, and others in recent years, that native pride and work ethic is still very much alive. In a sense, York not only reveres its past—but lives it."

I then turn to respected Civil War historian Scott Mingus, himself a proud York resident, for whom I have two important questions: Did burning the Columbia Bridge actually save the Union? And did the peaceful surrender of York Town to the invading Confederates in late June 1863 make York the only town in the North to surrender in the Civil War?

"Those are both questions historians love to debate," Mingus tells me. "Had the rebels crossed the river successfully, who can say what would have happened? Their original plan was to burn the bridge themselves to destroy the northern supply lines and beat the Yankees in Copperhead country. This also partially explains why the citizens of York pragmatically surrendered their town to Gordon's approaching army and why his men left the town intact, treating York citizens with surprising respect. It's a complex and fascinating story that had an unexpected outcome. When the people of Columbia took the decision out of their hands and set fire to their own bridge, the rebels turned around and went back to Gettysburg, which they'd previously occupied. That set the stage for the most important battle of the Civil War."

I am pleased to learn that Mingus and McClure are collaborating on a new collection of York County stories—*Civil War Stories from York County,*

Pa.—and intrigued to discover how Mingus, a relative newcomer who relocated here from Ohio in 2001, views the city's future.

"When I came to York twenty years ago," he says, "this was still pretty much a closed society heavily influenced by the emigrant culture of its past. But that's started to change in recent years with the influx of new people and ideas in an old city that has finally begun to appreciate its unique place in American history—the place where we formally became a nation with a constitution, followed by a Civil War that nearly tore that nation apart but ended when events took a different turn.

"When you walk the streets of this city," he sums up, "you can't escape feeling how so much unique history happened here."

The next day, following the author's advice and an excellent breakfast of "panhas" and "dippy eggs" at Round the Clock Diner on aptly named Memory Lane in East York—just one short block off the Wagon Road—I spend a couple useful hours in the York County History Center, which Mingus recommended visiting, and its outstanding Revolutionary War gallery, time-traveling to the autumn of 1777 before I set off on my self-guided tour.

As Jim McClure points out in *Nine Months in York Town*, colonial York Town was little more than a poor country village with muddy streets and roughly seventeen hundred residents living off the land when John Adams and other delegates of the Second Continental Congress began arriving here on September 30, 1777. They had left Lancaster after just one day before following their flight from British-occupied Philadelphia, hoping that by placing the Susquehanna River and Washington's Continental Army at Valley Forge between themselves and British General Charles Cornwallis's three thousand troops, a measure of security would allow them to formally create a nation.

Most delegates arrived alone on horseback or in small groups, following the Monocacy Road from Wright's Ferry to the town's High Street (today's Market Street). The weary delegates included both John and Samuel Adams; John Hancock, the newly married president of Congress; South Carolina's Henry Laurens; Virginia's Richard Henry Lee; Robert Morris (financier of the revolution); and thirty or so other delegates from thirteen newly designated "states," accompanied by a retinue of servants and slaves who quickly filled up the town's modest inns or bunked with local families, placing enormous stress on York's limited resources.

Long days of discussion and argument ensued at the county courthouse as delegates got down to the hard business of producing a workable constitution for a collection of individual states that had their own needs and agendas shaped by divergent views on everything from slavery to commerce. Newlywed Hancock found the long hours so taxing, he complained in a letter to his bride, Dorothy, "I sat in the Chair yesterday & Conducted the Business Eight Hours, which is too much. And after that had the Business of my office to attend to as usual. I cannot Stand it much longer this way." He also sent a friendly note to his friend Robert Morris asking for several bottles of Madeira. "I care not the price," he pleaded, "for I feel awkward not to have it in my power to ask a friend to take a glass."

As the weeks dragged on and a steady cold rain turned York Town's dusty streets to a soup of mud, a weary John Adams complained to wife Abigail that the Congress's inability to reach consensus over taxation and divisions among free Northern states versus Southern slaveholding ones was slowly draining his spirit. "War has no charms for me. If I live much longer in Banishment, I shall scarcely know my own Children. Tell my little ones, that if they will be very good, Pappa will come home. I will crawl home upon my little Pony and wait upon myself as well as I can."

A needed ray of sunshine came in late October, however, with news of General Horatio Gates's stunning victory over British forces at Saratoga. As delegates awaited confirmation of General Burgoyne's surrender of six thousand British and foreign troops, John Adams excitedly wrote to a colleague, "We have heard Rumors that filled us up to the stars . . . " And to wife Abigail: "We are out of patience. It is impossible to beat this suspense." The official word arrived on Halloween, delayed for nearly two weeks by an army courier who allegedly stopped en route to court a young woman— proof that all's fair in love and war.

"The church and courthouse bells in York Town rang for hours," recounts McClure of the moment the news was confirmed from the steps of the York Courthouse, regarded by many as the first major turning point of the Revolutionary War. Horatio Gates was subsequently awarded the position of head of the Board of War and feted by the citizens of York, who days later celebrated Congress's official Proclamation of Thanksgiving and Praise, extending a tradition begun by the Pilgrims in 1676 to the thirteen states. As a result of Gates's victory, the adoption of the Articles of Confederation and ambassador Franklin's persuasive charms, the once hesitant French would soon consider joining the American cause, forcing the British to shift their strategy to an ambitious Southern campaign that would ultimately prove disastrous. It also inspired convention delegates to finish their primary business in York—the writing of a formal constitution.

"Many [delegates] assert that the very salvation of these States depends on it," urged Cornelius Harnett, the merchant delegate from Wilmington, North Carolina, pointing out that "none of the European powers will publicly acknowledge them free and independent, until they are confederated."

Inspired to move with dispatch, Congress achieved agreement on thirteen principal articles by November 13, and appointed a committee to prepare the final draft of the document. Two days later, delegates had a chance to read over the draft written by Pennsylvania delegate John Dickinson, making only a few minor changes.

Short and simple, the Articles granted all thirteen states—optimistically referred to as a "League of Friendship"—the right to remain sovereign and fully independent, with Congress held as the last resort on matters of dispute between states. It also allowed the new "United States of America" to hold the obligation to make foreign treaties and alliances and maintain armed forces and coin money. The delegates also agreed to a system of state-by-state voting and a proportional state taxation scheme based on land values, but left issues of state claims on western lands unresolved. To a man, the delegates understood that their fledgling constitution was inadequate and still needed work. But with the British occupying Philadelphia and the Continental Army mired down at Valley Forge, the flawed Articles at least gave anxious patriots—not to mention watching foreign powers—the first framework of a national government.

Ironically, perhaps the biggest unresolved issue centered on the document's First Article: the official name of the new confederation of states.

The secretary of Congress originally proposed "The stile [*sic*] of the Confederacy shall be 'The United States of America,'" but after some quibbling, "Confederacy" was changed to "Confederation."

"The time had come," writes McClure. "Congress adopted the Articles of Confederation. It was up to the thirteen colonies—now states—to ratify Congress' action."

Henry Laurens sent the handwritten document of the Articles to Lancaster printer Francis Bailey, requesting three hundred copies, which made their way back to York Town on Friday, November 28. Laurens had them tied in bundles and distributed to each delegate for his state, urging delegates to lay the fledgling constitution before their state legislatures "at the earliest opportunity."

Just over a month after its adoption, the state of Virginia was first to ratify the new constitution. Several other states ratified the Articles during the early months of 1778. But when Congress reconvened in June that year, delegates learned that Maryland, New Jersey, and Delaware remained holdouts. The Articles required unanimous approval by all thirteen states. Smaller states wanted larger Southern states to relinquish their claims on western lands before voting to ratify. New Jersey and Delaware eventually agreed to conditions of the revised Articles in November 1778 and February 1779, leaving only the state of Maryland as the remaining holdout. Irked by Maryland's recalcitrance, several state legislatures passed resolutions that established a national government excluding the state of Maryland, though Congress ultimately abandoned this approach. It was only when British raids on Chesapeake Bay communities dramatically increased, prompting Maryland to seek aid from the French navy, that Marylanders finally took the advice of the French to ratify the Articles. About this same time, the state of Virginia agreed to relinquish its claims on western lands. The Maryland legislature ratified the Articles of Confederation on March 1, 1781.

Though its work product was notably flawed—there were no provisions for judicial and executive branches designed to create a system of checks and balances, for example, no power to regulate commerce, levy taxes, or enforce laws—most historians credit the delegates of York Town with at least creating the nation's first constitution, a workable baseline for the growth of functional democracy at the greatest moment of peril for America.

"Whatever the defects of the Articles of Confederation," wrote historian Edmund Burnett, "they constitute nevertheless an important, a necessary, stage in the development of an efficient constitution, even as the confederation under them was an important, necessary step in the progress toward a more perfect union."

By the end of the soggy spring of 1778, green shoots of hope were sprouting everywhere. With strong support from France's dashing young Marquis de Lafayette, George Washington survived a cabal that challenged his leadership and signed two game-changing treaties of alliance with the French, while a host of congressional actions stabilized the finances of the war. Washington's revitalized army—drilled into an effective tactical fighting force by Baron Von Steuben—began to make major gains against the enemy, prompting a stream of desertions from the British army.

On June 6, Congress officially rejected peace proposals submitted by British Lord William Howe and Sir Henry Clinton. Twelve days later, almost nine months to the day after Congress began evacuating Philadelphia, the British Army abandoned the city, allowing American forces to reclaim it within hours.

The Second Continental Congress conducted its final session at the York County Courthouse on June 27, pledging to soon discuss important improvements to the Articles of Confederation. Returning legislators found their beloved Pennsylvania State House ransacked but quickly went about placing the house in order. The Liberty Bell—spirited off to a hiding place in Bethlehem for the duration of the British occupation—would soon return.

One day after Congress reconvened in Philadelphia, Washington's improved Continental Army won a narrow victory over Sir Henry Clinton's retreating forces at Monmouth, New Jersey, a well-publicized battle that made his position as commander in chief unassailable. Within days, Washington would be hailed as the "Father of the Country" for the first time in print.

Despite the scarcity and widespread ruin left in the wake of the British occupation, on July 4, eighty delegates, military leaders, and important officials gathered at City Tavern for an elegant dinner to celebrate the anniversary of America's independence. At the head table, a large baked pudding held a crimson flag that bore symbolic images: an eye representing the providence of God; a label with an appeal to heaven; and a man holding a sword in one hand and the Declaration of Independence in the other. No record exists of how the liberty pudding tasted that evening. But the taste of freedom was sweet.

"An orchestra played as the dignitaries ate," recounts Jim McClure in *Nine Months in York Town*. "The dinner ended with [Henry] Laurens offering 13 toasts accompanied by the roar of cannons after each toast. That night boisterous crowds enjoyed brilliant fireworks. William Ellery, a signer of the Declaration of Independence from Rhode Island, marveled that Americans could celebrate their independence on the very streets the British had occupied just days before."

"What a strange vicissitude in Human affairs!" Ellery was moved to pen.

What's equally impressive and important to many Yorkers is that, eighty-five years later, almost to the day, the citizens of the town found themselves captive to another event that shaped the course of American history.

In late June 1863, as part of Robert E. Lee's second attempt to invade the North and earn a victory on Northern soil, more than 11,000 Confederates arrived in York County, occupying the town of 8,605 residents. Two weeks earlier, Lee's 70,000-man Army of Northern Virginia routed Union troops in the Second Battle of Winchester and pushed north into the Great Valley of Pennsylvania, taking possession of a sleepy farming and college town named Gettysburg with relative ease.

Immediately Yorkers spirited livestock and valuables into hiding and clogged the Wagon Road to cross the Columbia Bridge. A York jeweler named Francis Pollack packed silver from his shop into coffins, planning to bury them temporarily in the graveyard of Christ Lutheran Church. A shoemaker named Jacob Emmitt did the same with his stock of shoes.

One enterprising businessman posted signs in his windows reading "Smallpox," in hopes of deterring Confederates and thieves.

Several citizens hid horses in their houses and cellars. A girl who received a horse and buggy for her sixteenth birthday begged passing Confederates who were confiscating horses from farms to spare hers. "The soldiers told her if she could play 'Dixie' on her piano, they would be on their way. To their surprise, she knew the tune and played it for them." The rebels departed without the horse.

All told, the invaders would collect more than a thousand farm animals from York County citizens, mostly horses meant to pull supply wagons. But a surprising number of encounters between York residents and the Confederates unfolded peacefully, with the rebels confiscating food and grain but respectfully leaving horses for farmers who had fields to work.

The Union Army's own seizure of assets and damage to personal property, meanwhile, rivaled—and in some cases exceeded—that of the invading Southerners. "Fear of the Rebels sometimes turned to surprise when they proved to be well-behaved and gracious," write Mingus and McClure, "and joy when the Federal soldiers arrived would turn to shock and disgust when they openly robbed York Countians. As hundreds of Yorkers found out, hunger knew no distinction, blue or gray. Nor did thievery, gluttony, and greed."

To deal with the threat, a summit was held at Jacob Altland's house in the hamlet of Farmers, west of town on the gravel-packed turnpike between Gettysburg and York. Confederate Brigadier General John B. Gordon—recently a conservative candidate for governor of Georgia—met with a delegation of York civic leaders called the Committee for Safety on that Saturday evening, June 27, to discuss the terms whereby rebel troops would peacefully enter the town the following morning. The word "surrender" was never spoken during their discussions.

For his part, Gordon provided assurances that all "persons and property" would be protected on the condition that the rebels would be provisioned while remaining in the area. The gentleman general requested that all "rum shops be kept closed and promised that his men would 'be shot like dogs if they insulted a lady.'"

That Sunday morning, Gordon's brigade of eighteen hundred troops moved out early on the Wagon Road into York, confiscating horses as they went, kicking up clouds of dust that could be seen for miles. They reached the outskirts of downtown by 10 a.m. "Until then," note McClure and Mingus, "few Yorkers had ever seen a Rebel soldier." As they arrived, church bells were ringing, and well-dressed citizens lined the sidewalks on their way to services. A twenty-five-year-old lieutenant colonel with the 57th North Carolina named Hamilton Jones Jr., an attorney before the war, recorded in his diary: "They stopped and gazed at the troops as they passed with something like stupefaction, but there was no sign of alarm."

Many Yorkers skipped church that morning. "The ladies went to their homes," Jones recorded, "and during our stay there they were rarely ever seen again on the streets. The men, however, mingled freely with the Confederate officers, and there was little or no sign of apparent bitterness. They drank together and discussed the war and many other subjects together."

This presents an extraordinary picture to the mind: sons of the same nation, now brothers at war, pausing to share a drink and news, and agree what a shameful thing had come to pass.

On the morning of its occupation—the largest Northern town to surrender to the Confederates during the Civil War—General Gordon himself led his men to the heart of the town, stopping only long enough to take down the Stars and Stripes that floated high atop a tall flagpole in the center square—now Continental Square—before proceeding on to Wrightsville, where he planned to cross Columbia's historic covered bridge into Lancaster County. (Thanks to Old Jacob Miller, he discovered a bridge in ashes.)

My friend Dave Kochik laughs when I tell him I've walked from the American Revolution and the Civil War to York's industrial age in just two days.

We meet for a late lunch at the White Rose Bar and Grill, directly across Beaver Street from York's own historic Central Market House, before I'm due to make tracks for Gettysburg.

Dave is another friend from the golf world whom I promised to call whenever passing through his hometown. He and his wife, Pat, parents of two and grandparents of five, are both retired schoolteachers who worked in the city and county public school system for more than three decades. For many of those years, Dave taught American history and later served as a middle school principal in the inner city. After retiring in 2000, he taught education technology at York College of Pennsylvania. He and Pat are college sweethearts with fifty-one years of marriage and a shared passion for golf between them. Pat is not with him this day, however, because she's playing in a season-ending golf tournament.

"So, what was your favorite moment or thing in York?" Dave asks, ever the curious schoolteacher.

I mention my delight at York History Night, the infectious pride and passion of the city's history-loving citizens, and the thrill of learning about the creation of America's first constitution.

"But the York Agricultural and Industrial Museum pleased me the most," I admit.

The museum is housed in a former turn-of-the-century printing-press factory across the street from William Penn High School. Shortly after the doors opened that morning, staffer Parthena Bowman—whose double-great-grandmother was a "Bauman" who immigrated from Germany—thoughtfully gave me the Triple-A discount entry price of thirteen dollars plus a York Peppermint Pattie and sent me off on a journey through York innovation that led from revolutionary farm implements to the digital computer invented by a local man named George Stibitz.

I'm eager to share more about it, but the November afternoon is already growing dark and I have a specific question to ask. I've seen York's impressive golden-age mansions all over town, but also blocks of minority and mixed-race neighborhoods that appear to be seriously struggling. What does he make of the city's social challenges?

He sips his porter beer and tells me that economically struggling places between Philadelphia and Pittsburgh are sometimes referred to as "Pennsyltucky," a hybrid of the forgotten industrial North and the impoverished Appalachian South.

"When Pat and I came here in 1967, there were so many big-time factories operating, you didn't need a college education to make a good living. You went to work where your father or mother worked and that was that. But every bit of that is gone now, and young people have to go elsewhere to find the decent-paying jobs, better education, and economic opportunities. Many York kids just don't see a way out because there are no role models left for them."

That's the bad news, he says with a gentle head shake.

"The good news," he continues, "is that many of the migrants we see coming here from Central and South America are hardworking folks eager to make a living. Some probably know more about York history than many lifelong citizens do. This is a place that has welcomed immigrants for hundreds of years, York's real legacy. The immigrant spirit is still very much alive here, maybe stronger than ever among this new generation of newcomers."

I'm pleased to learn this, and as we part, I ask him to give my best to Pat, hoping her day on the course was a good one. Next time through town, I'll bring my clubs.

As a chilly darkness settles over surprising York City, I realize that there's one last stop to make. The eternal eighth grader in me demands it.

I find my way to an empty Brooks Robinson Plaza, where I find my boyhood baseball hero frozen in bronze, the work of sculptor Lorann Jacobs. The world's greatest infielder is signing a baseball for a pair of kids about the same age I was when I fell in love with Brooks Robinson, an adopted son of the Great Wagon Road.

PART THREE

BROTHER AGAINST BROTHER

TWELVE

THE GETTYSBURG
GOSPELER

A COLD NOVEMBER RAIN CHASES ME OUT OF THE NIGHT AND INTO THE brightly lit lobby of the Gettysburg Wyndham, where I discover a lively crowd of Union officers and their hoopskirted ladies partying like it's 1860 all over again.

It's the eve of Remembrance Sunday and the 154th reading of the Gettysburg Address. I am here at the invitation of a Gettysburg living institution who probably knows more about the mystery and meaning of Lincoln's most famous speech than anyone on earth.

His name is Gabor Boritt, a seventy-eight-year-old Hungarian-born academic who escaped both the Nazis and Communists after World War II to become one of America's leading Lincoln scholars and the founder of the prestigious Civil War Institute at Gettysburg College and author of more than a dozen outstanding books on the Civil War, including my own favorite, *The Gettysburg Gospel*, published in 2006.

Professor Boritt's *Gospel* begins where more than a hundred other books on the Battle of Gettysburg end: in the ruined landscape left in the wake of withdrawn armies; a once-peaceful farming town littered with the dead and dying, half-buried human corpses, dead horses and farm animals, utterly destroyed homes, severely damaged businesses, burned-out orchards, and fields scorched beyond recognition, a physical and spiritual devastation that would take years—even decades—to fully recover from.

Professor Boritt sets the scene:

The land itself seems to wail. Nothing but suffering. Sights, sounds, smells unbearable. Horror. The piles of limbs dripping blood, the dying, the dead. Hell on earth.

Named for an early Wagon Road tavern owner, Gettysburg, Pennsylvania, holds an outsized place in American history due to the extraordinary events that unfolded there over the first four days of July 1863, when this quiet market town of twenty-four hundred residents, home to a Lutheran seminary and college, became the staging ground for the most decisive battle of the American Civil War, a conflagration that left eleven thousand soldiers dead and twenty-five thousand wounded, with ten thousand simply "missing in action," ten times the number of American casualties on D-Day in 1944.

Though the war would drag on for another seventeen months, ultimately claiming more than 750,000 lives, most Civil War historians regard the South's defeat at Gettysburg as the major turning point of the war, providing a much-needed victory for a struggling Union Army and foiling Robert E. Lee's second attempt to invade the North in order to destroy Yankee supply lines, feed his hungry troops, and seize key Pennsylvania towns—a daring ploy meant to persuade Abraham Lincoln to accept peace terms favorable to the Confederate cause.

Instead, one of the bloodiest battles in American history—ironically waged over America's eighty-seventh birthday between ninety thousand Union and seventy-five thousand Confederate troops—ultimately preserved the Union and provided the backdrop for Abraham Lincoln's finest moment, a transcendent hymn of democracy once memorized by every American schoolkid, including this one.

Professor Boritt cites the US Christian Commission that took stock of conditions in the aftermath of the battle as calling it "a scene of horror and desolation which humanity, in all the centuries of its history has seldom witnessed." Ditto an army medical officer's report that was even blunter:

"The period of ten days following the battle of Gettysburg was the occasion of the greatest amount of human suffering known in this nation since its birth." The government, Boritt sums up, "was utterly unprepared for the greatest man-made disaster in American history."

And yet, in this grim tableau, a new beginning rose from the ashes, the moving and once little-known story of how Abe Lincoln's epic last-minute decision to journey to Gettysburg—just four months after the battle—resulted in a brief 272-word speech that lives at the heart of the American experience like no other piece of public oratory: an enduring plea for universal renewal and recommitment to democratic principles that helped a mortally wounded nation begin to heal from the wounds of its greatest ordeal. It is my hope that Boritt can tell me more.

At his invitation, this is why I've come. To sit at the elbow of a distinguished historian—himself a spiritual Wagon Road immigrant—and be drawn a bit closer to my favorite president and the speech I once memorized as a grammar school kid.

Before this, however, it's party time in hoopskirts and blue Union wool.

As I check in at the hotel front desk, I eavesdrop on a pair of impressively bewhiskered Union officers standing a few feet away with cocktails in hand, chatting about the endlessly ongoing debate over Confederate statues, specifically an item in that day's *Wall Street Journal* that mentions activists allegedly determined to remove every trace of Confederate remembrance from America's most beloved battlefield.

"The park service has stated over and over that no statues of any sort will ever be removed from the battlefield. But some people just won't let it be," says the older general. "They come back every few years with the same goal to rob Gettsyburg of its full meaning." He sports a thick salt-and-pepper mustache and a pair of world-class muttonchops that remind me of Abner Doubleday, the railroad surveyor who *didn't* invent baseball but *did* command the first shot in defense of Fort Sumter, and offered one of the smoothest comebacks ever to an indignant superior who demanded to know what all the sudden uproar was about. "A trifling difference of opinion between us and our neighbors opposite," he'd artfully replied. "And we are trying to settle it, sir."

"That would be a sad day," agrees the younger general, rattling the ice in his tumbler. "Gettysburg is sacred ground, even for those whose people fought on the losing side. It's one of the few places where we probably *should* have Confederate statues."

Since my own view on rebel statues is more or less still evolving, I'm interested to hear the thoughts of these dapper blue-belly reenactors who clearly have some skin in the debate.

I turn to them with notebook drawn.

"Sorry, gentlemen. I couldn't help hearing what you guys are talking about. What about down in Richmond, where the city fathers removed every Confederate statue along Monument Avenue?"

They look at me as if I might be a rebel spy disguised in faded Levi's, a St. Andrews Links ball cap, and dripping Orvis field jacket.

General Doubleday shakes his head. "I can't speak for the people of Richmond. But there are fourteen hundred statues and monuments on the field here at Gettysburg from every state that had soldiers in the fight. This battlefield was created to honor the dead from both sides. They were all Americans, brother against brother."

I dutifully jot this down.

"You a reporter?" asks the other general.

"Used to be. Now I just play one at reenactment events."

I politely inquire his name. He smiles and shakes his head.

"Forgive us, sir," injects his older partner with a lovely touch of nineteenth-century formality. "Tonight, we prefer to remain securely placed in July 1863. In other words, blissfully unfamiliar with contentious words over statues and monuments on a battlefield which is, in truth, many decades away from being created."

He explains that this annual Gettysburg Ball—happening at that moment in the hotel's main ballroom—is the highlight of their historic reenacting year, "the Super Bowl of the reenactment year, if you will," and will be followed by the annual reading of the Gettysburg Address in the morning. "Hope you understand. It's nothing personal. This is simply who—and what—we are gathered to celebrate this evening."

Surrounded by a sea of brass buttons and heavy blue wool, I fully appreciate his point. Sensing that neither is willing to slip out of character, I ask which historic Union officers they are portraying.

The older one smiles. "Who do you think?"

I change my mind from Doubleday, thinking he might instead be George Gordon Meade, who Lincoln placed in charge of the Army of the Potomac three days before the Battle of Gettysburg. Or maybe, given those impressive muttonchops, he's Ambrose Burnside, who birthed the word "sideburns."

By his stiff mien, as if prepared to be insulted, I choose "Fighting" Joe Hooker for the younger man, he who distinguished himself at Antietam but lost his nerve—and subsequently his command—after Lee outfoxed him in western Virginia.

"Nope," he says brightly, sounding pleased. "Neither one."

"Sometimes, we're not even sure," adds the older man with a smile.

They do tell me that they are longtime members of the Sons of Union Veterans, a national organization with more than seven thousand proud members from every state in the Union and several European countries. They will participate in four different events over the next two days, beginning with the annual Gettysburg Ball tonight, followed by an annual SUV breakfast in the morning, a traditional fife and drum parade through the town center, and a special ceremony at the Wilson monument on the battlefield before the reading of the Gettysburg Address at the Soldiers' National Cemetery.

"And on that note," adds the gracious elder, "I think we'd better get back to our wives in the ballroom before they run off with better-looking and much younger officers." He offers a dignified little bow straight from the nineteenth century. "Whatever you write," he adds with a wink, "I do hope you will be kind to us."

I thank them for their time and make for the elevators at the end of the lobby hallway, still dripping on the carpet, thinking how my brother, Dick—the Civil War nut who knows the heroes of the Southern cause chapter and verse—would relish this scene, even though he would be the only true rebel sympathizer in the house.

Suddenly, I hear a buzz of friendly voices from an open ballroom doorway. When I poke my head in, I'm delighted to see Pulitzer Prize–winning author Ron Chernow signing copies of his bestselling biography of Ulysses S. Grant. Having recently finished his book and thoroughly enjoyed it, I'm tempted to get in line to purchase a second autographed copy as a Christmas gift for my rebel-loving brother, but suddenly I spot a more familiar head rising above the crowd that belongs to General Grant's boss. My favorite president himself.

The real Abe Lincoln was known to like the press and enjoyed manipulating writers to serve his purposes. So it's no surprise that this Lincoln, who looks impressively like the original, standing alone at the end of the room's buffet table, nibbling cheese and crackers, with a glass of something sparkling pink in his hand, is happy to shake my hand and provide his real name. He's George Buss, a life sciences teacher who hails from Freeport, Illinois, site of the famous Lincoln-Douglas debates. He is on hand for a second year in a row to read Lincoln's address at the dedication service in the morning, he explains, having succeeded his close friend Jim Getty, who performed the task for more than thirty years. At six foot four, Buss is almost a dead ringer for our sixteenth president.

"Growing up in Freeport, I had a natural affinity for the president because friends and neighbors always told me I looked so much like a young Mr. Lincoln," he explains, when I point out the resemblance. "That fueled my interest to learn all I could about him, especially his rise from obscurity to public attention beginning with his campaign debates with Stephen Douglas. So much was at stake for the country at that moment over the Dred Scott case and Missouri Compromise. Their debate over the expansion of slavery into the new territories," he adds, "is what really put Abe Lincoln on the map.

"That's why the Gettysburg Address is more important than ever. It changed the course of American history—and gives us a sustaining blueprint for improving our imperfect Union."

He sips his pink wine and wonders if I'm part of an official group connected with the ceremonies tomorrow or just "your average American Civil War fan willing to brave the elements."

When I mention Gabor Boritt and the Great Wagon Road, his craggy Lincolnian features light up.

"Oh, wonderful! In that case, you will be in perfect company tomorrow. Gabor is a dear old friend and a marvelous teacher. Nobody knows the story of the Gettysburg Address better than Gabor. His own story, as you may well know, is living proof that the words Lincoln spoke here continue to be heard by people around the world."

I thank him and wish him good luck and clear weather in the morning.

"By the way," he says, as I turn to leave, "I've heard of the Great Wagon Road. I just can't remember where it runs exactly."

I explain that when he reads the Gettysburg Address in the morning, he will be looking straight down from Cemetery Hill upon it, less than a mile away, today's Route 30 through Gettysburg Center. It's the road thousands of immigrants took west in the eighteenth century, I explain. My standard elevator speech seems to get briefer with each stop.

Mr. Lincoln looks surprised, maybe even touched, by this small revelation.

"Thank you for telling me that, sir. My own ancestors came this way on their way out to Illinois in the early 1800s. Do you think they might have traveled it?"

"Almost certainly," I tell him. "Good luck tomorrow, sir."

As Gabor Boritt makes plain in *The Gettysburg Gospel*, facing an approaching reelection campaign in 1864 that even the friendliest newspaper pundits believed he was destined to lose, politics played a significant role in Lincoln's decision to travel to Gettysburg to consecrate the new Soldiers' National Cemetery that November.

"For Lincoln to be reelected," Boritt sums up, "people had to endure the hardships of war and still maintain the will to fight on. For the country to be saved, the war had to go on. And the bereaved—the whole country was bereaved—needed consolation of the highest order." For this reason, Lincoln had been invited by the recovering town's civic fathers to offer a few "appropriate remarks" to place that aspirational hope in motion.

As public wartime events go, the consecration of a new national burying ground would be neither simple nor easy to stage. Though the spirits of Gettysburg's citizens were buoyed by the proposal of the new Soldiers' National Cemetery and early word that the president himself might appear to dedicate the grounds, thousands of hastily buried Union bodies had yet to be exhumed from hasty graves, identified if possible, and transferred to their new resting places atop the cemetery's highest space, to be arrayed in semicircular formation determined by state.

Moreover, as grave diggers began their grim task—more than thirty-five hundred bodies would ultimately be removed and reinterred by the end of that winter—the town prepared for an onslaught of dedication visitors, running the gamut from grieving families still in search of missing loved ones' remains to what one observer described as "curious grief tourists," as they hastily repaired homes and spruced up the streets around the Diamond in town center, restocking shelves and reopening shops. One New York newspaper predicted fifty thousand might descend on recuperating Gettysburg for the October 23 consecration ceremony.

Problems beset the event's planners, however, from the beginning with a scheduling snag from Edward Everett, the nation's most beloved orator, who was invited to give the main address but reported that due to unspecified illness, the initial October date simply wouldn't work. He proposed an alternative date of November 19 to organizers. Meanwhile, several of the nation's leading poets, including Henry Wadsworth Longfellow (whose son served in the Union Army) and William Cullen Bryant, declined invitations to compose a special ode for the consecration ceremony, as did prolific John Greenleaf Whittier. To make matters worse, as late as middle October, the White House had yet to confirm whether President Lincoln himself would bother to show up.

Nevertheless, by month's end, cabinet members, Northern state governors whose troops fought at Gettysburg, plus several foreign ambassadors made plans to attend the highly publicized event. At least twenty-three newspapers agreed to send reporters as well, and the Baltimore and Ohio Railroad put on several special trains from Baltimore, Philadelphia, and New York to handle the expected crush of travelers. In Gettysburg itself, a large platform for dignitaries rose atop Cemetery Hill while an aggressive committee composed of local businessmen promoted an air of patriotic fervor. A towering hundred-foot flagpole went up on the Diamond. "Patriotic bunting sprouted all over town," recounts Boritt, " . . . and a great graphic *Panorama of the War* depicting the Civil War battles from their start in South Carolina to the present moment arrived for exhibition"— predecessor of the magnificent cyclorama painting of the battlefield that would, in time, dazzle generations of future Gettysburg visitors. "Pilgrims started arriving early," writes Boritt. "The town was in a frenzy, fast filling up with visitors."

As late as five days before the ceremony, David Wills, the Gettysburg attorney who had hired Scottish horticulturist William Saunders to design the cemetery's stately layout and personally written invitation letters to scores of dignitaries, still had no firm confirmation that Lincoln would appear. As a precaution, he invited Secretary of State William Seward to serve as a stand-in if the president failed to show.

"It was only a day or two before the ceremonies before he actually decided to come," Professor Boritt reminds me as we sit together bundled up against a brisk north wind beneath clear skies on the fourth row of seats at the cemetery, awaiting the start of the 154th reading.

Over the past twenty minutes since we rendezvoused in front of the stage, a stream of Professor Boritt's former students, neighbors, and Lincoln colleagues have appeared to greet their celebrated mentor, reunions that are touching to behold. This charming, diminutive scholar with his bright dark eyes and vibrant features seems genuinely thrilled to catch up with old friends, colleagues, and former students with hugs and laughs, but between these touching encounters, Boritt is curious to know about my own experiences with Gettysburg. I mention a couple visits with my history-loving papa in the early 1960s and an unexpectedly chaotic one with my wife and our four young children when we stopped off on our way home to Maine from a Southern vacation.

"With school starting up, I thought it would be great to introduce our three small boys and one teenage daughter to the glory of Gettysburg," I explain. "What a mistake."

During a ninety-minute narrated driving tour of the battlefield, somewhere around the site of Pickett's Charge, three boys arguing over Pokémon figures and a teenage daughter sulking over missing the first day of field hockey practice and thus in danger of failing to be named co-captain of the team finally got the best of their old man. I stopped the car, got out, and continued the tour alone and on foot. A little while later, our car eased up behind me, and my wife, Wendy, explained that there were four deeply sorry children in the car who wished to apologize to their father "for ruining his day at Gettsyburg."

Gabor Boritt smiles.

"It's not always easy to light the flame for young folks. Sometimes it takes years. If I may ask, did your daughter get to her practice on time?"

"We were only a day late. But Maggie was still named co-captain of the team."

Not long ago, I add, she phoned to wish her old man good luck on the Wagon Road, adding that she had "really fun memories" of our first family visit to Gettysburg.

"I think she must have meant the ghosts the kids all swore they saw at the inn by the battlefield where we stayed that night," I joke to Boritt. "None of us slept."

"So, you see?" he cheerfully replies. "An important seed was planted. Sometimes that's all it takes."

I wonder, in the moment, if he's thinking of his own journey here.

Thanks to a fine documentary made by his middle son, filmmaker Jake Boritt, called *Budapest to Gettysburg*—filmed during the time his dad was writing *The Gettysburg Gospel*—I know about the remarkable road that transformed Gabor Boritt into a "living treasure and hero of Gettysburg," as President George W. Bush once described him.

Born into a Jewish family in Budapest at the start of World War II, he grew up living in a single room and playing on bloodstained floors in a hospital on the edge of the city's ghetto. His father joined the resistance against the Nazis and his grandfather's family was deported to Auschwitz and murdered, and after his mother died and his father was imprisoned, he was sent to live in an orphanage. At sixteen, he joined the student-led Hungarian Revolution, a popular uprising he described as "euphoric" until it was crushed by the arrival of Soviet tanks less than a month later, costing the lives of fifteen hundred Hungarians and sending two hundred thousand of his countrymen abroad to seek political refuge. Boritt and his older sister, Judith, were among them, crossing the border into Austria, where they lived in a refugee camp for months.

As a teenage refugee, he arrived in New York City—"the dirtiest place I'd ever seen," as he once told a biographer—and was advised that the *real* America was somewhere "out west."

So, he set off for South Dakota and picked up a pamphlet of Abraham Lincoln's selected writings in order to practice his English. He was immediately taken by the mastery of Lincoln's language, the depth of his moral clarity, and the fact that he rose from poverty to the American presidency. It became his North Star of sorts. In 1962, he earned an undergraduate degree in history from Yankton College, followed by a master's degree in American history from the University of South Dakota one year later. A doctorate from Boston University followed. He went on to teach history to American troops during the Vietnam War with a special focus on the Civil War, and began work on his first book, *Lincoln and the Economics of the American Dream*, a groundbreaking work in the late 1970s that helped revive both scholarly and public reading interest in Lincoln's story. (A survey of leading Civil War scholars lists the book as one of the ten most important books about Abraham Lincoln ever published.)

In 1981, after a stint teaching at the University of Michigan, Boritt came to Gettysburg College to teach history as the nation's first fully funded chair for the study of the Civil War. Among other things, he started the respected Civil War Institute and helped establish the fifty-thousand-dollar Lincoln Prize in 1991, an award considered among the most coveted for the study of American history. Its first recipient was Ken Burns for his popular PBS project, *The Civil War*.

A short time later, Boritt was awarded the National Humanities Medal from the National Endowment for the Humanities, with a citation that reads in part: "His life's work and his life's story stand as testament to our nation's precious legacy of liberty."

One bit of romantic lore perpetuated by sensationalized newspaper reports, repeated by some of Lincoln's own early biographers, holds that the president jotted the Gettysburg Address on a scrap of paper (later discovered on the floor) during his short train ride to Gettysburg, suggesting the immortal words simply emerged from the ether of his genius at the eleventh hour.

Another version claims that Lincoln worked on the address sporadically over the days leading up to his arrival, putting the final flourishes on it late at night after giving an impromptu speech from his balcony to boisterous crowds while billeted at David Wills's home on the Diamond; a year after the ceremony, Lincoln's own attorney general claimed that the day his boss left Washington for the four-hour trip to Gettysburg, half the speech was already written and safely in his pocket, which he finished late at night at the Wills house or early the next morning, too late to fully memorize.

This is just one of the beguiling mysteries Gospeler Gabor Boritt skill-fully examines, noting that where and when the 272 immortal words were written may matter little to the modern ear that hears them today. The speech remains the stuff of a presidential historian's dreams, one of the enduring mysteries that lifts the Gettysburg Address to an almost Homeric pitch of meaning, regardless of its origins.

As Boritt's *Gospel* recounts, on the beautiful autumn morning before the ceremony, Lincoln toured the still-festering battlefield as crews re-spectfully paused from exhuming and identifying bodies. Afterward, he and Seward returned to the Wills house, where, according to John Nicolay's rec-ollection, Lincoln finished writing the final version of his speech.

A short while later, he stepped out into the square to rousing cheers from the massive crowds, many of whom had stayed up all night to catch a glimpse of him. With the Marine Band at the head of the procession, the parade moved slowly up to Cemetery Hill three-quarters of a mile away. Be-fitting the solemnity of the occasion, people lining the route up Baltimore Street removed hats and bowed their heads to the passing president, who carried his own famous hat with a mourning band attached in memory of his own recently deceased son Willie.

After an opening prayer by a local minister and the playing of "Old Hundred" by the Marine Band (which included the father of nine-year-old John Philip Sousa), imposing, white-haired Edward Everett, former congressman and president of Harvard College, America's most admired patriotic orator, gave a two-hour verbal history of the "great battle for dem-ocratic principles," including a remarkably detailed day-by-day account of the Gettysburg battle, recounted largely from memory. Everett concluded his speech by putting forth an original argument against the right of seces-sion and offered a vision of how history, future Americans, and the rest of the world would come to regard the importance of what transpired at Gettysburg:

> *Wheresoever throughout the civilized world the accounts of this great war-fare are read, and down to the latest period of recorded time, in the glorious annals of our common country, there will be no brighter page than that which relates the battles of Gettysburg.*

The last word was left to Abraham Lincoln.

Following another musical interlude by the singers of the Maryland Musical Association, the sixteenth president of the United States—already standing, still hatless—was introduced to respectful applause.

"We will never know the exact words he used," writes Gabor Boritt, "but the minor variations that would come down to posterity did not change the substance of what he said—not for the people at the cemetery or for those who would subsequently read his words in the newspapers: *Four score and seven years ago our fathers brought forth upon this continent a new nation, conceived in Liberty, and dedicated to the proposition that all men are created equal . . . "*

Newspapers broadly reported that Lincoln's audience stood quietly at the end of his short address—"as one would after a prayer," one writer noted.

A similar silence befalls the sacred burying ground as we watch the keynote speaker and distinguished historian, Lincoln scholar, and former Gabor Boritt pupil Harold Holzer rise to give a brilliant address that helps crystalize my own thinking about the fate of Confederate statues.

"We gather here to remember a great speech in a sacred spot," Holzer begins. "But Gettysburg is not only a final resting place for those who here gave their lives that this country might live; it is also an outdoor sculpture gallery with more than thirteen hundred monuments—Meade and Lee; Longstreet and Buford; Wadsworth and Warren. These statues recall a time when valor more than values elevated subjects onto pedestals. And when— let's admit it—the real issue that ignited the words Lincoln echoed here— all men are created equal—remains a promise unfulfilled.

"Today, as we remember Lincoln in his finest hour, a speech that went on to inspire statues of its own, we face a challenge and exploration of countless other statues to collective memory itself. Do we embrace the memory? Do we revise it? Or do we simply erase it?"

Over the next twenty minutes, Holzer makes an eloquent plea for moving with utmost caution and care in the conversation about revising the landscape of Civil War statues and battlefield memorials, wherever they stand.

"Our Civil War past still haunts us," he acknowledges. "But obliterating relics that testify to it cannot change yesterday—while learning from them *can* change tomorrow." Lincoln did more, he reminds the assemblage, than any single figure of his time to end slavery by enacting the Emancipation Proclamation.

A possible solution to the continuing furor over objectionable statues, he adds, is to consider moving them to museums, cemeteries, and battlefields where they can be used as a valuable teaching device to provide a more honest story of time and circumstance.

"Might we here resolve to slow the rush to judgment, to consider the genuine benefit of art for art's sake, and to consider that wonderful alternative—context! Why not *explain* statues rather than reducing them to dust! Why not add new information and computer screens to tell full stories. For when we blow up memory altogether, and leave no trace of it for our children or theirs, we forget who we were, why we care, and how we can become something even better."

Out of the corner of my eye, I see Professor Boritt, nodding.

What comes next is a lovely surprise, not to mention a powerful way to underscore Holzer's argument.

"Gabor Boritt, who is with us today"—here he pauses, allowing for strong applause—"was born in Budapest, a city that has been occupied over time by Nazis and Communists. His own family fell victim to both rounds of terror." But even in Budapest, Holzer explains, after decades of turmoil, Hungarians refused to destroy the public art that was raised to celebrate villains. Instead, they created something called Memento Park, "where old statues of discredited people are arranged in permanent display instead of erasing the painful memories of the past, compelling people to comprehend, remember and—above all—learn from the past.

"Maybe," Holzer concludes, "we can be strong enough to do that here."

As the sustained applause dies down, it is time for the "Big Lincoln Moment," as one of Gabor's former students seated nearby describes the annual reading.

A hatless George Buss steps forward as Abe Lincoln, his voice possessing the same fluting, high-pitched Midwestern cadence that falls off at the end of each sentence, described by some as eerily similar to that of the former Illinois log splitter.

As he speaks, I feel my throat unexpectedly tighten, and I stumblingly recite the words I once memorized for a long-ago Presidents' Day, feeling a powerful rush of emotion and pride that makes me wish every American alive today could be sitting here with us.

As we make our way out of the cemetery, the Gettysburg Gospeler pauses and takes my arm. "So, what did you think?" he asks quietly, almost urgently.

Clearing my throat, I admit that this was one of the most moving public ceremonies I've ever witnessed. I just wish my wife, Wendy, had been here to see it with me.

"Maybe," he says with his impish smile, still holding my arm, "you should come back someday soon and bring her to see our farm."

Following the Lincoln Fellowship Annual Luncheon (during which I learn that there are more statues and monuments of Lincoln than any other American; more than 280 of them scattered across thirty-six states, several of which are currently under threat to be removed) we rendezvous for an early evening dinner at the Hotel Gettysburg with wife Liz and several of Gabor's former students who work for various historical preservation entities and the National Park Service.

It's a pleasure to sit and listen as this remarkable historian and his students reminisce and share stories of their work projects and related adventures.

The evening concludes with the fifty-sixth annual Robert Fortenbaugh Memorial Lecture at the Majestic Theater in downtown Gettysburg, presented by Duke University history professor Thavolia Glymph, on the under-recognized role enslaved and free Black women unionists played in the fight for ending slavery. It's an eye-opener too.

As we step out beneath a crisp autumn moon to say goodbye, I marvel at my host's physical stamina and thank him for an unforgettable day.

"You are most welcome," he says, reaching for my hand. "I ask only one thing of you. Perhaps someday soon you will return and tell me about the people and stories you find along the Wagon Road. This interests me greatly!"

I've known Gabor Boritt less than twelve hours, yet he makes me feel as if I'm one of his students.

I tell him that I would be honored to do so.

"Wonderful! Bring your wife and come for lunch. Liz and I restored an old farmhouse from the late 1790s that looks across Marsh Creek at the site of Pickett's Charge. The house had broken windows and no doors when we moved in many years ago. When a reporter from *The New York Times* came for a visit, he actually stepped through the floors!"

I laugh, and he smiles.

"Please don't worry. We've fixed the floor since then. Liz is a wonderful cook!"

THIRTEEN

RISING FROM THE ASHES

O N MY WAY TO THE ANTIETAM NATIONAL BATTLEFIELD. I STOP IN Chambersburg, Pennsylvania, to gas up and grab lunch. This is where the Great Wagon Road departs from the Lincoln Highway and turns southwest to follow beautiful, meandering US Highway 11 through Pennsylvania's Cumberland and Virginia's Shenandoah Valley to Roanoke, part of a much-longer federal highway that stretches 1,645 miles from the US-Canadian border in upstate New York to a national wildlife refuge east of New Orleans, Louisiana.

A forty-mile stretch of Highway 11 from Harrisburg to the Maryland state line—the route Moravians from Bethlehem took to Carolina, crossing at Harris's Ferry on the Susquehanna—is called the Molly Pitcher Highway in honor of the plucky young wife of a Continental cannoneer who heroically took over loading and firing her dead husband's cannon during the crucial Battle of Monmouth in 1778. (Though some Rev War geeks contend Molly Pitcher was merely a symbolic name that represents several heroic females who served in battles alongside their husbands, records show that a real Molly Pitcher remarried and settled in Carlisle and served with distinction in the state's general assembly.)

During the two decades I regularly traveled this way between our homes in Maine and North Carolina, I grew to love the "back way home" over historic Highway 11 to avoid the miserable traffic congestion around

Washington, DC, opting for the sweeping views and small towns of the lush Cumberland and Shenandoah Valleys. Curiously, though, I never fully appreciated my attraction to the old road and places along it until I discovered that Highway 11 was built directly over the colonial highway my ancestors took to Maryland and the Carolinas in the eighteenth century. Now gravitational pull suddenly made sense, a spiritual geography that spoke to a child of wilderness travelers. Today, even though Highway 11 closely shadows busy I-81 and briefly joins the interstate in scattered places, the historic highway retains much of its lovely rural character as it passes through pastured hills, handsome valley farms, and the main streets of some of the prettiest towns and villages in America.

As I gas up, with time to kill before my late-afternoon appointment thirty miles down the road, I'm embarrassed to realize that I've probably driven past Chambersburg a hundred times in my life without stopping to learn about this old Pennsylvania town. With a couple hours to spare, I decide historic Chambersburg clearly merits a closer look, especially since the original path of Highway 11 passes straight through the center of town.

The one story I recently learned about it comes from James McPherson's masterful work on the Battle of Antietam, *Crossroads of Freedom*. Two weeks after the Union's victory at Antietam, Confederate General Jeb Stuart led eighteen hundred Confederates on a daring daylight raid of Chambersburg, the seat of Franklin County, safely evading Union troops to steal twelve hundred horses, destroy railroad equipment, and seize a dozen prisoners plus several enslaved persons, suffering only two casualties before safely returning to rebel lines. Stuart's main objective to cripple the Pennsylvania Railroad bridge at nearby Scotland failed, but the incident dampened the euphoria unleashed by a desperately needed Union victory at Antietam.

And so, I follow the sight line of one of the tallest church steeples I've ever seen to the handsome municipal town square, park in front of a stately Presbyterian church, and duck into the chamber of commerce office across the street, where a friendly receptionist helpfully directs me on to the Franklin County Historical Society–Kittochtinny museum over on East King Street, two blocks away.

There I am taken kindly in hand by a society volunteer and discover that Chambersburg—originally called Falling Spring—began as a trading post built by Wagon Road Scots-Irish settlers on a hunting trail used for millennia by Native American tribes known as the "Virginia Path." From there, it evolved into the Great Philadelphia Wagon Road, bisecting the Cumberland Valley from Harris's Ferry (later Harrisburg) to Hagerstown and the Valley of Virginia. Due to the settlement's strategic position on the most heavily traveled road of early America, more than two-thirds of Falling Spring's population fled the violence of the French and Indian War. When the Treaty of Paris was signed in 1763, granting Britain sovereignty over all lands east of the Appalachian Mountains, Falling Spring quickly rebounded.

During the Whiskey Rebellion (1791–1794), true to their natural Scots-Irish passion for freedom and homemade whiskey and intense dislike of any authority under heaven, local citizens protested George Washington's order of conscription to put down the rebellion and even raised a defiant "liberty pole" in the center of town, a symbol of freedom that originated with Roman senators upon the assassination of Julius Caesar in 44 BC. The defiant structure was finally hauled down, the story goes, just hours before President Washington himself stopped off to spend the night with a local surgeon while en route to battle whiskey rebels around Carlisle, said to be the first time a sitting US president commanded troops in the field.

A decade later, in 1808, Chambersburg was officially incorporated, named for the town's founding patriarch, a Scots-Irish immigrant named Benjamin Chambers, whose three sons, James, William, and Benjamin Jr., were among the first non–New Englanders to join other patriots during the Siege of Boston in 1775 and went on to serve with distinction in several key Revolutionary War battles.

Because of its key location on the heavily traveled road, the town soon became a prominent stop on the Underground Railroad, home to an active community of free and enslaved Blacks and a largely sympathetic white populace that funded some of the nation's first public schools for Black children.

Prior to John Brown's raid on the federal arsenal at Harpers Ferry in October 1859, Brown and several of his fellow conspirators stayed at a residence on East King Street (it still stands, a few paces away from the society's front door) with Brown posing as a mining engineer and accumulating a cache of gunpowder and weapons under the guise of buying mining equipment. Prior to the raid, which was meant to spark a national slave uprising, Brown supposedly met with Frederick Douglass at a local rock quarry only to be warned by the famous abolitionist that his plan was a guaranteed suicide mission. After the Harpers Ferry raid during which Brown was captured and ten of his fellow raiders were killed, including sons Watson and Oliver, five others escaped and later turned up briefly back at the house on East King Street before being recognized, arrested, and tried. That December John Brown became the first man in the United States to be executed for treason.

At the museum, I learn that Chambersburg was subjected to three different raids by Confederate forces, each one worse than the one preceding it.

The second one came in late June 1863, a week before the battle of Gettysburg, as elements of Lee's army moved up the Wagon Road toward Carlisle. There, a second cavalry brigade occupied the town to finish the job of destroying the Cumberland Valley Railroad as well as the bridge at nearby Scotland. Another in July 1864, conducted by Jubal Early's troopers, proved to be the most devastating of all. When it was learned that the local bank had sent its cash reserves out of town for safekeeping, and was thus unable to provide the heavy ransom demanded by Early's rebels, the Confederates set the town ablaze, including its handsome Doric-columned county courthouse, purportedly in revenge for the burning of the Virginia Military Institute and farms down in the Shenandoah Valley by Union troops earlier that summer. Among the few buildings left standing in Chambersburg was the Masonic Temple, which was guarded by order of a Confederate officer who belonged to the Masons. As a result, "Remember Chambersburg" became a popular battle cry for the Union Army.

General Jubal Early was eventually accused of war crimes for burning down the town—believed to be the only Northern town to suffer that fate during the Civil War. Reconstruction took more than thirty years, and every year around July 30, according to the museum volunteer, the town holds a service of remembrance to honor its Civil War soldiers and Franklin County veterans from other wars at the fountain and statue of a Union soldier in the center of town.

I spend a delightful hour poking around the handsome downtown district, admiring Chambersburg's tidy redbrick streets, prosperous shops, and mix of Second Empire and late–Gothic Revival architecture, before I duck into the Main Street Deli for an excellent Reuben sandwich and use my phone to read a piece by one of my favorite political commentators, *New York Times* columnist David Brooks, about modern Chambersburg and the genteel conservatism of Franklin County, a reflection on traditional so-called Red America. "The conservatism I found in Franklin County is not an ideological or a reactionary conservatism," he writes. "It is a temperamental conservatism. People place tremendous value on being agreeable, civil, and kind. They value continuity and revere the past."

This is good to know, reminding me of my own family roots back in rural North Carolina, people who care about God, country, and being a good neighbor.

After lunch, long addicted to poking my nose into any house of worship, I find my way to the Central Presbyterian Church that dominates the town square. There, a friendly staffer shows me the historic sanctuary, and recounts the construction of the structure following the Civil War and how most of its beautiful Tiffany windows even survived a terrible fire in 1938.

"No known Confederates involved with that one," he jokes. As we sit, he tells me a charming story about the church's extraordinary steeple, which soars 186 feet above the town. Its construction was funded by a wealthy local woman who earned the moral indignation of several female members of the congregation, who railed that she'd shamefully underwritten an architectural phallic symbol in the middle of town. Miss Sarah Wilson's response to her critics was pure Presbyterian steel: "If God wanted it to come down, then it would. If He didn't, then it would stand."

Before moving on, I drive a few blocks north on Main Street to have a look at Wilson College, formerly a women's institution modeled after Vassar College that's still affiliated with the Presbyterian Church, named for the same plucky matron. The college was founded during the same years the town rose from the ashes following the Civil War, yet another example of the Presbyterian passion for spreading the Gospel and public education along the Wagon Road.

The campus is lovely: handsome stone buildings and grassy quads still green beneath mature hardwood trees even as the last of autumn's leaves filter down. The sight of students walking in pairs to afternoon class, laughing and chatting, seems eons from Chambersburg's fiery past, the perfect image for a town that rose with biblical determination from the ashes.

I'm glad I finally dropped by to have a look. But it's time to get on to the blood and horror of Antietam.

FOURTEEN

ANTIETAM

PEOPLE WHO COME HERE *FEEL* THIS HISTORY," SAYS SHARON MURRAY.
She pauses and smiles. "Some have ancestors who died or went missing here just four or five generations ago, almost within living memory. Think about that for a moment. For many of them, this is sacred ground, and the battle is part of who they are. Being a guide here is about telling the stories of the brave Americans who served and perished on both sides. I'm honored to do that. Telling stories keeps them alive."

Murray, an elegant, gray-haired woman of sixty-two, glances over the soulful contours of the Antietam National Battlefield, thrown into golden relief on this late November afternoon. On a single autumn day in 1862, more than twenty-three thousand Union and Confederate soldiers were killed or wounded or went missing in action here, in a battle that would alter the direction of the Civil War, often described as the bloodiest day in American history.

Having met Murray only moments before, I ask her what she likes most about her historic position as Antietam's first female battlefield ambassador.

"Let me think about that for a bit," she says as we drive the short distance up the Hagerstown Pike past the Dunker Church to the southern edge of the infamous cornfield where the first phase of the battle took place.

She opens our tour by describing Antietam Battlefield's own struggle to survive.

Along with the historic Civil War battlefields of Gettysburg, Vicksburg, Shiloh, Chickamauga, and Chattanooga, Antietam was created by an act of Congress in 1890, and maintained by the US War Department until 1933, when all five military parks were transferred to the newly created National Park Service. Rising patriotism and growing public interest during and after the Second World War gave a boost to the nation's historic preservation movement, Murray explains, yet in the late 1980s and early '90s, Antietam Battlefield found itself in a fight for its life due to a building boom in Maryland's Washington County that landed the battlefield on the National Trust for Historic Preservation's list of most endangered historic places in America.

The battle to save Antietam might have been lost if a local grassroots preservation group called Save Historic Antietam Foundation hadn't sprung up to keep the battlefield and surrounding private lands free from development, fueling its campaign with the battle cry "Don't Gettysburg Sharpsburg," a reference to the rampant commercial exploitation that inevitably mushroomed around the town of Gettysburg. "We didn't want the 19th century character of Sharpsburg to be polluted by the smell of hamburger grease from fast-food joints and neon lights flashing at motels," founding member Dennis Frye of SHAF told the *Herald-Mail* in 2016.

Thanks to the foundation's tireless work and collaboration with the American Battlefield Trust over nearly a decade of public and private activism, nearly ten thousand acres—three thousand in the park proper and seven thousand surrounding it—were eventually granted protection. About 60 percent of this property was acquired since 1990. During this period, SHAF's members used original battlefield maps to clear brush, remove fences, and restore the battlefield's rolling hills and open fields to make it look much as it did that fateful September of 1862. Today, as a result, Antietam is widely considered the best-restored battlefield in America. A short time before my visit, the foundation also acquired forty additional acres between the Cornfield and Dunker Church, where some of the most savage fighting of the day took place in the opening hours of the battle. Since 2021, the American Battlefield Trust has acquired and preserved an additional fifty acres.

With this background, Murray opens a large ringed notebook filled with

maps of the battle and harrowing photographs of the conflagration's aftermath taken by Alexander Gardner and his assistant James Gibson, colleagues of Washington photographer Mathew Brady. The images shocked
the sensibilities of Americans both North and South when they began to
appear in print, and remain some of the most powerful images of war's horror ever published.

"Very good," Murray says with a solemn smile. "Shall we go join the
battle?"

Three months before Antietam, fifty-five-year-old Robert E. Lee took
charge of the struggling Army of Northern Virginia and saved the Confederacy from collapsing.

Vastly outnumbered by a well-equipped, well-fed Union force commanded on the Virginia Peninsula by George Brinton McClellan, Lee's army
had luck on their side when Union troops came within three miles of seiz-
ing the capital city of Richmond only to have their commanding officer lose
his nerve and halt an advance that might have ended the war. "If General
McClellan is not going to use the army," a frustrated Lincoln reportedly
declared when he heard the report, "I would like to borrow it for a time."

Meanwhile, Lee and his lieutenants—defying conventional military
logic—adopted a swift hit-and-run strategy that saved Richmond and
pulled off a succession of stunning rebel victories topped off by the Second
Battle of Bull Run in late August, where Stonewall Jackson routed a dispir-
ited Army of the Potomac so badly that Lincoln sacked its commander and
withdrew the army to the outskirts of Washington over concerns that the
national capital itself was in danger.

"These were dark, dismal days in the North," writes James McPherson
in *Crossroads of Freedom*, his masterful account of the Battle of Antietam,
"perhaps the darkest of many such days during the war." As panic spread
through the streets and government corridors of Washington, Northern
newspaper editors openly expressed their fear that Lee's victorious troops
were likely to soon surround Washington and Baltimore, bringing the war
to an unhappy conclusion.

Robert Edward Lee had something just like that in mind. With congressional elections two months away and Union troops back on their heels,

he calculated that a long-anticipated invasion of Northern soil, beginning with the state of Maryland—a slave-owning state where there were many residents sympathetic to the cause of Southern sovereignty—would rally support from so-called Peace Democrats who opposed the war and provide his famished, weary army with much-needed provisions and a chance to feed itself off the late-summer bounty of the Cumberland Valley.

It would also draw the enemy's demoralized troops away from the defense of Washington before fresh Federal recruits could be properly trained for action, enabling him to select the time and place for a decisive battle on his own terms. A victory, he knew, would send a powerful message to the watching governments of Britain and France, both of which were reportedly on the cusp of granting official recognition to the Confederacy, even considering providing military assistance.

Time and fate, however, were not on Lee's side, beginning with the condition of his army. Though morale among his troops was high from a summer of hit-and-run successes in the field, many of his soldiers were in desperate physical condition, half-starved and exhausted from long marches and poor rations. Many were barefoot. Given these circumstances, the longer the war dragged on, the more likely the North's huge advantage in manpower, money, and vastly superior industrial capacity would eventually win out. A decisive knockout blow was needed.

On September 4, long rebel infantry lines waded across shallows of the Potomac River at Leesburg, entering the state of Maryland as a band on the far shore welcomed them with "Maryland, My Maryland," a popular secession hymn that referred to Lincoln as a "tyrant" and urged proud native Marylanders to take up arms against the "Northern aggression."

"By the sixth and seventh, the rebels are in Frederick, twenty-five miles east of Antietam," explains Sharon Murray. "But here is Lee's main problem: he wants to use the Shenandoah Valley and Wagon Road as a main supply and communication line. The problem is, there is a Union garrison at Martinsburg on the Wagon Road to the west and another at Harpers Ferry to the south."

With the Union Army getting reorganized under General McClellan outside Washington, the most fateful decision Lee makes, Murray allows—long debated by military historians—is to once again divide his army into several parts as they cross into Maryland, sending James Longstreet's troops toward Boonsboro and thence to Hagerstown, Stonewall Jackson's battle-tested corps to attack the federal arsenal at Harpers Ferry, and Jeb Stuart's cavalry to protect the Army of Northern Virginia's rear flank as it moves toward the tiny Potomac River town of Sharpsburg. On September 9, Lee detailed this strategy to his field commanders in infamous Special Order 191, with the plan to reassemble his army around the hamlet of Sharpsburg. On September 13, however, a lost copy of the order—mysteriously wrapped with two cigars, found by a smoldering rebel campfire—came into possession of Union General George McClellan, placing Lee's fragmented army in peril.

Perhaps Lee's largest miscalculation, Murray points out, was believing that Lincoln's controversial decision to reinstall George McClellan as the commander of the reconstituted Union Army of the Potomac would require many weeks to whip itself into an effective fighting force before giving chase to the rebels. In terms of personality and battlefield vision, the thirty-five-year-old Union officer was the polar opposite of Lee—a vain young field commander who fancied himself to be an American Napoleon, disliked by most of Lincoln's cabinet and even the president himself for his tendency to hesitate from committing to the fight when the moment was ripe. But at the same time, he was beloved by the troops under his command.

"McClellan, for all his faults, is a brilliant organizer who quickly reforms the Army of the Potomac quicker than Lee or his generals expect," Murray explains.

On September 14, three pitched battles were fought over possession of three South Mountain passes guarded by outnumbered rebel troops. By nightfall, Lee ordered his forces to withdraw from South Mountain and consolidate around Sharpsburg, claiming the favorable high ground positions west of Antietam Creek with their backs to the Potomac River and a lone crossing ford if escape was needed.

Within a day, Murray says, summing up the preparations as we arrive at the infamous Cornfield, site of the first engagement, "McClellan has moved his own powerful army into key positions east and north of the Confederate lines, Union forces roughly outnumbering Lee's troops by a two-to-one margin [eighty-five thousand to forty thousand] with three hundred cannons versus 240 for the Confederates."

At 5 a.m. on a foggy September morning that happened to be the seventy-fifth anniversary of the signing of the US Constitution, the bloodiest day in American history began.

Over the next three hours, Murray captivatingly recounts the battle, taking me over blood-soaked ground, sharing intimate testimonies from soldiers on both sides of the battle and the horrors of the bloodiest day through her compassionate and deeply informed perspective.

On an average, three hundred thousand visitors a year come to Antietam National Battlefield, which is peanuts compared to the estimated two million who flock to Gettysburg. Only about six to seven hundred visitors choose to take a guided walking or driving tour of the most thoroughly restored battlefield in the nation with a park ambassador like Sharon Murray. This is a pity.

She walks me to where sleepy-eyed Joe Hooker began his massive dawn assault on Lee's left flank, moving against three divisions commanded by Stonewall Jackson with an intense artillery exchange that led to savage point-blank fighting that raged for almost four hours, spreading from the cornfield of Miller's farm to the Dunker Church and the West Woods across Hagerstown Pike, a shifting battle that finally ebbed in late morning with more than thirteen thousand casualties, including the loss of two Union commanders. "There were eight thousand casualties in the Cornfield alone," Murray explains. "Roughly one every two seconds. The Cornfield changed hands six times."

This was followed by a walk through a sunken farm road worn down by years of wagon traffic in the middle of the Confederate lines where so many casualties were suffered by the time the scene of the fight subsided around 1 p.m. that the old road became forever known as Bloody Lane, a place where dead bodies were so thick underfoot, as one commander reported, one could pass through it without touching the ground.

From there we move on to the southern end of the battlefield where Ambrose Burnside's four divisions spent more than three hours attempting to cross Antietam Creek over a 125-foot stone bridge that would forever be known as Burnside Bridge.

Following two failed attempts to seize the bridge from four hundred

Georgia sharpshooters who held off twelve thousand Union attackers, a tactical flanking maneuver and charge of the bottlenecked bridge by the combined Fifty-First Pennsylvania Infantry and Fifty-First New York Volunteers Brigade finally proved successful, allowing Burnside to focus on surrounding Sharpsburg, ideally cutting off Lee's only means of escape over the Potomac.

"After getting across the bridge," Murray explains as we stand by the historic "witness tree," a beautiful old sycamore that still stands at the site, "Burnside attacked approximately two thousand Confederate troops on the outskirts of Sharpsburg with eight thousand men. What saved Lee's bacon was the fortuitous arrival of A. P. Hill's light division from Harpers Ferry late that afternoon. Hill slammed into Burnside's exposed left flank, which was manned by green troops, and rolled his line up from left to right. By dark, Burnside's command had retreated to the hills overlooking the bridge and the fighting was over."

One could say, she adds, that Lee's troops were essentially on the ropes several times during the day.

The battle ended around five thirty that afternoon. By the next morning, Lee was prepared for a final Federal assault that never materialized. Instead, during the improvised truce, both sides began recovering and exchanging their dead and wounded. The Union suffered 12,410 casualties with 2,108 dead and 225 missing. Confederate casualties were 10,316 with 1,547 dead and 306 missing in action. Nearly 2,000 Union soldiers and 1,500 Confederates were housed in makeshift hospitals in every church and private home from Sharpsburg to Hagerstown. Six generals died in the fight, three Union and three Confederate. In total, more casualties occurred during the Battle of Antietam than on any single day in the nation's history.

Though the battle was technically considered a draw by military historians, the Northern press proclaimed a much-needed victory for the Union by ending Lee's first attempt to invade the North. Among the loudest voices of praise was George McClellan himself, who boasted on many occasions in the coming years that he had "saved the Republic" through his deft management of the battle. (Some historians tell a different story.)

By the evening of the eighteenth, Lee began quietly withdrawing his forces across the Potomac River, which gave him the chance to rest his troops and regenerate his battered army. President Lincoln was disappointed that McClellan's troops did not pursue Lee with more vigor, missing the opportunity to deliver a crippling blow. After the fall elections, Lincoln removed McClellan from his command.

More importantly, five days after Antietam, eager to capitalize on perceived momentum, Lincoln chose to issue his preliminary Emancipation Proclamation, which changed the legal status of 3.5 million African Americans in the Confederate states from enslaved to free. With the stroke of a pen, a struggle over Southern independence was transformed into a fight to end slavery. The proclamation also provided for the recruitment of former slaves into the armed services of the United States.

The governments of Britain and France quietly shelved their proposed support of the Southern cause.

"No other campaign and battle in the war had such momentous, multiple consequences as Antietam," James McPherson concludes in *Battle Cry of Freedom*, pointing out that the important Union victories to come at Gettysburg, Shiloh, and other crucial places across the South might never have happened without the fateful turn of events at Antietam.

As we start back to the park's visitor center, I'm curious to know how Antietam became such a passion for Sharon Murray, a slightly different slant on the question I put to her at the start of our walk. So I ask.

Like others I've met on my Wagon Road journey, hers turns out to be a love story, a personal awakening that began with a trip she and her late husband, Dale Robinson, a fellow history lover from Idaho, took during the summer of 2003. They visited the key Civil War battlefields of Harpers Ferry, Gettysburg, and Antietam. "It was a vacation that changed my life," she says.

Following Robinson's death from metastatic colon cancer, Sharon, a career mining engineer, decided to retire and move east. "Quite literally, I woke up one day a few years later—this was now 2009—and decided that I didn't want to do what I was doing anymore. What I *wanted* to do was something—anything—at Antietam Battlefield, though I had no idea what that might be. When I told my family that I was considering a move to Maryland, where a Civil War battlefield was going to be my retirement plan, they didn't believe me. I think they thought I was joking," she allows. "Maybe I was feeling the same sort of compulsion my Scottish ancestors felt when they arrived in Pennsylvania well before the Civil War and headed west. But whatever it was, Antietam was calling me back."

And so, in 2010, Sharon Murray sold her home in Boise, Idaho, loaded her beloved Rottweiler, Shiloh (named after the Shiloh battlefield in Tennessee), into her Ranger, and drove twenty-five hundred miles due east to find a new life on an old battlefield in Southern Maryland.

"I had no idea what I would find. That was the beauty of it. I just had this powerful sense that Antietam was where I was supposed to be."

Starting as a volunteer at the visitor center, she eventually became the park's first certified female battlefield ambassador, part of a select group of volunteers that cleans headstones and repaints the park's War Department tablets and historic markers around the battlefield. During the park's busiest summer weeks, Murray and a partner even do a demonstration firing of a reproduction twelve-pound Napoleon cannon on a field near the visitor's center. She and a staff colleague have also "adopted" four sets of cannons to keep their carriages clean and painted. "It's a little like having a thousand-pound baby," she quips as she walks me to my car.

I'm pleased to learn that she is writing a book about the remarkable life and times of a heroic Union cavalry officer named Benjamin Franklin Davis. The eldest of six orphaned brothers from Louisiana—three of whom fought for the Confederacy—Davis graduated in the same West Point class as Jeb Stuart and Dorsey Pender and cut his teeth fighting Indians in New Mexico and California as a captain in the US 1st Cavalry before accepting an appointment as a colonel in the New York Volunteers Brigade. In charge of six cavalry regiments as Stonewall Jackson's troops tightened the noose around Union forces at Harpers Ferry, he led his horse soldiers on a successful daring break for freedom that wound up capturing an important Confederate supply train near the Maryland town of Williamsport on the Potomac. "Like so much of the action at that time, this happened on the Great Wagon Road," she points out, bringing the story full circle, adding that Davis's tale is emblematic of the Civil War in general and Antietam specifically, a conflict that savagely pitted "brothers against brothers and other family members. There are many such stories here at Antietam. Davis died at Brandy Station in June 1863. He was just thirty-one years old."

I see the emotion in her eyes as she says this.

(Murray's book on Davis, *An Ornament to His Country*, was published in 2023. In October 2024, she began she began her fifteenth year as an Antietam ambassador and was presented with a folded US flag that flew over the battleground and a plaque honoring her years of service, a rare honor bestowed on volunteers.)

Before I can ask anything more, she says, "I've been thinking about your original question. I'm not sure I can put it into words. I came here late in life, a journey I never expected to make. It's no exaggeration to say, however, that this has become my life's work, the best thing I've ever done. I'm fortunate to be living this battle every day of my life."

I thank her for such a wonderful afternoon, for sharing half a dozen heartbreaking stories like that of Benjamin Franklin Davis, and for widening my understanding of the battle in such intimate and personal terms.

"Isn't all history personal to someone?" Sharon asks, using words I've heard several times in my journey.

"Being a Southerner, you might have had a relative in the Confederacy," she adds. "Maybe even one here at Antietam."

I admit this is a possibility, explaining that as a kid attending family gatherings back home, I occasionally heard vague whispers from the elders about a relative who might have fought for the Confederacy. Both the Dodsons and Tates were said to be antislavery Methodists, however, probably due to the strong Quaker influence of the area, which seemed, according to my dad, to make this an unlikely possibility. Even so, he sometimes joked about having a "Lost Confederate" in the family tree, though he never had a name for him. If this shadowy figure really existed, I tell Murray, it's my hope that this trip may somehow reveal his identity or finally debunk the story.

"Good luck solving the mystery!" she offers with a grin. "That's the wonderful part of our national story. It's full of surprising people and turns of events."

I thank her for illuminating America's bloodiest day.

"You're most welcome. I assume you know about the illumination?"

I shake my head.

"No, ma'am."

She explains that something called the Annual Antietam Memorial Illu-mination takes place on the first Saturday of December. "I believe this year is the thirtieth edition of it. It's a remarkable memorial event born here at Antietam. Volunteers place twenty-three thousand luminaries across the battlefield. It's beautiful and deeply moving. Thousands of people come from all over the world to experience it. Many come back year after year. You should check it out sometime."

"I'll be back in two weeks with my wife," I tell her.

FIFTEEN

THE GREAT ILLUMINATION

A **FEW DAYS LATER, I TRACK DOWN A FORMER PRESIDENT OF THE HAGERS-**
town–Washington County Convention and Visitors Bureau named
Georgene Charles, who got the idea for what some call "The Great Illumination" from a remembrance service that had several hundred schoolchildren
place luminaries on every headstone at a Hagerstown cemetery. "It was so
beautifully done and brought a lot of attention to our area," Charles tells
me. "That got me thinking why we couldn't do something similar and on a
much larger scale at Antietam."

Despite initial reluctance over fire concerns, the park service came on
board with the first event in 1988, when hundreds of local volunteers, including six hundred Boy Scouts from three neighboring states, fanned out to place
twenty-three thousand lighted votives across the entire Antietam Battlefield
at dusk on the first Saturday of December. "The scoutmasters explained that
each luminary represented a life lost here," Charles explains, "and told the
kids the story of Antietam. Generations of children have learned about it, as
a result, a wonderful living history lesson. It really took off after that."

Thirty years later, there's a waiting list of folks eager to volunteer, and
similar memorials at Gettysburg, Valley Forge, and other historic battlefields have popped up. Antietam's groundbreaking illumination, however,
has been featured in numerous national magazines, recognized as one
of the top 100 free public events in the nation. A candle company from

Medina, Ohio, that dates from 1867 provides a special Antietam candle for each paper bag—without cost—and scouts spend up to six hours placing the votives around the battlefield. "They also camp out in the park," Charles says, "whether it's a cold starry night or a rainy warm one. We've had snow and sleet, but we always find a way to get it done, even if it means having to move it a week or so."

The annual opening ceremony before the luminaries are lit features a bagpiper and honorary chairs that have included governors, members of Congress, cabinet secretaries, and military dignitaries at the battlefield's Clara Barton Monument. "I never get tired of hearing that opening ceremony, especially the bagpiper," Charles tells me. "It's all about remembering what happened here, the lives lost, the lesson of history.

"By the way," she adds, "if you're coming this year, you might want to arrive a bit early. The line to drive through the battlefield gets lengthy very quickly."

She isn't wrong.

After a morning of checking out the historic Jonathan Hager House (circa 1734), which sits directly on the Wagon Road in Hagerstown, followed by an afternoon exploring the quaint market town of Shepherdstown, West Virginia, just across the Potomac—where Union and Confederate soldiers recovering from their wounds attended the same Episcopal church for weeks after the battle—Wendy and I grab a bite to eat at a popular pub on Main Street in Sharpsburg as the sun begins to set. There, we fall into a friendly conversation with two couples from Ohio and New Jersey respectively who annually visit the Antietam illumination as part of their holiday traditions. "It's impossible to describe it if you haven't ever seen it," says a fellow diner at an adjoining table, who turns out to teach history at a New Jersey community college. "It never fails to bring tears to my eyes," adds his wife. "Even after nine illuminations."

By the time we reach the end of the line of cars inching their way into the battlefield from Maryland State Highway 34, we are five miles from the park entrance. Traveling at the speed of a horse-drawn farm wagon, it takes us two hours to pass through the illuminated battlefield.

But the night is clear and cold and the stars over Antietam shine like diamonds scattered on black velvet.

Hardly a word passes between us as we creep past campfires tended by scouts at the edge of the road near Bloody Lane and take in the sweeping landscape illuminated by twenty-three thousand tiny flames. At one point I put on Samuel Barber's elegiac Adagio for Strings and see Wendy wiping her eyes.

During this solemn passage, I find myself thinking about my German ancestors who passed this way before the American Revolution, traveling south over the same road that brought General Lee's army to near ruin.

According to Kessell family lore—my late mother's people—a trio of immigrant brothers from southern Germany named John, James, and Peter came down the Great Wagon Road from Pennsylvania to Hagerstown sometime before the American Revolution, eventually moving on to establish a mountain settlement in today's Hardy County of West Virginia, not far from the town of Moorefield.

A comprehensive genealogy commissioned by my cousin Jeannie Harner Roswell in 1994, however, tells a different story. Based on the *Record of Indentures of Individuals Bound Out as Apprentices, Servants, Etc.*, found in the archives of the German Society of Pennsylvania, sometime between October 3, 1771, and October 5, 1773, a "bound boy named Michael Kessel, N.A. in the leather trades," arrived in the city of Philadelphia from southwest Germany. The "N.A." designation simply meant that no age was officially recorded, a common practice for children traveling unaccompanied as indentured servants, which means that young Michael was probably a teenage apprentice in the tanner trade, sponsored by a patron he was legally apprenticed to. His surname turns up again a decade later, in May 1782, in the records of the Lutheran church in Hanover, Pennsylvania, along with a wife named Dorothea and a son, also named Michael. Since no further references appear in the church records, the family is presumed to have migrated to Hardy County in West Virginia a short time later, where they appeared in the county records of April 12, 1814, "deeding all the land we own in the County of Hardy, in consideration of our love and affection and one dollar" to another son, Jacob, "128 acres situated on the middle mountain between South Fork and South Branch Potomac."

One thing became clear from reading through the voluminous four-hundred-page genealogy report on the Kessells. They were thoroughly gifted at procreation. Every Kessell family unit seems to have produced at least a dozen children, creating a large and spirited clan of mountain folk who seeded the rugged hills of eastern West Virginia with hundreds of their own kind.

My own branch evidently came down eight or nine generations from the first Michael Kessel through Jacob to James Kessel Sr., my double-great-grandfather, whose modest headstone I found on a summer afternoon two decades ago in the Kessell family cemetery. His son James Wilbur Kessell (with an added "*l*"— either by design or a clerical error somewhere along the way) for whom I'm named, and his first wife, my grandmother, the former Maggie Roadcap, produced eleven children of their own, eight girls, three boys, all born on Kessell Mountain. My mother, Janet Virginia Kessell, was their final child. Two years after her birth, my grandmother died in the Spanish flu epidemic in 1922. Until about age six, my mom was raised by her six older sisters and a German-speaking grandmother. At school age, however, she moved to Cumberland to live with my Aunt Fanny and her husband, Gerald Lancaster. (For the first eight years of my life, surrounded by eight blond, bighearted German aunts, I mistakenly believed that my stern but loving Aunt Fanny—twenty years my mom's senior—was my grandmother.)

I cherish my memories of the boisterous Kessell clan from annual summer and winter visits to their various camps and households in West Virginia and Maryland, where I hiked and fished and learned to shoot rifles and snow skied and was even allowed to drink beer when the uncles gathered by the pump house, where kegs of National Bohemian were cooled on Fourth of July weekends. Tubing down the rapids of the South Branch with my cousins was an annual summer rite that my brother and I never grew weary of. Ditto the stick of dynamite our Uncle Russ once set off up on the mountainside at dusk to celebrate the nation's birthday.

Whatever the season, the food, laughter, beer, country music, and family stories flowed like the Potomac at flood stage anytime Kessell kin gathered. In truth, they were much more adventurous and fun than my sweet but bland Methodist and Southern Baptist Dodson relatives back home in North Carolina. Perhaps because of her rowdy hillbilly family's passion for living full and loving big, my mother, the baby of the family, grew up to become a superb singer who won the Miss Western Maryland Pageant in 1938 and was invited to fill in for Miss Maryland, who was unable to perform some of her duties that year. My mom also won the Miss Congeniality award and found herself singing on the radio in Hagerstown after graduation from Cumberland High School, selling big-band records in her spare time at Mc-Crory's department store back in Cumberland.

About that same time, she met my father, a young reporter and ad sales-man for the *Cumberland Times-News*, and dumped her wealthy fiancé, a scion of the local coal business named Earl, who owned a snazzy Stutz Bearcat automobile. Brax Dodson didn't own a record player but returned to buy big-band records until Janet Virginia Kessell finally agreed to go out with him. They got hitched at the St. Paul's Lutheran Church in summer 1942, not long before my dad shoved off to train as a glider pilot for the Eighth Air Force. My mother went to work for an admiral in Annapolis and was approached by Tony Martin, the Hollywood actor and singer, who'd heard her recording of "Stranger in Paradise" and invited her to join his touring musical show. The story goes that when my feisty Southern Baptist grandmother Beatrice Taylor Dodson (supposedly a descendant of Zachary Taylor) caught wind of it, she hopped on a train from Greensboro to Annapolis to persuade my mother that a career with Tony Martin was not an option for a proper new-lywed young woman. My mom turned down Martin's offer.

As we drive back across the Potomac River to our Bavarian-themed hotel after the Great Illumination, Wendy touches my arm. We haven't shared words for well over an hour. Each lost in our own world of thoughts and memories.

"That was possibly the most moving thing I've ever experienced," she says, breaking the silence. "I can understand why people come back to see it every year."

She wonders what I'm thinking.

I tell her that I'm suddenly missing the big wintry clan of German aunts and uncles I loved so much as a kid and teenager. Sadly, they are all gone. Miss Congeniality was the last to go.

She takes my hand.

"Isn't that why you are traveling the Great Wagon Road—to remember stories about them?"

She's right, of course. As Sharon Murray reminded me that soulful November day at Antietam, it's stories that keep them alive.

PART FOUR

AWAKENINGS

SIXTEEN

APPALACHIAN SPRING

HE SITS ON A GARDEN BENCH OUTSIDE THE MUSEUM OF THE SHENANDOAH Valley in Winchester, gazing at pear trees in bloom, dressed in the green woodland hunting frock and tricorn hat of a Southern colonial militiaman. His large hands rest calmly on the knob of an elegantly carved walking stick.

After being off the road for weeks attending to my busy life and work, I'm spending this beautiful April morning walking the grounds of the historic Glen Burnie House, the restored home and grounds of Winchester's founder, James Wood.

As I approach, he remains as still as a statue, evidently lost in thought.

"You look like a fellow waiting for the revolution to begin."

He glances up with a half smile, white-haired, ruggedly handsome, intelligent pale blue eyes behind rimless spectacles.

"I hear that quite often, friend."

He explains that he is waiting to meet a school group set to arrive for one of his presentations. I ask what kind.

"I tell the story of Liberty Man, Abel Johnston. He was my fourth-great-grandfather. A true American patriot during the American Revolution."

"Maybe I should join your class. I'd like to hear about that."

He pats the bench. "My group is running late. Take a seat."

His name is Rev. Larry Wilson Johnson, an eighty-year-old resident of nearby Warren County, and a retired bishop of the Anglican Church. Over the next twenty minutes, the story he spins is the kind of lovely surprise I am beginning to realize is commonplace along the Great Wagon Road. Best of all, it involves my own home state, North Carolina.

In 1777, a young farmer named Abel Johnston married a woman named Ann Johnson. Abel was nineteen, Ann just seventeen. They lived on a farm on the banks of Middle Creek in a township called Pleasant Grove on the coastal plains of eastern North Carolina, not far from present-day Raleigh, where they raised tobacco and cotton. At that moment, North Carolina was a hotbed of patriot rebellion. The year before, loyal Scottish Highlanders made a daring broadsword charge across a partially dismantled wooden bridge as hundreds of North Carolina patriots quietly waited in the woods with cannons and muskets poised. The loyalists were routed, marking the first significant victory for the patriot cause of the American Revolution, effectively ending British authority in the colony.

Not long after the Battle of Moore's Creek Bridge, Abel Johnston joined the fight as a militia horseman, leaving home with his Brown Bess musket and a tomahawk that belonged to his father during the French and Indian War. Over the next six years he saw action in several key engagements across the Cape Fear region and Southern Theater under the command of notable generals Nathanael Greene and Daniel Morgan. "The North Carolina militia fought all the way from Camden to Guilford Courthouse," Larry Johnson explains, "including the key battles at Cowpens and Kings Mountain, ending General Charles Cornwallis's plan to divide and destroy the Continental Army. Abel Johnston was right in the thick of it."

As a son of Guilford County who learned the story of Britain's failed Southern Campaign as a boy, I can't resist interjecting: "They followed the Great Wagon Road to Guilford Courthouse."

Liberty Man looks surprised. "Yes, they did, as a matter of fact. So, you know about the Great Wagon Road, do you?"

"Learning more every day."

I mention that I'm traveling its recovered path to Carolina, talking with folks like him who are caretakers of the old road's stories. His blue eyes light up.

"What a marvelous idea! Part of my family also came down it to Carolina."

The Johnstons, he explains, were English settlers who arrived at James-town and filtered down to North Carolina in the early 1700s. "The German part of the family, however, followed the Great Wagon Road to Mecklen-burg County [NC] in the 1740s, eventually settling in Cleveland County. They were named Huss. But it's the Johnstons who populate my story."

I apologize for the interruption.

Liberty Man smiles. "No worries, I like it when the kids interrupt me. It means they are paying attention."

At war's end, Private Johnston rode home, stopping to bathe himself in Middle Creek before presenting himself to his wife. He'd been gone more than half a decade, having left as a teenager and returned a seasoned sol-dier, with six years of warfare under his buckskins. He resumed farming and "became a father of seven children whose own children would be named Nathanael Greene, Benjamin Franklin, and Thomas Jefferson Johnston in honor of the Founding Fathers and defenders of our freedom." In recogni-tion of his six years of service, North Carolina awarded Johnston one hun-dred pounds sterling and a pair of land grants totaling three hundred acres each. After her husband's death in 1829, Ann Johnston never remarried, but lived to the ripe old age of seventy-eight.

"Unfortunately, she spent two decades after Abel's death struggling to obtain her husband's rightful pension," her fourth-great-grandson explains. "She had testimony from veterans who'd served with Abel, men who by then were in their upper eighties, interrogated by a panel of three judges. After that the authorities insisted that she needed to provide a legal marriage certificate to prove they were married. Problem was, in those days, official marriage certificates were quite rare, especially in the rural South. Important docu-ments were spelled phonetically, which may explain why the T in 'Johnston' eventually got dropped. Ann found people in their nineties, however, who'd witnessed their marriage." He pauses and shakes his head. "Unfortunately, she died before she could produce enough proof to satisfy the government."

It was the discovery of his ancestor's unsuccessful quest, he tells me, that changed Larry Johnson's life.

Some years ago, his daughter had phoned to say she was applying for membership in the Daughters of the American Revolution, and had been in contact with a genealogist who'd unearthed a mother lode of Johnston family connections going back to pre-revolutionary times. "She was so excited by this research and sent me a large package that I dropped on my home office desk and sadly left unopened for several weeks."

Finally, on a snowy winter afternoon without much to do, Johnson decided to open the package to see what had gotten her so fired up. "I began reading the materials, all written by hand, and could not put it down! About three hours later, the hair was still standing up on my neck and there were tears to my eyes. It was a true awakening. I suddenly knew what I had to do."

In 2010, Johnson applied for his own membership in the Sons of the American Revolution and eventually became president of the local chapter near his home in Warren County, Virginia. He also had the inspired idea to bring his ancestor Abel Johnston back to life as Liberty Man, an artistic resurrection that began by commissioning an Indiana firm specializing in authentic historical costumes to dress him as a backcountry North Carolina Revolutionary War militiaman. Not long afterward, a friend gave him a beautiful reproduction of a Brown Bess musket.

"That's when I became Abel Johnston and created a program about the history of the war and our fight for freedom around his personal story," Johnson explains. "Quite frankly, I had no idea if anyone today would even be interested. I just knew it was something I had to do. Fortunately, it caught on."

The first Liberty Man program debuted in 2013 in the children's room of the Page Public Library in Luray. "I set up a display of Revolutionary War battle flags and eighty items that a typical colonial militiaman would have used during service in the war. I also brought my twelve grandchildren there to make sure I had a live audience," he remembers with a laugh. "I hid behind the bookshelves as they came in looking totally confused, completely ignoring the displays. The older ones, in fact, were checking their smartphones, clearly prepared to be bored. I heard one of them loudly complain, 'Why are we here?'"

At that moment Liberty Man appeared with his Brown Bess in hand. "I'd like to welcome you all to the past," he told the gathering. "I'm your fourth-great-grandfather from the Revolutionary War, Abel Johnston, two hundred and sixty-five years old. I've come back to tell you what our family and many others like it did to gain our nation's freedom."

As he began his presentation, curious library patrons filtered in to fill the room's empty seats. "I told them Abel's story and explained how ordinary Americans came together to achieve our country's freedom. I showed them copies of the US Constitution and Bill of Rights and talked about who wrote these incomparable documents and why they were still important today. Soon there was not a cell phone being used except for taking photos. That was the beginning of Liberty Man."

Word quickly spread, and soon the innovative program was in demand. Veterans and school groups, civic and historical organizations, church groups and book clubs across the region wanted to learn more about Liberty Man, everyone from assisted-living residents to preschoolers before nap time. As a teaching device, Johnson began bringing along a replica of the Declaration of Independence and inviting his audiences to sign it. As a pastor, he also brought the sacraments to veterans and shut-ins along with meditations based on Bible verse John 15:13—"No greater love than to lay down one's life for one's friends."

Though he is now officially retired as bishop of the Virginia Anglican Church, I learn that Johnson is still performing Liberty Man many times a year, including a recent star turn at the 246th anniversary of Valley Forge. He's also featured on a YouTube channel and distributes DVDs of his programs to audiences promoting democracy's story at the grassroots level, a Johnny Appleseed of American liberty.

I wonder, as we sit together, why he thinks audiences young and old are so drawn to Liberty Man.

"Because his is a timeless story, one that every American can relate to one way or another. Each of us wants to know where we came from. From our earliest days America was a rootless society, always on the move—the very reason for the Wagon Road you're traveling! But human beings need roots to achieve a true sense of their identity. I think there is a yearning for that identity among all Americans these days. The world is so unsettled. This country is so bitterly divided. I think my presentations simply educate and maybe even inspire tolerance in folks once they know that most of us came from someplace else to find new life and liberty in the American wilderness."

I congratulate him on his quest and wonder aloud where *he* comes from. The answer turns out to be at least as interesting as that of his fabled ancestor.

Larry Johnson grew up in a small town in Harnett County, working in the tobacco and cotton fields just like his revolutionary ancestor. At nineteen, he enlisted in the military to fight as a marine. "When I got out of service in 1960, like a lot of kids in America, I basically had no idea what to do with my life or how to get there." After attending Campbell College on a basketball scholarship and moving on to the University of North Carolina to earn dual degrees in history and chemistry, Johnson's first job was working in a pilot program for the Raleigh public school system designed to stem the city's high dropout rate.

With no guidelines on how to proceed, Johnson based his teaching on the principles of discipline and self-respect he learned in the Marine Corps. After a year, his work caught the eye of Governor Terry Sanford, a trailblazing figure in the development of North Carolina's progressive public education system. "One day out of the blue Governor Sanford asked me to come see him at the state capital. So, I dressed up all my kids, coat and ties and shoes polished, and took them with me to meet the governor. The governor's security people were alarmed to see a bunch of former juvenile delinquents descending on them. But Sanford was an Eighty-Second Airborne vet. He loved it. He and the kids really hit it off."

A few days later, Johnson received a call from the state superintendent of education asking if he could install his innovative program in every school district across the Old North State. They tripled his salary and made him the industrial coordinator for a groundbreaking program that established working apprenticeship programs in 115 public schools across the state. It became the basis for a cooperative education curriculum that helped inspire the creation of North Carolina's highly regarded community college system, today one of the leading in the nation.

Two years later, he was summoned to Washington, DC, by the secretary of education and tasked with overseeing a national vocational tech program for forty-nine states. Over the next two decades, Johnson's cooperative education system enrolled more than five million kids in life-changing programs. Soon after, California Governor Ronald Reagan tapped him to write the vocational training policies manual for his presidential administration.

In the midst of all of this, Johnson earned a master of education degree from NC State followed by a doctorate in divinity in the Anglican Church.

"After that," he says with a gentle smile, "I suppose Liberty Man might have been inevitable, a case of 'once a teacher, always a teacher.' I often think back to that slow winter day when I finally read the genealogical report on our family roots that my daughter sent me. The timing was perfect, God-sent, I think. Liberty Man has given me many years of joy—and hopefully to others as well."

As he says this, a yellow school bus is drawing up in front of the museum. Moments later, a stream of kids begins trooping off, chattering like magpies.

"I think your next audience has arrived," I point out.

"Very good," he says, rising on his walking stick. "You were almost as good a listener as the kids," he adds with a wink.

Long before white men arrived on the North American continent, powerful indigenous tribes occupied the spectacular Shenandoah Valley, which geographically stretches from the banks of the Potomac River at Harpers Ferry in the North to Rockbridge County in the South, a broad fertile valley spread between the Blue Ridge and Allegheny mountains that was used for hunting and making war by Iroquois and Algonquin-speaking peoples for millennia. It is named for a majestic river that is one of the few in North America that flows south to north owing to the lower elevation of the northern portions of the valley; thus, south is the *upper* valley, north the *lower*, a geological anomaly I never could keep straight as a scout hiking and camping in the forests of the Shenandoah. A charming legend sources the valley's name from an Indian word meaning "Daughter of the Stars," though archaeologists generally believe it actually stems from an obscure Iroquois tribe called the Senedos.

By 1716, only the hardiest of European settlers lived in sight of the eastern range of the "high mountains," as the misty and mysterious Blue Ridge range was then called. But Virginia's ambitious governor, Colonel Alexander Spotswood, a highly educated man who embraced many progressive ideas of his day, was convinced that the colony of Virginia needed room to grow. Eager to explore beyond the Blue Ridge, pursuant to Sir Walter Raleigh's vision of a "New English Nation," Spotswood set off from Williamsburg on August 1 that year at the head of a large exploration party of sixty-three horsemen he dubbed the Knights of the Golden Horseshoe, including a retinue of white and enslaved servants, in hopes of finding a great inland lake believed to be the source of the James River and determined to claim whatever else he found in the name of the English Crown—hopefully gold.

After slashing their way through dense forests that included "hells" of tangled mountain laurel as the land ascended, enduring occasional skirmishes with hostile Indians along the way, the expedition finally reached the summit of a high Blue Ridge mountain pass on September 5. The knights took their first view of a spectacular valley that rolled westward for twelve miles before reaching a low ridge (Massanutten Mountain) and a view of the hazy Allegheny Mountains beyond. "It was indeed a breathtaking sight," writes Williamsburg historian Parke Rouse Jr. "To the east lay English America, descending to the sea. To the west, as far as they could see, lay the unsettled heart of North America, still a mystery to all except Indians and a few daring Europeans."

Inspired by the panorama of a wide valley that appeared to be as fertile as it was beautiful, the proud governor made a toast to the king and royal family, then led his knights down the mountainside to the lush floor of the valley, traveling seven miles across grasslands taller than the head of a man and laced with game trails and clear free-running streams, until they reached the banks of a beautiful river winding north. On the far bank Spotswood buried a wine bottle containing a document that claimed the land for King George I, and portentously named the river the Euphrates. That evening, the knights feasted on wild turkey and fresh-killed deer plus plums and blackberries gathered from the river's edge. "We had a good dinner," party member John Fontaine confided to his diary. "And after it we got the men together and loaded all their arms, we drank the king's health in champagne; and fired a volley." Having nothing else to do, the party continued to drink and discharge muskets. " . . . We toasted the Princess's health in Burgundy, and fired a volley, and all the rest of the royal family in claret, and fired a volley. We drank the Governor's health and fired a volley . . . " recorded Fontaine.

The next morning, Spotswood thanked his loyal knights and turned for home, leaving behind half a dozen rangers to further explore the valley. In the process, the explorers came across a wide trail where trees had been notched by a hatchet. "This was the Southern trading path of the powerful Great Lakes Indian tribes," notes Rouse. "The so-called Great Warrior's Path to Carolina." Less than three decades later, the Great Path would be given a white man's name—the "Great Waggon Road," the "way south" to tens of thousands of brave and hearty European settlers.

Back home, Spotswood was happy to spread the fiction that he and his knights were the first white men to lay eyes on the Valley of Virginia, but in truth, the governor was aware that French trappers and missionaries had been exploring in the valley at least since 1632, foreshadowing a growing menace from France's steady encroachment into the Appalachian range from the Ohio River Basin. The Great Warrior's Path also had its own legacy of Indian violence stemming from centuries of raids and tribal wars between the powerful Iroquois of the League of Six Nations and the Algonquin-speaking Shawnee of the northern woodlands and Siouan, Cherokee, and Catawba tribes of South Carolina, conflicts that had reached their peak around 1674. By 1700, many of the Native American residents of the valley had been either wiped out by these tribal wars or pushed farther west, where they came under the influence of the aggressively acquisitive French. To his credit, Spotswood advocated a policy of fair treatment to the remaining Indians of the valley, though it wasn't until the signing of the Treaty of Lancaster in 1748 that the matter was finally settled, establishing the right of colonial settlers to use the "Indian Road" that five years later William & Mary mathematician Joshua Fry and Thomas Jefferson's father, Peter, officially surveyed and identified on their groundbreaking map of Virginia.

Another decade would pass before a surge of Quaker, German, and Scots-Irish immigrants from Pennsylvania would arrive in search of cheaper land and more opportunity, lured to the wild beauty and fertility of the Shenandoah Valley by generous land grants from Lord Fairfax and later Virginia's governor Gooch. Ever skeptical of English ambitions, the Presbyterian Synod of Philadelphia formally wrote Gooch in 1738 to inquire about "civil and religious liberties" in his colony, and get assurances that Scots-Irish settlers would be guaranteed freedom to worship as they pleased in Anglican Virginia. Gooch replied that Virginia welcomed all religious settlers and had long been "inclined to favor the people who have lately removed from other provinces, to settle on the western side of our mountains . . . " fueling the concerns of skeptics that industrious German farmers and feisty Scots-Irish settlers were going to be used as human shields against threats of Indian attacks on English settlements. Nevertheless, the declared embrace of religious tolerance encouraged a steady immigration, and the frontier town of Winchester—the first English-speaking town established west of the Blue Ridge mountains, built on the remains of a former Indian settlement called Shawnee Springs—would soon become home to some of the oldest Lutheran, Presbyterian, Quaker, and Anglican churches in North America.

"For such a relatively small town, we do seem to have an awful lot of colorful history, due in large part to the Wagon Road," confirms Nick Powers, curator of collections of the Museum of the Shenandoah Valley, as we head for his favorite pub in Winchester's handsome Old Town district.

Following a tour of his spectacular museum, Powers is treating me to a driving tour of the city's historic sites, including places where young George Washington lived; the serenely beautiful Mount Hebron Cemetery, which holds the remains of hundreds of Confederate and Union soldiers who perished during five major Civil War engagements fought in or around Winchester; and the historic Handley Regional Library, a Beaux Art gem on West Piccadilly Street in Old Town. He even takes me out to see Apple Tree Ridge north of town, where he grew up, a fine rural setting first occupied by Quaker farmers who used prisoners captured during the French and Indian War to harvest apples. His father, an emergency room physician, not surprisingly, is a serious student of Winchester history and avid collector of period antiques.

"So essentially I had no option but to follow him into history," Powers quips as we navigate Old Town's narrow brick lanes. "Basically, everywhere you look in Winchester there's a plaque, a statue, or a monument of some kind to remind you of the town's role in the development of early America, including the three major conflicts that shaped this country."

He means, of course, the French and Indian War between Britain and France (1754–1763), the American Revolution, and the Civil War, all of which played out in different ways on these narrow streets. Not only did a young George Washington cut his teeth here as a surveyor and ranger, he also served as the ambitious military officer placed in charge of mounting colonial America's first response to the French threat from the Ohio territory. Eighty years later, because of its strategic location on the busiest road through the Valley of Virginia—by that point known as the Great Valley Pike—Winchester would be repeatedly assaulted and occupied by Confederate and Union troops.

It's my understanding from a mutual friend who curates collections for Old Salem's prestigious Museum of Early Southern Decorative Arts that Nick Powers hails from one of the oldest families in Virginia. As we settle over beer and crab-cake sandwiches in a noisy Union Jack Pub, I wonder if this is true.

"It is true," he confirms. "Our family goes back quite a long way here. I suppose that helps explain our generational love affair with Winchester history."

A man named Edward Powers, he points out, served as the first jailer of Winchester in 1740, just two years after the settlement became Frederick Town, named for the new county carved out of the Old Dominion's sprawling Orange County. The first clerk of the county court was Colonel James Wood, a Scottish immigrant who began building his Glen Burnie homestead in 1735, laying out twenty-six half-acre lots near a clear limestone spring. Wood's homeplace was used for the town's early governmental affairs. Today it serves as the beautifully restored and expanded home of the Museum of the Shenandoah Valley.

In March 1748, just past his sixteenth birthday, George Washington, eager to gain experience on the frontier in hopes of furthering his career as a professional soldier, came to Frederick Town as part of the surveying team sent by Lord Fairfax. The town and region were destined to shape the abilities and character of the future Father of America.

"Leaving Winchester a decade later," notes Virginia historian Garland Quarles, "young George Washington had become a seasoned leader of men, who had known defeat, debilitating illness, the intrigues of army life, the frustrations of inadequate support, the mortal dangers of battle, and all the other irritations and uncertainties which he was later to experience as Commander-in-Chief of the American forces during the Revolution."

In 1752, the Virginia House of Burgesses granted the colony's fourth town an official charter, naming it Winchester in honor of Lord Fairfax's friend the Earl of Winchester. One year later, freshly minted Major George Washington, now twenty-one, was sent out with a seasoned scout named Christopher Gist to warn the French to stay out of western lands claimed by the English king.

"Why the governor picked a twenty-one-year-old major of the Virginia militia for this mission—a man who spoke no French, had little formal education, and utterly lacked diplomatic experience—may not seem intuitively obvious," writes Fred Anderson in *The War That Made America*, a short history of arguably America's least known war. "Young Washington, however, had several qualifications." Most notably, he had the backing of his family's powerful friend Lord Thomas Fairfax, who liked his work as a surveyor and knew that Washington was determined to make his name as a backcountry leader, willing to undertake difficult missions in the wilderness in the dead of winter, hoping to earn the respect of his superiors.

The French politely received young Washington. Then told him to bugger off.

The next summer, newly commissioned Lieutenant Colonel Washington was sent back to the western wilderness by the Burgesses of Williamsburg, leading a small army of local volunteers he'd had difficulty raising, determined to underscore the British claims by force of arms if necessary. Following a disastrous encounter in which a French emissary from Fort Duquesne was savagely murdered by a Seneca chief accompanying Washington's party, the young officer ordered a crude circular stockade to be built around a storehouse he aptly named Fort Necessity, fifty miles south of the forks of the Alleghany and Monongaghela Rivers (today Pittsburgh). Within weeks, more British troops arrived to strengthen the force in preparation for a planned assault on Fort Duquesne—one that abruptly ended when six hundred French-Canadian militiamen and a hundred Ottawa Indians allied with the French launched a surprise attack on Fort Necessity that left thirty of Fort Necessity's defenders dead and seventy of Washington's troops wounded.

Washington was forced to capitulate to terms and sign a document of surrender written in French that amounted to a confession of assassinating the peaceful French envoy.

Many historians regard this incident as the spark that ignited the French and Indian War, part of a broader Seven Years' War between the English and French for global domination. A humiliated Washington returned to Winchester to try and rebuild his shattered Virginia militia, which had suffered numerous desertions in the aftermath of the fiasco. Ultimately, disillusioned by the politics of Williamsburg and his own failings, he resigned his command and returned to private life to concentrate on farming.

The following year, in March 1755, Parliament dispatched a sixty-year-old former colonel of the Coldstream Guards, Brigadier Major General Edward Braddock, to finish the job Washington botched. He was authorized to raise a formidable force composed of British army regulars and colonial militiamen to drive the French trespassers back to the Ohio once and for all. Owing to his hard-earned knowledge of the terrain, not to mention a desire to restore his military reputation, Washington signed on as an aide-de-camp to Braddock. Before the campaign got underway, Benjamin Franklin warned the pompous British commander that Indian fighters had their own way of conducting battles in the colonial backcountry, advice Braddock blithely dismissed, predicting no force on earth could stand up to the mighty British Army—least of all "savages and their French friends." It would be, Braddock confidently predicted, a quick fight.

He was right. With troops and volunteers sent from several adjoining colonies, such as militia from North Carolina that included a gangly young Yadkin Valley wagon teamster and blacksmith named Daniel Boone (just two years older than George Washington) and a feisty young wagoner from Winchester named Daniel Morgan (who would later prove himself to be a brilliant battlefield tactician and superb leader during the American Revolution), Braddock's slow-moving force of two thousand struggled to traverse the narrow forest footpaths meant for packhorses instead of wheeled artillery and heavily loaded supply wagons.

On July 9, 1755, as the expedition crossed the Monongahela River to the sound of traditional fife and drum, they marched straight into an ambush by several hundred French-Canadian sharpshooters and their Indian allies. Braddock had dismissed Washington's suggestion to send Allied Indian scouts ahead to assess the state of French preparations. And while his troops battled gamely for several hours, as did the general himself, losing four horses under him before being mortally wounded in the back, nearly half the expeditionary force was killed or wounded. The fortunate ones escaped by means of a hasty retreat orchestrated by Washington, who miraculously survived the slaughter with only three horses shot out from under him and several bullets piercing both his coat and hat. To save themselves at the peak of the fight, volunteers Boone and Morgan cut their wagon teams loose and fled on horseback. Wounded stragglers would be left to die by the road or be mutilated by the victorious Indians, who broke into barrels of confiscated rum and celebrated by taking scalps.

Braddock died on the grueling march back to Winchester and was buried in an unmarked grave on the road by order of Washington to prevent his body from being found and mutilated by the Indians.

Back home, a short time later, Washington was further tasked by the Burgesses to protect three hundred miles of backcountry settlements along the Shenandoah Valley, a job that would occupy him for the next three years.

"Washington's years in Winchester were probably the most formative of his public life, and yet the least known by Americans," Nick Powers explains after telling me this story; as a teenager, Powers developed a comprehensive guided tour called Walking Washington's Winchester for his Eagle Scout project. The popular tour is still in use today.

On the heels of the disastrous Braddock mission, Washington had even greater difficulty recruiting and training a well-functioning militia, prompting him to resort to harsh penalties that included five hundred lashes for quarreling, a hundred for drunkenness, even hanging a deserter or two to impose discipline on his disordered troops for the duration of the Virginia border war, 1755 to 1758. His primary responsibility, however, was overseeing the planning and construction of Fort Loudoun to protect the people of Winchester, a formidable redoubt with four bastions he modeled on plans he found in the Library of Congress. The fort was never completed, though French spies warned their superiors that it was probably impregnable. Washington eventually oversaw the construction of more than fifty forts strung along the Shenandoah Valley and in present-day West Virginia aimed at protecting western settlers from Indian attacks.

The effort was visible but not always appreciated by the community.

"Even before his early military failures, young George wasn't terribly liked by some of the citizens of Winchester," Powers tells me. In letters to friends, he adds, the future Father of America referred to the town as "this vile post" and singled out the "obstinacy and dastardliness" of Winchester's Scots-Irish settlers in particular.

Still, the fact that the future Father of America found the people of Winchester more than a little disagreeable didn't prevent him from running to represent them in public office for the first time in 1755. In total, young George would run three times for the House of Burgesses from Frederick County, losing the first time, according to legend, due to his firm opposition to Winchester's many "tippling" houses and taverns. "In truth, he probably lost because he was a political outsider in the valley; his name may have been put up by friends without his knowledge, and because he was absent on election day," Powers clarifies, "he was away performing his job to secure the Virginia frontier. His opponents showed up offering free spirits. It wasn't even close. Washington came in third."

After three years, though, loyal supporters of Washington—absent once again on polling day, this time leading the British assault to recapture Fort Duquesne—showed up to represent him at the polls by proxy, bringing along fifty-nine gallons of rum punch, thirty-four gallons of wine, and forty-six gallons of beer to encourage the voting spirit. Washington's troops reached Fort Duquesne only to find it abandoned by the French, effectively ending their threat to the Virginia frontier, but back home in Winchester, he won election to the House of Burgesses in a romp. "His friends and supporters 'chaired' his proxy, Colonel James Wood, through the streets of Winchester to celebrate," Powers explains. "Proving the power of a timely drink." Washington would win a second term in 1761.

As we head back to the museum, I wonder if the people of Winchester share Nick Powers's infectious enthusiasm for their rich and surprising history, which is probably as colorful as any single place on the entire Great Wagon Road.

"I think they do today. But that wasn't always the case."

He explains that a controversial decision in 1970 to demolish a historic property called the Conrad House on Cameron Street to make way for a new municipal building galvanized Winchester's fledgling preservationist movement, resulting in the establishment of an organization called Preservation of Historic Winchester that has saved dozens of historic properties in Old Town over the past forty years, seeding appreciation of local history and fueling an ongoing economic engine in the process. Winchester's annual Shenandoah Apple Blossom Festival in April, he explains, has grown to be a citywide celebration of local history, arts, and culture that draws an estimated fifty thousand visitors to the town and region each spring.

Eager to hear more about the region's origins, I meet Shenandoah University history professor Warren Hofstra for supper at the historic George Washington Hotel downtown. Having read his excellent book *The Great Valley Road of Virginia*, I am curious to know more about the earliest settlement of the valley and the road that fueled it.

"Before it became the Great Philadelphia Wagon Road and the Great Valley Road," Hofstra says as we occupy a small table in a quiet corner of the dining room, "it was, as you probably know, used by the Iroquois and other early native peoples for hunting, trading, and making war for millennia. It was inevitable, however, that once the first European settlers began to arrive in this area, drawn by the unique physical attributes of the Shenandoah Valley—its fertile limestone soils, abundant game, rich rivers and forests, its protective ridges, and so forth—the floodgates opened to make the valley an irresistible attraction to thousands of immigrants and settlers, particularly the Germans and Ulster Scots, who expanded the road and shaped the culture of the frontier as they went."

Over dessert, Professor Hofstra recounts the story of the fabled "sixteen families"—more than one hundred men, women, and children who arrived with wagons and livestock, led by an enterprising Palatinate German immigrant named Jost Hite. Among the first European settlers to enter the region, Hite's party reached the valley in 1731, ten miles north of the confluence of the Shenandoah and Potomac Rivers.

There, Hite settled on a parcel of 5,018 acres between today's Winchester and neighboring Stephens City, part of a larger 40,000-acre tract in the Shenandoah that he and a partner purchased from the Virginia Council with the condition that at least one family per thousand acres would be settled on the land within two years, clearly meant to be a buffer against Indian attacks. Borrowing a page from William Penn, Hite hired an agent to post advertisements in both English and German back in Philadelphia, promoting land for sale at a rate of three pounds per hundred acres. According to one story, he even sent his eldest son to Ireland to find buyers for his land.

"The Wagon Road's importance to the emerging American story can't be overstated," Professor Hostra thoughtfully sums up. "It's really only rivaled by the Camino Real connecting Santa Fe to Mexico City."

My final day in Winchester begins just after sunrise with a plan to Walk Washington's Winchester, beginning at the statue of young George Washington that stands outside his surveying office at the corner of Braddock and Cork Streets. En route there, however, I stop for coffee at Steamy's Café on West Piccadilly. Local scuttlebutt has it that Steamy is a Winchester institution (as he himself quickly confirms), a trim, lively character who chatters away as he darts around behind the counter of his narrow eatery, fashioning bagel sandwiches and frying bacon. I happen to be the first customer through the door.

"Coffee makes all things possible! Gotta have my patented Winchester bagel! Nothing like it in the civilized world!" he barks at me over Pat Benatar's "Ring of Fire" blasting on the shop's sound system. As he toasts my bagel, Steamy tells me about growing up "in the county outside town" and "roaming around the wide world, checkin' things out, doing this and that" before finding his true calling in life by opening the "best breakfast place in Frederick County."

"Know that song?" he cheerfully shouts at me. I glance up from my walking guidebook having realized it will lead me past the Hudson River house on Braddock Street where Thomas "Stonewall" Jackson made his headquarters at the start of his successful Shenandoah Valley Campaign in 1862.

"I do. Johnny Cash wrote it. He was a descendant of the Great Wagon Road."

"Never heard of it, brother. What's that?" Steamy squints, his hands flashing as he creates a mammoth everything bagel stuffed with egg, cheese, and bacon. The door jingles and a woman wearing a bright blue Valley Health sweater steps in as I attempt an abbreviated version of my elevator speech. But Steamy cuts me off.

"There she is—my *favorite* customer!"

He hands me my bagel sandwich over the counter and whispers: "I tell people what they want to hear. I am the secretary of truth."

"I've heard of that road," the woman in blue pipes up, having overheard my pitch. "Isn't that up in the mountains near the Skyline Drive?"

"We *are* in the mountains—or least the valley between the mountains," Steamy reminds her.

With Pat Benatar still wailing, I explain to her that US Highway 11— which passes directly through downtown Winchester—was constructed over the Great Valley Road and the original Great Wagon Road that preceded it, following the Great Warrior's Path leading back to unrecorded time.

"Wow," she says, gently blowing on her coffee. "That's good to know."

"You still happily married?" Steamy asks her.

She grins. "Sure am. Just not that happily."

They both laugh. She mentions that her daughter is in town for the start of the Apple Festival, which kicks off this very morning.

"Streets are gonna be crazy this weekend," predicts Steamy. "I love it."

The door jingles again. The morning coffee crowd is suddenly streaming into Steamy's, so I head for the door.

"Here," says the secretary of truth, leaning over to hand me something else across the counter. "Take a free blueberry muffin for that Wagon Road you're trying to find."

I finish both muffin and bagel—for the record, excellent if not the best in civilization—by the time I reach stop number seven on Nick Powers's Washington Walk: Mount Hebron Cemetery on East Boscawen Street, the site of the ruins of Winchester's first Lutheran Church (1764) and the burying ground where Daniel Morgan's remains were moved to from the Old Stone Presbyterian Church in 1868.

Since ruins sometimes speak, I find Morgan's grave and stand for a bit, hoping I might hear the voice of a frontier hero. I first heard his name as a kid on one of my family's battlefield trips to the Cowpens Battlefield in South Carolina, where Morgan engineered one of the most stunning victories of the Revolutionary War.

Alas, the only sound I hear is morning traffic from a couple blocks away, so I pay my respects and make my way to a roundabout where schoolkids with backpacks and cell phones are crossing a plaza. There, I'm delighted to find an oversized Daniel Morgan in bronze standing by the Old Stone Presbyterian Church. A large brass plaque at his feet lists his many accomplishments.

Morgan is the patron saint of colonial badass overachievers, a rebellious teenager who ran away from his New Jersey birthplace to become a teamster hauling freight along the Great Wagon Road. He earned the nickname "Old Wagoner" even before joining the ill-fated Braddock campaign, where he not only survived five hundred lashes for punching a superior officer who smacked him with his broadsword—a penalty that would maim ordinary men—but also managed to avoid (along with fellow wagoner Daniel Boone) being killed and scalped by French sharpshooters and their Indian allies.

When the American Revolution broke out, Morgan was among the first to answer Washington's call, leading a group of Shenandoah rangers to Boston called the Morgan's Rifle Company. The deadly sharpshooters dressed in frontier hunting shirts that struck terror in the hearts of British regimental troops. More important to America's fortunes, Morgan turned out to be a brilliant commander and tactician who executed daring engagements out of the box, including attacks disguised as Indians and hit-and-run tactics that helped win the critical battles at Saratoga and Cowpens. Repeatedly passed over for promotion by his superiors (probably due to his noted indifference to ranking officers), Morgan was finally awarded a special gold medal by Congress after the war, along with the title "Thunderbolt of the Revolution." He returned to Winchester and helped put down the Whiskey Rebellion in western Virginia and died a wealthy man on his own birthday in 1802.

I move along to see the site of Fort Loudoun and Washington's Well, famously dug 103 feet through solid limestone rock, then press on to Stonewall Jackson's Headquarters on Braddock Street, where I take the morning's first tour of the house with a pair of British couples winding up their five-day driving tour of the Shenandoah Valley's famous Civil War battlefields.

"We Brits are rather *embarrassed* by our own civil war," confides Toby from Gloucestershire as we stand together in the silent upstairs bedroom where Jackson wrote soulful letters to his wife, Anna, back home in Lexington during his successful Shenandoah Valley Campaign of 1862. The conversation pauses when our guide points out that it was during their correspondence that Jackson learned that his own sister had disowned him for joining the Confederacy, but resumes again as we make our way through the house.

"What I love about you Americans, on the other hand," Toby continues as we enter a room where Jackson's work desk stands, "is that you make a jolly good show of your bloodiest battlefields. We're thinking of coming back for the big reenactment at Cedar Creek next October. I'm told it's quite a show. Have you seen it?"

"Yes. Many years ago. But I'm more of a Rev War guy," I confess.

Toby grins. "Why you colonial *devil!*"

My response is truthful, but as soon as I say the words, I can't help but feel the truth behind them.

Probably because of my time with Gabor Boritt, and having experienced the winter candlelight of Antietam, I've suddenly had enough of the enduring romance and faux pageantry of a horrific Civil War that killed more than half a million of my countrymen and supposedly ended 154 years ago. Perhaps this is also a delayed reaction from growing up in several small towns across the segregated South of the 1950s, following my dad's newspaper odyssey from Texas to Mississippi and home to the Carolinas, where the mystique of the Lost Cause of the fallen Confederacy was never far from many minds, lips, and open affections of neighbors, teachers, and preachers who seemed to view the War Between the States as little more than a cruel assault on genteel Southern values and civilization.

Toby of Gloucester, of course, doesn't need or wish to hear any of this complaint, which I suddenly think of as my "Confederate Blues" on the spot. Standing in Stonewall Jackson's office where he directed the first of many military campaigns that made him a fabled figure in newspapers across America and abroad, I resolve to skip the many commercial roadside Civil War museums, tourist traps, and popular battlefield reenactments that lie in wait on the road to Roanoke.

Before leaving Jackson's headquarters, however, I purchase a rare print of illustrator N.C. Wyeth's haunting portrait of Jackson for my big brother. It was originally commissioned for a popular Civil War novel published in 1910, about the time public interest in the Civil War led to a resurgence of defiant statues on public squares across the South, funded by Ku Klux Klan chapters and white supremacists, meant to send an unmistakable message to Southern citizens of color.

Oddly enough, Wyeth's portrait seems to convey a starkly different message. One of tender uncertainty and even spiritual foreboding, depicting an anxious leader standing by his horse in a cloaking mist, perhaps prefiguring his own mortality and the bleak irony of dying of pneumonia a week after being accidentally shot by one of his own troops during the Battle of Chancellorsville in May 1863, a staggering blow to the Southern cause. When I look at the portrait, I see a man who had his own case of the Confederate Blues, perhaps thinking of his estranged sister, perhaps suffering doubts and a doomed sense of loyalty to his homeland, just thirty-nine years old at the moment of his death.

For what it's worth, Jackson's widow, Anna, reportedly disliked Wyeth's mystical portrayal of her late husband and refused to accept the painting from its creator.

Which, in a sweetly perverse kind of way, makes it okay for me to purchase a print of it for my big brother, Dick, who sees something truly noble in Jackson's life and sacrifice. Besides, Wyeth is my favorite childhood illustrator. His rendering of Jackson reminds me of the soulful Scottish kings and colonial heroes depicted in the lavishly illustrated histories of Scotland and the Revolutionary War that were a big part of my boyhood in the sleepy South.

On a happier note, my final stop in Winchester is the historic Patsy Cline House, which is a mild cure for my Confederate Blues. Cline's modest childhood home sits in a blue-collar neighborhood at 608 South Kent Street, the ideal place for a lifelong gospel, bluegrass, and country music fan like me to conclude a hike through three hundred years of Winchester history.

Due to the start of the Apple Blossom Festival, a line of white-haired seniors, mostly female, waits patiently outside the small Greek Revival house where Patsy resided with her mother and little sister from 1948 to 1957. I join the queue and fall into conversation with an elderly woman and her daughter down for the day from Cumberland, Maryland, my late mom's hometown. The daughter, Libby, who is about my age, explains that her mother, Joyce, is a Winchester native who attended the first Apple Blossom Festival as a little girl back in the 1940s, and once saw "Miss Patsy" perform with her first Maryland country band at a club in Hagerstown. The two have made a pilgrimage to Winchester every other spring since the mid-1970s. "Your basic mother-daughter bonding thing," says Libby with a smile.

They ask about my interest in the Songbird of Winchester.

"My mom wanted to be her," I say.

Briefly, I explain my mother's dream deferred, how she was offered a gig singing and acting but was saved from the road to ruin by my feisty Southern Baptist grandmother.

"If she'd chosen Hollywood over my dad, I probably wouldn't be here today."

"Did she keep singing?" Joyce, who looks to be in her eighties, reminds me of my late mother. Big blue eyes and silky silver hair.

I answer honestly that my mom cut a couple records then called it quits, choosing to follow my dad's newspaper career, and two small boys, across the Deep South of the 1950s.

"Was she happy with her decision?"

"She was one of the happiest people I ever knew. But she loved Patsy Cline's music. I think she identified with her, possibly because of the career she never had and Patsy's that ended too soon. They even shared the same first name—Virginia."

"That's a wonderful story," Joyce is moved to say, gently dabbing her eyes, just as the line begins to move. We finally cross Miss Patsy's threshold.

Virginia Patterson Hensley was born in Winchester Memorial Hospital in September 1932 and lived in this small frame house—a former log cabin dating from the early nineteenth century—longer than she lived anywhere. Her mother, Hilda, was a gifted seamstress who made her daughter's stage costumes. Her father was a maintenance man who took a job at Washington and Lee University in Lexington when Patsy was young. "That's where Patsy got exposed to music for the first time," a docent named Margie explains on our walk through the tiny house. "Big bands came to the college on weekends and her house was right on campus. She heard female singers for the first time and started singing herself out in the yard."

At seven, Patsy asked for a radio. At eight, a piano, which she taught herself to play by ear. When the family moved to Winchester, she enrolled in the ninth grade at Handley High and found a job as a clerk at Gaunt's Drug Store. The pharmacist took a shine to her and helped her get on a local radio station to sing live. Not long afterward, she joined a popular local country band and performed across the region through the early 1950s, convinced by the band's leader to adopt the stage name Patsy Cline after marrying her first husband. Patsy's big break came in 1957 when she won Arthur Godfrey's televised *Talent Scouts* competition singing "Walkin' After Midnight." That same year, she served as Apple Blossom Queen back home in Winchester, wearing a rhinestone-studded cowgirl outfit made by her mother.

Like many great country singers, Patsy's unique, sultry voice lofted her to stardom and eventual heartache. She survived divorce and years of records that flopped until, finally, in the early 1960s, she remarried and moved to Nashville with her two children, where she regularly appeared on the stage of the Grand Ole Opry and released a record turned down by Brenda Lee called "I Fall to Pieces." The record became a runaway hit, topping the country charts and even crossing over as a hit in pop music.

After Cline survived a car cash that nearly killed her, her follow-up hit was a song called "Crazy," written by Willie Nelson. Patsy initially didn't like the song but recorded it anyway. It was released in October 1961 and raced to the top of both country and pop charts, establishing Patsy Cline as the new Queen of Country Music.

On March 3, 1963, she performed a benefit gig at the Soldiers and Sailors Memorial Hall in Kansas City in a show that included George Jones, Dottie West, and the Clinch Mountain Boys. Her three performances were standing-room-only affairs. The next day, she opted to fly home to Nashville rather than endure the sixteen-hour car ride Dottie West offered. The plane went down in bad weather ninety miles from home; her beloved wristwatch and a Confederate flag lighter were later recovered from the wreckage. An old friend who shares my passion for traditional country music once told me that Nashville legend Marty Stuart has a unique item in his twenty-thousand-piece country music collection: the boots Patsy was wearing when she died. In 1973, Patsy Cline became the first solo female artist to be inducted into the Country Music Hall of Fame. Today she is considered one of the most influential singers of the twentieth century.

I spend just over an hour checking out the Patsy Cline House, which today is owned by a nonprofit organization called Celebrating Patsy Cline, Inc., which opened the museum in 2011. I enjoy the grainy recordings and videos spanning her performances from Arthur Godfrey's show to her peak of stardom but find her sequined evening gowns and custom-made cowgirl outfits made by her mother kind of sad. Hilda Hensley eventually moved across Kent Street to raise Patsy's children, Julie and Randy. Patsy's childhood home sat empty and neglected for many years.

I wander into the Cline kitchen, where—being America—all sorts of Patsy memorabilia and tchotchkes are for sale, including replicas of her famous US postage stamp, souvenir ink pens, copies of her on the cover of *Life* magazine, postcards and tapes of her bestselling albums and records, brightly colored Patsy T-shirts, and other perky Patsy doodads. I learn from the shop clerk that a crew from the BBC recently dropped by Patsy's house to film a segment on her for their documentary on Scots-Irish music in America.

"You know? I had no idea country music and bluegrass music came over here with settlers from Britain," she says. "They told me the Scotch brought that form of music with them to America and spread on down the road to the hill people of Appalachia. Can you believe that?"

"I believe I read that somewhere."

I skip the elevator speech but do point out that America's enslaved people brought the first banjo with them from West Africa—the quintessential instrument of bluegrass and country music.

She gives me a very Patsy-like smile. "Well, isn't *that* somethin'. They didn't tell me that!"

Through the back door, I see Joyce having a quiet moment on the house's tiny back porch, gazing at something across the yard.

I step out. She points at a tree in bloom. "They say Patsy's mother planted that beautiful lilac tree over there in memory of her daughter."

"My mother would like that," I say. "She was also a big fan of white lilacs."

Joyce gives me a maternal smile and touches my arm.

"Unlike Patsy, honey, I think your mama made a very good decision."

SEVENTEEN

THE PAST CANNOT BE UNREMEMBERED

ON A COOL, CRISP SATURDAY MORNING, MY WIFE, WENDY, JOINS ME AT historic Belle Grove Historic Plantation in Middletown for an event called *Inalienable Rights—Free and Enslaved Blacks Crafting a Life in the Shenandoah Valley*, the latest in a series of African American living history programs sponsored by the National Trust for Historic Preservation and an organization called the Slave Dwelling Project that are designed to revise and expand the story of enslaved people in Virginia.

Belle Grove Plantation was the home of Major Isaac Hite Jr., a veteran of the Virginia colonial militia who was present at the surrender of the British Army at Yorktown in October 1781. His grandfather Jost Hite was the immigrant linen weaver from Germany who led the first group of Wagon Road settlers to Virginia's Shenandoah Valley in 1732. After returning from service in the revolution, Isaac Jr. married Nelly Conway Madison (younger sister of the future president) of Montpelier plantation in 1783, and expanded the family's extensive land holdings in Middletown to more than seventy-five hundred acres. The elegant Palladian-style manor house, built with design input from Thomas Jefferson, was said to be the finest home west of the Blue Ridge mountains, commanding wide views above fertile limestone fields of the northern Shenandoah Valley: "Meant to be seen and stamp its serene presence on the rural landscape," as an early visitor described it.

At the peak of influence around 1800, Belle Grove Plantation was a powerhouse of regional economic and political influence, boasting more than a thousand acres of highly productive wheat fields, livestock, a major milling operation, and even its own whiskey distillery, entirely dependent on the labor of enslaved individuals. Not surprisingly, given the mansion's strategic location directly on the busiest toll road of the Civil War era—the Valley Pike by that point was an improved gravel byway—the plantation was occupied by several different Union generals during major battles that took place around Middletown and Winchester between 1862 and the autumn of 1864, including the last great battle of the Shenandoah Campaign that took place on the grounds of Belle Grove in October 1864, the Battle of Cedar Creek.

Two weeks before this gathering of local archivists, historians, and social activists, Belle Grove's neighbor, the nonprofit Cedar Creek Battlefield Foundation, staged its annual fundraising event on the plantation's rolling fields—the 154th-anniversary reenactment of the Battle of Cedar Creek—which annually attracts hundreds of dedicated Civil War buffs and reenactors from across America. Having reached my quota of Civil War reenactments for one lifetime, I'd chosen to skip the battle in favor of a more timely gathering that coincides with the 400th anniversary of the first enslaved people arriving on Virginia's shores and the simultaneous publication of the 1619 Project, which has produced a firestorm of debate among academics, political pundits, and social theorists left, right, and center over the question of whether systemic racism and the legacy of slavery remain a shaping force in modern American life. With similar programs designed to set the record straight on enslaved populations simultaneously happening at Thomas Jefferson's Monticello and James Madison's own Montpelier plantation, a long overdue awakening, many believe, might finally be at hand.

For this reason, I've invited Dame Wendy to join me to serve as an extra set of eyes and ears at this first-of-its-kind Belle Grove event, a deal sweetened by the opportunity to spend a couple nights at the historic Wayside Inn a few miles up the road in Middletown, one of the two oldest inns on the Wagon Road and a favorite haunt of young George Washington.

The first surprise of the day comes when Wendy wanders off to have a look at Belle Grove's bedrooms and I drift within earshot range of a conversation between several folks who are admiring artist Charles Peale Polk's portraits of James Madison Sr., Major Hite, and his wife, Nelly, in the main parlor room of the house. "For such privileged folks, they all look pretty unhappy," observes a middle-aged woman wearing a wool bomber jacket and cherry-red beret. A man near nods, pointing out that life on the western frontier was difficult for rich and poor alike, also that nineteenth-century portrait painters preferred their subjects not to smile. He turns out to be a longtime valley historian and Belle Grove docent named Wayne Sulfridge.

When I introduce myself to him and mention my interests in the Hites and the evolution of the Great Wagon Road, he gives me a broad smile.

"My goodness! Are you related to Stephen Dodson Ramseur?" he asks excitedly. "I can show you the room where he died. It's an amazing story. Let's go there."

In truth, I've never heard of Stephen Dodson Ramseur. But since we seem to share a name and I'm naturally prone to follow any historian who promises a good story, without hesitation, I follow Sulfridge to the mansion's nursery, as does the curious woman in the red beret. The docent points to a framed sketch on the wall that depicts a dying man lying on a cot being attended by several uniformed men who appear to be Union officers.

"An extraordinary encounter took place right here," he says, launching into the story.

In the aftermath of Union Major General Philip Sheridan's successful "scorched earth" campaign that decimated Shenandoah farms and mills feeding the Confederate war machine, he explains, the final and most decisive battle of the Shenandoah Valley began on the grounds of Belle Grove Plantation early on October 19, 1864, when Confederate Major General Jubal Early's cavalry launched a surprise attack on Sheridan's seven encamped infantry units, driving them back and inflicting heavy damage. The attack, launched days before the presidential election, was timed to influence the outcome of the vote in favor of a Peace candidate willing to negotiate terms with the rebels.

Summoned from his Winchester bed, Sheridan and his aides rode furiously to Middletown in time to rally their troops. Their ferocious counterattack won the day for the Federals, all but securing Lincoln's reelection in the process and delivering, as many Virginia historians believe, the killing blow that assured the demise of the Confederate rebellion.

"A popular young Confederate major general was severely wounded in the battle," Sulfridge continues. "The Valley Pike was so congested with people and troops trying to flee the scene of the battle, the Yankees were able to catch up to the rebel ambulance wagon bearing him. Discovering his identity, they brought him here to the house. He was an 1860 West Point graduate from a small town in North Carolina, just twenty-seven years old. While he was mounting his third horse of the day and trying to rally his troops, a bullet struck his right side, passing through both lungs. It was a mortal wound he could not have survived for long. His name was Stephen Dodson Ramseur."

I glance at the sketch, considering the possibility of a connection. The name, after all, is similar, and there is a small town called Ramseur less than fifteen miles from my home in the western Piedmont of North Carolina. It suddenly occurs to me that this fellow might even be the Lost Confederate Dodson elders loved to whisper about. Is the enduring mystery to finally be solved? What a surprise awakening *this* would be.

Before I can mention this all to Sulfridge, he pushes on with the story.

"Word quickly spread over the battlefield that Dod Ramseur—that was his nickname, by the way—had been brought to the mansion mortally wounded. Some of his closest friends from West Point rushed to his bedside to pay their final respects."

One of them was Wesley Merritt, a Union cavalry officer and member of the West Point class of 1860. After the war, Merritt became superintendent of the academy and served as military general of the Philippines during the Spanish-American War prior to retiring in 1900.

Other notables reached the dying man's bedside. "The last man to speak to Ramseur before the opiates took effect and he lost the ability to speak," Sulfridge adds, "was another close friend from West Point who was commanding the artillery battery of the Union's Eighth Corps—Henry du Pont. Of the Delaware du Ponts."

Another officer who came to say goodbye to his friend had been a cadet in the class directly behind Ramseur and Merritt. He was commanding his own Union cavalry unit that day at Cedar Creek. "That's him in the picture," says Sulfridge, pointing. "George A. Custer."

As the youngest major general in the Confederate Army lay dying, the beret lady and I learn, he was wearing a white wildflower pinned to the breast of his uniform, a symbol of his new status as an expectant father. Back home in North Carolina, Ramseur's wife was due to give birth to their first child at any moment. "He planned to ride straight home after the battle to see his new child. A prearranged signal was designed to let Dod Ramseur know when the baby was born," Sulfridge confirms. He received this news before the battle, but the message didn't include whether he was the father of a baby boy or girl, and he died never knowing. His colleagues laid him out in Belle Grove's library and even allowed Confederate prisoners to file in to pay their final respects.

In 1920, the North Carolina Historical Commission and the NC United Daughters of the Confederacy erected a monument to the youngest general of the Confederacy at the intersection of Belle Grove Road and Highway 11, a simple stone column with a polished granite cannonball on top. I'd noticed the striking monument as we entered the plantation's grounds that morning and wondered who or what it memorialized.

"At the dedication of the monument," the historian adds, finishing the tale, "the principal speaker was a gentleman in his eighties, now a former senator from Delaware named Henry du Pont."

Sulfridge pauses, allowing that to sink in for a moment before continuing.

"The guest of honor who unveiled the monument that day was a woman now in her mid-fifties. Her name was Mary Ramseur. The daughter Dodson Ramseur never got to meet."

The woman in the red beret gently gasps. "That's amazing," she sniffs.

Sulfridge smiles and nods, then glances at me. "Yes, it is. But it serves to remind us how this terrible war between friends and neighbors and even family members touched every American life—even to this day. Hopefully never again."

I nod in agreement, intrigued to think that a longstanding family mystery may (or may not) have been solved, though something tells me the names are merely coincidental. No breakthrough here, I decide, though it merits further inquiry.

At that moment Wendy steps into the nursery and touches my elbow. "Babe, the speakers are starting downstairs. Maybe we should go get our seats."

As we troop downstairs to the exhibition room where the event's speakers are being introduced, Wendy whispers, "That looked pretty intense back there. Is that woman okay?"

"I think so. We heard an interesting story. I'll tell you later."

"The executive director just told me an unbelievable story too. Ever heard of Slavery's Trail of Tears?"

I ask if she means Andrew Jackson's Trail of Tears, the forced displacement of sixty thousand Cherokee, Choctaw, Seminole, and Chickasaw Indians from their native Southern homelands beginning in the 1830s.

"No. I mean half a million African slaves who were marched in chains with their families from Virginia down the Great Wagon Road to the slave markets of New Orleans prior to the Civil War. Their story never made it into the history books."

She tells me that, in the spring of 2015, Belle Grove's executive director Kristen Laise was finishing her workday and closing the museum's gift shop when a writer named Edward Ball phoned to inquire about Belle Grove's enslaved community—specifically wondering whether members of it may have been sold to slave traders at some point in the plantation's history.

"We get calls regularly from historians and folks interested in family history," Laise told me later. "But when I looked up Mr. Ball, I discovered that he was the author of *Slaves in the Family*, a groundbreaking book that changed the conversation about race and won the National Book Award twenty years ago. He was planning to follow the route of a notorious slave-trading company from Arlington across the South and wondered if he might come by for a conversation about the Belle Grove's enslaved community."

As it happened, a similar conversation was already underway at Belle Grove. Not long after Laise joined the staff as executive director in 2013, she'd taken a life-changing trip with three board members to the National Trust's annual conference in Savannah, Georgia, where attendees were introduced to the groundbreaking work being done by Charleston historian and National Trust field coordinator Joseph McGill with his Slave Dwelling Project, an innovative program created in 2010 to raise awareness of the lost narrative of an estimated one million enslaved people by inviting guests to spend nights in former slave dwellings.

"That experience was powerful and life-changing for all of us," Laise recalled. "It quickly became our mission to research the Hite family's enslaved population and place a human face on slavery here in the Shenandoah Valley. In every respect, this work has been a true awakening and a long-overdue reckoning."

The effort soon involved the work of an archaeologist from James Madison's Montpelier plantation and geology students from James Madison University who, using ground penetrating radar, discovered the location of graves in the slave cemetery on the grounds. Simultaneously, Laise and her staff began researching the letters and early documents of the Hites, discovering a newspaper ad from October 1824, placed by Isaac Hite, master of Belle Grove, that proposed to sell off "60 slaves, of various ages, in families," offering reasonable credit terms to potential buyers.

The research work of Laise and her team produced a significant database of names that could assist those in search of lost enslaved ancestors, a process that was of great interest to Edward Ball when he arrived the morning after their initial conversation.

"I gave him a walking tour of the house and shared our work with him, which was beginning in earnest at that time," recalled Laise. "He was a lovely, self-effacing man who explained that he hoped to tell the stories of people who endured this horrible, forced march to New Orleans if he could find the route taken. It was a shocking but largely unknown event, ignored by historians of the period."

With that goal in mind, she suggested that they look at a modern road map. "I showed him how historic US Highway 11, which runs right past Belle Grove's property through the heart of the Shenandoah Valley—the original Great Wagon Road—passes through several Deep South states to New Orleans. It was quite an aha! moment—obviously one of the country's primary slave-trading routes."

The visit later found its way into Ball's riveting account of following the route, which appeared in the November 2015 issue of *Smithsonian Magazine*:

> *The Slave Trail of Tears is the great missing migration—a thousand-mile-long river of people, all of them black, reaching from Virginia to Louisiana. During the 50 years before the Civil War, about a million enslaved people*

moved from the Upper South—Virginia, Maryland, Kentucky—to the Deep South—Louisiana, Mississippi, Alabama . . . [a forced resettlement that was] 20 times larger than Andrew Jackson's 'Indian removal' campaigns of the 1830s . . . bigger than the immigration of Jews into the United States during the 19th century and even the wagon-train migration to the West, beloved of American lore. This movement lasted longer and grabbed up more people than any other migration in North America before 1900.

In the piece, he vividly recounts men shackled to each other, followed by wives and children, who trekked through the heat and dangers of the Southern wilderness from the depleted "tobacco South to the cotton South," a commercial boom fueled by the invention of the cotton gin and rise of "King Cotton."

Ball estimates that as cotton replaced played-out tobacco as the South's leading cash crop, nearly four hundred thousand people were uprooted and sent to the Deep South states from Virginia and surrounding states in chained marches between 1810 and 1860. He quotes University of Virginia historian Maurie McInnis, who calculates that the sale of people in Richmond in 1857 alone amounted to $4 million—"That would be more than $40 million today."

As the author pointed out to Kristen Laise, several prominent American historians knew of the infamous "coffle trains" but, owing to the scarcity of details, never attempted to write the story of Slavery's Trail of Tears, an argosy of anguish and vanished lives that never reached the pages of mainstream American history.

"Maybe the most interesting thing to us," Laise now explains, "was the section after Belle Grove where Edward Ball visited tourist centers and shops up and down the valley asking local people if they knew anything about the chained slave coffles that traveled through the valley. Most had no idea what he was talking about." *People do know, however, about Civil War battles,* Ball writes. *The bloodletting here has a kind of glamour. A few people launch into stories about the brave Confederates. A few bring up their own ethnic lore. Well, Germans and Scots Irish settled the Shenandoah, that's who was here . . . Oh, my, the Scots Irish—they were made of brass.*

His narrative included the role played by the Great Wagon Road.

The gang headed down the Great Wagon Road, a route that came from Pennsylvania, already some centuries old—"made by the Indians," in the euphemism. Along the way, the coffle met other slave gangs, construction crews rebuilding the Wagon Road, widening it to 22 feet and putting down gravel. They were turning out the new Valley Turnpike, a macadam surface with ditches at the side . . . Today the Great Wagon Road, or Valley Turnpike, is known as U.S. Route 11, a two-lane road that runs between soft and misty mountains, with pretty byways. Long stretches of U.S. 11 look much like the Valley Turnpike did in the 1830s—rolling fields, horses and cattle on hills. Northern Shenandoah was wheat country then, with one in five people enslaved and hoeing in the fields. Today a few plantations survive. I stop at one of the oldest, Belle Grove. The Valley Turnpike once ran on its edge, and the coffle of 300 saw the place from the road. Relatives of President James Madison put up the stone mansion at Belle Grove during the 1790s, and it lives on as a fine house museum run by a historian, Kristen Laise. A walk through the house, a look at the kitchen where all the work was done, a walk through the slave cemetery, a rundown of the people who lived and died here, white and black—thanks to Laise, Belle Grove is not a house museum that shorts the story of slaves.

A powerful line near the end of his stunning odyssey lodged itself permanently in my Southern head: "The past cannot be unremembered."

"This museum is an example of setting the story straight," says Adeela Al-Khalili. "Our goal is to recognize the sacrifice and humanity of these forgotten enslaved Americans and write them back into the American story."

Al-Khalili, a retired public-school teacher, and her good friend Dee-Dee Liggins, historian and board member of the historic Josephine School Community Museum, sit with me on an unseasonably warm afternoon in a prim white clapboard structure on the outskirts of Berryville, Virginia. It was built by the descendants of former Clarke County slaves who established the hamlet of Josephine City after the Civil War. Al-Khalili's compelling Belle Grove presentation on the school and the unique community of former slaves who created it is the reason I've come for a closer look and deeper conversation.

In 1995, the simple one-story, two-room schoolhouse, built in 1882, was placed on the Virginia Landmarks Register and National Register of Historic Places. A few years later, a historic roadside marker was raised at the corner of Josephine Street and Church Street in Berryville, the county seat. It read:

> To improve the lives of former slaves, Ellen McCormick, widow of Edward McCormick of Claremont, established this African American community of 31 one-acre lots early in the 1870s. The lots . . . sold for $100 each. . . . By 1900, Josephine City had become an oasis for Clarke County's African American residents and included a school, grocery store, gas station, boarding house, restaurant, cemetery, and two churches.

"That sign," says Al-Khalili calmly, "is a perfect example of what I would call whitewashed American history, a story that reflects what many white people up till now wished to believe—namely that a white woman's generosity toward the lives of her freed slaves allowed them to create a life of their own. It suggests that without the help of whites, Black people were incapable of taking care of themselves. Josephine City is living proof that the exact opposite is true."

Al-Khalili and Liggins, whose roots reach back to the community's founding, further explain why McCormick's motives were anything but philanthropic. "The true facts of the settlement, uncovered in recent years, reveal that McCormick's motives were entirely self-serving," says Al-Khalili. "By the end of the war, tobacco was failing, and the widow McCormick's farm needed money to avoid foreclosure. Her property went up for auction twice without being purchased. Like many white plantation owners, including those at Belle Grove, she was in serious financial trouble."

Liggins provides an important addendum to the story. "One of her former slaves, a freed Black woman named Josephine Williams, approached Ellen McCormick about the possibility of former slaves purchasing their own land for one hundred dollars a plot. She was a seamstress who'd put away enough money to buy two lots from the widow. Twenty-four other former slaves did the same thing, including a man named Thomas Laws, who purchased his lot with money he earned moonlighting by selling vegetables from his garden. The community named the self-sustaining settlement in honor of Josephine Williams, becoming one of the first in America of its kind. One of the first things the residents did was build a schoolhouse for its children. The school became the cultural center and heart of the community. The residents knew that education was the true road to freedom."

From there, Josephine City flourished, the women contend, because of the combined skills and competency of the community's industrious residents. "These newly freed people created their own insular community where racism would never inhibit opportunity," Al-Khalili goes on. "They were determined to make a way out of no way for themselves and their descendants."

The original schoolhouse, the cornerstone of the community, served as an elementary school until it was relocated a short distance from its original site in 1928 to make room for the Clarke County Training School complex, which provided high school education to African American students.

In 2003, the schoolhouse was moved to its current spot in the community's historic district, becoming the first museum devoted to the history of Clarke County's African American community. Liggins's grandfather Robert Ligons and other former residents and members of the community filled the structure with historic photos and timely artifacts, colorful displays, and period exhibits that tell the story of a community's determination to exist and thrive, highlighted by narratives of residents who went on to important public careers. A poster that catches my attention lists the names of 4,735 people once enslaved in Clarke County, refuting a popular belief that the Shenandoah Valley had relatively few slaves owing to its rich limestone soil and frugal German farmers. "The kids are always amazed when they see that figure," says Al-Khalili. "This was just one county in *one* state, mind you."

"Times have changed but we're still growing and adding to our story," Liggins observes as she shows me around the tidy two-room museum. A fifth-generation resident, she returned to her hometown a couple decades ago to take care of her ninety-two-year-old mother, and became a lynchpin of the community's Improvement Association that saved the schoolhouse from a planned demolition, pushing for other civic improvements when Josephine City was annexed to the town of Berryville in 1989.

A major victory occurred in 2014 when the State of Virginia's Department of Historic Resources replaced the offensive historic marker with an accurately updated account of Josephine City's evolution. Moreover, during the years Confederate statues were being quietly removed along Richmond's Monument Avenue, Liggins, Al-Khalili, and other residents even persuaded Clarke County officials to add a meaningful display that honors the sacrifices of African Americans to stand beside the generic Confederate soldier that keeps watch on the county courthouse lawn in Berryville, a small but important victory that will allow for a full and unbiased story to be told in the future. My friend Neil Ronk would be pleased.

Adeela Al-Khalili is a youthful Black woman of seventy-one, a beautiful mother of six—three girls, three boys—who lives on Clarke County land that her husband's great-uncle acquired one hundred years ago. "I think my children are still a little angry with me because I pushed them so hard to get educated and become citizens involved with their society," she allows with a laugh. "But then, I was a demanding elementary school teacher for twenty-five years. I'm pleased to say they've turned out well. Their father and I are very proud of them, and I think they appreciate the work I do."

In her role as a board member of the Josephine School Community Museum, Al-Khalili routinely speaks to civic organizations and conferences around the country about the historic school's living legacy and the importance of getting the story of race in America correct. "That's why events like the one at Belle Grove are so important. The truth is right under our feet. But the story has been buried for hundreds of years. It must be dug up and told. That event, in fact, brought you here."

She's right. For a moment, we sit together in the warm silence of the old schoolhouse, surrounded by two hundred years of photographs and artifacts that tell the generational stories of the heirs of the Josephine School Community.

She breaks the silence by asking where I went to elementary school.

I tell her how I attended first grade in Florence, South Carolina, a town that was—in my mom's own words—Dixie in aspic. "We lived there for a year and a half in the late fifties after my father lost his newspaper in Mississippi. My mother had a second miscarriage. A kind Black woman named Miss Jesse came to help her get back on her feet and take care of my brother and me. I loved Miss Louise. She took me to the grocery store and taught me to dance in the kitchen to gospel music playing on her transistor radio. Without question, she saved my mother's life. I also know for a fact that she's the reason I love gospel music to this day."

I suddenly wonder if I've shared too much.

"That's a fine memory," Al-Khalili says, smiling. "And very true to that shameful era."

She glances out at the schoolyard through the open doorway. Dragonflies circulate like mythic messengers over the golden afternoon lawn.

"I'm a Yankee from Philadelphia. When I came down here thirty years ago, I was shocked to learn that the Civil War was still being waged by so many white people, in both subtle and overt ways—white supremacy politely disguised as nostalgia for the past."

She tells me about a road trip her family took when she was young, a rude awakening of a different sort. "My parents were from Dublin, Georgia. We had relations there. One time we took a family road trip to visit our relatives down there, three cars full of Black people. We knew we would probably be stopped by police. My dad, a cabdriver back in Philly, coached everyone on what to say. My mother wouldn't let my sister and me use the colored bathrooms along the way because they were so incredibly foul. She made us pee in the woods. I cannot let go of how insane that was. Imagine that today. It seems like another lifetime ago."

It does seem like a lifetime ago, we agree. And yet. *The past cannot be unremembered.*

We talk about school boards that are suddenly banning books by the bushel and nearly coming to blows over a bogeyman called critical race theory; politicians and TV wags stoking white-hot panic in their audiences over an utterly paranoidal concept called "replacement theory," not to mention leaders who play footsie with white supremacists and seem to embrace every conspiracy theory that comes along the pike.

"Is this why you're traveling the Great Wagon Road?" she finally asks with another easy smile. "To see how far we've come—or have yet to go?"

"Both, I suppose."

She gives me a strong mama hug, pointing out that "our ancestors are watching," a lovely reference to the enslaved who have gone before—and still observe us.

"For me, this is a labor of love," she says. "Juneteenth was not an accident. We are slowly awakening in America. I truly believe that—unearthing one true story at a time. That's our job. That's your job too."

She gives me another strong hug. I kiss her cheek. She smells like spring flowers.

"We can only move forward," she says, "because we're finally talking about this stuff."

EIGHTEEN

NARROW PASSAGE

FIFTY MILES DOWN THE ROAD, I STOP TO SEE MY FRIEND ED MARKEL AND HIS wife, Ellen, who own and operate the historic Inn at Narrow Passage, believed by some to be the oldest surviving inn on the Great Wagon Road.

I met Ed several years ago during a fly-fishing trip with an old friend on the North Fork of the Shenandoah River, which borders the inn's spacious lawn near the historic valley town of Edinburg. Heavy rains upcountry had forced the river to jump its banks and ruined our day of fishing, flooding the inn's lower meadow in the process. When the sun finally reemerged around five o'clock, our consolation was the opportunity to sit with Ed on the lawn with a bottle of good bourbon and learn how Narrow Passage got its name and bloody reputation, a story that illustrates the challenges of life for settlers on Virginia's early frontier.

Owing to the extreme narrowness of the Wagon Road as it passed the inn's front door through tightly bunched hills, Ed explained—"a road barely wide enough to accommodate a single wagon at a time going one way"— the isolated location became notorious for ambushes by highwaymen and hostile natives. Ed pointed out a small state historical marker down by the bridge (underwater at that moment) that described Narrow Passage's violent early history.

"The historical marker originally read 'Site of Virginia's Last Indian Outrage' but the state changed the language a few years ago to avoid giving offense to any individual groups," he explained with a shrug. "Though I'm sure the settlers massacred here wouldn't be terribly concerned about political correctness."

The original marker referred to a particularly gruesome incident in early summer 1764 when a group of local women and children assembled on the property of a German farmer named George Zeigler (sometimes spelled Sigler) on Narrow Passage Creek, seeking protection from increasing Indian attacks on area settlements in the aftermath of Pontiac's Rebellion, a war that erupted when a loose confederation of Iroquois warriors launched waves of attacks on western settlers designed to halt British expansion into the frontier.

A History of the Valley of Virginia, published half a century later, graphically described the violence set on those who took refuge with farmer Zeigler: "An old man named Sigler was with them. Five Indians attacked them. Sigler, after firing and wounding one in the leg, clubbed his gun and fought to desperation. While he was thus engaged, the women and children made their escape, and got safe to the fort. Sigler broke his gun over the heads of the enemy, wounded several of them pretty severely, and received himself several wounds, but continued to fight until he fell from loss of blood, when his merciless enemies mangled his body in a manner shocking to behold."

I let that sink in as we sat on the evening lawn sipping whiskey and watching the North Fork slowly recede. I asked Ed how he and wife Ellen came to own the historic inn.

"Sometimes I ask myself that very question," he replied with a chuckle. "It's been a forty-year adventure for Ellen and me and our three grown children, that's for sure."

The inn's original owners were unknown, he explained, but the enterprise probably began as a crude one-room log ordinary on the primary north–south road the Moravians and others followed to western North Carolina in the 1750s. By the time Stonewall Jackson used the original part of the inn as his headquarters during his successful valley campaign a century later, the original log structure had been expanded to include several rooms and a popular tavern. Jackson's stay there is memorialized by a famous painting titled *Headquarters at Narrow Passage*, the work of historical artist John Paul Strain. A signed and numbered copy of it, depicting Jackson meeting with his mapmaker in the snowy yard of the inn, hangs over the piano in the inn's reception room.

"We had people lined out the door when the artist came here to sign copies of that painting," Ed recalled, pointing out that the young woman shown in the painting holding a cat as she stands on the inn's balcony above Jackson and his mapmaker was named Daisy McGinnis, the innkeeper at that time of the war. "Almost every structure in this part of the valley was burned by Sheridan's Union troops in short order. The inn only survived because there was nothing else for miles and both sides needed to use it."

In peacetime, the inn became a girls' school for many years. "Probably because there weren't any decent structures still standing in this part of the valley," Ed speculated. "After that, it basically sat empty for God knows how long until Ellen and I came along in the 1980s."

At that point in his story, the bottle was empty and our long day on the river officially ended. As we went off to bed, Ed urged us to "Come back someday when the river is running normally and I'll tell you the rest of the story."

Two years later, I'm eager to hear the unfinished tale.

As we sit in the same wooden chairs overlooking a meadow with late-blooming wild phlox and yarrow, sans bourbon, I ask Ed if he remembers his first sight of the abandoned inn.

"Oh, golly, I sure do. Never forget it! The place was a desperate ruin, a complete disaster, totally uninhabitable. It had sat empty for God only knows how many years—*decades*, at the very least. Part of the building had actually burned and I couldn't even find the entire foundation. I remember lifting Ellen up to peek through broken logs and her saying 'Oh my goodness, Ed. This is *terrible*.'"

But something about the place spoke to the Markels, particularly Ed. It was 1983, and he had just bailed out of the corporate world as CEO of a company that manufactured industrial electric wire in the suburbs of Philadelphia, his hometown. The shared dream of the couple was to find either a country inn or a small-town hardware store to purchase and build a new life for their three young children in a "safer rural America."

"I grew up near Philadelphia and attended Germantown Academy, you see, the first public school in America," Ed explains. "That's probably where my love of American history got into the bloodstream. Also, we lived for years in Valley Forge and both Ellen and I belonged to lots of organizations that were engaged in historic preservation. But Philly's suburbs were changing at a rapid rate, becoming more urban and violent by the year. So, like the original Wagon Road travelers, we cashed out and left it all behind to find a better life for our kids. Friends thought we were crazy."

He shakes his head. "Indeed, there were moments when we wondered if they might be right. We had to travel a long way to get here. We looked at dozens of places from Vermont to North Carolina. None were right. Nothing spoke to us. Frankly, we were getting frustrated when we happened to be passing through Narrow Passage and heard about this place. It was everything we ever wanted."

"A crumbling ruin," I prompt the witness.

Ed laughs and bobs his head. "Yep. It was even *worse* than that. But you could *feel* the history here. Some old things in this world, you know, have a living presence, like a soul of their own, if you know what I mean. Anyway, we kept returning to have a look at this crumbling ruin, as you call it, asked around and eventually located the family that owned the property—they were descendants of McGinnis, by the way. We made them an offer. They accepted and we loaded our three young ones into the station wagon and headed to western Virginia. Crazy, huh? Just like those original Wagon Road settlers heading off into the blue unknown. We sunk everything we had into this place, heart and soul and no shortage of money."

Over the next thirty-five years, year after year, the dream of life in the country took shape as the Markels lovingly rebuilt, updated, and expanded their historic inn ("Starting out, we all lived in just two rooms for years— real pioneers!"), adding rustic porches and architecturally appropriate additions that eventually included a cozy conference center plus a dozen new guest rooms. "Ellen did all the gardens. She became an expert at that." Ed beams. "When we opened for business on Labor Day of 1985, we had people lining up to stay. They've come from all over the world ever since, including every state in America. Many still come back every year—especially the Washington crowd. Looking back, it's been better than I ever could have imagined. They're like family to us—even the politicians!"

"Best of all," he adds, "our kids grew up here able to enjoy a rare quality of life not many young people get in America anymore, right here on the Old Wagon Road. I think that means a lot to them." Jennifer, his oldest, is now a science teacher at a top academy in Leesburg, Virginia, where oldest son, Keith, serves as deputy city manager. Their second son, Ryan, does contract work for the federal government. "It's kind of top-secret stuff," Ed confides with a grin. "But all three are residents of [nearby] Loudoun County. No big cities for them."

It's a slower, quieter life, and there is really only one thing that worries my friend Ed: the changing tastes of the American hospitality business.

"When we started up there were only a few motels in Woodstock and Edinburg along Highway 11. We were the only historic inn between Harrisonburg and the Wayside Inn up in Middletown. The growth of Interstate 81 has brought more franchise motels and people in a rush to get places. Some travelers seem to prefer convenience over anything else. Historic inns everywhere, I've read, are all having a difficult time thanks to Airbnb."

He notes that there are presently more than six hundred Airbnb establishments scattered across Shenandoah and neighboring Augusta Counties alone. "My friends in the rotary can charge fifty or sixty bucks a night for an Airbnb. We're over a hundred for a nice room with a view of the river. Hard to compete with that."

As we sit beside Ellen's fading gardens in the morning light of late autumn, Ed glances at the North Fork, now peacefully flowing past the meadow below us. "I fear it may be a sign of the times that historic full-service inns like ours are in danger of going the way of the Conestoga wagon. Fortunately, for the moment at least, we still have a loyal base of customers who come every year to fish and hike or just enjoy the peace and quiet we still have out here in the Passage. Being one of the oldest inns on the Great Wagon Road helps. As long as history still matters to some folks, we'll be here."

Before moving on, I ask Ed to keep the lights on at least until I return with my wife and fly rod. The Inn at Narrow Passage is our kind of place.

Ed grins and winks. "We'll be waiting for you. Hopefully not at flood stage."

The narrative works of historical artist Keith Rocco have been favorably compared to the best of Frederic Remington, Alphonse de Neuville, and

Howard Pyle. His impressive body of work includes more than eighty historical paintings scattered across thirty sites for the US National Park Service and every major public collection of historical military art in the nation
and several foreign countries, including the US House of Representatives,
Gettysburg National Military Park, the Pentagon, and the US Army War
College.

Rocco's commissioned murals for the Wisconsin Veterans Museum
in Madison and the Abraham Lincoln Presidential Library and Museum
in Springfield, Illinois, and the First Division Museum at Cantigny Park in
Wheaton, Illinois, are considered masterpieces of visually narrative storytelling. With battlefield subjects ranging from the Napoleonic Wars to the
Korean conflict, painstakingly rendered to evoke the agony and historical
accuracy of ordinary men at arms, his work is some of the most admired and
important in the world.

I was introduced to it by a dear old friend from Richmond named Isabel
Correll, a major force in Virginia's spiritual and historical life, who gave me
her copy of Rocco's bestselling 2009 book *The Civil War Art of Keith Rocco*
not long before she passed away at age ninety. I phoned the artist on a lark
as I approached Narrow Passage, shamelessly dropping Dame Izzy's name
and asking if I might stop by just to say hello and talk a little art history.

Rocco couldn't have been more welcoming. "Come on up this afternoon
and we'll have a glass of wine and I'll show you my studio," he proposed.

As we settle with glasses in his gorgeous studio, which overlooks a pasture behind the house where the Roccos' horses Missy and Rafi are peacefully grazing, I mention Isabel Correll's recent passing and how I promised
her I would look up her favorite artist as I traveled by on the Great Wagon
Road.

"I'm sorry to hear she's gone," Rocco says, "but I'm glad you could stop
by. Love to hear more about the road . . . "

I give him a slightly more detailed version of the elevator speech before
turning the conversation back to his passion for art, history, and authenticity.

I can't help but look around as we talk. His studio is a bright and airy
space filled with eighteenth-century rifles, military sabers, replica uniforms
from several seventeenth- and eighteenth-century wars, and authentic personal battlefield artifacts collected during the artist's extensive research

trips to battlefields at home and abroad. Thinking of my own home office filled with memorabilia from all over the world of golf, I wonder aloud what role these artifacts might provide him as an artist.

"Artifacts are important because they transport you *into* history—to the people who created a moment in history," he replies. "I think of my painting, in fact, as a two-dimensional time machine and have come to believe that you can't understand history until you hold a genuine artifact in your hand. It could be a simple canteen or an officer's sword, a uniform belt buckle or a spur, anything lived and genuine. The details are important. They grant authenticity. People who seriously collect antiques understand this. The artifact or item survives to tell us a story about the people who possessed them. I try to add their authentic details into my visual narratives."

To emphasize the point, he indicates a cup filled with soil from a famous battlefield for a current project. "It even helps me get the color of the ground correct."

"Do you remember the first artifact you collected?"

Rocco smiles. "I sure do. I purchased it on my first visit to Gettysburg during an eighth-grade graduation trip. My dad was a World War II veteran who had a strong love of military history that he shared with me. I was one of those kids who grew up with toy soldiers and watching TV shows and documentaries on the Second World War in the late 1950s and '60s."

Following a tour of the battlefield with his school group, Rocco and his classmates were granted twenty minutes to do some souvenir shopping. He made a beeline for an antiques dealer in search of an authentic Civil War artifact. "The man sold me a canteen, a cartridge box, and a scabbard and bayonet. I was so excited to own them, though I later learned they were actually post–Civil War artifacts, probably from the Indian wars out West. As a result, I learned a valuable lesson about detail and authenticity and was basically hooked."

His first authentic Civil War artifact came at age sixteen, a cavalry saber purchased for twenty bucks from a bookstore in Oak Park, Illinois, not far from his home in Cicero.

By that point, a passion for sketching and drawing had evolved into oil paintings of landscapes and battlefields. "Around the eighth grade, my parents gave me a set of oil paints. My first paintings were done on the backside of canvas wallpaper and weren't very good. But I was drawn early to the works of Michelangelo, Vermeer, Delacroix, and Rembrandt—the amazing way they captured light and details in such a human context."

He studied art at Northern Illinois in the 1970s. "But I dropped out because everything being taught was non-representational. I stopped painting completely but picked up my brushes several years later. If it's in you, as they say, it's in you. Every artist learns this one way or another." By the 1980s, he'd made up his mind to quietly pursue the path of historical narrative art influenced by artists like Remington, Jean-Louis-Ernest Meissonier, Alphonse de Neuville, N.C. Wyeth, and Howard Pyle. Pursuant to that goal, he supported himself as a commercial art director in the ad agency world of Chicago. "I did work for all the vices," he wryly notes. "Sugary cereal, cigarettes, and alcohol. I drew the line at prostitution."

During that period, he took a few of his paintings to an antique figurine show and sold them. "That's when lightning struck, so to speak. People seemed to relate to my history-based military subjects."

His work was soon in high demand from private collectors and top historical museums and organizations. These days, 80 percent of his work comes from commissions, including two large murals of the US Army's First Infantry Division landing at Omaha Beach on D-Day that he's putting together for the McCormack Trust.

Given that a sense of place often means as much to an artist's creativity as his subject matter, I'm curious how Keith and Libby Rocco came to settle on a ridge of serene pastureland just off the Great Wagon Road.

"God brought him here," Libby says, laughing as she joins us. "And there was just too much history for him to think of ever leaving." For Libby, her family has been along the Wagon Road since the 1740s.

Keith smiles at her and nods. He moved to the area in 1992, two years before the couple met. "I'd lived in Chicago for thirty-seven years and was ready to start something new. I'd been coming out here to the Shenandoah for a few weeks every summer. I'd do a show, drive around, and visit battlefields and galleries. I'd seen enough of Virginia to know that I didn't wish to live east of the Blue Ridge mountains—a little too steamy during the summers for me—so I chose the Woodstock area."

One day in 1997, new friends invited him to play in a tennis tournament. Libby was in the group.

"The first time I saw Keith, he was sitting on a bench wearing a fedora, and I thought, 'He's not from around here.' When he told us he was a painter," she remembers, "I thought that meant he painted houses."

Her family, he discovered, had the deep roots in the area, dating from an ancestor in 1740 named Augustus Coffman who fought in the French and Indian War and was given a land grant on Narrow Passage Creek.

Libby recently retired from running her own insurance company but still heads up the annual Old-Time Festival in nearby Edinburg. "In the past," she explains, "we've had living Civil War encampments and displays from the Daughters of the American Revolution. Last year, though, we had a 1950s theme that included a sock-hop dance. Keith's role was to drive folks around town in a 1940s cab. He was one popular guy!"

Later, as the conversation winds down and the couple walks me to their front door, we pass a Keith Rocco work that stops me in my tracks. It's a large painting of a Plains Indian bearing down in a cloud of dust on a Great Plains buffalo, bow and arrow aimed for the kill. *Buffalo Hunter*, a twenty-four-by-thirty Keith Rocco original, was inspired by a visit to the Cody Heritage Museum in Wyoming, yet another thing we have in common. I once spent an enchanting day at the same museum with my young daughter, Maggie, during a cross-country summer fly-fishing and camping trip.

As a guy who also fell in love with history in the eighth grade, I dare to inquire if this Rocco masterpiece might be for sale.

The artist smiles and tells me the price.

He laughs when I admit that, oddly enough, I've yet to purchase any kind of souvenir or object on my journey down the Wagon Road to remember it by, though *Buffalo Hunter* would suffice very nicely.

"All things are possible," he says. "Drop by again when you finish the road and maybe we can talk."

NINETEEN

ANGELS OF THE ROAD

AFTER SEVERAL WEEKS OFF THE ROAD TO CELEBRATE CHRISTMAS AND THE New Year with my family and tend to my day job, I'm thrilled to be on my way to see Jeff and Beverley Evans, the Wagon Road's premier auctioneers and collectors of early American decorative arts, especially since Mully is now riding shotgun with me. As we take a backcountry road to their place in Rockingham County, we pass a fellow struggling to push a riding lawn tractor out of the ditch.

I turn around to see if I can lend a hand. Mully hops out to supervise the operation.

"Can't believe this durn thing crapped out on me. Just spent two hours tuning her up," he says with a pained grin as we push what must be the oldest John Deere lawn tractor in existence out of the ditch and up a long gravel driveway that leads to a white house and a weathered red barn with a faded Confederate flag draped on its side.

As we reach the barn door, the man stands up and rubs his back. "Thanks for your help, buddy. I got this dad-blame psychotic nerve that give me fits when the weather turns."

What a perfect name. *Psychotic nerve.*

"No problem. I've got one of those too."

He grins, wipes his hands on a rag, and offers a hand. His name is Dwight. A faded sign above the barn door reads "Small Engine Repair." Unshaven and skinny as a Great Depression grave digger, a soiled Virginia Tech cap atop his flecked graying head, Dwight appears to be in his late thirties or early forties, too old to cry but too young to die. He glances down the yard at the Pearl.

"That's one fine old road angel you got down there, buddy. Ain't seen a Roadmaster in years."

"She's a real pearl."

Dwight rattles out a nicotine cough. "Know what you mean. Lemme show you what I got like it."

He opens the barn door and Mully, never one to wait for a formal invitation, scoots ahead to scout the premises.

"Good-lookin' dog," says Dwight. "Smart, I reckon."

"Smarter than her owner."

"How old?"

"Almost fifteen."

"Still huntin'?"

"Only for table scraps."

In the back of the heated workshop, beyond a lighted worktable freighted with machine parts, an entire northern wall of shelves groans with tools, machine parts, and metal boxes. In the middle of a floor littered with small engines and several lawn mowers in various states of repair, sits a vehicle under a dusty gray car cover. The space reeks not unpleasantly of oil, dust, and engine parts, the sweet decay of automotive time.

"Check it out. Here's *my* road angel."

As he tugs off the cover, I half expect his angel to be a fireball-orange Plymouth Duster with the Stars and Bars on its roof.

But instead, it turns out to be a deep maroon Corvette Stingray coupe in apparent mint condition.

"*Wow*. What year?"

"Nineteen sixty-five. Got her at the auto auction over in Richmond nine years ago, a gift to myself after Iraq. Been slowly rebuildin' her. Got a few things to fix yet but I'm finally gettin' close. She's got four hundred twenty-seven horses, four-barrel carb, low compression. Probably the most powerful engine you can get on the street."

He opens the 'Vette's driver's-side door and invites me to sit behind the wheel. A small silver cross dangles from the rearview mirror.

"Original leather," he says as I slide in. "Good radio too. Crank'er up if you want."

The deep throbbing engine sounds like a rumble of war from the automotive gods. I let it run for a few moments before killing the engine.

"My brother's dream car," I say, rather pointlessly, reaching up to touch the dangling cross.

"That was my mama's. She passed 'fore I got home. Daddy wasn't in good shape either. So, I took over the shop."

Though I'm more of an aging-Subaru than vintage-sports-car type, I can't help but sit for several moments in this iconic American car, enjoying the smell of the original leather, both hands on the steering wheel, imagining a highway to the horizon.

"Only hadder out a couple times. She's almost ready for a big ride, though."

"Where will you go?"

"That's easy."

He scratches his unshaven chin.

"Out to see old Crazy Horse."

I climb out and shut the 'Vette's door, a resonant thump. Does he mean the statue in the Black Hills of South Dakota?

"That's it. Some Polish fella spent his whole life carving it out of a mountaintop. My grandmother told me about Crazy Horse when I was a kid. My grandfather, see, met her out in Wyoming during the war. He was a mechanic at the air force base. She was a teacher at the Wind River Indian Reservation. They met at a USO dance. She was actual Shoshone. He was Southern Baptist. Can you believe it? But they run off and got hitched. I spent a summer with 'em when I was nine or ten. Best summer of my life. They took me up to Dakota to see Crazy Horse. He's the warrior who wiped out George Custer. They put him on a postage stamp. I thought about Crazy Horse a lot when I was over in Iraq. He had a vision quest to save his people. I vowed if I got home alive, I'd go out see old Crazy Horse again. Just to say thanks."

I'm surprised how moved I am by his vision quest. Every road warrior, I suppose, needs one.

We walk back outside. Mulligan has finished her official inspection of the premises and sits halfway down the gravel driveway, watching crows in

Dwight's stubbled cornfield. November is ending. I'm tempted to ask about the faded flag on his barn, but I know that the answer will be heritage and history and maybe something worse. My dear friend the Rev. Ginny Bain Inman, a gifted Episcopal priest, likes to say that one loves God by loving one's neighbor, regardless of how you find him, and that faith is far more process than perfection. The Hebrew scriptures talk about entertaining angels unaware. Meanwhile, down here on earth where we all momentarily reside, I've learned that you rarely change a mind with a poke in the eye.

Instead, I simply tell him that we have something besides road angels in common.

"Yessir? What's that?"

I tell him about my father's grandmother, Aunt Emma, the Catawba foundling.

"So, you got some Indian blood too, buddy."

"I feel it sometimes."

He asks where I'm headed.

"Down the Old Wagon Road to see some friends in Broadway."

He wonders what that is, the Old Wagon Road.

I tell him and he offers a lopsided grin. "No way. You know, my other grandmother—mama's people—told me they come here way on back from Ireland or maybe Scotland, not sure which. But she said they was good at farmin' and making babies and half-decent whiskey. Church people, though. Good people."

"I know the type. That makes us both sons of the Wagon Road."

Since he's a vet with a road vision, I mention Jim Webb's 2004 book *Born Fighting: How the Scots-Irish Shaped America*, which notes how the Ulster Scots were the backbone of America's westward expansion, born fighters who cherished freedom and participated in every war America ever fought.

"Maybe I'll have to get me that book," Dwight says.

"Hold on."

I walk back down to the Pearl and pull my dog-eared copy out from my briefcase and walk back to the barn and hand it to Dwight.

"It's kind of marked up with my notes," I explain, "but it could be good reading on your way out to see Crazy Horse."

Dwight thanks me, flipping through its pages.

"I ain't much for readin' books. But I'll read this. I might have to keep on goin' till I see the Pacific Ocean. Always wanted to see that too."

"Well, wherever you go, take care of that *psychotic* nerve," I say.

"You do the same, buddy."

Jeff Evans smiles as I explain why I'm an hour late. He and his wife, Beverley, are showing me around their spectacular early eighteenth-century stone farmhouse set in a rolling meadow just outside the town of Broadway. "I've probably only met a couple hundred like him in my years as an auctioneer," he says, referring to my new friend Dwight. "True salt of the earth. Everywhere out here in God's country."

The Evanses are road angels of a different sort, preserving everyday items of early American life from the Wagon Road and well beyond. They have been described as our nation's leading specialists in Southern decorative arts and general Americana, including eighteenth- and nineteenth-century glass, ceramics, and fine antiques. Their home is essentially a museum of early American treasures, a collector's dream house of spectacular furniture and decorative pieces made in the Shenandoah Valley.

"I like to say we're simply into old houses full of old objects," Jeff remarks as he leads me from room to room past two-hundred-year-old pie safes and ornately painted blanket boxes, shelves filled with beautiful and simple glassware and historic ceramics, stately tall clocks, and German schranks (cabinets) with gorgeous Fraktur paintings. He confirms that the house is essentially a private collection of more than twenty thousand pieces of early American domestic life they have collected over five decades traveling Southern highways and back roads.

"Everything in this house basically came from three counties," Beverley adds. "Augusta, Rockingham, and Shenandoah."

"We reside happily in the past," Jeff chimes in. "And that's pretty much the chief appeal to us. These things were made with people's hands, with care and love, meant to outlive those who owned or made them and be passed on through generations. It connects us to this place. We feel an obligation to preserve them because you feel like you know these people. Everything in here has a story."

In this I hear echoes of Alexandra Kirtley: "They tell the story of brave and resolute immigrants on the move, determined to preserve their language, culture, religion, and traditions in the American wilderness. Best of all, they give us a vivid picture of these newcomers to America, their daily lives and dreams. The Great Wagon Road was essential to creating that new American story."

"When we started out," Beverley explains, "we didn't intend for it to be wall-to-wall furniture and folk-art museum. Because of Jeff's work and my interest in antiques and my love of folk art, it just kept expanding. It can really draw you in."

She smiles. "You are probably thinking this house looks like a nightmare to keep dusted. Honestly, I dust the house only a couple times a year. If you don't move anything, you know right where the dust is."

No stranger to old houses and antique auctions, I'm curious to know how all of this came about—*their* shared passion for history and a lifestyle and thriving business rooted in the historic past.

Jeff's love for old things, he tells me, began with collecting arrowheads and old bottles around his family's auction house near Mount Crawford in the eastern part of Rockingham County, which is surrounded by Mennonite farmlands. His parents started their Green Valley Auctions business in 1967, when Jeff was six. "My mother drove me around to see every historic house in the county. My dad started the Shenadoah Flea Market at the auto auction in Harrisonburg in 1972. Every Saturday I would attend local estate sales, take stuff home, wash it up, and sell it at the flea market the next week."

At twelve, Jeff called his first auction; at thirteen he was a fully licensed auctioneer. He conducted his first professional auction before graduating high school, and started his own business in 1979, Jeffrey S. Evans & Associates.

He and Beverley met in high school French class. Her interest in old things—in particular antique quilts—came from her great-grandmother. "When we got married, we decided that we needed a place of our own." She wanted a historic house, something pre-1850, made of either stone or handmade brick. He wanted something "that looked old and only half an hour from work."

Someone told them about the old Sites house on four hundred acres in

Broadway, built by a man who came down the Wagon Road from Philadelphia in 1784. A traditional German stone house with a rare center chimney had replaced the property's original log house sometime in the early nineteenth century.

"A family named Kline lived in the house from 1870 to 1954," explains Beverley. "And then it just sat empty for decades until a woman from Broadway purchased the house with plans to restore it in 1976."

"She did manage to get it on the National Register of Historic Places, but the restoration never happened," Jeff says, picking up the tale. "The stack was starting to crumble, and the porches were falling off. It wasn't for sale, but we asked permission to look at it."

There was no running water or electricity.

"Animals were actually living in the house," Beverley adds with a laugh. "Skunks, raccoons, even sheep downstairs."

"Luckily, no one had stolen the doors and mantelpiece. They were original and beautiful. A miracle. Original Shenandoah Valley door hinges—the best in the valley."

Two weeks after they got in to see the house, the owner offered to sell it to them for exactly what she paid in 1976—forty grand, including eleven acres of land.

Their first job was to clear trees and shrubs that enveloped the house, then install an electric fence around it to keep the animals out.

The couple hired a trusted contractor from Staunton with a handshake deal and started a restoration that took three full years. "We lived out of an upstairs bedroom for a full year during the restoration," Beverley remembers. "A simple mattress on the floor." There were issues with the county over what could be preserved and what wasn't building code. They put sawdust on the two-hundred-year-old floors to allow workers' feet to clean them as work progressed; repaired the rotted windowsills with fiberglass wood; and even managed to save most of the house's original plaster walls.

"Our firm rule became: if there's any way to save it, we save it," recalls Jeff. "Any doubt, save it too."

With one small exception: because the house originally had a separate kitchen owing to the danger of fire, they replaced a dogtrot connector with a modern kitchen, though it looks as authentic as a Quaker pie safe. They also turned the garage into a charming guesthouse and built a beautiful spring-house log house in order to host seminars on decorative arts. The likes of MESDA, Winterthur, the Museum of the Shenandoah Valley, and *Country Living* have all availed themselves use of the facility for seminars and special events. Their attic contains a spectacular resource library on historical decorative arts and design—including several books authored by Jeff.

Since conducting their first catalog auction in 1995, the Evanses have sold many of the most important estate and landmark collections for some of the most prominent consignors in the world. The company logo is inspired by a painted decoration found on a hanging cupboard from around 1800 that brought the highest price in the history of their catalog auctions. The panel features a leaping six-point stag painted by early Shenandoah Valley artist Johannes Spitler in red, white, and blue, and fetched a record price for painted American furniture: $962,000. The couple also holds the record for the most expensive Spitler blanket chest sold at auction: $356,000. Both Evanses also serve on multiple boards of directors of historical organizations in the region, and Jeff has worked as an appraiser and consultant for Virginia collections at the Woodrow Wilson birthplace in Staunton, the Jackson House Museum in Lexington, and the Museum of the Shenandoah Valley in Winchester, among others. He regularly lectures on American glass and decorative arts around the country and is headed off to Pennsylvania within days to do just that.

"Now *that's* a vintage car," Jeff says as he walks me to the Pearl with one of their half dozen cats following us. "I see you've got a good traveling partner."

Mully sits calmly waiting on the Pearl's front seat, eyeballing the cat.

"I do. She's vintage too."

Beverley wonders what our next stop on the Wagon Road happens to be.

"Staunton. I have a history there."

"Great place. So do I," Jeff says. "That's where I was born."

"You and Woodrow Wilson."

They thank me for dropping by and Jeff invites me to attend one of their future catalog auctions.

I mention that the last time I attended an auction I dropped two grand on an oil painting of cows in a pasture that hung at the 1904 world's fair. "Old things are seriously dangerous for me."

Jeff laughs. "In that case, you should *definitely* come."

Before Mully and I push on for Staunton, a fine old Wagon Road town where I made a life-changing decision forty years ago, there's a place I'm eager to see that's not too far away. It's called Singers Glen, the so-called birthplace of Southern gospel music.

Though winter is closing fast and dusk is upon us, according to Jeff Evans, the village of Singers Glen is only a fifteen-minute drive through Cooter's Store and Turleytown. There a Mennonite music teacher and composer named Joseph Funk founded America's first sacred music printing house in 1847. All I know about Funk is that he was the son of Anabaptist settlers who fled the horrors of Europe's Thirty Years' War and became the first man to publish shape note hymnals and sacred choir music. I have no clue what to expect in Singers Glen but am curious to see where Southern gospel music was born. Perhaps there's even a gospel-themed motor inn that accepts dogs and features guest rooms named for stars of the gospel music firmament.

To my surprise, or maybe not, Singers Glen turns out to just be a pretty hilltop hamlet no bigger than the hips on a corn snake, with four churches and a general store, a small post office, and no gospel-themed motel. This is just as well. When I find it, even Funk's National Register homeplace is closed up tight for the night. Someday I'll return and learn more about its place in American music history.

In the meantime, we turn back for Highway 11 with Shenandoah Valley resident Mary Chapin Carpenter singing about being between the here and gone, a perfect anthem for an old man's drive through the winter night with his dog.

Half a dozen miles later, as we reach Highway 11, a roadside marker informs me that Abraham Lincoln's father, Thomas, was born three miles back the way we've just come from.

As fellow road angel Mary Chapin likes to say, the road only goes one way. And you can't go back.

PART FIVE

REVELATIONS

TWENTY

SMOKE & MEMORY

SNOW IS FALLING IN DOWNTOWN STAUNTON WHEN I PARK ON BEVERLEY Street a few minutes before the opening of the Woodrow Wilson Presidential Library and Museum.

It's Friday, February 2.

My 67th birthday.

It's also the 369th birthday of Nell Gwyn, the London stage actress and longtime mistress of King Charles II, the monarch who gave Pennsylvania to young William Penn. Wildly popular with the public, witty, extravagant, beautiful, and completely illiterate, Gwyn shared the king's bed for sixteen years and bore him two sons, both of whom became lords. She was said to be his most trusted adviser on matters of state and business. So, I probably owe her a belated debt of gratitude for the opportunity to travel the road of my ancestors.

Across the street, a smoke shop is about to open for the day, with a display window full of fine handmade European pipes. Hooking Mully to her lead, I cross over so I can take a closer look. Both my father and his father were pipe smokers. Back home, a couple of their favorite pipes and three of my own, in fact, sit on my writing table. In truth, I mostly appreciate the craftsmanship of handmade pipes and only fire mine up on cold winter days, which somehow bring me closer to the two men I miss most. I'm nowhere near the smokers they were, though I've always found the scent of pipe smoke pleasing and enjoy a talent for making perfect smoke rings that delighted my children when they were sprouts.

My grandfather Walter Dodson, for whom I'm named, was the quietest man I've ever known, a skilled carpenter and electrician who worked on road crews putting up electrical lines across the rural South of the 1920s, a gentle fellow of few words who seemed unusually at peace with the world, especially with a fishing rod in his hands and his pipe or a cheap King Edward cigar in his mouth. According to my father, Walter's heroes were Franklin Roosevelt and Chief Sitting Bull, possibly because his mother, Aunt Emma, may have been a Native American. "The day after Roosevelt died down in Georgia," my dad once told me, "your grandfather took a rare day off work and stood by the railroad tracks in Greensboro waiting for the train bearing the president's casket to pass through town. I think he stood there for half a day smoking his pipe, waiting to pay his respects."

I've come to Staunton in search of my father's own favorite president, however, Woodrow Wilson, a son of the Great Wagon Road who was born a few minutes after midnight on December 29, 1856, in the front bedroom of an elegant brick house owned by the local Presbyterian church on the eastern fringes of town. He was the third child of Janet Woodrow and Rev. Joseph Ruggles Wilson's four children.

Wilson's mother was a Scottish immigrant and his father the son of Scots-Irish settlers. But Tommy, as they called the baby, would never get to know the sweet Shenandoah town until he was a grown man. Not long after his birth, Reverend Wilson accepted a better-paying position as pastor of the Presbyterian parish in Augusta, Georgia, where Wilson would live until age fourteen, shaped by the fever of Southern rebellion.

Founded in 1747, the town of Staunton is named in honor of Lady Rebecca Staunton, wife of Virginia's royal lieutenant governor Sir William Gooch. In its early years, it established itself as a major north–south center of trade in the remote American backcountry, also serving as the westernmost courthouse in British North America prior to the revolution and even briefly as the capital of Virginia when British occupation threatened Richmond in 1781. Young Thomas Jefferson had his first law office in Staunton, which may explain why so much of the historic town today looks as if he designed it. By the time the Virginia Central Railroad arrived a century later, Staunton was a booming manufacturing center with factories producing carriages, wagons, and agricultural supplies, a major transportation hub that annually sent tons of grain and tobacco to Europe.

Due to its central location in the fertile heart of the Shenandoah Valley, Staunton became a vital staging area and supply depot for the Confederacy during the Civil War. In summer 1864, a force of ten thousand Union troops descended on the town to sever enemy supply lines, destroying the railroad tracks and burning the town's handsome train station along with many private homes, warehouses, and factories, looting its retail stores in the process.

Today, tastefully restored Staunton can make claim to be one of the coolest small towns in the South if not America at large. It's home to historic Mary Baldwin University, a spectacular American Shakespeare Center, several historic hotels and inns, a serious preservation movement, a thriving foodie scene, and a bustling Main Street of locally owned shops that *Architectural Digest* cites as one of the most beautiful in America.

With Mully settled on her favorite wool blanket for a midmorning nap in the car, I set off for the Wilson Presidential Library and Museum to see if I can learn why Wilson was my old man's favorite president. Was it because he was the first Southerner to be elected president after the Civil War? Or maybe because Wilson steered the country through the horrors of the First World War and advanced a revolutionary idea called the League of Nations, providing the inspiration for the creation of the United Nations decades later?

Historians and biographers still find Wilson a beguiling paradox, a fellow whose lofty vision of a world made safe for everyone runs parallel to his human shortcomings. Perhaps this day will yield an answer.

By sheer luck, the first person I bump into opening the doors of the Wilson museum for the day is the complex's youthful curator, Andrew Phillips. The first question I ask Phillips is how pretty Staunton came to be home to Wilson's library and museum, a place where he spent only a tiny fraction of his life.

"Good question," he cheerfully says, noting that even though Wilson lived here only a very short time before the family relocated to Georgia, he maintained a strong spiritual connection to his hometown for his entire life, returning often with both his wives and daughters. "He spoke of it fondly throughout his public life, and famously observed that a man's rootage is more important than one's leafage. He clearly believed that was important, perhaps the reason he was such a proud son of Staunton."

Phillips gives me a brief history of the facility. Not long after Wilson's election to the presidency in 1912, he and first wife Ellen returned to Staunton on his birthday to spend two nights in the home where he was born. They were reportedly welcomed by several thousand citizens. Following the president's death, a dozen years later, wife number two, First Lady Edith Bolling Galt Wilson (whom Wilson married less than a year after Ellen succumbed to Bright's disease in 1914), returned to Staunton to support a plan by Wilson's former cabinet members and prominent locals to transform the old church manse into a presidential birthplace museum. "She basically wanted to create a shrine to the memory of her husband, beginning with where he came from," Phillips explains.

With help from the trustees of Mary Baldwin College, the Woodrow Wilson Birthplace Foundation was officially incorporated in 1938, opening doors to the public in 1941 with a personal dedication by President Franklin Roosevelt. Three years later, much of its endowment was coming from a popular film about Wilson's life. Two decades after that, the fully restored property was designated a National Historic Landmark, followed two years later by recognition from the National Register of Historic Places. The adjacent eight-thousand-square-foot museum opened its doors to the public in 1990, containing eight galleries that average twenty-five thousand visitors a year. The top attractions are an authentically replicated World War I trench and the president's own 1919 Pierce-Arrow automobile. Many of Wilson's papers—those not claimed by the Library of Congress—are housed at the Woodrow Wilson Library on Staunton's East Beverley Street. The library, I learn, is closed this snowy Friday morning.

"Otherwise, your timing is great," says Phillips. "We're celebrating the centennial years of Wilson's presidency. There's no better time to take a good look at the man and the relevancy of his presidency in today's world. Considerable reconsideration of his work by presidential scholars and the museum is currently underway. Our mission statement has also changed. We are trying to be a site that tells not just what Wilson did or didn't do but how consequential his accomplishments and failings were to a rapidly changing world, including his financial reforms, his role in leading us to war, and his failed vision for the League of Nations. Wilson's legacy touches all of these topics and much more. We make no excuses," he adds, "for the racism that darkens his legacy. Our guides tell his story objectively and honestly."

Phillips is curious what bring me to the museum on a cold, snowy morning.

I mention my late father's admiration for the man and my own interest in Wilson's Wagon Road roots, leaving out that Staunton also happens to be the place where I had something akin to a spiritual awakening in 1983.

Phillips smiles. "Funny how our fathers shape our lives, isn't it?"

He mentions how his father's passion for Civil War history inspired him to earn a bachelor's degree in history at Gettysburg College before taking a master's in museum studies at the University of Washington that ultimately landed him in Staunton in 2014. "Because my focus was slavery and American memory, we put together a tour of the house that focuses on the lives of the enslaved people who worked here during Wilson's time and before. We're proud of our work on this project. History is a living study that deserves perpetual analysis and unbiased objectivity."

At that moment, he notes, archaeology students from nearby James Madison University are working with the museum staff to unearth and identify additional artifacts from the property's smokehouse and stables.

I ask if he knows Professor Gabor Boritt.

Phillips lights up. "Of course, absolutely! Professor Gabor is an old friend and my favorite professor at Gettysburg College. I first met him when my father and I went there for the orientation. His own immigrant story is amazing, isn't it? I loved my years in Gettysburg. It's probably the only college town in America where it's perfectly normal to see someone carrying a musket or cavalry sword to class."

Given his love of American history and current position as a modern caretaker of a complex presidential life, it's only natural to get his take on how we should look at admired historical figures that seem deeply flawed in the context of today's world.

Not surprisingly, Phillips has a ready answer.

"One thing I've come to believe is that figures and events in our history need to be remembered in the context of their own times. Wilson is a prime example. There are many things we can admire about his vision and leadership, but also factors we cannot condone from the perspective of today's world. We can only study and learn from his mistakes. The best and worst presidents seem to happen at pivotal points in history where change and conflict intersect. Maybe that's the definition of true leadership—or at least its challenge. There may be no better example of this dichotomy than Woodrow Wilson, who was born before the Civil War and died after the First World War. During that time, there were seismic changes in the world and American life."

With this useful introduction, I spend the next ninety minutes following the story of Tommy Wilson's remarkable journey from his humble start in Staunton to his death in 1924.

As noted, Wilson's formative years took place during the Civil War down in Augusta, where, unable to read until age ten—probably due to dyslexia—his handicap transformed him into a slow but deliberate reader who was deeply inspired by his father's intellectual sermons and the incendiary public rhetoric of the day. Among other shaping influences, he had watched with awe as Confederate troops marched off to war and was proud of the fact that his father signed on as a company chaplain.

By the time he arrived at Princeton in the late 1870s, Wilson was a keen debater and student of American politics, destined to edit the school newspaper and form his own debating club, which exposed him to new ideas and a hunger for more. Though he arrived at Princeton an avowed segregationist, as he later took pains to point out, he left a passionate student of Edmund Burke, a statesman and philosopher who opposed the slave trade.

After graduation, Wilson studied law at the University of Virginia (and unsuccessfully courted his first cousin Hattie back in Staunton) to prepare for a career in politics. After a couple of unfulfilling years as a lawyer in Atlanta, however, he abandoned his law practice to pursue a graduate degree in government and history at Johns Hopkins. He also married the daughter of a Georgia Presbyterian preacher named Ellen Louise Axson in 1885. She would give him three beloved daughters, Margaret, Jessie, and Eleanor, in a marriage that was generally believed to be warm and happy (despite Ellen's bouts of depression and an affair Wilson was rumored to have had along the way).

In 1885, he began a career teaching history and politics at Bryn Mawr College. Three years later, he moved on to Wesleyan University. Two years after that, he returned to teach politics and history at Princeton, where he rapidly became the highest paid and most popular member of the faculty. In 1902, he was the unanimous choice to be named Princeton's president and, once appointed, promoted several academic and far-reaching financial reforms that elevated the school's stature and made Wilson a star.

Such highly visible success attracted the attention of the kingmakers of the state Democratic Party, who convinced him to successfully run for governor of New Jersey in 1910, where he pushed through a handful of sweeping parliamentary and social reforms that landed him on the presidential ticket just two years later.

In 1912, running on a "New Freedom" progressive platform based on individualism rather than government, Wilson prevailed in a hard-fought, three-way presidential contest between himself, former Progressive (Bull Moose) Party candidate Theodore Roosevelt, and Republican William Howard Taft, collecting only 42 percent of the popular vote—one of the lowest popular totals ever—of forty states in the electoral college.

He is remembered as a president of several "firsts"—the first (and only) to have earned a PhD degree; the first to have served as a college president; the first to hold a press conference and give an annual State of the Union address before Congress; even the first to throw out a baseball at a World Series game.

More important, though, he successfully maneuvered several major pieces of legislation through Congress that included reduced tariffs on imports for the first time in half a century, offset by legislation that established the first graduated income tax, and created the Federal Reserve System to give the nation a more stable money supply. These achievements were followed in 1916 by antitrust legislation that mandated the Federal Trade Commission to oversee unfair business practices, plus laws that regulated overseas shipping and provided the first government loans to struggling farmers. The regulations prohibited child labor and established the five-day workweek for railroad workers, a cultural shift in American labor that would spread to the broader workforce within a decade.

There were also significant contradictions. For a man who instituted segregation across the rank-and-file government offices, Wilson also nominated the first Jewish justice to the Supreme Court, Louis Brandeis, destined to become one of the court's greatest jurists. He initially opposed passage of the Nineteenth Amendment, which gave women the right to vote, but later supported its passage thanks to lobbying by his daughters.

As World War I consumed mainland Europe, Wilson successfully campaigned for reelection on the isolationist slogan "He kept us out of war." Not long after taking the oath of office for a second time, however, on April 2, 1917, he asked the new Republican-dominated Congress to declare war on Germany, committing more than two million American troops to the fight in Europe. It was the first time America had ever sent soldiers abroad to defend foreign soil. More than one hundred thousand would fail to come home.

When the conflict ended a year later and the armistice was signed, Wilson went to Paris to promote America's hopes of building lasting international peace through a program of fourteen points that included a "general association of nations . . . affording mutual guarantee of political independence and territorial integrity to great and small states." The press gave his visionary idea a shorthand name—the League of Nations.

After months of lobbying for his plan in France, Wilson presented the Treaty of Versailles and his fourteen points to a US Senate dominated by isolationist Republicans. "Dare we reject it and break the heart of the world?" he rhetorically asked. The Senate rejected the idea by a margin of just eight votes. Many historians today believe rejection of Wilson's grand scheme of peace—choosing instead to unleash stern retribution upon Germany by our bitter European Allies—sowed the seeds for the Second World War.

The League of Nations was Wilson's greatest hope and biggest failure—though the idea would take root and flower as the United Nations several decades later.

In a desperate effort to save the treaty, against his doctor's orders, Wilson decided to take his lofty plan directly to the American people on a grueling national whistle-stop campaign to mobilize public support. He spoke for several hours each day during the cross-country trip, which stretched on for weeks and, ultimately, proved too much. Following a speech in Pueblo, Colorado, in which he proclaimed that 80 percent of Americans supported his League of Nations, the president suffered a devastating stroke from which he never recovered.

Incredibly, for seventeen months, behind closed doors, Edith Wilson and Wilson's chief of staff kept the true state of the president's condition hidden from the American people. To this day, many believe Edith Wilson served as de facto president during the latter days of her husband's term, studying his papers and making decisions she believed her husband would sanction.

"Woodrow Wilson," sums up his biographer H. W. Brands, "lived too long and then died too soon." Following a slow recovery from his stroke, he continued to promote the treaty and the League of Nations even as many Americans adopted a strong isolationist mood. In 1920, the Congress passed the Eighteenth Amendment, which prohibited the sale of alcohol in the United States, a measure Wilson strongly opposed. But it was the beginning of the Jazz Age in America, a period when the public turned against the lofty idealism that Woodrow Wilson represented, as his influence irrevocably waned.

The Wilsons retired to a quiet house on Washington's S Street above Dupont Circle, where the ailing president talked about mounting a third presidential campaign that never materialized.

He died peacefully on February 3, 1924.

Though I am familiar with many of these facts from excellent biographies by A. Scott Berg and H. W. Brands, the Wilson presidential museum provides a welcome refresher course—and personal context—that intimately connects me with memories of my dad and his newspaperman's passion for history. The day's big question, however, remains largely unanswered—why Opti's thing for Woodrow Wilson?

A surprising answer comes in the museum gift shop, of all places, as I'm poking about for some modest Wilsonian knickknack to commemorate my own birthday in Staunton, and come across a sleeve of official Woodrow Wilson presidential golf balls.

"Did Wilson play golf?" I ask the gift shop manager, Lissa Dod.

"My goodness, yes!" Dod declares with zeal, pulling something out of a drawer that turns out to be a six-page treatise titled *Wilson and Golf*.

The first line is the clincher. "Woodrow Wilson is estimated to have played twelve hundred rounds of golf during his 8-year presidential term." That's four hundred more, I realize, than golf-mad Dwight Eisenhower played during his two terms in office, and nine hundred more than golf-crazy Barack Obama!

The article provides a comprehensive account of Wilson's addiction to the Scottish game of his ancestors. For a bloke who played so devotedly, it's somewhat baffling that W.W. (same initials, by the way, as my grandfather) rarely broke 100 with his game and once produced a score of 164 strokes, committing to his diary afterward: "One of the worst golf days I have had since I began." At one point, he memorably forced an aged (and slightly baffled) Ulysses S. Grant to tag along and watch him hit balls. After Wilson missed the ball with a swing, the old general dryly remarked, "It does seem to be good exercise. But what is the *ball* for?"

Like many golfers, however, Wilson used the game to get his mind off work and the daily pressures of life, a way to ease stress and get some exercise, often accompanied by his first wife, Ellen. After her death, he played alone for a time, typically taking to the fairways in the late afternoon. One of his first meetings with widow and Washington socialite Edith Galt came following a round of golf: the two soon went off to the Homestead Resort in Hot Springs, Virginia, for their honeymoon, playing golf every morning during the visit.

Up until the moment of his stroke in 1919, wherever he went on official business, Wilson's golf clubs went along, including to Paris for the signing of the Treaty of Versailles. After the stroke, Wilson's doctor and chief aides falsely spoke to the press of the president's "improving condition and keen desire to get back on the course," in order to obscure his real condition. He never made it to the first tee again, but he favored his old golf cap to the end of his days, wearing it on several occasions when guests came to visit on S Street, where his golf bag hung in the library.

There's even an annual golf tournament that supports the work of the museum and library, I learn from Lissa Dod, at which point a light bulb goes on in my head. Perhaps *golf* is the simple answer I seek.

Suddenly, I can see it: my dad's admiration for a flawed but self-made fellow Southerner who strove for an impossible vision of world peace only to come up short and find spiritual comfort in a lonely and inscrutable game invented by crafty Presbyterian shepherds that's meant to underscore man's utter fallibility in a world predestined to fail.

Whatever the truth of it, in honor of my old man's admiration for W.W. and a delightful morning at his museum, instead of golf balls or a presidential coffee mug (neither of which I need or want) I fill out a membership form for the museum's League of Friends, the support organization that provides 80 percent of the museum and library's funding for educational programs that promote Woodrow Wilson's ideals of international peace, domestic reform, and an informed citizenry.

Mully is still snoozing in a patch of sunlight on her travel blanket when I get back to the car. The snow has stopped and the noon sun has bobbed out, rapidly melting the snow. Reluctant to wake the old girl, I slip across the slushy street to have a second look at the pipes in the smoke shop window. Almost every drawing I've ever seen of early Wagon Road travelers shows someone—old geezer or young boy—thoughtfully smoking a pipe of some kind, a small source of comfort far from home in an uncertain wilderness.

Drawn by smoke and memory, I return to my car with an elegantly carved Italian Mastro Geppetto briar pipe and a small pouch of mild Virginia burley tobacco called Shenandoah Blend, where I find Miss Mully sitting up, bright-eyed, ready for her midday walkabout.

I pack my new pipe, fire it up, hook her up again to the lead, and set off in search of a pub somewhere in town where, four decades ago, I received a cosmic nudge from the universe that changed my life.

One afternoon in the spring of 1983, I phoned my dad from Vice President George Bush's office to tell him I no longer wanted to be a journalist.

Bush and I were friendly from traveling together in the 1980 presidential election, and I was in Washington, DC, to interview for my dream job at the newspaper where my old man was working the year I was born. Unfortunately, after nearly six years as one of the youngest staff writers at the *Sunday Magazine* of the *Atlanta Journal-Constitution*, the oldest Sunday magazine in the nation (where Margaret Mitchell reportedly worked when she wrote *Gone with the Wind*), I was weary of writing about murder and mayhem in the Sodom of the South. I'd just turned thirty.

"Let me ask you something," Opti asked calmly after I'd poured out my tale of premature career angst. "When was the last time you played golf?"

"I think Carter's polls were still good."

He suggested that I change my flight plans back to Atlanta. He'd pick me up in Raleigh. The next morning, he was waiting with my dusty Haig Ultra clubs in the back seat of his car. We drove straight to Pinehurst and played historic No. 2, where I barely broke one hundred.

Afterward, we sat on the Donald Ross porch drinking beer and talking about everything except my early midlife career crisis.

"So why do you want to give up journalism?" he finally asked.

I joked that journalism was supposed to be good for democracy, but it was making me feel crappy. "I'm sick of making a living on the sorrows of others," I lamented, pointing out that so many of my pieces were about Southern conmen, race violence, and murder victims in a "City Too Busy to Hate," as Atlanta styled itself.

Opti came back with: "Here's a thought. If you could do anything, what would that be?"

I quipped that I'd love to be a professional golfer but couldn't break a hundred. Or maybe a NASA astronaut—the first English lit major to walk on the moon. Short of these goals, I thought I might move to Vermont, a place I'd never been, and learn to fly-fish.

He simply smiled and observed that he would hate to see me give up writing.

"You may laugh at this," he added, "but have you ever thought that you're just writing the wrong things? Instead of subjects that you hate, why not write about things you love?"

I did laugh. It was vintage Opti. As was the kicker.

"In my experience, Bo, if you tell the universe what your heart really desires, you might be surprised by the results."

I looked at his wonderful old face and steel-blue eyes. My dad possessed the same calm demeanor and ease with the storms of life as his own father, a trait that endeared my old man to everyone who knew him. I could only dream of achieving this kind of grace someday, somehow.

He knew what was really eating me.

It was the tenth anniversary of my girlfriend Kristin's murder, an event I'd never spoken about to anyone, much less come to terms with. My big journalism break in Atlanta had come not long after her murder, and writing, not talking, had offered me the chance to delve into the darkest corners of the human heart. As my wise old man instinctively knew, I'd been trying to outrun a ghost.

A week after that, I withdrew my name from the Washington job, handed in my resignation to my wonderful editor at the *Sunday Magazine*, and headed for a trout stream in Vermont.

Halfway there, at the suggestion of an older writer friend, I stopped off for a few weeks at the Virginia Center for the Creative Arts in the Blue Ridge mountains to start work on a novel about a south Georgia farm family. The project was destined to fail. My heart really wasn't in it. But that failure was the key to finding my future.

At the art colony, I made a trio of friends that included a gifted young female novelist named Carole, a brilliant young film composer named Paul, and a roguish eighty-year-old poet named Phil, a widower and former professor of mythology on his way to work as a Peace Corps volunteer in East Africa.

The four of us spent many afternoons hiking together in the George Washington National Forest, slaking our thirsts afterward at a pub in downtown Staunton. During his last couple days before shoving off for Kenya, Phil the Poet gave us each a book from his portable library. "You strike me as a young fella about to take a hero's journey," he said to me that final evening at the pub, as he handed me a well-worn book. "Consider this food for the journey. You'll need it. Trust your heart and the universe to lead you."

It was a well-worn copy of Joseph Campbell's *Hero with a Thousand Faces*, the 1949 spiritual classic on the symbolism of mythology. Campbell was one of Kristin's favorite authors.

I was startled to hear Phil's words, because they were eerily like the ones that came from my father's own mouth just six weeks before.

That November, I found a small cabin heated by only a woodstove on the banks of the winding Green River outside of West Brattleboro, Vermont, and acquired a golden retriever pup from the Windham County Humane

Society. A short time later, my New York publisher introduced me to one of his favorite authors, a wonderful fellow named Judson Hale, the editor of *Yankee* magazine, who invited me to become the first senior writer and only Southerner in the legendary magazine's eighty-year history.

It was the smartest move of my career. I made great friends and wrote about things I loved—history, poets, improbable adventurers, and eccentric Yankees. In the spring, I took up fly-fishing and playing golf on an old nine-hole course in Brattleboro where Rudyard Kipling supposedly played during the time he lived and worked in the area. Several Kipling books sat on a bookshelf in my bedroom back home in Carolina.

It all seemed somehow connected. I even started attending church again.

Looking back, living alone with my dog Amos during that intensely cold first Northern winter was exactly what my soul needed, the happiest winter of my life up till then. Together, Amos and I took long walks every evening over snow-crusted roads, and I came to deeply love the Arctic night sky with stars that glittered like polished diamonds. I even saw the Northern Lights for the first time. Best of all, I read—or reread—every book I wanted to read including all of Joe Campbell's works, the essays of Ralph Waldo Emerson, and a dozen other writers, poets, and philosophers.

Was I on a hero's journey? To this day, I'm still not certain. All I know for sure is that my life took a wonderful turn toward healing and the "kingdom within" after my time with my hiking pals in Staunton.

Unfortunately, Mully and I are unable to find the pub where this cosmic "aha" moment with Phil the Poet and the others took place.

Pretty Staunton has grown dramatically. And maybe so have I.

Heading back to the car, we stop at a gourmet bakery on West Beverley for coffee and an afternoon muffin. The young woman running the place makes a show over Mully, offering the old girl an organic homemade dog biscuit. She's happy to accept.

Half an hour down the highway, I see a sign for historic Cyrus McCormick Farm and Workshop in Steeles Tavern, another place I've driven past for years and always intended to someday check out. No better time than now.

The former 625-acre farm, originally called Walnut Grove Farm, is the ancestral home of inventor Robert McCormick, the grandson of Scottish immigrants. His son Cyrus Hall McCormick turned his father's modest grain thresher into a mechanized reaper that was eventually hailed as one of the ten most important inventions in history. Patented in 1834, the world-famous McCormick reaper was credited with changing agricultural production worldwide, able to do in an hour what twenty field workers took a full day to accomplish. Today, the farm is an agricultural research and extension center, owned and operated by Virginia Tech since the mid-1950s.

Curiously, not a soul is around on this now-mild winter afternoon to expand upon the McCormick saga, though I glean a great deal from the excellent mounted displays presented on the walls of the restored log workshop where farm mechanization was born, including a spectacular replica of his original grain reaper.

The exhibit explains that, tinkering in the blacksmith shop below, young Cyrus built his first reaper at age twenty-two and spent the next six decades of his life revising and improving the prototype of the modern-day farm combine. More than one hundred reaper machines came from this modest log workshop until McCormick decided that the Midwest—soon to be hailed as the "breadbasket of the nation"—provided a better marketplace for his wondrous newfangled machine.

In 1847 McCormick relocated to Chicago and opened the first of his factories for manufacturing the improved McCormick reaper, founding the world's largest farm equipment company in the process. Three years later, his pioneering mechanical reaper was being used (and copied by competitors) in every state in America. By the time he captured the Grand Prize of Honor at the Paris International Exposition in 1855, despite being mocked by the London *Times* as "a cross between an Astley Chariot and a wheelbarrow," McCormick's reaper was known by farmers around the world, hailed as one of the "greatest inventions of mankind," by a jury of judges in Paris.

Unfortunately, the Great Chicago Fire of 1871 left McCormick's Chicago factory in ruins. But in true American fashion, the elderly inventor and businessman made a spectacular comeback, partnering with his son and namesake to create International Harvester, the world's largest farm equipment company.

Before moving on, Mully and I follow a circular hiking path that winds through the McCormick property, following a small stream that feeds the waterwheel of the restored gristmill, reminding me of George Washington Tate's lost mill on the Haw. As we walk, the late-afternoon sky turns a deeper shade of gold laced with ribbons of purple as small brown-headed birds dart through the winter-bare trees along the path. We find a last good sunny spot to sit for a spell as the chilly afternoon slips into shadows around us.

With my best friend by my side, and Joe Campbell, Phil the Poet, and pipe-loving Opti the Mystic still on my mind, there is no rush to be anywhere else.

I pack and relight my new pipe with Shenandoah Blend and puff contentedly as my dog and I watch the foraging winter birds, even managing to send a few reasonably decent smoke rings into the still but chilly air that would have delighted my goslings once upon a time.

What a fine birthday it has been.

TWENTY-ONE

COUSIN STEVE

MR. DODSON," HE SAYS WITH A SLOW SOUTHERN DRAWL, "DO YOU HAVE A minute?"

"I do. How can I help you?"

It's middle March, the Pearl is gassed up, and I'm backing out of my driveway when this call comes, excited to be heading back to the GWR after a month at home attending to life, garden, and magazine deadlines. My wife has taken to telling friends that I have a hidden love life up in the Blue Ridge hills, a mistress named the Great Wagon Road.

At the other end of the line, he clears his throat. "You don't know me, sir, but a little bird tells me you are writin' about the old road that brought our Irish and Scottish kin here to North Carolina way back yonder. That pleases me to hear. I figure you might be curious to know more about our shared ancestor George Washington Tate."

He suddenly has my attention.

I learn that his name is Steve Lynch. He explains that we are cousins through our shared double-great-grandfather, George Washington Tate, the fellow whose vanished gristmill on the Haw planted the seed of the Great Wagon Road in my head almost six decades ago. It was Tate's own double-great-grandfather, also named George, I've learned since, who traveled from the docks of Philadelphia to the Hawfields of Piedmont, North Carolina, in the mid-eighteenth century. But this is the extent of my knowledge about these important ancestors.

Lynch mentions that he owns a small museum in his backyard near the historic Alamance Battleground south of Burlington that is dedicated to "both George Washingtons—America's first president and our George Washington Tate." He invites me to come over some afternoon to have a look. "You might be surprised to see what I've got."

"How about tomorrow?" I propose, happy to delay visiting my mistress in the hills by a day.

This is the latest in a string of revelations. Just three days ago, my father's first cousin Roger Dodson, a retired missionary who shares my fascination with the mystery of Aunt Emma Dodson's origins and inexplicable suicide, brought me something incredible: the only known photograph of Aunt Emma, found buried in an old Dodson family album. To my eye, the placid features of my grandfather's mother look distinctly Native American. I also suspect that dear Roger Dodson may be the "little bird" who opened this unexpected hidden door to Cousin Steve, possibly drawing both of us one step closer to the truth.

I offer to bring the photograph of Aunt Emma to Steve and ask if he has heard the stories about her.

He chuckles. "Yessir, Brother Jim. I heard all about her when I was a'growin' up. I do believe the stories about her are true. But you come over tomorrow round about two and I'll show you some things that may help clear things up a bit."

Lynch, seventy, turns out to be a decorated Vietnam vet, retired police detective, and longtime DA investigator, a thirty-third-degree Mason and descendant of one of North Carolina's signers of the Declaration of Independence. He's also a grade A certified American history geek and serious military collector for whom the past is not just alive and kicking but a source of daily happiness that he enthusiastically shares with visiting school and community groups as well as individuals who find their way to the most charming backyard museum in North Carolina.

This tribute to a pair of George Washingtons sits in a well-tended garden less than a mile from where a group of ragtag farmers and local militiamen fought against British colonial rule in a skirmish known as the War of

Regulation in 1767, regarded by some historians as the opening shot of the American Revolution. Lynch Lodge, as he calls his tidy museum, is housed in a pair of sturdy Amish-built sheds artfully fused together and fronted by a porch where Lynch and his wife, Betsy, often sit and admire a garden that features a tall American flagpole and live boxwood shrubs rooted from cuttings from Thomas Jefferson's own Poplar Forest estate, George Washington's Mount Vernon, and the Governor's Palace at Williamsburg. Even Cousin Steve's bushes have historical provenance.

Inside, I find an unbelievable array of historic artifacts and original documents, paintings, and maps, not to mention hundreds of vintage collectibles bearing the likeness of America's first president—everything from commemorative tobacco tins to antique liquor bottles to presidential fireplace andirons; china plates with portraits of Mount Vernon and Martha Washington; a first-edition twin-volume *History of the American Revolution* featuring the writings of our founding president; plus at least a dozen statue heads including a brass bank sitting on a shelf below Gilbert Stuart's famous unfinished portrait of Washington.

"A fella I visited who owned a plantation house down in Little Washington gave me that rare print years ago. Just lifted it off the wall and sent it home with me," Cousin Steve explains, shaking his fluffy silver head. "Can you believe that?" He moves on to an original newspaper clipping of Washington's obituary from December 1799, cleverly hidden behind a rare gilt-framed portrait of Washington from 1786 holding a copy of the US Constitution on his lap.

I ask what it is about Washington that so fascinates him.

"Well, Brother Jim, he was our first president and decided he didn't want to be a king. You gotta like a fella like that. He was also a dedicated Mason. I wish politicians today would emulate the way George Washington lived and looked at the world."

He pauses and smiles.

"Also, I'm rather partial to the name."

With this, he hands me a copy of the only known photograph of George Washington Tate, taken late in life, a well-dressed older gentleman with thinning gray hair, kind but weary eyes, and a grimly resolved smile. A silver watch chain dangles from his dark vest.

"That was taken after he came home from the war," Steve explains. "Probably about the time he received a patent for improving Cyrus McCormick's reaping machine."

"Wait," I say with a laugh. "Slow down. You mean the Civil War?"

"Yessir, Brother Jim. He was a colonel in the North Carolina Forty-Sixth Infantry."

Steve shows me official documents from both national and state Civil War databases that confirm that George Washington Tate joined the Confederate army on February 22, 1862—the *other* George Washington's birthday—and was assigned the starting rank of major in the Eleventh Brigade of the North Carolina Forty-Sixth Infantry Regiment, the so-called Burke Rifles from Orange and Chatham Counties. He served under the command of a man who had previously been an officer in the British Army and left his post as a professor of history for the University of North Carolina to take up arms in the rebellion. At that moment, George Tate was a thirty-three-year-old father of four, third-degree Master Mason of the local Masonic Temple, gristmill owner, and Methodist church elder. His middle daughter, Mary Emma Tate, my great-grandmother, would have been either two or four years old during this time, depending on which of her conflicting recorded birth dates is accurate.

"By the way," adds my host, "those are his too. They went with him to the war."

He nods at items hanging above his desk: a plain silver pocket watch on a chain (seen in the photograph) and a portable fork and spoon darkened by time. I stand looking at them in one hand, Tate's clear-eyed photo in the other, recalling what Keith Rocco said to me about artifacts connecting us directly to people and events of the past, items of living history. Indeed, at that moment I am feeling like a kid who has stepped through a portal into the ambered past, equal parts astonished and darkly thrilled at this discovery of my family's "Lost Confederate" who came home from the war and allegedly never spoke of his service, most likely because many of his Dodson kinfolk were opposed to secession and slavery on religious grounds.

Cousin Steve explains further that local Lynches and Nelsons—a pair of Scottish immigrant clans that intermarried with the brothers Tate—also signed up to fight that winter of 1862, heirs of immigrant families that also came down the Great Wagon Road to Alamance County about the time George Tate and his younger brother made the trip through the frontier in the mid-1700s. He shows me a document that indicates that the brothers were in fact among the first settlers of the Hawfields, as this part of the northern Piedmont was then called, and that George's first son, James, married Margaret Nelson, daughter of David Nelson, on May 16, in 1785. They had eight children.

"This is the same branch of Nelsons that went on to Texas after the war—Willie Nelson's people, which makes us directly related to Willie." Cousin Steve clearly relishes my reaction to these surprising details, which keep on coming.

As it turned out, G. W. Tate's regiment initially saw limited rearguard action until it joined Lee's second attempt to invade the North in middle summer 1863, at which point he led 617 men into battle on the first day of the Battle of Gettysburg at Seminary Ridge, suffering two hundred casualties in the process. On day three of the fight, July 3, the Burke Rifles joined an all-out assault on Major General George Meade's deeply entrenched troops on Cemetery Hill. Lee's own general in charge of the assault, Lieutenant General James Longstreet, presciently questioned the wisdom of sending nine infantry brigades—twelve thousand men—three-quarters of a mile over open fields under heavy Union artillery bombardment and murderous rifle fire, a disaster that came to be known as Pickett's Charge, which suffered 50 percent casualties and effectively ended Lee's final attempt to invade Pennsylvania, underscoring the decline of Confederate fortunes. An additional one hundred of Colonel Tate's troops from the NC Eleventh were killed or wounded in the disastrous assault. (Perhaps this explains the psychic chill I felt on the beautiful December afternoon Wendy and I visited Gabor Boritt and his wife, Liz, at their beautiful farm overlooking the site of Pickett's Charge, a month after my big day at the Gettysburg Address.)

In any case, Cousin Steve's documents provide the rest of the story. During the Eleventh's hasty retreat to Virginia, with more than half of its numbers missing, dead, wounded, or captured, 86 of the regiment's soldiers were captured by Union cavalry as they attempted to recross the Potomac at Falling Waters. Despite such losses, the reinforced regiment went on to fight at the siege of Petersburg, Spotsylvania Courthouse, and the

Wilderness Campaign, losing an additional 182 men before joining Lee at Appomattox Court House in April 1865.

Colonel George Washington Tate reportedly resigned his command on April 3, three days before Lee signed the articles of surrender. The North Carolina Eleventh Infantry Regiment finished the fight with just eight surviving officers and seventy-four enlisted men. "Old George changed out of his uniform before the surrender and rode home to start his civilian life and never mentioned his years in the war," Cousin Steve solemnly confirms. "He'd done his part. And then got on with life."

As we stand in momentary silence, I feel a deep sense of gratitude to have finally solved the mystery of the family's phantom Confederate. It's so overwhelming, in fact, I almost miss what Cousin Steve casually dropped about Tate "reinventing" Cyrus McCormick's famous grain reaper machine.

"You're not going to believe this," I tell him with a shake of the head, "but I've just come from McCormick's Farm on the Wagon Road. My dog and I had the entire place to ourselves."

He grins. "How 'bout that, Brother Jim. Reckon it's good that I called you. Looky here . . . "

He points to a large gilt-framed US patent hanging on the wall above his desk, an ornate government document granted to Georgie Washington Tate in 1878. An official citation reads: "For significantly improving the production capacity of Cyrus McCormick's famous grain reaping machine from 1840."

"Tate's version of the machine—the only one that was ever granted its own patent, by the way—tripled the machine's production capabilities, revolutionizing American farming," Steve explains. "This was a fellow who came home from a terrible war and made a real difference in people's lives. I like to think that redeemed him. That's why I think of him as our family's own George Washington."

He then shows me a detailed map of Orange, Alamance, and Guilford Counties that Tate officially surveyed and drew for the state in 1891, plus an early newspaper clipping about his successful mill and furniture shop on Haw Creek. A pastoral illustration depicts a turning waterwheel headlined "George Tate's Mill" and a poem titled "Grandpa's Mill," with a concluding stanza that goes: "The water's no longer falling / the stones no longer grind / But the Old Mill is still running / If only in my mind."

"He really was one remarkable fellow," my host muses. "A jack of all trades—artisan, tinkerer, inventor, soldier, map and furniture maker, and church elder—even an accomplished artist. Check this out."

I follow Steve back to the front door, where an oil painting of a light-house on the Carolina coast is displayed on an easel. "That's the famous Hatteras Lighthouse. This painting hung for many years at the state history museum. I got it from a collector who picked it up when the museum sold off some of its older pieces."

"Wait," I say, struggling to catch up with this runaway narrative. "The newspaper clipping said Haw *Creek*. Wasn't Tate's mill on the Haw River?"

"Nossir. They're different. The creek leads into the river." He shows me the map again. Tate's Mill is clearly designated on Haw Creek.

I explain how, as a kid, I was shown the remains of Tate's mill in the Haw River. Fickle is the memory of an awestruck thirteen-year-old.

"It may have been the creek that fed the river that you saw," Steve explains. "They're very close. Both are a major water source. I know an old fella who can take us directly to George's mill. It's still visible," he adds. "Maybe someday we'll go find it together."

It's a date, I agree.

As he walks me to the door, Cousin Steve Lynch wonders how long it will take me to finish my journey down the Wagon Road. I'm already start-ing my third calendar year of travel, I sheepishly explain, a case of balancing my boyhood fantasy with the realities of life and work.

"I do plan to follow it till the string ends, however," I add, using an old reporter's slogan.

Steve grins. "I like that! Bet our Scottish ancestors said that same thing as they came down that old road. Hold on, wait a second! There's something I want you to have for your travels . . . "

He walks back to his desk, removes a small item from the shelf, and returns with it in his hand. He places it in my palm: a well-worn Confeder-ate Army brass belt buckle stained by time or blood or both, bearing the familiar raised CS insignia.

"This belonged to our double-great-grandfather, who took the same road home that you're traveling. I want you to have it."

For a moment, I have no idea what to say. I simply thank him for an extraordinary afternoon of family revelations.

Cousin Steve smiles with visible emotion. He takes a moment to find his voice.

"Brother Jim, we share a love for American history and a remarkable man. That's in our blood and heritage. So, you take old G.W.'s belt buckle with you on down that road, however long it takes. Then come on back here and we'll go find his long-lost mill together."

TWENTY-TWO

THE GHOSTS OF LEXINGTON

OVER EASTERN VIRGINIA FRIED OYSTERS AND A LOCAL BREW CALLED DEVILS Backbone at the swanky Georges Inn, I meet my friend the Rev. David Cox for a late lunch. We are in Lexington, the picturesque Wagon Road town of 7,500 residents, home to Washington and Lee University and the Virginia Military Institute.

David and I met three years ago on a crisp mid-October afternoon not long after the faculty of Washington and Lee voted overwhelmingly 188 to 51 to remove Robert E. Lee's name from both the university's name and the historic chapel the general had built during the five years he served as Washington College's president following the Civil War.

The news cast a national spotlight on Lexington and fueled a major backlash from W&L alumni, including major donors who threatened to cease financial support of the university, a private liberal arts institution that has produced several Supreme Court justices, twenty-seven US senators, sixty-seven US representatives, thirty-one state governors, a Nobel laureate, and several winners of the Pulitzer Prize in its long and distinguished history.

I came in late 2019 hoping Cox, author, former rector of R.E. Lee Memorial Church, now Grace Episcopal Church, professor of history and religion at nearby Southern Virginia University in Buena Vista, could provide perspective on the controversy and maybe help me resolve my own complex feelings about Lee, one of the most tragic figures of the Civil War. I began by asking a straightforward question: Did Lee's actions after the war somehow redeem him in any way?

"In a sense, that is the very question that haunts many who've struggled to come to terms with his service and postwar life," Cox tells me on that gorgeous October Saturday. "Given Lee's role as the commanding Confederate general who led an armed rebellion against the United States, is he worthy of being remembered for the genuine good work he did after the war? Or is his sin of insurrection beyond redemption?"

"In your opinion, which is it?" I'm curious, having finished both of Cox's outstanding books on Lee's spiritual life and namesake chapel.

My learned lunch mate smiles. "If you'll pardon the unintentional pun, it's not an easy black-or-white issue. How about we take a walk after lunch and you can decide for yourself."

Over the next two hours, as the afternoon shadows lengthen and roars from W&L's football stadium echo through the cozy lanes of the town, my host walks me all over the beautiful campus detailing the school's beginnings as a pioneer institution called Augusta Academy, established by Scots-Irish Presbyterians in 1749. The academy relocated to Lexington in 1780, chartered as Liberty Hall Academy in the wake of patriotic fervor.

Liberty Hall admitted its first African American student in 1795, a free Black man named John Chavis, who fought in the revolution before going on to study at the College of New Jersey (Princeton University) and become an ordained Presbyterian minister. One year later, a gift of twenty thousand dollars from George Washington saved Liberty Hall from insolvency, at that time one of the largest gifts ever given to an American educational institution. In gratitude, the trustees renamed the school Washington Academy. In 1813, the school was rechartered as Washington College. One year later, an eight-foot statue of George Washington by sculptor Matthew Kahle was placed on top of Washington Hall on the campus's historic Colonnade, hence to be known as "Old George."

Prior to the Civil War, Washington College students raised a Confederate flag in support of Virginia's secession, and some of its students even joined the Stonewall Brigade. During a brief occupation of Lexington by

Union forces, Captain Henry du Pont refused to burn the school's stately Colonnade in deference to the statue of Old George atop Washington Hall.

In the aftermath of the war, the college was in shambles, along with the state at large. An equally destitute Lee turned down a surprising number of business opportunities in favor of taking the job of rebuilding struggling Washington College.

"What's not widely known, however, which certainly speaks to Lee's character, I think, is that he initially hesitated to take the job in Lexington," Cox reminds me as we walk, "fearing he might not be physically up to the task or, worse, would burden the struggling institution with the long shadow of a defeated secessionist. At his wife Mary's insistence, however, he turned down other opportunities, including a couple from Northern colleges, and accepted the job in Lexington."

"Lee came to Lexington with the overarching objective of promoting peace and reconciliation in the theoretically reunited nation," writes Cox in *Lee Chapel at 150*, "a goal that could only be accomplished by rebuilding the South. Restoring prosperity would rely on people who were trained to know what they were doing. The college could equip them for their jobs. But attaining the larger goal of genuine peace also depended upon people of character, people of what the Revolutionary generation of his father called 'virtue.' Lee saw in his college the opportunity to promote both qualities in his students, who then could lead the South, and the nation, in both practical and principled ways."

That newfound humility was on full display when the newly appointed president arrived in September 1865. Unknown to Lee, the college's trustees had organized a lavish inauguration event to mark the school's new era, including a brass band accompanied by young girls robed in white and bearing chaplets of flowers, who welcomed the new president and invited dignitaries from across the nation.

"But Lee would have none of it," writes Cox. "All he wanted was to take the oath of office and get to work."

And work he did. Over a short tenure of just five years before his death, Lee reimagined the basic purpose of American higher education. In place of the college's traditional focus on training ministers, teachers, and lawyers, he instituted a much broader curriculum that—radical for its day—could equip students to pursue whatever vocations they aspired to by introducing an elective system of courses that included Practical Chemistry, Experimental Philosophy, Practical Mechanics (funded by a ten-thousand-dollar grant from inventor Cyrus McCormick), Applied Mathematics, Modern Languages, and History and Literature, as well as advanced training in civil engineering, astronomy, geology, natural history, business, and journalism. As Cox points out, "Lee and his faculty aspired to meet the wants of the country and Southern education by trying to give the broadest and most thorough development to the practical and industrial sciences of the age."

One of the most telling things about Lee's forward-thinking vision, Cox explains, was the fact that so many of his fresh educational ideas were later embraced by other reform-minded programs of younger presidents at Harvard and Cornell. Though Lee's deep religious faith shaped every aspect of his Lexington life, among the new president's first acts was to abolish mandatory chapel attendance by students, which Harvard and Yale also did decades later. Ditto mandatory learning of Greek, which Lee believed had little practicality when rebuilding a nation devastated by civil war.

In 1867, Lee oversaw the construction of a new college chapel designed to hold everything from daily chapel services to visiting lectures, concerts, and graduation ceremonies. The beautiful Victorian Romanesque revival brick chapel with its arched medieval windows, probably the work of Lee's son George Washington Custis Lee, was destined to play a large role in the future of Washington and Lee University. It not only became the spiritual and social epicenter of the campus but also housed Lee's personal office in the basement. Soon after Lee's death in 1870, his friends and family commissioned a statue of Lee asleep on an unnamed battlefield by sculptor Edward Valentine. The work proved too large for the basement room where Lee was first interred, so an apse was added to the chapel where the altar stands in a traditional Christian church. Upon its unveiling in 1883, the statue became the chapel's most notable feature. The basement of the chapel became the Lee family crypt.

During our campus walk, my generous host shows me every space of stately Lee Chapel, including the old general's basement office, the famous

Valentine sculpture of Lee in repose, the Lee family crypt, and even the spot where the general's beloved horse, Traveller, was interred.

As we leave the building, Cox stresses that Lee never intended for the stately brick chapel with its elegant steeple and classic arched Norman windows to bear his name. It was his preference for it to simply be called College Chapel, a place meant to hold daily chapel for the students and faculty, host graduation ceremonies, and provide a meditative space for generations of famous visiting speakers ranging from poets to presidents.

"Whatever else can be said about Robert Edward Lee," Cox sums up, "he embraced a living faith that has forgiveness at its core. There is no question that he probably saved Washington College from an unhappy fate."

Cox says this as we are standing in Lee's office in the chapel, preserved exactly as he left it to go home for a meal before a meeting of his fellow leaders of the Episcopal church on September 28, 1870. It was a tedious meeting. As he rose to say grace over the family, he couldn't speak. They fetched his army cot, set it up in the dining room, and placed him there. He never recovered, dying on October 10.

Days after his passing, in gratitude for his service, the board of trustees unanimously voted to add Lee's name to that of the college's original benefactor, George Washington.

"How do you think Lee would have felt about that?" I ask Lee's most interesting biographer as we stand at the edge of the campus looking at President Lee's former home.

"I'm not sure he would have wanted that honor," Cox replies. "He was a genuinely humble man who detested the culture of the Lost Cause that was springing up around him and only intensified with his passing. I think he wished to be simply remembered as a good man who may have somehow redeemed himself in the eyes of the world—and more importantly, his God—by helping to save a promising college that was destined to become one of the country's leading universities. I place the period there."

It seems like the perfect coda. But then, as we shake hands, my thoughtful host reflects: "However you choose to interpret his life and legacy, Robert E. Lee lives on in the minds of many as either a classically flawed hero or tragic failure. He was probably both. That will probably never change. By the way, his beloved horse lives on too."

Cox points to the stable doors beside Lee's former residence.

"When the general and Mary Custis Lee resided there, that was where Traveller lived until he died at age twenty-five. According to W&L lore, the stable doors are always standing open because, as generations of W&L students believe, Traveller lets himself out at night to wander through the town looking for his master."

It's a spooky thought, and I keep it in mind when I join a group of tourists that evening on a popular Lexington Ghost Tour led by a dandy dressed in the top hat and shabby silk waistcoat of an undertaker from a Dickens novel. The first story out of his mouth is the Traveller tale I heard from David Cox. He also mentions that Rockbridge County was a hotbed of Scots-Irish settlers who filtered down the Great Wagon Road to become the backbone of both George Washington's colonial militia and Lee's Confederate army.

Most of the tour, however, focuses on the life of Thomas "Stonewall" Jackson, commencing at the steps of the only house Jackson ever owned, on East Washington Street, during the years he worked as artillery instructor at the Virginia Military Institute. At the base of the steps, I notice a stone marker that curiously reads:

GEN. JACKSON CSA
Teacher and Gardener
1863

While living here, Jackson reportedly taught Black children to read and write in the basement of the Lexington Presbyterian Church, just one block from his front door. I first learned this surprising fact from a newspaper colleague whose father served as head pastor of the church for many years. The fact that he was evidently also a dedicated gardener makes me think there's possibly more to admire about my brother's Civil War hero beyond his battlefield brilliance.

The finale of the ghost walk leads us to Jackson's grave in the Oak Grove Cemetery (formerly called Stonewall Jackson Cemetery), where our guide tells the story of Stonewall's untimely demise in May 1863 from friendly fire at Chancellorsville. To this day, he adds, the general's ghost can still be seen walking slowly through the town's graveyard on moonlit nights.

"What about Little Sorrel, *his* horse?" pipes up a jolly fellow taking slugs for warmth from a pint in his windbreaker pocket.

"Oh yes, lest I forget, you can go see Little Sorrel down at the VMI Museum," our grave digger guide informs him. "He was Jackson's favorite horse, a tough little mount who was captured by the Yankees several times and returned to Confederate troops out of respect for his famous owner." Little Sorrel outlived his owner by two decades, he adds, and was a big hit at county fairs and rebel reunions, where Southern ladies would snip pieces of his mane for their jewelry. When the horse finally died, his remains were shipped to the Virginia Military Institute's museum "down the street," which had him stuffed and displayed.

On our way out of the cemetery, a young woman walking beside me at the rear of the group giggles nervously and points to a bearded figure in a Confederate officer uniform walking parallel to us among the headstones. As more people take notice, more nervous laughter erupts and the pace to the exit gates noticeably quickens. The effect is a big hit.

I'm half tempted to go after the ghostly rebel for a quick autograph, but he disappears as rapidly as he appears, confirming N.C. Wyeth's supernatural portrait of the man in the mist.

Now, three years later, it's good to learn and see that peace and change have finally come to pretty Lexington. Long gone are the Confederate flags, and Lost Cause iconography that used to adorn Lee Chapel, now renamed University Chapel, which is undergoing its third major renovation. Pretty Lexington is no longer haunted by reunions of the United Daughters of the Confederacy or gatherings of rowdy unrequited rebels as it did for over a century. Even the stolid Hotel Robert E. Lee has been artfully transformed into an upscale boutique hostelry called the Gin Hotel, popular with well-heeled hipsters and young professionals. Maybe best of all, the school's trustees eventually voted to keep the name Washington and Lee unchanged, a sign that past and present can peacefully coexist with visible mutual acknowledgment.

Equally pleasing to me, my good friend David Cox, a youthful seventy-five and grandfather of six, is more enthusiastic than ever about teaching American history to young students, having expanded his own curriculum to include classes on Race in America and America's Founding Mothers and Fathers.

"It's really been a fresh start. There are still a few ruffled feathers on both sides of the debate," he allows as we dine on delicious oysters and Devils Backbone ale. "But it's worth remembering that a similar crisis occurred back in the 1980s when Washington and Lee went coed. A lot of angry donors said 'never again'—which lasted until their granddaughters began applying for admission. That was a debate over who comes to the university. I saw this one as a debate over the identity of the school itself."

"How do you feel about the changes?"

Professor Cox smiles and takes a moment to finish his beer.

"You know, as an educator," he says, "I am careful not to render an opinion. In fact, I don't really have one. First and foremost, I am a devoted friend of this community and a historian. I will say, however, one thing I feel rather strongly about is that it is unfair to judge people of the past by our standards today—for that robs you of the context of history, the opportunity to show how we may, or may not, have progressed as a society. I remember something the president of the Civil War center in Richmond said when she spoke from the chapel pulpit during all the turmoil—an African American woman, no less. Please imagine, she said, how people one hundred and fifty years from now are going to be thinking about what we do today.

"I think that is a very good principle to live by," Professor Cox adds.

He wonders how my Wagon Road odyssey is going.

Slowly, I admit. But I wouldn't have it any other way. "The people I've met, the things I've learned, the stories I've heard . . . it's been a life-changing experience."

"The healing power of history," says Professor David Cox.

And with that, we order another round of the Devils Backbone.

TWENTY-THREE

THE BRIDGE OF GOD

ACCORDING TO AN ANCIENT LEGEND, A GROUP OF MONACAN INDIANS, A prehistoric woodland tribe of Eastern Siouan descent, were fleeing fierce Algonquin warriors when they came to a mighty gorge and prayed to the Great Spirit for deliverance. A stone bridge miraculously appeared and took them to safety. The grateful tribe named it the "Bridge of God."

Later, word spread of a wondrous landform unlike any other in the known world that came to inspire generations of adventurers and artists to set off into the wilderness of the James River region to have a look at this natural wonder of arched stone that soars fifty-five feet higher than Niagara Falls—including, according to lore, a daring youth named George Washington.

To this day, twenty-four feet above Cedar Creek, which flows beneath the arch, the initials "G.W." are clearly carved into the stone. Historians have debated its authenticity forever.

When he first laid eyes on the bridge in 1767, Thomas Jefferson wrote in his travel notebook that the bridge was "a Wonder of the New World— the most sublime of nature's works." Looking down for about a minute, he recorded, "gave me a headache." Eight years later, on July 5, 1774, Jefferson purchased the bridge and 157 acres from King George III for twenty shillings with plans to build a rustic lodge near the arch for an inspiring getaway spot. It never came to pass. Rockbridge County, however, was created and named after Natural Bridge just four years later. In 1809, an aging Jefferson put his sublime work of nature up for sale but found no buyers.

After the bridge became a popular destination for artists and landscape painters (eventually including the likes of Frederic Edwin Church and later Hudson River school landscape artist David Johnson) Jefferson's heirs were finally able sell the property to a new owner in 1833. He built a crude accommodation called the Forest Inn to serve growing numbers of "bridge seekers." A succession of inns and owners followed. So did presidents and other famous folks, including Herman Melville, who compared Virginia's great rock arch to the breeching white whale in *Moby-Dick*.

In the 1890s, a wealthy character named Colonel Henry Parsons erected the Natural Bridge Hotel on an adjacent hillside, anticipating the growth of backcountry "tourism" as roads improved and America's desire to see the nation's natural wonders took root. The hotel featured luxury rooms, a mineral health spa, fine dining, and a swimming pool.

It was still in operation when my parents honeymooned there in the summer of 1942, not long before my dad shipped off to the war in Europe. I have a photo of the newlyweds posing on the deck of the hotel swimming pool; Miss Western Maryland sits on her skinny groom's shoulders, both grinning with the unassailable optimism of youth in a world dissolving into chaos.

Years later, in April 1963, the original Natural Bridge Hotel caught fire and burned to the ground. In just two years, it was replaced by a grander brick affair that opened with pomp and ceremony. About that same time, I made the first of many visits to Natural Bridge, where I first heard the legend of the Bridge of God from my father and remember being amazed (and not a little frightened) that we'd driven directly over the arch on Highway 11 to get there. In 1998, Natural Bridge was designated a Natural Historic Landmark by the US Department of the Interior, and eighteen years later became the thirty-seventh state park of the commonwealth of Virginia.

Having visited the bridge many times in my life, I'm inclined to skip the park this lovely spring morning and make tracks down Highway 11 to the Star City of Roanoke, where I have a dear friend and a special church to check out.

But as Mully and I pass the Natural Bridge exit, something prompts me to turn around and go back, perhaps the simple sudden awareness that at my age—to quote those timeless poet philosophers Seals and Crofts—we may never pass this way again.

An hour before the official opening time, the reception center parking lot is empty save for a motor home, where its occupants are apparently sleeping. Since dogs are allowed on park premises with leads, I hook up Mully and head for the winding stone steps that descend past the two-thousand-year-old arborvitae to Cedar Creek at the base of the bridge.

As always, the first sight of the mighty stone arch rising above us stops me in my tracks. It does seem like the prehistoric architecture of the gods. Even Mully glances up with mild interest.

I'm pleased to see that young George's mark is where I left it, high up and safely unmolested by time and vandals, prompting us to move along the creek past the rebuilt Monacan village to the Lace Falls, where we sit for a while on a stone wall watching the water flow, a perfect reminder that time and nature wait for no man and his dog. I find myself thinking, however, about the Moravians who were believed to be the swiftest travelers of the Wagon Road, according to their well-kept diaries, and wonder if even they paused long enough as they crossed the arch to peer over the edge before pushing on to Big Lick, the colonial name of an early settlement that would be called Roanoke a century or so later.

This supernatural setting, especially at this early hour, speaks to the myth-loving kid in me. No wonder Jefferson desired to own it, and my own parents came here to celebrate their marriage vows, embracing something truly sublime. When we lose our myths, said Madeleine L'Engle, we lose our place in the universe.

On the way back to the reception center, Mully and I meet an elderly couple walking hand in hand to view the falls. They stop and give her head a scratch. Hank and Shirley are from Atlanta, I discover, my old stomping ground. They have a golden retriever named Jasper back in their van.

"We weren't sure you could bring dogs down here even on a leash," Shirley explains. "Jasper's young and full of energy."

Hank is a retired banker; Shirley works for the CDC. I learn that he proposed to her by the Lace Falls in 1977, right out of the navy. This is their first trip back to the Bridge of God. They are on their way to Connecticut to spend a few weeks with their four grown kids and nine grandchildren.

"But we couldn't pass here without stopping," Hank provides. "It's even more impressive than I remember."

We slip into talk about Atlanta. They own a house in the Morningside neighborhood. I lived for a time in nearby Virginia Highland. Once upon a time we were neighbors, though it feels a lifetime ago.

But then Shirley surprises me. "I remember reading your stories in the *Sunday Magazine*. I wondered where you went."

I'm both surprised and touched by her memory.

"If I may ask," says Hank, "why did you leave town?"

The short answer is that I'd been there almost seven years and never taken a vacation, I explain. I wanted to learn how to fly-fish. Though I'd never been to Vermont, that seemed like the best place to go.

The more complicated answer, which I'd shared with only one other person (my wife, Wendy), is that a week or so after my dad and I had our life-changing conversation about writing on the Donald Ross porch in Pinehurst, I'd awakened in the darkness of my Midtown Atlanta bedroom to find Kristin standing at the foot of my bed. I later told myself it must have been just a vivid dream, but the visitation was so powerful and lifelike, decades later I'm convinced that she was really standing there speaking to me. Crazy, I know, but I've lived long enough not to discount such healing encounters from people who lost loved ones that returned to provide comfort or—as in my case—a message. As she stood there looking as beautiful and alive as ever, she smiled.

"Pook, it's time for you to leave here and go north. That's where you'll find what you are looking for. I'll always love you."

"Pook" was her pet nickname for me. After she vanished, I sat still in my bed and wept, wishing I'd had the courage to attend her burial service.

Naturally, I'm not about to share anything about this to these two nice people who remember my time in Atlanta. I simply give them the short answer.

Hank smiles. "Did Vermont work out for you?"

"Without question."

I start to tell them about how, during the year I lived on the Green

River in West Brattleboro, I went to work for *Yankee* magazine and met a young woman fresh out of Radcliffe named Alison. We soon got married and moved to a forested hill near the coast of Maine, where we built a post-and-beam house, and I planted my first garden, and we had two beautiful babies.

But I suddenly realize that I'm rambling, probably sharing way too much. (Mully's expression seems to confirm as much.)

"How wonderful," chimes Shirley. "I understand Maine is *fabulous.*"

"I meant to stay there for the rest of my life."

"You're not still there?" asks Hank.

Reluctantly—nota bene: *please* stop talking, Jim!—I explain that after a decade of marriage, amicable divorce, and remarriage, I had a chance to come home to the South and teach at a historic university in Virginia and start a couple arts magazines in North Carolina.

This makes Shirley smile. "So, you've come home again. How nice. Where are your babies today?"

Maggie is now an advertising executive and screenwriter in Los Angeles, I explain. Her brother Jack is a filmmaker and investigative journalist living in Israel.

"Seems pretty scary over there," says Hank. "Hope he's okay."

"He's a smart kid and a very good journalist," I assure them. "He'll be fine."

"Do you ever come back to Atlanta?" Shirley wonders.

"Only when I'm connecting flights at Hartsfield. My daughter Maggie's godmother lives there. I visit her whenever I'm passing through."

Hank nods. "Probably smart to get out when you did. Atlanta has grown much too big. Shootings every night on the news. We're talking about moving closer to our grandkids up North."

"Maybe Maine!" Shirley chirps brightly.

"I still have dreams about our house in Maine," I admit.

"Maybe you'll move back there someday."

"Quite possibly. Perhaps we'll be neighbors again."

Then it's time to go. The park is now officially open for business and tourists are streaming toward us from under the great stone arch, looking up and posing for selfies.

I wish them a safe trip and productive hunting up North.

They thank me for the conversation.

As we pass by George's colonial graffiti, my phone rings.

Talk about synchronicity. It's my son Jack, calling from the Negev desert, where he's working on an investigative story about the Bedouins, the ancient nomadic Arabs who are under threat of losing lands they've owned since the Ottoman Empire due to land policy changes by the Israeli government. I'm proud of my son's fearless work telling the story of forgotten people. His grandfather, the family's original newshound, would be proud too.

"I was just telling some folks from Atlanta about you," I tell him.

"Really? Who?"

"A couple senior citizens I met under the Bridge of God."

"What's that?"

"A wonder of the New World once owned by Thomas Jefferson. Your grandparents honeymooned here. It's right on the Wagon Road."

"Cool," he says. "How's the trip going?"

It's going well, I say. Better than I could have imagined. "How goes it with you?"

"Good," he says. "Getting work done."

He doesn't share details, and I don't ask, exactly how my dad and I typically chatted on the telephone during my dark Atlanta years writing about grieving families, unrepentant Klansmen, and the "Murder Capital of America." He would fill me in on my mom's work at the church soup kitchen or the latest antics of his golf pals, and I would tell him about the multiracial Little League team I was coaching or the sorry state of the Braves, never mentioning dozens of autopsies I'd recently witnessed or the militant survivalists I spent a couple days with at their illegal big-game preserve deep in the wilds of East Tennessee. It's a polite dance of evasion that three generations of Dodson ink jockeys seem to do with ease.

"Someday, maybe you'll make a documentary about the Great Wagon Road," I put to my talented son, not for the first time. "The stories I've heard are incredible. Amazing people."

"Cool. I'd like that," he says, also not for the first time.

"Well, dear boy, I love you. Please be careful," I say—just like my father before me.

"You too," he replies. "Love you."

As Mully and I climb the winding stone steps back to the reception center, I think how glad I am that we chose to stop and see the great Bridge of God perhaps one last time . . . also how proud my parents who celebrated their marriage in this spiritual place eighty years ago would be of their far-flung progeny.

Maybe the Monacans were on to something.

There is magic here, a bridge of stone that connects us to a higher world.

TWENTY-FOUR

THE BELLES OF BIG LICK

T'S A FULL HOUSE ON REFORMATION SUNDAY AT THE FIFTH AVENUE Presbyterian Church in Roanoke.

I've come at the invitation of pastor Vernie Bolden Jr., who would like me to meet members at this historic African American church that sits just blocks off Williamson Road, Roanoke's original main drag, laid directly over the Great Wagon Road. I've agreed under the guise of coming to learn about an unusual sanctuary window that honors the life of one Thomas "Stonewall" Jackson that drew national media attention in the aftermath of the George Floyd protests. But truthfully, I'm more interested to learn about a historic African American church that has deep roots in a handsome old city with a wretched racial past.

Church records show that Fifth Avenue was born in 1890, when the first "colored Presbyterian church" was organized and eventually built on a site formerly occupied by Roanoke's first (white) Methodist church in the 1870s. Roanoke was originally called Big Lick owing to its beginnings in the 1750s as a settlement near a salt marsh area—aka *lick*—where eastern buffalo, elk, and deer gathered to feed. Big Lick's early settlers were predominantly Scots-Irish and German farmers who found this part of the upper Shenandoah Valley with its rich limestone soil and abundant water resources to be the ideal stopping point. Others passed on through the Blue Ridge mountains via Maggoty Gap to North Carolina or took the

Wilderness Road—as did a young Daniel Boone—west to the wilds of Tennessee.

The first railroad line arrived in 1852, but growth was stalled by the outbreak of the Civil War. Residents of Roanoke County overwhelmingly endorsed the "War for Southern Independence," famously voting 850 to 0 in support of Southern secession, which may explain why the area lost so many sons during the war.

You'll often hear proud Roanokers say that a junction of regional railroads turned it into "Magic City" after the Shenandoah Valley Railroad and Norfolk and Western Railway merged in the early 1880s, after which the population jumped from seven hundred residents in 1880 to sixteen thousand just a decade later. Big Lick's grateful citizens voted to officially name the town Kimball after the railroad chief executive who orchestrated the stunning growth. But Kimball demurred and alternately suggested the name Roanoke—an Algonquin name meaning "shell money"—before building a luxurious railroad hotel in a former wheatfield overlooking the tracks.

During the year I served as writer-in-residence at Hollins University in 2006, I learned a great deal about this former nineteenth-century boomtown where many of my early Dodson antecedents settled after arriving on the Virginia coast in the late 1700s. Among Roanoke's least admirable distinctions, the city was among the first in the South to adopt Jim Crow laws, and by the turn of the century much of its Black population—estimated to be about 30 percent—lived in abject poverty on unpaved streets or in houses that lacked the basics of running water and electricity. Not surprisingly, the city had one of the largest Ku Klux Klan chapters in the United States.

In September 1893, just three years after the Fifth Avenue Presbyterian Church was organized (one of its trustees was named Charles Dodson—no relation as far as I know), a local mob stoked by inflammatory newspaper accounts surrounded the city jail and demanded "lynch justice" for a Black man being held for allegedly robbing and beating a white woman in the city's busy City Market district. Gunfire broke out, leaving eight dead and thirty-one injured, including the city's popular mayor, Henry Trout, who had vowed to protect the prisoner. The mob successfully snatched the accused assailant and hanged, mutilated, and reportedly burned his body, threatening to bury the dead man in Mayor Trout's front yard.

Hoping to shine up its image from such a dark legacy, in 1949 the Roanoke Merchants Association funded construction of an eighty-nine-foot illuminated star atop Mill Mountain to celebrate the upcoming Christmas season. The star quickly became a hit with locals and stayed illuminated throughout the year, earning a new nickname for resurgent Roanoke as "the Star City of the South."

I first saw the star during the summer of 1964, when my parents dropped me off to spend a summer weekend with my great-aunt while they attended a newspaper convention in Hot Springs. Aunt Lily was my grandfather Walter's beloved youngest sister. All I knew about her—explained en route over the mountains by my father with a cryptic smile—was that she had been a strong-willed beauty in her youth and something of the Dodson family's black sheep, having spurned several suitors before fleeing to Washington, DC, where she worked as a stage actress and theatrical seamstress.

By the time we met, Lily had been retired from a job in civil service for two decades and lived alone in a gloomy Victorian brownstone on Roanoke's First Avenue, an apartment filled with dusty antiques and Civil War memorabilia, including a Confederate cavalry officer's sword she claimed belonged to a Dodson ancestor who fought at Antietam and Gettysburg. There were also exotic paintings of classical nudes and wild beasts hanging on her walls, including the stuffed head of an antelope said to be a gift from her "favorite gentleman friend," who passed through town every winter with the Ringling Bros. and Barnum & Bailey Circus.

On my first night, Lily—a large-boned blond woman, endlessly talkative, swimming in White Shoulders perfume—took me via taxi to a Chinese restaurant in the City Market district where we dined with a snowy-haired "gentleman friend" she said had once been mayor of Roanoke. He talked about the recent Kennedy assassination and made a half-dollar coin appear from my ear, pointing out, as he did so, that another name for Roanoke was "Magic City."

The next morning, Lily took me to breakfast at the Roanoker Restaurant, a legendary diner where she seemed to be on a first-name basis with everyone from the owner to the head cook. After that, we drove up Mill Mountain to have a close look at the Roanoke Star. The taxi driver, an African American gentleman with a gold tooth, was named Ernie. Lily explained that he was also a part-time preacher, former navy cook, full-time house painter, and her "dearest gentleman friend in the world" and business partner who occasionally drove her to estate sales and farm auctions to buy artwork and antiques. Lily sometimes kept the finds, or gave them to Ernie to sell to collectors, splitting the profits. The Confederate cavalry sword was one of her discoveries, which she hinted might someday pass my way. This thought thrilled me.

On the Sunday morning of my visit, we went to hear Reverend Ernie preach at a little redbrick church, then on to lunch at the historic Hotel Roanoke in order to rendezvous with my folks for the drive home. Naturally, Lily knew the waiter; I was given something called a Roy Rogers and she was handed a small crystal glass. After we ordered our lunches, Lily discreetly removed a small silver flask from her purse and poured herself a bit of ruby sherry.

She looked at me and asked if I wished to have a taste.

Naturally, I said, yes, ma'am.

She asked how old I was.

Twelve, I lied.

She slid the glass of ruby wine across the table.

"Very well. Just a small sip, dear."

During the two-hour drive home through the Blue Ridge mountains, my folks were eager to hear about my weekend. I told them about Lily's many gentlemen friends and the interesting places she took me all over the Star City of the South, even mentioning the Confederate cavalry sword she had promised to give me someday.

I saw my dad glance at my mom. "Your great-aunt Lily is certainly a colorful character," he said. "She's lived a lot of places and has known a lot of interesting folks. She's the Belle of Roanoke for sure. Glad you enjoyed her, but here's the thing, Bo . . . "

Then, carefully, he revealed the true purpose of my visit with her. Great-aunt Lily was about to lose her home on First Avenue due to a hardening of the arteries—today it's called Alzheimer's disease. She was scheduled to move into a special care home in Raleigh around Christmastime and, as a result, would be coming to stay with us around Thanksgiving.

My mother chimed in, "And since your bedroom is the bigger bedroom, sweetie, we're hoping you won't mind giving it up to Aunt Lily when she's with us. You can bunk with your brother. It'll just be temporary."

A few months later, Lily arrived with a large wooden trunk and her sewing machine in tow. On the plus side, she told me stories about famous men she'd known—the actor David Niven, golfer Sam Snead—and, even better, kept boxes of Lorna Doone cookies hidden under bolts of fancy cloth in her trunk, which she was more than happy to share with me most days after school. One afternoon as we were having our daily cookie conversation, I asked her about the Confederate cavalry sword. Lily gave me a blank look, then dismissively waved her Lorna Doone cookie. "Oh, *goodness*, child. I gave that old thing to the church jumble sale ages ago. It wasn't worth a Confederate dime. I think I paid ten dollars for it at a yard sale up in Fincastle."

Predictably, as Christmas Eve approached, my German, clean-freak mother began to lose her mind over our private cookie sessions, but my father said all Aunt Lily needed was a good hobby, and so, he set up her sewing machine and she went to work behind closed doors. For several days nobody knew what she was making in there.

It turned out to be quilted floral potholders. Two *dozen* quilted floral potholders.

"Lily thinks you can sell them for Christmas money," said my dad.

I was mortified. Two pals from my Pet Dairy baseball team lived on our block, and so did my secret crush Della Jane Hockaday, whom I planned to soon give a mood ring.

"Look, sport," the old man reasoned, "Aunt Lily is here for only a couple more weeks. Just let her see you go down the block trying to sell them. You'll make an old lady very happy who has just lost her home. Lily is very fond of you."

I gritted my teeth and did it early on a frosty Saturday morning a week before Christmas, hoping none of my friends would be up yet. To my surprise, I sold a half dozen five-dollar potholders and made thirty bucks, though years later my mom let slip that she'd phoned every woman on the street beforehand to grease the skids, including Della's mom.

The next morning before church, my dad and I drove a large plastic bag filled with the remaining potholders to the drop-off box of the Salvation

Army store. He gave me an extra twenty for my trouble and insisted that I tell Lily, if she asked, that her beautiful potholders had sold out in just one morning.

But Lily never asked. Not long after the New Year, my dad drove his aunt and her big wooden trunk and sewing machine to her new place at the special home in Raleigh.

I got my bedroom back and never saw her again.

She passed away in the springtime two years later.

All of this comes flooding back as I sit in the handsome sanctuary of the Fifth Avenue Presbyterian Church, gazing at its controversial stained-glass window as the pews fill up around me. I am half convinced this is the same tidy redbrick church Aunt Lily brought me to in 1964 to hear Reverend Ernie preach. What a sweet irony that would be.

Prior to the service, I'd chatted with Michael Blankenship, who is being honored today as Fifth Avenue's "Man of the Year." He spent years meticulously researching, writing, and footnoting the church's impressive history, which pastor Vernie Bolden was kind enough to provide me with when I met him earlier in the week. "This nicely tells our family story," he said, "and even explains the somewhat complicated nature of our memorial Jackson window."

I took the history with me to supper that Saturday evening hoping to dine at the old Roanoker Restaurant in memory of Aunt Lily, but found it boarded up and for sale. Instead, I found my way to a corner booth at the K&W Cafeteria on Hershberger Road and read about how Fifth Avenue's founding pastor, Rev. Lylburn Liggins Downing, born a few months before the Emancipation Proclamation, grew up attending "blacks-only" Sunday school class at Lexington Presbyterian Church, where his parents had been taught to read the Bible by Thomas "Stonewall" Jackson. As a young man, Downing chose the ministry over medicine and took over the Fifth Avenue Presbyterian Church in May 1894, just days after graduating from Lincoln Theological Seminary. He would remain there for thirty-six years.

At its start, the church had seven members and offered its new pastor a weekly salary of two dollars. The first collection plate yielded sixty-seven cents. Two years later, with a growing reputation as a spellbinding orator

and gifted fundraiser, Downing presided over the opening of a new building on Patton Avenue, so impressive that *The Roanoke Times* took notice:
"The building is a splendid structure and reflects great credit on the colored
people of this city. Reverend L.L. Downing is doing much for the upbuilding
of his race in this section."

Attention came again when, during the summer of 1906, he installed
the Stonewall Jackson stained-glass window. With chapters of the Daughters of the Confederacy and affiliated Confederate organizations present,
the window's dedication included remarks from "Uncle" Jeff Shields, Jackson's body servant during the war and his Sunday school pupil prior to it.
Downing's parents were members of the same class of slaves that Jackson
had taught prior to the war, and in his own remarks to a packed church, he
counseled his fellow parishioners and Black folks in general "to be as chiv-
alrous and honest as you were in the days of slavery and uplift yourselves.
Those who want to get ahead will find the white man his best friend. There
is no reason why the races cannot work in harmony."

The window depicts an army camped on the banks of a river, with Jackson's attributed last words superimposed over the bucolic scene: "Let us
cross over the river and rest under the trees." According to Michael Blankenship, Downing told reporters from major newspapers across the nation
that "the memorial window tribute is in no way associated with Jackson as
a military leader but is purely and solely a recognition of his service as a
Christian and a faithful teacher of Gospel truth."

As he explained to me in the church library prior to the service, Fifth
Avenue's long and controversial history with the Jackson window is best
perceived as a window into another time.

"As Pastor Bolden likes to say, it's a complicated relationship with the
sins of the past. He once told a reporter that it represents an ideal of what
could be and what should be, instead of the reality of what is."

The storm passed for Downing, writes Blankenship, who became one
of Virginia's leading advocates for minority education during the Jim Crow
era—a middle school in Roanoke still bears his name—"and like Booker
Washington, Downing was an accommodationist who preached acceptance
of racial domination and discrimination, with the hope that there would
be personal and community elevation through hard work, education, and

material prosperity. Both taught a philosophy of self-help, self-control, racial solidarity, and racial harmony. Although Downing joined other activists locally to gently negotiate for better public facilities, he was not a civil rights leader. He never pushed for equality or challenged segregation, so he was not being honored as a champion of human rights."

A champion of populist ideas and progressive politics during this period, on the other hand, was a colorful white city councilman and future mayor named Benton Dillard, who improved city services for minority citizens and defended the public's right to protest. His son Richard went on to become a beloved professor of creative writing at Hollins College, and in 1965, he married one of his most promising former students, a young woman named Annie Dillard.

Reverend Downing died of a cerebral hemorrhage in February 1937, remembered by *The Roanoke Times* as "a believer in progress through education . . . The colored population of Roanoke has lost a leader whose spirituality and counsel it could safely depend on."

Just before services on a snowy November Sunday in 1959, Fifth Avenue Presbyterian's charming wooden church mysteriously caught fire and burned. Faulty wiring was officially cited as the cause, and only the controversial Stonewall Jackson window, the church's baptismal font, and a pair of flower stands survived. Two years later, a handsome new brick church was dedicated. Fifth Avenue's presiding pastor, the Reverend Curtis Kearns Sr., a staunch advocate of social justice and civil rights, was sharply at odds with the Downing family and others in the community who supported preserving the Jackson window as L. L. Downing's legacy, but a compromise was ultimately reached, allowing the window to be reinstalled with Jackson's name and words from the original dedication covered by an altar screen.

Men's Sunday proves to be a wonderfully spirited affair with vigorous preaching from guest minister Rev. David Dickey, whose sermon is titled "What Is Your Excuse?" preceded by an original poem called "A Father's Love" read by Michael Blankenship's son Joshua. Fifth Avenue's choir soon has the sanctuary rocking with lively gospel hymns and spontaneous "Amens" from the congregation. For the closing prayer, Pastor Bolden invites everyone to stand and join hands and face the person beside them. A prim elderly lady wearing a fancy hat with dried flowers takes my hand and smiles up at me.

"We thank you for the delicious food waiting for us downstairs," Bolden begins, "and for the fellowship of today and the soul food provided this day by the message of Reverend Dickey." He then asks us to repeat the following words: "Today is a good day. So, what is *your* excuse for not treating people right? For not loving somebody? For not believing in somebody? For not trusting somebody? We *have* no excuse!

"So, in God's name," he finishes, "we're gonna run out of here and tell everybody—we are *free* from excuses . . . Amen!"

A short while later, as I sit with half a dozen longtime congregants downstairs enjoying one of the best Sunday lunches I'd had in a long time, the subject of the Stonewall window never comes up or, for that matter, seems relevant. The folks at my table ask about my home, my family, and my travels on the Great Wagon Road. I tell them I'm pleased that most have heard of the road and know that it passes only a few blocks east of where we sit. I also tell them about my late great-aunt Lily, who may have brought me to their church when I was eleven—though I can't be sure.

"Child," declares a feisty young woman named Alicia, "what matters is that she brought you to church at that age! That's what the Lord cares about."

The table reverberates with amens and laughter.

An hour after the service, I meet my friend Cathy Hankla at her house in the city's historic Old Southwest neighborhood for an afternoon walk. Cathy is a gifted poet and longtime chair of the department of English at Hollins University, the faculty member largely responsible for my appointment as the school's prestigious Louis D. Rubin Jr. writer-in-residence in 2006, and by extension this trip.

On my first afternoon at the school, I ventured out Hollins's front gate for a short drive along Highway 11 and came upon a Virginia State roadside marker that read: "The Carolina Road, part of the Colonial era Great Philadelphia Wagon Road that brought settlers to Virginia and the Carolinas." The next afternoon, at a used bookstore in Roanoke's City Market district, I found a weathered copy of *The Great Wagon Road: From Philadelphia to the*

South; How Scotch-Irish and Germanics Settled the Uplands by Parke Rouse Jr. I was so taken with the subject that I read the book in two days and even attempted to track down the author, Colonial Williamsburg's longtime historian. Unfortunately, he'd passed away in 1997.

Still, a flame was rekindled.

Professor Hankla smiles upon hearing this story. We are having cold beers and a late lunch at the Green Goat after hiking along the Roanoke River Greenway, which winds through the Star City's historic Highland Park. One thing I'm struck by is how young and hip Roanoke now appears to be. We pass several racially mixed couples and a jogger wearing a T-shirt that reads, "Born Once. And That's Okay."

When I ask about this apparent transformation, Cathy smiles. "Like many places that resist change, time and nature have forced Roanoke to evolve. Instead of the railroad barons and race riots we now have big banks and giant medical centers, a large performing arts center, and lots of new highways, young people, and good colleges around the valley. I guess that's progress."

After lunch, we walk back to her exquisitely restored 1905 workman's Victorian bungalow in the historic district, talking about her recently published memoir that explores how human beings spend their lives searching for a sense of home, a place to finally come to. She wonders if I hadn't come to Hollins, would I have rediscovered the Great Wagon Road?

"Probably not," I admit. "I thought it was lost in time. Turns out, others were trying to find it too."

I mention a woman named Carol Fuller, a gifted genealogist who is on her own quest to document the original path of the Wagon Road. We met on a sleety afternoon in Boone near the end of my first year traveling the road. Having learned about my travels through a growing GWR grapevine, Carol was eager to tell me about a lively internet community she'd created called the Great Wagon Road Project whose stated aim was to document and confirm the historic road's precise path through Virginia and the Carolinas. According to Carol, who grew up hearing about the GWR from grandparents in her native Mount Airy, she and her volunteer army of researchers were hoping to achieve federal recognition for the most traveled road of colonial America. I promptly joined the effort and was impressed by the volume of information her colleagues turned up.

"So, you're both on a quest to find an old road that wasn't lost after all," says Cathy with a laugh. "Just waiting to be found."

As it happens, Cathy Hankla is something of a field expert on lost and found places.

Her latest book, a critically acclaimed memoir titled *Lost Places: On Losing and Finding Home*, explores how human life is shaped by nature and place, history and circumstance, including small moments of epiphany and restless urgings of the soul, a beautiful meditation on how the ache for home resides in all of us, as her fellow poet Maya Angelou once observed.

In Cathy's case, the journey was shaped by the small towns and rural landscapes of her native Southwest Virginia, and an odyssey to the mysterious Chaco Canyon in Northwest New Mexico, the cradle of Pueblo civilization. In a broader spiritual way, she invites her readers to explore their own inner landscapes, the endless urge to roam and seek hidden lost places of the soul.

"Home as a concept involves transformation," she writes. "My relationship to it—carrier pigeon's instinct to return—has never felt satisfied and stays enlivened by dreaming of what might be. My lack of a settled feeling or definition dovetails with a passage from Phillip Sheldrake in which he reminds us of Michael de Certeau's suggestion that we are all on a kind of perpetual pilgrimage that somehow parallels the mystical tradition; we experience dissatisfaction with final destinations or completed places and are driven ever onwards in a movement of perpetual departure."

As we arrive back to her place, we agree that many things in life seem eerily providential, perhaps written by an unseen hand, while others are just damn lucky. Our deep friendship is one or both things.

As we hug goodbye, I dare to ask this modern Belle of Big Lick if she's finally found *home*.

Cathy's coy smile makes me think of the endlessly curious country girl who grew up wandering Southwest Virginia's creeks and fields, studying the universe in the palm of her hand, absorbing the words and wisdom of her aunts and elders, seeking her own small place in an uncertain cosmos.

She finally answers my question.

"Time will tell. Call me when you get to the end of *your* road," she teases. "We'll take another walk along the river and compare notes."

PART SIX

THE ROAD HOME

TWENTY-FIVE

THE GREAT ROAD SCHOLARS

AFTER ROANOKE, CHANNELING MY MORAVIAN ANTECEDENTS, I PICK UP THE pace and encounter half a dozen of the most passionate and intriguing homegrown historians of the Great Wagon Road. I come to think of them as the Great Road Scholars.

The new stretch begins on an early December morning when I meet Dr. Francis Amos at his historic, boxwood-girdled home in Rocky Mount, a handsome Virginia hilltop town of five thousand in Franklin County, where Jubal Early practiced law before joining the Confederate rebellion. The stately white Amos residence was built by a friend of George Washington's named James Callaway in 1773, Dr. Amos tells me, to serve as an ordinary for the nearby Washington Iron Works, which produced everything from camp kettles to cannon balls for the Continental Army before the Battle of Guilford Courthouse.

Rocky Mount's retired family physician and longtime president of the Franklin County Historical Society, Dr. Amos has researched and written extensively on the Great Wagon/Carolina Road's path through Franklin and neighboring Henry County to the North Carolina state line, and graciously offered to drive me along the path taken by the Moravians in 1753. Before that though, we settle with a cup of coffee in his den, which he has transformed into a period-correct tavern that served early Wagon Road travelers, commercial wagoners, and patrons of the ironworks. His home also served as Franklin County's first court, where the gentlemen justices could slake their thirst after a long day's session.

"There was nowhere else around here for settlers and buyers to stay, much less get a good drink," Amos tells me, displaying a published list of beverages along with a copy of the tavern's original license, which advises that the establishment "Shall not suffer anyone to tipple or drink more than is necessary on the Sabbath."

Good Rum: 12p
Peach Brandy Whiskey: 8 shillings
Strong Beer: 1.6 shillings

"It was the tavern bartender's job to keep an accurate tally—to mind the number of pints and quarts a customer purchased and consumed," he explains. "You've perhaps heard the old phrase 'Better mind your p's and q's'? This is where that came from."

Amos also shows me a Spanish silver coin from the early colonial era—"a piece of eight," as such coins were called, that were legal tender in America until the mid-eighteenth century. "Our dollar sign comes, in fact, from the scrolled ribbon shown on the coin," he says. Finally, he shows me a formidable steel bar that swings down to lock the liquor cabinet at closing time. "That's where the word we use for such establishments today originated—the *bar*," he revels, gray eyes twinkling.

With this, Amos ushers me into his big Ford pickup truck and drives me along several winding back roads that cross the rural fastness of Franklin and Henry Counties, narrating the histories of the region and seemingly every historic house we pass in colorful detail, including the spot where John Boone's house formerly stood, a key stop on the stagecoach route of 1810. Eventually we turn down a narrow dirt road to the Blackwater Crossing by the Pigg River, named for John Pigg, a prominent early Wagon Road settler, and stop briefly in Waid Park, a beautiful public park that boasts well-tended ballfields and soccer fields, owned by Franklin County.

"The original Wagon Road ran right through here," Amos says matter-of-factly. "Before it received that name, of course, it was the Great Warrior's

Path. I sometimes like to sit and just imagine the Indian hunting parties, pioneers, soldiers, backwoods preachers, and Wagon Road settlers from all over Europe who came this way in search of a home. Kids playing ball here have no idea about the importance of this road. I think that's a tragedy. The Wagon Road was an artery pumping life into the heart of frontier America. I do think people today need to know about this history."

As we move on through rolling hillsides where most hardwoods have already shed their autumn leaves, passing just west of Ferrum College (home to the annual Blue Ridge Folklife festival, which Wendy, Mully, and I attended on an autumn Saturday a few years back; the annual coon dog water race is not to be missed), Amos tells me about falling in love with history as a youngster and cites an article that appeared in *The Roanoke Times* in the late 1970s about the Carolina/Wagon Road that fueled his bounding interest in the road's role in developing life in the Southern wilderness.

"That article got a lot of folks interested in learning about their ancestors, where they came from and how they got here generations back," he explains. Even before his official retirement, Amos became a dedicated activist of local preservation, serving as chairman of Franklin County's bicentennial celebration in 1986, actively purchasing and restoring several historically important properties that were in danger of being lost, including an old chapel near Penhook that dates from 1760.

While we roll past handsome farms and fenced pastures, I tell Amos about my buddy Craig Wagoner (perfect name) whose colonial ancestors settled on the Wagon Road in Franklin County and eventually struck off for Kansas a couple generations later. Drawn by his family's migratory story, Craig grew up hunting arrowheads in Kansas, which led to a passion for researching patterns of early settlement across Virginia and the Carolinas. It's made him a homegrown archaeologist, with a collection of arrowheads and artifacts from early American life that fills an entire room of his house. His work as a designer and builder of spectacular stone structures, as he once explained to me, keeps him "close to the ground, where you can always find something fascinating from a long time ago if you know what you're looking at."

"Sounds like somebody I'd like to meet someday," replies Amos. "An early love of history will do that to you."

A father of two grown sons and a pair of daughters, my companion's life has clearly been devoted to sharing a passion for American history with young people. He mentions a hyperactive ten-year-old named Zeb from a divorced family that he took fishing as a favor to the young man's worried mother. "Zeb couldn't sit still in school and concentrate. But that day he caught a twenty-four-inch catfish and got interested in the stories I told him about the history of this area, including the fact that his great-grandfather served in the Twenty-Fourth Virginia Regiment that was with Lee at Appomattox. I took him there too—to several history museums and battlefields as well. It was like a light bulb going on in his head. Zeb later invited me to his Cub Scout graduation ceremony and was soon making all As in school. Today he's a fine young man attending medical school."

"A young life enriched by learning history?"

"I've seen it happen over and over with young people," he continues. "The fortunate ones discover that history is far more interesting than fiction—or even the stuff on their mobile phones. When I can read or learn about something that really happened to living people—*my* people—events take on a whole new meaning that lead you someplace better. That's why sharing history with young folks is my joy, basically my life's work. You can study it endlessly because you can never learn it all."

A little while later we cross US Highway 58 near Horse Pasture and arrive at George Taylor Road, just above the North Carolina state line, not far from where Mully and I began this whole affair at a pull-over by the South Mayo River.

"Well, you're on your own from this point on," Dr. Amos says with a friendly grin. "Trust you can find your way home from here the way the Moravians did."

We shake hands and he winks.

"Just don't forget to mind your p's and q's."

Someone said the past lives beneath our feet.

This turns out to be the case with a couple old friends named Dowell Lester and Bill Collins, who know this part of the Wagon Road like the back of their own hands. Lester lives on the Amostown Road a few miles below the Virginia state line. A former manager of three different local textile mills who has studied the famous Moravian Diaries and Great Wagon Road in detail for decades, he is, among other things, a self-schooled expert on William Byrd's seminal *Histories of the Dividing Line betwixt Virginia and North Carolina*, an account of Byrd's expedition of 1728 to survey and establish the border between the colony of Virginia and the province of North Carolina. Byrd named the Mayo River for his chief surveyor, William Mayo.

Bill Collins, meanwhile, is a retired high school principal from Greensboro who served thirteen different public schools in four different North Carolina counties. His father was also a school principal for more than forty years.

Lester and Collins both attended North Stokes High School in the 1970s but found a late-in-life friendship through their shared passion for the Great Wagon Road, each having come to appreciate the role the road played in their family stories from researching their ancestors in slightly different ways.

Bill's focus was fueled by a grandmother who babysat him and his younger cousins while their parents worked. "We lived out in the country off Highway 89 and she told us stories about how she grew up here, including about her grandfather and three brothers who fought in the Civil War," he recalls. "She would take us for walks in the woods and show us plants that she picked to make natural medicines with. Her generation was so independent and close to the earth it made me want to know more about them."

Soon, he developed an interest in genealogy and traced his ancestry back to a French Huguenot named Fontaine, who fought in the Second Crusade; through the journal of an ancestor named John Fontaine, he learned that Peter Fontaine was William Byrd's personal priest. He also discovered early family ties to the Jamestown settlement and the James family who eventually migrated west in the nineteenth century, producing a gunslinging legend named Jesse.

"I found myself asking a fundamental question," he says. "How did these folks get here and settle where they did? I learned that in colonial times the oldest son normally got the house and property, and other sons were expected to move along," he tells me. "Girls were expected to marry. That's the story of early America, which I read about in journals and our old family letters. Once that gets into your bloodstream, why, you're off on a journey that never ends."

His pal Dowell Lester—who prefers to go by "Darrel"—had his own version of this awakening. "My people talked about the [Wagon] Road my entire life," he explains over a map from 1780 and several thick files of research materials spread out over the kitchen table in his house just off Amostown Road. "They were backwoods people whose kin lived directly on the road for hundreds of years, back to Indian days. I met them when I was a youngin' and my mama and daddy took us visitin'. Some of them were deep woods folks and didn't even have electric power in their homes, the last of a generation we'll never see the likes of again. But, brother, they could sit and tell stories and were completely self-sufficient. I grew fascinated by them. They were smart country people who passed their skills on down—farming, blacksmithing, gun making, whatever it was—just like their ancestors did. When I started researching them, I discovered that my fifth-great-grandfather came here from Britain and settled on land purchased from the king of England. The deed was written on a sheepskin."

Darrel's other family wing—Reformed Germans—came down the Wagon Road to the area in the 1760s, not long after a dozen Moravian "brothers" blazed an "upper" (and more direct) branch off the main Wagon Road through the Sauratown Mountains past Pilot Mountain to Bethania, the first Moravian settlement established in 1759. "These were the Ziglers," he recites. "Then come the Nances; they were Scots-Irish. My mother was a Nance. My daddy was a Lester. His mother was a Cox; they all came from original Wagon Road settlers, which means I do too."

The amazing thing, he emphasizes, is that the descendants of these Wagon Road families still reside along Amostown Road, which he is convinced is the original path of the road. Remarkably, nine different family lines stemming from Darrel's fourth-great-grandparents, he points out, still reside within a mile or two of his home. I joke that this must be a genealogical rarity in modern America. To illustrate how rare a phenomenon this is, however, Darrel shows me twenty-three family names on a six-foot map of the area that stands against his kitchen wall: "Every one of them came down the Wagon Road. And every one of these families are *still* living here.

"If you have one of these family names," he adds with a grin, "your people have been here for a couple hundred years, and you're related to almost *everybody!*"

He also tells me about a cache of letters he recently found in an old house just up the road that belonged to a family that his grandfather's sister married into. "That family had five sons who fought in the Civil War. It blew my mind to read those tender letters home from their sons and brothers, several of whom never got there. They ached to be home. That's how much life in this backcountry meant to them. Those that got home, never left again."

The family's homeplace in question, he explains, is still intact and full of artifacts from the eighteenth and nineteenth centuries. "It's like a museum in that house. You wouldn't believe it. Time stands still. An antique collector would go crazy. But that's sacred family stuff. Some of those heirlooms have been in that house for a hundred and fifty years. In my research, I've found dozens of houses along this road that are just like it—full of things from a faraway time, a lost time of American history, still here on the Wagon Road."

"I've been after Darrel," his old classmate Bill Collins puts in as he's leaving for another appointment, "to write a book about all that."

"It's comin'," Darrel assures him with a laugh. "Done written half already. That'll be my second one on the subject."

In 1984, Lester self-published a charming local history called *Seasons in Stokes: A Proud Look Back*, in which he recorded many of the stories of people and traditional practices in this part of rural northeast Stokes County. The book includes a detailed exegesis on the Great Wagon Road written by a skilled researcher named Bill McGee who did some of the first detailed work on the Wagon Road's various branches through Stokes, Rockingham, and Forsyth Counties, including the shorter "upper" route carved by the traveling Moravian brothers to Bethania in October 1753.

"C'mon," says Darrel, "I need to show you something."

He drives me a couple miles up the Amostown Road to a narrow bridge that crosses the South Mayo River. We stop in the middle of the bridge and he points down the river. "Look closely there and you can see the ford they all used when the wagons come down out of Virginia. That's where Byrd camped."

I stare for a moment. But the site doesn't match up to my memory of the winter day when Mully and I found what I believed to be the South Mayo ford. I relay my confusion to my companion.

Darrel smiles. "I know what you saw. It's just back a way. The wagons crossed there too. I'll take you there."

We turn around and drive maybe half a mile back to a small parklike area with a covered picnic shelter. The land belongs to the nearby Mayo Christian Church, a gift from Darrel's late mother. We drive across the grass and park by the shelter, then walk down to the water's edge through trees downed by recent storms. We are literally standing, he tells me, with one foot in Virginia and another in North Carolina.

Suddenly, the crossing looks familiar. Across the shallows, the telltale sunken roadbed rises up the hill through the forest. I have no doubt that if Mully were with me, she would take off like a shot up that old road.

"You okay?" says Darrel, picking up on my silence.

I nod. "I am. This is the spot."

"This is Crooked Creek," he clarifies. "It runs alongside the South Mayo. We're standing right on the Great Wagon Road. You can almost hear them wagons crossin' the creek, can't you?"

On the walk back to the car, he tells me that he's been invited to give a dinner presentation on the Wagon Road that evening to the Brown Mountain Boys at the Milk Bar in Walnut Cove. They are members of the Sons of Veterans of the North Carolina 2nd Infantry that fought in the Shenandoah Valley Campaigns and surrendered with Lee at Appomattox.

He invites me to tag along.

"One thing I've learned from many years of research on the road in this area," he says as we track down Route 704 from Sandy Ridge through Dodgetown, crossing the Dan River and on to Walnut Creek, "there are any number of branches that come off the original road, like the shorter route cut by the Moravian brothers made over to Bethania and Bethabara. Probably impossible to ever identify which is the original, though everybody has their opinions. I like to say they are all original because they all came this way about the same time. You can't blame folks, though. They have lots of pride in that old road, because it brought their kinfolk here way on back."

Half a dozen of the boys are already sitting around a private backroom table at the Milk Bar on Walnut Cove's main drag when we arrive. And what a sight they are. With their shaggy gray beards and bright red Brown Mountain Boys T-shirts with the Stars and Bars emblem, these aging sons of Confederate veterans look more like a ZZ Top tribute band.

Darrel introduces me as "a friend and working journalist who is writin' a book about travelin' the Great Wagon Road. I told him you fellas would probably have some thoughts on that subject that you might like to share."

For a moment, the air in the room grows still. They offer nods and muted greetings. Sensing their natural wariness, I choose not to take notes or tape Darrel's talk, which turns out to be one of the best presentations on the subject I've heard yet.

With the help of local artifacts ranging from original Byrd maps to ancient tomahawks, Rev War weapons to Civil War letters, that he's brought to illustrate his talk, Darrel tells a grand story of the Great Wagon Road's origins, from the Great Warrior's Path to the twenty-three different family homeplaces he's identified along the road of today.

"Folks ask me why I care so much about this stuff," he says as the program winds down. "The truth is, I was raised up in this history and am old enough to have known the last generation that had rich memories of what life was like out here in the backcountry of the South—or as my grandmother liked to tell us kids, 'I've seen everything from the hind end of a mule to landing the first man on the moon.' That's how quickly life moves along and why so much of our history can be lost or forgotten if someone like you and me don't work to preserve it. It's right beneath your feet if you take the time to seek out the story."

By my watch, Darrel's presentation has lasted well beyond the designated hour. And yet the Brown Mountain Boys listen intently to every word.

Following his talk, discussion shifts to more current events including how the national media has handled the toppling of *Silent Sam*, a bronze statue of a Confederate soldier that once stood on the campus of the University of North Carolina at Chapel Hill. Funded by the Daughters of the Confederacy in memory of the 287 UNC students who joined the Southern cause, progressive student groups long regarded *Sam*, erected in 1913, as a symbol of white supremacy and periodically protested the statue's presence.

Following the "Unite the Right" march in Charlottesville of August 2017, a yearlong sit-in protest took place that forced the North Carolina

Historical Commission to finally develop plans to relocate *Sam* to a museum or private property. On the night of August 20, 2018, as Chapel Hill police looked on, a group of activists pulled down *Sam* to a chorus of cheers and flashing cameras. Reportedly, only one person was arrested and charged with hiding his face in violation of the state's public gathering laws, a provision that ironically dates from the peak Klan years.

The Brown Mountain Boys devote several minutes to a thoughtful discussion of how their God-given right to celebrate their Southern heritage seems to be under assault by the mainstream media and the radical left. I listen quietly until their eyes shift my way.

"You being a big-city reporter and all," one of them says, "we'd be interested to hear your thoughts on the subject."

Before I can answer, a skinny member seated directly across the table blurts out, "You probably didn't have nobody in the fight, didja?"

"As a matter of fact," I reply, "I did."

With that, I take George Washington Tate's Confederate States belt buckle out of my coat pocket and lay it on the table. I've been carrying it with me ever since Cousin Steve Lynch placed it in my hand.

I tell them about my ancestor, who signed on with the Burke Rifles on George Washington's birthday in 1862 and fought from Gettysburg to the siege of Petersburg, returning home three years later as a full colonel a few days before Lee's surrender at Appomattox.

"So, what about *Silent Sam*?" asks another member at the table. "They yanked him down like he was a piece of trash, not a historic statue."

"You have a point. That kind of violent vandalism benefits nobody," I reply, hearing myself channeling the voices of Neil Ronk and Gabor Borritt. "I've come to believe military statues belong on the battlefields where the people they honor fought and died. If they are in a public setting and give offense to any particular American, I favor relocating them to private property where those who appreciate and value them may do as they see fit."

This response doesn't really answer his question, but at least the Brown Mountain Boys don't heave their peach cobbler at me.

To my surprise, when I thank them for allowing me to join their gathering, one of the graybeards hands me a memento of my visit—a Brown Mountain Boys T-shirt.

"Just something to remember us by," he says with a puckish smile. "In memory of your great-great-granddaddy's service to the South."

I'm touched by this gesture, and thank them for the conversation.

A few days later, on a cold and misty morning, Kyle Stimson meets me in the empty parking lot of the visitor center of Historic Bethabara Park, northwest of downtown Winston-Salem. Stimson, sixty-five, a rangy building contractor from Lewisville, is the author of *The Great Philadelphia Wagon Road in Forsyth County, N.C.: 1750–1770*. As a descendant of a fourth-great-grandfather who was mentioned in the historic Moravian Diaries, Stimson has offered to show me what he believes is the "true" path of the GWR across the county, including where it fords the Yadkin River near his hometown.

Stimson's early interest in the road, he tells me, was inspired by a state historic marker that went up in 1976 on the Bethania–Rural Hall Road to celebrate the route that brought the Moravians to the area in 1753.

"Then in 1987, the state's four hundredth anniversary, an article appeared in the local newspaper about a group calling itself the Great Wagon Road Preservation Committee." He immediately got in touch and found a welcoming group of history-minded folks that included the chief archaeologist for the Moravians, the aforementioned Bill McGee, and a distinguished Wake Forest historian, all of whom were eager to determine the road's true path to the Shallow Ford on the Yadkin.

"They were super people," he remembers. "Unfortunately, there was little agreement among the group on where the road passed through the county. It didn't take me long to discover that the information they had was all over the place. One lady from Rural Hall, for instance, claimed the road passed through her backyard based on the fact that older family members told her it did. She holds that view to this day." Though Stimson wasn't a trained historical investigator, he admits, he was determined to settle the debate once and for all. "It only took me thirty years," he says with a laugh.

He started with a deep dive into the Moravian Diaries and hundreds of state and local colonial-era deeds and records, followed by a road trip from Philadelphia to Georgia to pick the brains of local historians, county clerks, archivists, and museum curators, some of the same people I've met and interviewed. Like me, one of his prime inspirations was Park Rouse Jr., whom he met and interviewed at a historical conference in 1990 called the Great Wagon Road and the Scots-Irish Migration.

"Rouse told me something extraordinary. His recent research on the road had evolved since his Great Wagon Road book's publication . . . indicating that the traditional route he and other historians cited was wrong. It didn't go where they thought it did."

I take the bait. "So where does it go?"

Stimson smiles. "We'll save that for the end of the tour. It's a real surprise."

With that, we're off on a daylong, all-consuming magical mystery tour beginning at the spot where the historic road entered from Stokes County and followed a rough southwest line that roamed just north of downtown Winston-Salem through parts of Germanton, Old Town, and Pfafftown to Lewisville. Along the way, we make more than a dozen stops in urban neighborhoods, leafy subdivisions, ballfields, and patches of forest, even private driveways and shopping centers. At each stop, my enthusiastic host hops out and sets off with long strides, beckoning me to follow. In every instance, I find myself standing before what I've come to recognize as the remains of an old roadbed hidden by the accretions of modernity. "There it is!" he yawps gleefully. "*That's* the Great Wagon Road. Unfortunately, development hasn't been kind to history in these parts. That's why knowing exactly where the road runs is *so* vital."

In between these unexpected reveals, Stimson provides an encyclopedic narrative of the Old North State's colonial history that begins with Earl Granville's original tract of 1744, which gave the former lord proprietor ownership of one-eighth of the royal colony of North Carolina. Later, Granville's first big sale was to the Moravians of Pennsylvania, who purchased nearly one hundred thousand acres and dispatched a surveying party under the direction of Bishop August Spangenberg to North Carolina to determine the best place for the Moravians to settle. After several months of setbacks, the group decided on the lands of present-day Forsyth County, naming the site Wachovia after Moravian patron Ludwig Von Zinzendorf's Austrian estate Wachau.

"The thing to remember is that North Carolina is full of old backcountry roads and trading paths that were here even before the first Moravians came down the Wagon Road," Stimson reminds me. "As a result, there was always a great deal of confusion and debate over which one was the original. Folks have all sorts of claims and theories based on family memories and inferior maps. They're all wrong."

He mentions Rural Hall resident June Koehn (for the second time), the local resident who is convinced that the Great Wagon Road passed directly through her family's backyard. Koehn famously appeared in the *Winston-Salem Journal* explaining how she "stumbled" over a 1711 map that conclusively proved that the old road crossed her property and was unquestionably the original Great Wagon Road, though there were numerous doubters.

"She's completely wrong about that," Stimson sniffs. "Some people can't bear learning the facts."

Just for fun, I mention to my host that I spent a couple hours in Miss June's company yesterday at the Rural Hall public library. After she showed me piles of ancient maps and faded documents spread out over a pair of large reference room tables, we took a drive through town to her family property, where she pointed out what did appear to be a very old road and emphatically declared: "This is what people around here have *believed* forever, and I have proven it beyond doubt to anyone and everyone who has asked—except *one* man."

When I asked Miss June why this cause was so important to her, she added with emotion, "Because this is *our* history. Nobody can change that. The matter is completely settled. This *is* the Great Wagon Road!"

Stimpson shakes his head.

"As I told you, June and the newspaper are *both* wrong about the Great Wagon Road. Among other things, she says the Moravians *stole* the Great Wagon Road, whatever that means. The truth is that the road did not pass through Rural Hall and it didn't even pass through Salisbury and Charlotte as historians have long claimed. I'm going to show you the *real* path of the road," he promises. "It's going to blow your mind."

Remembering Darrel's comment about "many early wagon roads" that shaped the settlement of the region, I'm beginning to wonder if determining the "true" path of the GWR is a geographical impossibility, a case that can't be cracked, even one that's not all that important at the end of the day.

Even so, I keep mum until we roll into Shallowford Square in the center of downtown Lewisville, where a Nissen wagon sits in the town square on a street named the Great Wagon Road. Nissen wagons were created by a man named John Nissen in 1834, and though its resemblance to the iconic Conestoga wagon is unmistakable, there is one difference between the two: Nissen wagons were smaller, and lighter, and reportedly more maneuverable. The company produced nearly fifteen thousand wagons a year until the 1940s, when the rising popularity of automobiles diminished public interest in wagons of any kind.

During the short drive to the banks of the Yadkin River, he tells me about growing up in Lewisville, son of a postal mail carrier who went off to Campbell College to study philosophy and religion. "My grandparents lived right on the Great Wagon Road, which I heard about all my life," he adds as he leads me on a final brief hike through a field of blooming periwinkle to a historic sign erected by the NC Daughters of the American Revolution that reads "Daniel Boone Trail 1769." He points to the Yadkin River, glittering in the near distance. "This was part of the road down to the crossing spot that was used by frontier travelers going west, including the Boones," he says. "C'mon, I'll show you. The surprise begins there."

A few minutes later, we cross the narrow steel ridge that has replaced one that was washed away two decades ago to the community of Huntsville and Mulberry Fields Road, which Stimson insists Daniel Boone took west to the Wilderness Road.

"So, what's the big surprise?" I dare to ask.

Kyle Stimson grows serious. "The Great Wagon Road, as I hinted before, did *not* run from here to Salisbury as historians have believed for well over a hundred years. When I interviewed Parke Rouse in 1990, he told me that the road crossed here at the Shallow Ford but then followed Sherrill's Path through Mocksville and Statesville to Island Ford, passing well west of both Salisbury and Charlotte before entering upper South Carolina. In South Carolina, however, the road did indeed split, as historians agree, one branch going through York and Newberry, the other through Lancaster and Camden to Augusta. That much is true."

As a bonus for our long day spent chasing a mythical lost road, my host offers to show me the site where Daniel Boone built a honeymoon cabin for his wife, the former Rebecca Bryan. It stood on the banks of the river not far from Squire Boone's home at the Forks of the Yadkin.

A few minutes later, he points to a small clearing in the woods well off the highway. "Right over there is where the cabin was. It sat empty for years until it simply disintegrated."

It's just a clearing in the autumn woods. But I snap a photograph of it thinking how pleased Cousin Josie would be that I found my way to her hero's honeymoon cabin. It gives me a moment of surprising pleasure to picture her wise old face.

There is one more Great Road Scholar I need to meet before I cross the Yadkin River and decide which way to go. Johanna Brown, curator and director of collections for Old Salem Museums & Gardens, aka "Moravian Mama," meets me in the empty town square of Old Salem.

Some historians believe that Old Salem—a name that means "God's Peace"—was the most innovative town of frontier America, created thirteeen years after the Moravian brothers established a base camp at Bethabara in the mid-1750s and immediately began planning their version of a New Jerusalem in the vast ninety-eight-thousand-acre Wachovia tract in the wilderness sold to them by John Carteret, Earl of Granville, in 1752. Reportedly, Lord Carteret was deeply impressed by the industriousness and regimented religious lifestyle of Pennsylvania's well-behaved Moravians in their settlements at Nazareth, Bethlehem, and Lititz, and believed they would bring prosperity and a measure of protection to British interests in the wild Southern backcountry.

"From the Moravian point of view," Mama Moravian says as we set off from the square to walk the charming brick streets of what may be the best-preserved eighteenth-century archaeological town in America, "they wanted to be completely isolated so they could practice their faith and live the peaceful life they desired. This was something of a dichotomy, however, because the Moravians were such brilliantly skilled artists, craftsmen, and builders of almost everything, they envisioned creating a thriving commercial town where people in the expanding frontier could come to purchase their goods and would, in turn, support the mission of the church. Salisbury, where several trading routes crossed, wasn't far away."

Salem, Brown points out, was originally supposed to be created in a circular pattern with a town square at its center that fit founder Count Zinzendorf's communal vision. Pragmatically, however, the town wound up being designed along a high ridge above streams and forests, with individual houses liberally spaced for families and gardens, not unlike the town of Lititz in Pennsylvania.

"The designers made it clear that the town was not designed for farmers, but those with trades," she explains. "Education of the young was a high priority, with separate schools for boys and girls that equally taught science, mathematics, and history, disciplines shaped by the enlightened principles of Moravian philosopher and theologian John Amos Comenius, sometimes called the Father of Modern Education."

Advanced medical practices (including the art of blending natural remedies learned from the Cherokee Indians) and the music of their homeland were also important elements of cultural life in Salem. The town became home to several Tannenberg pipe organs, and was the first municipality in the Southeast to build a water system that furnished fresh running water to numerous town structures. One of them was the original Salem Tavern, built in 1771, which was constructed on the outskirts of the settlement to protect the congregation from the worldly influences of traders and travelers who stayed at the tavern. A brewery and distillery were also part of the thriving manufacturing trade that quickly developed, highlighted by gunsmithing (strictly for hunting and protection), shoemaking, tailoring, tin and pewter manufacturing, ironmongering (Moravian door hinges became treasured works of art), and outstanding furniture making and pottery that rivaled the finest decorative works of early German Pennsylvania.

One of the more interesting moments of our tour comes when Johanna Brown explains how the town's Singles Sisters became a major force with a highly successful laundry and bleaching enterprise that happened to be located on a site the town elders had proposed for raising Salem's permanent home church. To keep the two groups satisfied, the matter was submitted to "the Lot," a system the Moravians used to determine God's will in all matters spiritual and secular.

"The Lot was used for deciding everything from the location of the town square to marriages and accepting new members," Brown says by the home church's front doors. "Typically, three slips of paper were placed in tubes in a bowl. One piece read *ya*, a second *nein*, with the third left blank, meaning that more prayer and deliberation was needed." One of the more amusing episodes concerned a prominent fellow named John Vogler, a famous silversmith and watchmaker who went to the Lot several times in search of a wife and was never satisfied. In 1819, the church did away with the Lot for marriage, allowing Vogler to marry the woman of his choice.

A few minutes later, Johanna Brown and I stand together in the silent sanctuary of Old Salem's Home Moravian Church, which is handsomely decorated with fragrant beeswax candles and greenery for its upcoming annual Lovefeast that celebrates the birth of Christ. Dedicated in 1800 with clear glass windows, gorgeous wooden pews, and plain white walls, it powerfully reminds me of the home church I visited in Lititz on a summer afternoon just over three years ago. So much for a quick and breezy trip down the Wilderness Road of my ancestors.

I tell Mama Moravian how both churches feel like home—at least to me.

"Oh, so you've *been* here before?" she says with surprise.

"Yes, ma'am. Many times."

I explain that I am an Episcopalian who grew up with a Lutheran mother who never missed attending Old Salem's Moravian Lovefeasts.

"You know," she says, "I was raised Episcopalian myself but became a Moravian when I married my husband. In God's eyes we all come from the same spiritual root."

She wonders if I've ever attended the Easter sunrise service at Salem's God's Acre.

I nod. "Just once."

"Oh, I do hope you'll come back."

I mention how my girlfriend and I attended the sunrise service in the early 1970s, and a kind professor from Salem College loaned her his jacket and told us about the Moravians coming down the Great Wagon Road from

Pennsylvania, the first time I'd heard the name of the road since a winter day hunting mistletoe and bittersweet with my father on his grandfather's abandoned homeplace near Hillsborough.

"What a wonderful story," she replies. "How old were you then?"

"Thirteen. I decided that maybe someday I'd find and travel the Wagon Road just for fun."

Mama Moravian smiles. "And now you have. Has it been fun?"

"Everything an eighth-grade kid could ask for."

TWENTY-SIX

THE AMAZING TALE OF VALENTINE LEONARD

ON A CRISP SATURDAY MORNING IN NOVEMBER 2021, I BUMP INTO AN OLD friend and fellow history nut named Chris Garton at Greensboro's newly reopened historic downtown farmer's market. As millions of Americans are finally returning to something resembling normal life in the wake of the Covid pandemic, we spend a few minutes catching up and sharing lockdown stories that are now part of America's daily narrative.

"I have to ask," says Chris, "were you able to complete the Wagon Road before we learned to live life on Zoom?"

I explain that I'd just reached Charlotte and the Waxhaws when the world as we knew it shut down. But I'm now about to resume the journey at Salisbury, the colonial market town where the Wagon Road intersected the older Great Trading Path. I also mention that there suddenly seems to be no shortage of Wagon Road experts roaming the landscape who have their own ideas about where the original road passed through the Carolinas. In recent days, Carol Fuller's Great Wagon Road Project released its findings around a startling claim that the Great Wagon Road never even touched Forsyth County, but instead passed through lower Guilford and Davidson Counties before *ending* at the Catawba River, where it became the Great Trading Path.

Chris looks amused. She wonders which of the competing Road Scholars do I believe, and what path do I plan to follow?

I tell her that, having come this far, I plan to travel the traditional path of the road across the Carolinas described for centuries by colonial-era historians, including the road's eastern and western branches that cross South Carolina and reconnect at Augusta.

"That sounds very ambitious," Chris says with a laugh. "Maybe this will help—or just confuse you more."

She pulls a thick blue book out of her carryall and hands it to me, a 1927 edition of *Centennial History of Davidson County North Carolina*. It tells the remarkable story, she says, of her own Great Wagon Road ancestor, one Valentine Leonard, a German settler who came down to Davidson County in the 1750s, established the first Reformed German church in the region, and became a hero at the Battle of Guilford Courthouse in March 1781.

"I think he reflects the experiences of so many European immigrants who came down the Wagon Road and settled the Carolina backcountry. You might find his story very interesting."

One week later, on a cold, gray Saturday morning, I begin the final leg of my odyssey by attending the annual fall festival at historic Pilgrim Church in the rolling countryside just outside Lexington, the pretty Davidson County seat of government once known for making the finest hardwood furniture and (still) the best pork barbecue in the South.

Records show that Valentin Leonhardt, twenty-eight, a tailor by trade and son of the Palatinate region of Germany, took passage on the ship *Neptune* and arrived at the Port of Philadelphia on October 25, 1746, tarrying only a few days before taking the standard oath of allegiance to his new country and striking off for the Southern frontier. He took a wife named Elizabeth not long after arriving.

"Most of the German settlers in North Carolina came from the German settlements in Pennsylvania," notes the Davidson County history, "taking up residence in the modern counties of Guilford, Davidson, Forsyth, Rowan, Cabarrus and Catawba counties." There is no record of how long the Leonhardts stayed in Pennsylvania during this high tide of immigration. But like many of their fellow immigrants, the couple took several years to reach the Carolina Piedmont, during which they learned English and Valentin anglicized his original Huguenot family name from the Middle Ages to "Valentine Leonard."

In 1754, Leonard purchased a large tract of fertile land from an agent for Lord Carteret between Abbotts Creek and a creek that would soon bear his family name in an area known as the "Dutch settlement," where other Palatine immigrants would soon settle.

By that point, Leonard had become a wealthy farmer, fathering eight children and boasting a large herd of cattle and horses. At the outbreak of the Revolutionary War, according to the last will and testament he created before joining the patriot cause, his personal wealth included significant amounts of gold and silver, which he used to develop his home and surroundings—and start a church.

A charming story relates how he and a couple of companions from the settlement chose the site for a Reformed German church that would bear his name: "About three-quarters of a mile west of Abbott's Creek these gentlemen came to a beautiful spot in a grove of oak, hickory, and sugar maple trees, where was also a spring of sparkling water bubbling up," notes the history. Moved by the natural beauty of the spot, one of Leonard's companions remarked, in German: "God fashioned this place for a house of worship; here we must have a meeting house."

A short time later, in 1757 or a year before, "Leonard's Church" began as a crude brush-arbor structure on a rise of land within sight of Valentine Leonard's two-story "mansion house of immense hewn logs with a substantial cellar and wrought iron locks, hinges and window shutters." In time, the name would eventually be changed to the Church of the Pilgrims—or simply, the Pilgrim Church.

Sometime between 1757 and 1764, a substantial log structure made from local timber was constructed in the day's typical church design, one that featured a central gallery with a goblet-shaped, European-style pulpit at its center space, large enough to accommodate a single speaker. According to early church records, the Reformed congregation of Pilgrim Church welcomed local Lutheran and even Moravian ministers to its pulpit. For the next twenty years, in fact, the Reformed and Lutheran congregations shared the original Pilgrim Church structure (offering sermons alternately in German and English) until the Lutherans opted to construct their own church several miles away—it is still known to this day as the historic Pilgrim Lutheran Church.

Like many of his industrious German neighbors, Leonard was passionate about the life he'd found in the Carolina backcountry. So when the Revolutionary War broke out, at age fifty-five, he and five of his sons joined the patriot cause. "He was very influential in getting the German community to support the Revolution," notes a history of the Dutch settlement written by Rev. Everette Neese, a Leonard descendant. "This created great hatred for him among the Tories, many of whom were Germans loyal to England because of English assistance in getting to the New World."

The last battle in which Valentine Leonard fought was the decisive engagement between the forces of Lord Cornwallis and Nathanael Greene at Guilford Courthouse in March 1781, after which Leonard and his friend and neighbor Wooldrich Fritz returned home to get on with life.

Eight months later, the story goes, as he sat by his fireplace after supper, savoring the mild weather and evening light from his open Dutch door, "Suddenly a shot rang out at the open door . . . the good Christian man, the brave hero, the gallant soldier, fell to the floor mortally wounded." The assassins fled into the woods. They would never be identified.

Later that evening, Wooldrich Fritz was also shot and died instantly. Valentine Leonard lived for eleven days before succumbing to his injuries. The bodies of both men were buried side by side in the Pilgrim Church cemetery.

The first thing I do upon arriving at Pilgrim Church's annual fall bazaar is take a walk through its large cemetery to pay my respects. The land overlooks a serene lake with a beautiful hardwood forest beyond. It happens to be Veterans Day weekend and I hear gunshots from the woods, an eerie atmospheric addition.

It takes a while to find the graves of Leonard and Fritz. The cemetery is full of Wards, Sinks, Everharts, Truetts, Conrads, and Clodfelters, all good German names. Then, suddenly, dozens of Leonards appear with graves marked from the late 1700s to present day. Down the hillside, away from the other graves, with an unobstructed view of the lake, stands an elegant stone obelisk bearing a simple inscription: "Valentine Leonard. Born October 13, 1718. Died November 15, 1781. Aged 63 years old. The Heroes buried in this spot were assassinated in their homes by Tories near the close of the Revolutionary War. They were patriots and bravely fought for American independence."

At the feet of the obelisk lie two matching memorial stones bearing the names, birth dates, and death dates of Wooldrich Fritz and Valentine Leonard.

Of the dozen or so historic burying grounds I've wandered around during my four years on the Wagon Road, including those at Antietam and Gettysburg, this one feels much more intimate and personal, undoubtedly because most of the folks buried here were neighbors, family, and friends across many generations, many of whom probably never ventured far from home during their lifetimes. Walking among them, I remember my favorite lines from Thomas Gray's "Elegy Written in a Country Churchyard" . . . "Beneath those rugged elms, that yew-tree's shade / Where heaves the turf in a many mould'ring heap / Each in his narrow cell forever laid / The rude forefathers of the hamlet sleep."

A second gunshot in the woods and a chevron of honking Canadian geese flying low overhead return me to the moment. It's time to go.

Having arrived an hour later than planned and dawdled too long in the cemetery, by the time I reach Pilgrim Church's fellowship hall the fall bazaar is already winding down and all the homemade chicken pies, green bean casseroles, and chicken and dumpling dishes have sold out.

"Wish you'd gotten here two hours ago," sympathizes member Gene Edwards. "There's always a big crowd waiting for the doors to open. We went through three hundred pies and ninety quarts of chicken and dumplings in the first forty-five minutes."

He introduces me, though, to Pastor Richard Moore, who is busy selling homemade toys, and to ninety-one-year-old Francis Tibbey, who sells me a dollar ticket for the annual drawing for a beautiful quilt, handmade by a parishioner. Edwards also gives me a walking tour of the church, the fifth Pilgrim Church, he explains, to be built on the original site, a modern brick and steepled affair dating from the early 1970s. We start with the church's impressive history room, where Edwards shows me everything from original hymnals written in German to the re-created sanctuary with its unique goblet-style pulpit. In a locked glass case, he points out a strange carved wooden cylindrical device that figured importantly into the Valentine Leonard saga.

"When the killers came to kill him," Edwards explains, "they undoubtedly were also after his gold and silver. That wooden cylinder is where Valentine hid his gold and silver coins in the walls of his house. Supposedly only his daughters knew where it was hidden."

I ask how many members currently belong to historic Pilgrim Church.

"We once had around two hundred. These days it's down to about one hundred. Seems to be the fate of a lot of churches these days." He wonders if I've visited any other historic churches during my Wagon Road travels.

I'm happy to report that I've attended almost a dozen church services on my way down the road, a total that includes three Presbyterian, three Lutheran, two Methodist, two Episcopalian, and one Mennonite. Churches and taverns, I add, were among the most important public institutions of early colonial life, key places where a young nation's sense of community was fostered in the wilderness.

Gene Edwards smiles. "That makes only eleven. Maybe you should come tomorrow and make Pilgrim Church an even dozen."

Sounds like a great idea, I tell him, since I have no German Reformed on my dance card.

"I promise you will be made to feel very welcome."

The next morning, historic Pilgrim Church's opening hymn is "We Gather Together," a traditional Dutch Thanksgiving anthem that every schoolkid in America sang once upon a time when learning about the Pilgrims and their first Thanksgiving.

Pastor Moore gives a fine Veterans Day sermon titled "Love All People," reminding his flock of Jesus's greatest commandment in the book of Mark to "love thy neighbor as thyself," a scriptural charge, he says, that means "loving everyone the same regardless of personal income, religious beliefs, race, or politics. That *is* the truest measure of Christianity." This sentiment almost brings an involuntary "Amen" to my lips. Moore finishes his elegant meditation with one of my favorite bits from Micah 6, a verse commonly cited to spur the faithful in Christ to action during times of peril: "Do justice, love mercy, and walk humbly with God."

At service's end, several members want to hear about my travels on the Wagon Road, including LaVon Edwards and Margaret Truett. Truett will turn ninety on Valentine's Day and remembers growing up and hearing that the Old Greensboro Road, which passes the Pilgrim Church less than a quarter of a mile away—today US Highway 29—was referred to by elders as the Great Wagon Road. She wonders if I think this might be true.

I tell her that I know at least one prominent Wagon Road researcher who would absolutely agree with her elders. With so many early branches of the GWR crossing the Old North State, it's entirely possible that Carol Fuller and her band of Great Road contributors are correct that the Pilgrim Church sits just off the original road.

She smiles impishly and pats my hand.

"I *know* it's true, dear. Just wanted to hear *you* say so. Valentine Leonard and our ancestors sleeping out back are living proof that it was the old Wagon Road."

I chat for at least another twenty minutes with other members, some of whom encourage me to come back again and bring my wife. Gene Edwards wasn't exaggerating when he said the welcome would be warm and genuine.

At the door, Gene's wife, LaVon, also thanks me for coming.

"I'm sorry you didn't win the handmade quilt. But there's always next year's festival. Do come back and bring your wife."

I promise her I shall do just that, making sure I arrive before the chicken and dumplings and chicken pies all sell out.

Crossing the Yadkin River at the old Trading Ford, I next stop in historic Salisbury, the oldest continually populated colonial town in Western North Carolina, founded on 635 acres granted by Lord Carteret in 1755 at the intersection of the Great Wagon Road and older Indian Trading Path, or so generations of historians have claimed, making Salisbury and Rowan County a powerhouse of frontier commerce for the Scots-Irish.

I know this handsome town and its American Revolution and Civil War histories almost chapter and verse, but I am here principally to pose a couple follow-up questions to my good friend Dr. Gary Freeze, longtime Catawba College history professor and one of the most respected historians of the colonial South and the Great Wagon Road.

Weeks before I set off for Philadelphia in summer 2017, I had spent a couple days getting a crash course from Dr. Freeze on the region's complex frontier politics and geography of the road through the Carolinas.

"Salisbury was created because it was halfway on the migratory road between two colonies," he explained one noontime over a long lunch at the Sweet Meadow Cafe just off the city's busy main drag. "Halfway to Virginia, halfway to South Carolina, intersecting with the Great Trading Path, which made it one of the most important places on the entire Great Wagon Road."

The original reason for establishing a settlement here was to impose good English order on an untamed wilderness, "ideally creating a back-woods version of a proper English country town," he said. "It clearly didn't work out that way."

When North Carolina Governor Dobbs visited the rudimentary settle-ment in 1754 on his way to create a fort out west during a Cherokee uprising, Freeze explained, he found six or seven structures under construction in a rough village that would soon be named Salisbury after its English forebear. "Its good name was about as English as Salisbury would get thanks to a flood of arriving immigrants on the Wagon Road."

The newcomers, he explained, fell into two major groups. The first were industrious German farmers who planted crops and soon opened a trade road to Charleston to sell their cheese, butter, grain, and indigo in ex-change for farming supplies and other essentials of life. They would settle on the eastern flank of the Wagon Road all the way to Charlotte. The sec-ond group, on the western side, were Scots-Irish settlers who were famous for taking possession of land simply because they believed it was their God-given right and obligation to do so.

"Dobbs describes the Scots-Irish settlers as a Covenanter community influenced by a maverick Presbyterian minister and ultra-Scottish nation-alist named Alexander Craighead who was chased out of Pennsylvania by William Penn and came down the Great Wagon Road to Sugar Creek (near present-day Charlotte) using the power of Calvinism to bitterly oppose anything English." Craighead raised a Presbyterian church on the Cowpas-ture River in Sugar Creek and taught his followers "to hate any English lord or bishop that would make them bow their heads. Because when you bow your head, the English will cut it off."

Even after his death, Craighead's radical beliefs about freedom and resisting British authority continued to infuse and shape the politics and character of the Carolina backcountry and the rural South in general for the next two hundred years.

"Among other things, this intense antipathy for the British and anything that smacks of government authority will fuel—and ultimately decide—the Revolutionary War in favor of America, not to mention the Confederacy that follows less than a century later."

This restless energy also led to the creation of the Mecklenburg Declaration of Independence, which called for independence from Britain in May 1775, roughly a year before a similar declaration was signed in Philadelphia. An authenticated copy of the Mecklenburg Declaration, however, has never been found, though it remains a subject of intense debate among colonial historians to this day.

After showing me several historic spots and traces of the old road that are still visible around and along US 29 south to Concord and Charlotte (including a vast ancient caldera in which the modern city of Charlotte sits today), Freeze urged me to drop by historic Thyatira Presbyterian Church—organized 1750—in the rolling countryside a few miles west of Salisbury, to get a sense of the foundational impact Scots-Irish values had in shaping the life and culture of the backcountry of both Carolinas.

"It's a beautiful old church. Make sure you check out the church cemetery," he advised. "I often take my students there because it's been called the Westminster Abbey of Rowan County due to all the important folks buried there. Not to mention the unexplained pirates."

Not long before I set out for Philadelphia, a church elder named Glenn McCorkle invited me to attend Thyatira's annual summer homecoming service. Having attended a similar Presbyterian homecoming at historic Bethesda Church in Aberdeen in the neighboring Sandhills—another hotbed of Scottish settlement—I looked forward to a presentation of clan flags, a fine sermon, and a delicious covered-dish luncheon afterward.

The highlight of the day, however, was when Glenn McCorkle showed me around the well-kept cemetery of his ancestors, early settlers, and other illustrious colonial figures that included John and Jean Knox, immigrants from Scotland and grandparents of US President James Polk, who committed seven sons to the revolution; his own famous ancestor Dr. Samuel E. McCorkle, a Princeton grad and Thyatira Church minister who helped found the University of North Carolina; and half a dozen Revolutionary War officers; as well as Elizabeth Gillespie Steele, who owned the Salisbury tavern where

Nathanael Greene famously spent the night with British General Cornwallis hot on his heels during their so-called Race to the Dan in 1781. According to Salisbury lore, Steele presented Greene with a couple sacks of coins—her life savings—in support of the rebel cause, and allowed him to scratch a treasonous insult on the back of the tavern's painting of King George III during his flight through town. This was a story I'd heard all my life and hoped someone at Thyatira might tell me more about. I'd always heard that the painting had mysteriously vanished. When I mentioned this to McCorkle, he smiled and said, "On the contrary, it's here. I've saved that for last."

We completed the tour of the beautifully maintained cemetery standing by four mysterious "pirate graves" set off by themselves in the oldest section of the burying ground. No stone bore names, but three of the monuments featured a skull and crossbones and a fourth had menacing crossbones over its face.

"No one knows how and why these got here. We're a long way from the sea," McCorkle explained. "One theory some folks have advanced is that they were victims of violence on the road or maybe a plague of some sort. The stones could be a warning not to come too close."

"What would history be without a mystery pirate?" I said.

McCorkle nodded and smiled. "Now, let me show you something very special."

He led me to the Thyatira Heritage Museum, adjacent to the church sanctuary, where he showed me early church documents and the church's most prized possession—the well-traveled portraits of King George III and wife Queen Charlotte. He opened a locked security cabinet and delicately took out the painting of the monarch, allowing me to hold Thyatira's most precious artifact.

"Turn it over."

On the back were the words, written upside down in script, "O George hide thy face and mourn." Beneath that were the initials "N.G."

"It's that way because Greene had it upside down when he wrote on it," my host explained, chuckling.

"So, it never actually vanished?"

"Oh yes. It did vanish. For quite a long time."

The mezzotint portraits, he explained, hung on Elizabeth Steele's tavern wall even when Lord Cornwallis showed up just hours after Greene had fled north to gather his scattered Continentals and militias to prepare for an encounter at Guilford Courthouse. My host handed me a small bound booklet titled *The Traveling Monarchs* by Beulah Davis.

"Take this with you. The story's all here."

After Elizabeth Gillespie Steele's passing in 1790, the story goes, the paintings began their long journey to Governor David Swain's mansion in Raleigh, and then to his presidential office at the University of North Carolina, where they hung on the wall until his death in 1868. Upon his widow's death, the paintings were sold at public auction and purchased by a Raleigh schoolboy named William Andrews for a "few cents," who proudly displayed them on the wall of his own home until his death; his widow moved to California and the king and queen effectively vanished until the late 1970s. At that point, an enterprising descendant of both Francis McCorkle and Elizabeth Gillespie Steele, an archivist named Norman McCorkle, tracked down the paintings to a fine arts gallery in Palm Springs, California, which was selling them both for fifteen hundred dollars.

Fortunately, another McCorkle/Steele descendant named Pauline McCorkle Neel and her husband, Locke, an avid historic preservationist, came forward to authenticate and purchase the paintings. They returned them to Thyatira Church in 1980, and funded the construction of the highly secure Heritage Museum where the king and queen safely reside today.

"That was the first great story I found on my Wagon Road travels," I explain now to Gary Freeze, five years after our first visit. Freeze, today retired and doing historic research for several local attorneys and organizations, wonders how many folks I've interviewed along the road since our first meeting.

Latest count, including the good folks at the Pilgrim Church, is well over 100, I explain.

"Good stories?"

"A moveable feast of colonial America," I confirm. "I've even found home-grown historians who can't agree where the Great Wagon Road originally ran."

Freeze sips his sweet tea and smiles. "Oh, really? Where do they say it runs?"

I mention Kyle Stimson's Sherrill's Path and Carol Fuller's firm asser-
tion that the Great Wagon Road ended in colonial Salisbury.

Freeze looks amused. "Everyone wants to place their stamp on history,
I suppose. Unfortunately, they're both dead wrong. As it happens, I grew
up on Sherrill's Path and probably know about it better than anyone alive
today. It was indeed a very old trading road and Indian hunting path, one
taken by lots of settlers and soldiers. But the patterns of settlement and
commerce prove that the original Great Wagon Road not only passed directly through Salisbury and Charlotte, as long held by every credible colonial historian of the past century, but did indeed go on to Georgia."

He seems pleased when I tell him that, until proven otherwise, I'm
choosing to follow the traditional route to Georgia, including both branches
across South Carolina, the latter of which will enable me to return home to
Greensboro over the branch of the road Lord Cornwallis took to Guilford
Courthouse in his fabled Race to the Dan with General Nathanael Greene.

"What an excellent way to finish the journey," he agrees. "Ending where
you began."

"You sound like the Gospel of Thomas."

"Well, hasn't it been something of a spiritual pilgrimage for you?"

"More than you know."

Like any good mentor, Dr. Freeze wonders what I've learned during my
Covid-interrupted pilgrimage, now approaching five years.

"All history is personal to someone."

"How true," says Professor Freeze. "Especially for someone whose ancestors came down the Great Wagon Road."

TWENTY-SEVEN

THE BEECH ISLAND BOYS

WHAT I'M GOING TO TELL YOU MAY COME AS A BIG SHOCK," BETTIS RAINS-
ford Sr. says pleasantly before we line up for lunch. "Contrary to common belief and the claims of generations of historians, the Great Wagon Road did not pass through the state of South Carolina."

I smile and nod my head. By now I should probably not be surprised by anything I read or am told about the old colonial road I've been chasing for close to five years. But in this particular setting, the idea that the Wagon Road doesn't exist at all in the Palmetto State is quite a statement.

I've just finished giving a well-received, hour-long talk on my Great Wagon Road travels to members of the Beech Island Agricultural Club, one of the oldest continuously operating grange organizations in the United States. Following my talk, several of Rainsford's fellow members were eager to share their own stories of ancestors they believe came down the Great Wagon Road to South Carolina during the eighteenth century.

Beech Island is an all-male club founded by South Carolina Governor James Henry Hammond and eleven local farmers in 1856, originally created for the "diffusion of agricultural knowledge and regulation of illegal slave traffic." At the time, founding members agreed to pay five dollars a year in dues and gather on the first Saturday of every month to discuss agricultural news and related issues over a barbecue lunch. One hundred and sixty-six years later, with the pleasant scent of pig butts roasting over a pit of coals just outside the modest tin-roofed meeting hall, some might say this is simply a gathering of good old boys memorializing a lifestyle that's gone with the wind.

Though its founding fathers were antebellum farmers, the club's current membership is quite occupationally diverse, composed of local ministers and physicians, public educators, municipal and state government officials, leading businessmen from both sides of the Savannah River, and no shortage of lawyers and serious historians.

A glimpse of the club's roster of monthly guest speakers includes the likes of John D. Rockefeller and President William Howard Taft, with a liberal sprinkling of prominent artists, athletes, authors, inventors, governors, and even Supreme Court justices. Testament to the club's lofty social stature on both sides of the Savannah River are the hundreds of framed photographs of former prominent members from across the region that adorn the walls of their modest cinder-block meeting hall set deep in the forest.

"You have to be legitimately dead to get your photo on the wall," a long-time member named Roy Simpkins explains to me with a wry grin. "Truthfully, I might be the only *real* farmer in the club, which is why we began letting in local undertakers a while back on the theory that they are the ultimate planters."

The jokes keep coming.

One of the most prominent photographs displayed behind the speaker's podium belongs to Robert Edward Lee. When I ask another elderly member ahead of me in the buffet line if Lee was a Beech Island member, he explains that the photograph has been on the wall longer than any living member can remember. He thinks it's there because Lee came to speak to the club after the Civil War to promote his "little ol' college up in Virginia."

"You know," he adds with his slow Southern drawl, "we've only missed two Saturday meetings in our entire history. One was due to Covid; the other was due to the *wah*-uh." At which point he smiles and winks. "That would be the *wah*-uh between the states, of course."

The member behind me tilts forward and says with a gentle snort, "That's not true, of course. He just loves to tell that to gullible Yankees."

The invitation to speak to the Beech Island Boys, as I've fondly come to think of them, was arranged by local history-loving friends from the world of golf. Augusta, Georgia, is not only the historic terminus of the Great Wagon Road but also the home of Augusta National Golf Club and the Masters Golf Tournament, my usual stop on Washington Road.

This time, however, in the generous company of Erick Montgomery, executive director of Historic Augusta, a longtime Beech Island member, I'm taking a deep dive into two and a half centuries of the old river city's history, from its liberation from British occupation by local "Sons of Liberty" in 1781—orchestrated by "Light-Horse" Harry Lee (Robert's daddy) and South Carolina's own beloved military hero Andrew Pickens—to the city's rebirth as an inland capital of King Cotton prior to the Civil War. After showing me the city's nine neighborhoods on the National Register of Historic Places and learning of my soft spot for historic churches, my host showed me the Springfield Baptist Church—oldest African American church in America— and even snuck me into the sanctuary of Saint Paul's Church, the Mother Church of Augusta, at 6th and Reynolds Streets, established by the English at Fort Augusta in 1751, destroyed and rebuilt five times after three wars and the Great Augusta Fire of 1916.

Later that evening, on my own recognizance, I took a candlelight Christmas tour of Woodrow Wilson's boyhood home at Telfair and Seventh, learning about Tommy Wilson's penchant for playing tricks on the household staff and the pride he took in watching his papa, pastor of the adjacent First Presbyterian Church, march off to war as a chaplain with local Confederate troops. The next day, I'd spent a couple interesting hours in Augusta's outstanding Museum of History learning about everything from the first settlers who arrived via Wagon Road to the life and times of hometown R&B legend James Brown.

In a sense, lunch with the Beech Island Boys amounts to the proverbial "end of the road" of my Great Road odyssey, though I still plan to follow the "eastern branch" of the historic Wagon Road home to Greensboro in the footsteps of Cornwallis and Greene, the so-called Race to the Dan that hastened the end of the Revolutionary War.

That is—if the road even exists in these parts.

During lunch, Bettis Rainsford, who hails from nearby Edgefield County and has become involved in the Palmetto State's ongoing celebration of its role in the American Revolution, provides me with a copy of a recent historical paper in which he explains why the Great Wagon Road never existed in the Palmetto State. The outbreak of the French and Indian War, he argues, slowed traffic to a trickle on the Wagon Road from western Pennsylvania to North Carolina, but dramatically increased traffic into North and South Carolina as settlers came south to avoid the bloodshed in the middle Atlantic region. However, the Cherokee war in the Carolinas that broke out in 1760 effectively ended settler migration for several years before resuming in 1763 and growing dramatically up through 1775. Rainsford notes that prior to 1730, South Carolina had no significant development beyond sixty miles from the coast, but that by mid-century, the burgeoning populations of Pennsylvania, Delaware, Maryland, Virginia, and North Carolina had begun to eye the rich backcountry lands of South Carolina and the attractive inducements for settlement offered by the colonial government. At that point, he adds, the Great Wagon Road and other roads from the north had reached the border of South Carolina and were beginning to funnel settlers from northern colonies into South Carolina.

"What is clear from all of the contemporary evidence," he writes, "is that once in South Carolina the 'Great Wagon Road' ceased to be considered a single and dominant road, but instead divided into many paths or roads fanning out across all the South Carolina backcountry. From what we have been able to determine from looking at contemporary sources, no one in the colonial area thought of any of the paths or roads through South Carolina as being a truly dominant one, as they had of the Great Wagon Road in Pennsylvania, Maryland, Virginia and, to a lesser extent, North Carolina."

To support his thesis, he notes that not only do most historians of the South Carolina backcountry never mention the Great Wagon Road, per se, but modern studies of families that settled in the Palmetto State before 1800 suggest that another well-traveled colonial road due east of where the Great Wagon Road allegedly ran—more or less following the present-day path of US Highway 1—was also significantly responsible for the state's immigration growth from northern colonies.

"Thus, in answer to the question of *where* the Great Wagon Road was in South Carolina," my genial lunch companion sums up, "we are left with the conclusion that the Great Wagon Road, as such, really did not exist in South

Carolina. Instead, there were *many* roads that constantly changed over the period from 1750 to the end of the century."

He appears pleased—and not a little surprised—when I mention that I agree with his conclusions, noting that the wide geographic spread of historic towns and places across the Palmetto State that claim some provenance with the road, many of whom even mention it by name in their early histories, suggests to me that the mythology of the nation's first immigration highway is far more important than any quest to prove or disprove the old road's original path.

Just for fun, though, I mention how I followed the traditional "western branch" of the Wagon Road through York and Chester to the delightful college town of Newberry ("City of Friendly Folks")—where I spent two days checking out its handsome historic (1881) opera house and upscale art shops on Main Street—and plan to take the "eastern branch" through Camden, Lancaster, and the Waxhaws home to North Carolina.

Newberry's sparkling new historical museum is housed in the town's elegant former central post office building. There, Director Ernest Shealy walked me through a host of impressive exhibits and artifacts that told the story of how Quaker and Scots-Irish immigrants from Pennsylvania settled the county in the 1750s. "They arrived on the Great Wagon Road," he explained, "which was locally called the Carolina Road, used by merchants who kept a brisk trade with Philadelphia and Charleston." As it turned out, I'd just missed the museum's annual "living history" tour, during which Shealy pointed out visible traces of the original road that passed through the area as it rambled on toward Edgefield and ultimately Augusta.

"That simply proves my point," Rainsford interrupts. "It's the history that happened along these multiple old roads that matters most to the creation of South Carolina and its vital role in winning the Revolutionary War."

He tells me about the state-wide Sestercentennial Commission chartered by the South Carolina General Assembly in 2018 in partnership with the American Battlefield Trust. They're planning a series of special 250th-anniversary events across the state that tell the story of South Carolina's essential role in winning the American Revolution.

"To be frank, up to till now," he confides, "we've not done a very good job telling our story to our own people, much less outside of South Carolina.

We plan to change that in the coming years. Our history is a great untold story."

I congratulate him on the effort and agree that South Carolina has a wonderful story to tell; I know a good deal of it thanks to a father who was keen on Revolutionary War history and took my brother and me to Camden, Kings Mountain, and Cowpens battlefields during the years we resided in the state. Being a longtime Rev War freak, I've been back to all three battle-fields several times in my life.

My new friend looks even more pleased.

"So *you* have a history here too. How marvelous! Therefore, you know how South Carolina helped shape the outcome of the war."

"I do indeed. It shaped the way I look at the world today," I add. "That's an untold story too."

After lunch, eager to head for Camden, I thank the Beech Island Boys for their hospitality and strike out over backcountry highways that bypass the sprawling suburbs of Columbia, the state capital, leading me through a stark but beautiful winterscape of longleaf pines and scrub oaks, dormant peach fields and shuttered roadside produce stands, cinder-block Free Will Bap-tist churches, and sleepy crossroad junctions that bring to mind one of my favorite Wagon Road stories about the isolated South Carolina backcountry.

In 1766, a newly minted Anglican priest and poet named Charles Wood-mason passed this way, attempting to save the lost souls of the region. Woodmason was a reactionary product of the First Great Awakening and wave of "New Light" preachers sweeping through Eastern America in the mid-eighteenth century, finding their most fertile ground in the vast South-ern backcountry. Early on, Woodmason achieved financial success as a planter and Charleston merchant and even published poems that lauded the inquiry of the Scientific Revolution in America, particularly Ben Franklin's discovery of electricity. Upon the imposition of Britain's detested Stamp Act, however, Woodmason's business interests nose-dived, prompting him to return home to England to become an ordained priest of the Church of England in April 1766.

Soon after he returned to America, determined to bring salvation to the untamed wilderness of both Carolinas, he reportedly traveled thousands of miles on horseback for half a dozen years through the most violent and unsettled parts of both colonies—preaching to, marrying, and baptizing thousands of settlers while condemning the unstructured and highly emotional evangelism of his fellow Baptist, Methodist, Presbyterian, and Moravian ministers. (Woodmason is even believed to have had a hand in stirring up loyalist tensions that led to the Regulator's War at Alamance Battlefield in 1766, a preview of the much larger conflagration to come.) The journals he kept during his remarkable odyssey, however, provide a darkly amusing picture of what the earnest young preacher was up against in the fierce Scots-Irish backcountry.

One of his early stops was at Pine Tree Hill, today known as Camden, which provided a bitter taste of things to come.

"The people around," he wrote, are "of abandoned morals, and profligate principles—rude—ignorant—void of manners, education, and good breeding—no genteel or polite person among them—save Mr. Kershaw, an English merchant settled here."

On he rode, a holy warrior railing against secret papists and Presbyterian preachers, dangerous Dunkers and—worst of all—wild-tongued Free Will Baptists. "Among this medley of religions True Christianity is not to be found. And the perverse spirit of the Presbyterians displays itself much more here than in Scotland. It is dangerous to live among or near any of them—for if they cannot cheat, rob, defraud or injure you in your goods, they will belye, defame, lessen, blacken, disparage the most valuable person breathing . . . They have almost wormed out of all people the church people who cannot bear to live among such a Vett of Vile unaccountable Wretches."

At one memorable stop, a band of "rude fellows" repeatedly interrupted his Sunday sermon by herding fifty-seven dogs into the church sanctuary "(for I counted them) which in time of service they set fighting, and I was obliged to stop—in time of sermon they repeated it—and I was obliged to desist and dismiss the people."

Adding to Reverend Woodmason's moral disgust, in some backcountry communities he found women who were "half naked or completely without covering and beyond reach of shame." Deep in the rural fastness of South Carolina, he wrote despairingly: "Nor is this a country or place where I wish any gentleman to travel or settle . . . The ignorance and impudence is so very high, as to be past bearing. Very few can read, fewer can write . . . they are very poor—owing to their extreme indolence for they possess the finest country in America and could raise but everything. They delight in their low, lazy, sluttish, heathenish, hellish life, and seem not desirous of changing it. Both men and women will do anything to come at liquor, cloths, furniture rather than work for it—hence their many vices—their gross licentiousness, wantonness, lasciviousness, rudeness, lewdness, and profligacy they will commit the grossest enormities before my face and laugh at all admonition."

Given these barriers, it's remarkable that the circuit-riding preacher, by his own account, managed to serve thirty different churches across two states and baptize hundreds of lost souls during his peripatetic ministry, covering six thousand miles through a wilderness he clearly regarded as hell on earth.

In 1768, he finally abandoned his holy quest, admitting, "It will require much time to Model the Manners and Morals of these Wild Peoples," before moving on to accept posts at loyalist Episcopal parishes in Virginia and Baltimore. (There, he eventually gave a controversial sermon in tribute to the Crown in February 1776 that prompted a local patriot committee to suggest that he might wish to make tracks out of town to save his own skin.)

Father Woodmason returned to England a short time later and spent the balance of his days serving as a journeyman Anglican preacher.

As I gas up the Pearl on the outskirts of Camden on a backcountry highway that he might well have traveled, a man about my age is doing the same thing for his faded pickup truck. A young black retriever sits patiently waiting on the front seat.

"Love that wagon," he says. "They don't make 'em like that anymore, do they?"

"It's a relic. Nice dog. I used to have one like her. What's her name?"

"Midnight. I can't go anywhere without her."

"I know the feeling."

Mully has been gone for only five months. But an unfillable hole in my heart remains.

Our last trip together came the summer after Covid when she went with me to find Andrew Jackson's birthplace—claimed by both North and South Carolina. On the way, we attended the eleventh annual Pirate Day festival on the grounds of the Museum of the Waxhaws on the Wagon Road.

By that point, Mully's legs were beginning to falter. As I visited with museum coordinator Kathy Wright to learn how Pirate Day had grown out of a popular long-running outdoor drama called *Listen and Remember*, which told the story of the formation of the Waxhaws Colonial Settlement by Wagon Road Scots-Irish settlers and the subsequent birth of President Andrew Jackson in the area, Mully waited for me in the shade outside with a painted mermaid named Beth, who graciously offered to hold her leash and give her water.

According to Wright, both the Great Wagon Road and older Trading Path merged in Waxhaw, becoming the primary route by which thousands of Northern settlers made their way to York, Lancaster, and the rest of South Carolina.

The showpiece of the museum was a handsome farm wagon from the eighteenth century.

As we stood looking at it, Wright spoke up: "Every time I look at that wagon, I try to remember that it belonged to real people traveling through a terrifying wilderness with their families and probably everything they owned crammed into one small space. It must have been so uncomfortable and terribly lonely at times."

"The smart ones brought along a dog for security and companionship," I pointed out, mentioning that dogs frequently appear in paintings of back-country travelers.

Wright is curious how my journey along the Wagon Road has gone.

"Quite nicely. My old wagon has lots of room and even air-conditioning. I also have the best dog ever for company. She's traveled half the road with me."

Such fateful words.

Two months later, a kind lady vet arrived in our backyard as Mully completed a slow final circuit of our Asian garden on trembling legs. It was late afternoon, the time of day when we often sat together watching the light fade and birds feed in our garden. This time was different, a final farewell. She sat down by the bench where I sat and looked up at me with her soulful brown eyes, clearly aware that my heart was breaking. I stroked her head and thanked her for nearly seventeen years of incredible friendship. Then she lay down and placed her chin on my foot. Wendy was standing a few feet away, already weeping. As the powerful narcotic did its job, my eyes filled too. A few days later, I scattered her ashes in the garden that's now named for her.

After gassing up the Pearl, I spend a silent hour walking the Camden Battlefield, missing Mully like a fever that won't break, remembering how she came here with Wendy and me for the annual reenactment of the Battle of Camden. We were in the company of a wonderful storyteller named Paul David Reuwer, a local judge and respected Rev War historian who is one of the principals of the annual event, wisely staged each November rather than in the furnace blast of midsummer when the actual battle took place, in August 1781.

Reuwer not only graciously walked us through the battle and its aftermath but finished our time together with a tour of the nearby historic Quaker cemetery, where so many on both sides fell and were buried.

"After the Battle of Camden there were many who feared the cause of liberty was gravely endangered," he said at one point. "Fortunately, the backcountry of the Carolinas and an unlikely military genius named Nathanael Greene would rise up in the nick of time and have something different to say about the outcome."

Following the British army's capture of Savannah in December 1778, Georgia was reestablished as a royal colony, and an ambitious campaign aimed at pacifying the Carolina backcountry by rallying the region's many loyalist citizens got underway. With Savannah as a staging ground, a large military force under British general Sir Henry Clinton surrounded and subsequently captured Charleston, the South's largest port city, in May of 1780, taking several thousand Continental troops prisoner and placing them on offshore prison ships, nearly the whole of George Washington's Southern Command. Patriot militias that pledged no further involvement in rebellion against the Crown were freed and sent home.

With American forces decimated and in retreat, Clinton dispatched fresh troops into South Carolina's interior to fortify key British outposts at Camden and Ninety Six under the command of veteran Lieutenant General

Charles, Lord Cornwallis, a well-educated British aristocrat who privately held sympathies for the American cause but proved his chops by previously driving George Washington's troops out of New Jersey.

On the heels of Charleston's surrender, Cornwallis sent a fast-moving legion of dragoons led by his protégé, Lieutenant Colonel Banastre Tarleton, to track down a group of surviving Virginia regulars and fleeing militia under the command of Abraham Buford before they could reach the safety of North Carolina. Tarleton overtook the Americans at Waxhaws, named for the ancient Indian tribe that inhabited the border area between North and South Carolina. What happened next is still subject to historical interpretation. In his postwar memoirs Tarleton claimed the Virginians failed to surrender and fired point-blank at his charging cavalry, and in the resulting melee, most of Buford's exhausted troops were savagely hacked to death, including many who were killed as they attempted to surrender. The so-called Buford Massacre tagged Tarleton with the nickname "Bloody Ban" and ignited backcountry fury, especially after Clinton subsequently issued a proclamation that anyone refusing to support the loyalist cause would be considered a rebel or enemy combatant subject to death. Farmsteads and plantations were promptly set ablaze.

The major flashpoint came at a crossroads settlement of Pine Tree Hill/Camden, where Cornwallis gathered his large and superbly equipped army to begin a major effort to push remaining Continental troops and patriot militias permanently out of South Carolina and possibly North Carolina and Virginia as well.

"Camden was the jewel in the crown of British outposts," writes Andrew Waters in his 2022 book *To the End of the World*, a brilliant account of Britain's failed Southern Strategy and the subsequent Race to the Dan between the armies of Cornwallis and General Nathanael Greene, "for it controlled the southern terminus of the Great Wagon Road, the main thoroughfare leading south from Pennsylvania."

Meantime, still reeling from the fall of Charleston, and with the war at a stalemate in the North, an anxious American Congress turned to semiretired General Horatio Gates, the "Hero of Saratoga," issuing him a mandate to revive the foundering Continental Army and push the British out of the South Carolina backcountry.

Ignoring the advice of local partisans who suggested that he march his battle-weary, half-starved Continental regiments from Maryland and Delaware down the Wagon Road through Salisbury and Charlotte, "a region friendly to the Patriot cause," as Waters notes, "where the Continental Army was more likely to find supplies and reinforcements," Gates foolishly opted to take a more direct route to Camden through the notorious Pine Barrens of the border region, "a desolate, unpopulated region of sand, pine, and swamp area covering both North and South Carolina."

Pushing his exhausted army eighteen hours a day, with little food or rest, adding 2,100 North Carolina militiamen to his force just twelve miles north of Camden, Gates ordered an all-night march and dawn assault on the larger British force, resulting in a devastating defeat at the hands of Cornwallis's veteran Twenty-Third and Thirty-Third Regiments of Foot.

Gates lost more than half his army before escaping on horseback and fleeing to Hillsborough in Piedmont, North Carolina. As Waters sums up, "On August 16, 1780, Charles, Lord Cornwallis, lieutenant general of the British Army, conquered the South."

On paper at least, the sweeping British victory cleared the way for Cornwallis to rally backcountry loyalists and march the most powerful army in the world through the backcountry of both Carolinas to destroy remaining patriot strongholds and put an end to the war.

From Camden, I cut across country through the Sumter National Forest to Chester and turn onto US Highway 321 north, a road many believe to be part of the original Great Wagon Road, hoping to visit one of the state's few Rev War places I've never been to.

Brattonsville was the plantation home of a wealthy Whig patriot named William Bratton, site of a smaller but no less important engagement that helped revive patriot hopes that terrible summer of 1780.

A week before the American debacle at Camden, a Pennsylvania-born loyalist captain in Tarleton's legion named Christian Huck, who owned a well-earned reputation for roughing up colonial women and hanging relatives of backcountry patriots, was dispatched to round up and eliminate rebel leaders in the area where Cornwallis's massive army would soon be arriving.

After reportedly murdering an unarmed boy who was reading his Bible

and burning the home and library of a Whig leader and influential Presbyterian minister in Chester County, Huck's troops destroyed the ironworks
of Whig William Hill in nearby York and descended on Bratton's plantation
with thirty-five dragoons, twenty New York Volunteers, and sixty loyalist
militia, infamously placing a reaping hook to the neck of Bratton's wife,
Martha, in a failed attempt to learn her husband's whereabouts. Huck and
his men promptly took three neighbors of the Brattons' as well as Colonel
Bratton's older brother, Robert, into custody, placing them in a corncrib
under guard to await hanging in the morning.

They never got the chance. At dawn the next morning, using intelli-
gence gained from a Bratton family slave and other residents, a hastily organized patriot force of 150 militia attacked Huck's sleeping encampment
from three sides. In the surprise attack, Huck was fatally shot in the head as
he attempted to mount his horse and rally his men, many of whom surrendered or fled. The Tory toll was high. In his report to Cornwallis, Tarleton
reported that only twenty-four of his men managed to escape. Patriot losses
amounted to just one dead and one wounded. The four prisoners were lib-
erated from the corncrib.

News of "Huck's Defeat" spread like wildfire through the Carolina backcountry and had an outsized impact on the direction of the war, according
to South Carolina historian Walter Edgar, who cites the patriot victory at
Brattonsville as a major turning point in the American Revolution in South
Carolina. "The entire backcountry seemed to take heart. Frontier militia
had defeated soldiers of the feared British Legion," he writes, citing it as a
key link in the chain of rapid successes that led to patriot victories at Kings
Mountain and Cowpens.

Before I push on to find a motel near Kings Mountain for the night, I
stop to have a look at the historic Brattonsville's Plantation House, which
was used in the filming of the 1990 Mel Gibson film *The Patriot*, one of my
favorite movies. According to the calculations of Forsyth County historian
Kyle Stimson, the roadbed of the Great Wagon Road literally ran right past
the front porch of the house. Today, the ten-acre property is a living history site that features thirty colonial and antebellum structures and a pair
of house museums chronicling life in the Southern backcountry. Unfortunately, the grounds are closing as I arrive, but a thoughtful staffer points out

a narrative walking trail through the battle site of Huck's Defeat and agrees to give me fifteen minutes to walk it.

Maybe it's due to the late hour of the day or the fact that I'm tired and missing my dog, but all sorts of unexpected memories and emotions have bubbled up during the long drive across South Carolina's soulful back-country.

During my years traveling the Wagon Road, every time someone shared a story of how their ancestors fled troubles and traveled the road to find a new home and a better life in the South, I often found myself thinking about a similar journey my own family made during the late 1950s, a flight to out-run trouble that resulted in a strange but oddly beautiful year we wound up living in Florence, South Carolina.

I wasn't exaggerating in the least when I confided to Bettis Rainsford that the brief time my family lived in South Carolina shaped my life in an important way, including how I look at the world today.

TWENTY-EIGHT

THIS WORLD IS NOT
YOUR HOME

IN LATE 1957, AFTER A SUCCESSFUL CAREER AT MAJOR NEWSPAPERS IN WASH-
ington, DC, and Dallas, Texas, my dad saw his dream of owning his own
newspaper in coastal Mississippi disappear in a single afternoon. He'd just
returned from purchasing a new printing press in Tampa when he found
that his silent partner in their fledgling enterprise had cleaned out the company bank accounts and disappeared to parts unknown.

Matters quickly got worse.

A couple days later, my mother suffered a late-term miscarriage and
nearly died. Later that week, my dad's only sister, Irene, died in a car wreck
on an icy road outside Washington, DC.

Decades later, during a golf trip to Scotland, I asked him how he managed to survive such a devastating time.

Not surprisingly, Opti the Mystic smiled. "You simply do what you must
do, Bo. I had two young boys and a dangerously ill wife to take care of." So,
he picked up the phone and called a colleague from his years in Washington
who got in touch with a newspaper publisher he knew in Wilmington, North
Carolina. "A week later, when your mom left the hospital, we put you boys
and Amber the dog in the car and drove all night to North Carolina."

I was four years old. The only memory I have of this overnight flight
was stopping in the morning somewhere in the Great Smoky Mountains

west of Asheville for breakfast at a roadside diner on the Cherokee Indian reservation. My father purchased my brother and me "real" Indian moccasins in the gift shop. As we left the restaurant, snowflakes were falling. It was the first time I'd seen snow.

My dad's new job in the advertising department of the Wilmington *Star-News* was well below his many years of newspaper experience, but Wilmington became our family sanctuary for a year. I attended kindergarten at St. Paul's Lutheran Church and my mom slowly got better. My brother and I sang in the cherub choir at church and watched our dad play Balthazar in the church's annual Christmas pageant. We went to the beach often and spent a wonderful week at the Hanover Seaside Club near the Lumina Pier at Wrightsville Beach.

The next summer, just before school started, Dad found an executive position at a newspaper in Florence, South Carolina. We briefly lived in an old house with a large porch near the "whites only" swimming pool in a large city park, before moving to a smaller brick house with a carport in a neighborhood off Cherokee Road.

I liked Florence. It was sleepy, quiet, and very green. I received my first bicycle and could ride it up and down our street as much as I wished. Also, a family named Dodson lived right next door, though they were no relation to us. They had a son named Roy Dean, who was my brother's age, and a daughter named Debbie, who was my mine. We started the first grade together at the Royall School and learned that a famous man lived on the estate directly behind our backyard. His name was Melvin Purvis, the FBI agent who captured John Dillinger and locked up "Baby Face" Nelson and lots of other big-time gangsters. Several times that year, Debbie and I snuck onto the Purvis property hoping to see the famous G-man but encountered only his elderly gardener, who gently shooed us off the property.

For all my efforts over two full summers, I never even caught a glimpse of the famous G-Man beyond the back fence.

That autumn my mom suffered another miscarriage.

An older Black woman named Miss Louise came to help her get back on her feet and look after my brother and me.

I liked Miss Louise because she often took me with her to the Piggly Wiggly supermarket in her powder-blue Dodge Dart and dialed up Southern gospel music on a small transistor radio perched in the window above the kitchen sink while she cooked supper. When my mother—a former beauty queen who "couldn't boil eggs," as my dad liked to say—got back on her feet, Miss Jesse stayed on to teach her how to cook.

One evening while they were cooking together, Miss Louise insisted it was high time I learned to "feet dance." As a lively tune played from the kitchen window, she placed my bare feet on top of her shoes and shimmied me around the floor. I remember how my mother laughed and laughed.

Another evening, my dad's boss from the newspaper came to supper. He was a tall, pale man in a gray wool suit who rattled loose change in his pants pocket. As Miss Louise and my mom cooked supper together, he stood in our kitchen talking about a civil rights protest up in Charlotte by the NAACP.

I was sitting at our kitchen dinette table just listening. I had no idea what a "civil rights protest" meant.

At one point, my dad's boss looked at me and rattled his pocket change. "Tell me something, Jimmy crack corn. Do you know what NAACP stands for?"

"No, sir," I replied.

"It stands for Nigras Ain't Actin' Like Colored People."

He chuckled. So I laughed too.

My mom quietly said, "Jimmy, could you please come with me for a minute?"

Taking me painfully by the ear, she walked me down the hall to the bathroom, shut the door, and made me sit on the closed toilet seat. I watched her unwrap a new bar of Ivory soap. She held the bar soap under my nose.

"Pay close attention," she said evenly. "I'd better never hear that word come from your sweet little mouth. Is that understood?"

"*What* word?" I protested.

"*Nigra*," she said. "That's how supposedly educated white people down here say 'nigger.'"

It was shocking to hear *that* word come from her mouth because it was strictly forbidden to use in our household.

I remember telling her that lots of kids at school used both words.

"That may be, mister. But I'd better never *ever* hear either of those awful words come from your lips or you'll be sitting here with a bar of soap in your mouth until the cows come home."

It was a moment when everything changed. What, to that point, had seemed like a peaceful green paradise, I came to realize, was something very different for my parents.

One afternoon on a trip to the Piggly Wiggly, I asked Miss Louise why so many white people were mad at Black people. (I wasn't even allowed to use "colored.")

She gave me a tender look. "Child, some people just born with a lot of fear and anger in 'em, baby. But let me tell you something. This world is not your home. There's a much better place waitin' for us all."

Even though I'd attended weekday Bible school that summer at the Lutheran church, I wasn't sure what she meant. It would take me many years, in fact, to realize what she was telling me. The words took on new meaning after my girlfriend Kristin's murder and I heard them in my head often during my dark passage as a journalist in Atlanta. I've probably thought of them a thousand times in my life, anytime I find myself unmoored by the sorrows of this world, including during my pilgrimage down the Wagon Road when I heard stories of travelers who lost family members to violence or disease.

Sadly, several months after my mother learned to cook and Miss Louise left us, we learned she was in the hospital suffering from pneumonia.

By that point I was halfway through the second grade, though strangely I can't remember my teacher's name.

It was almost Christmastime. My mom took me to see Miss Louise in the "colored wing" of the hospital and we brought her Whitman's candies and a new powder-blue bathrobe, Miss Jesse's favorite color. I remember a little Christmas tree with tinsel sitting on a side table near her bed.

A few days later, we learned that Miss Jesse had "gone home to Jesus."

My mother and I attended her funeral service at a small brick church somewhere out in the countryside. To my surprise, there were other white people there. The choir sang several gospel songs including the one that Miss Louise sometimes sang when she ironed our clothes. I never learned its name but a line of it went "In the shadow of the trees, my sweet Lord and Savior stands and waits for me." To this day, I can hear her humming it as if she's right next to me, sprinkling our clothes with water sloshing back and forth in her Coke-bottle sprinkler.

It is far from fashion to even speak of having had someone like Miss Louise in your life, a holdover from the apartheid South in which I grew up. To my eternal regret, I never learned her last name. To me she was simply "Miss Louise."

But I will never forget the nurturing impact she had on my family's life. On me.

She's the reason I love old-timey gospel music. The reason I dance rather badly. The reason the scent of Ivory soap nauseates me to this day. The reason I cook collard greens at the holidays, the recipe passed down from my mother, who eventually became a fine "Southern" cook. In small but important ways, Miss Louise not only restored my mother's health but carried my family through the most challenging days of our lives.

Not long after her funeral, we moved home to Greensboro because my dad got a new job with the top advertising firm in the state of North Carolina. He soon created the state's first major travel campaign, called "Variety Vacationland," which aired with a snappy jingle that proved impossible to forget.

A few days after we arrived, he took my brother and me to get library cards and walk the Guilford Courthouse battlefield. It was then that I became a kid obsessed with the American Revolution, particularly the story of how Nathanael Greene outfoxed Lord Cornwallis in their famous Race to the Dan.

In the wake of the Camden debacle, the American Congress granted George Washington the authority to appoint Horatio Gates's successor. He turned to his loyal friend Nathanael Greene, a bookish Rhode Island Quaker and former Continental Army quartermaster chief whose lifelong passion was studying military history and the flow of North American rivers.

Greene would arrive at the shattered Continental Army's camp at Charlotte in early December 1780 to find a military force that was in no condition to face Cornwallis's rapidly advancing juggernaut.

"On the ride south to join his army," Andrew Waters writes, "Greene turned to his most potent weapon—his mind."

Aware that the formidable British Army wasn't a machine built for swift pursuit through an unpredictable wilderness, Greene devised an unorthodox plan to split his outmanned and undersupplied army to fight a hit-and-run partisan war in places of his own choosing, keeping rivers between his army and the larger British force. He ordered his scouts to determine every viable river ford across upper South Carolina and all of North Carolina, including the Dan River in northwest North Carolina and the Trading Ford on the Yadkin River at Salisbury, "the funnel point," as Waters notes, "of the Great Wagon Road."

Among other smart moves, Greene recruited "Light-Horse" Harry Lee and his veteran cavalry and chose Daniel Morgan, the charismatic former Wagon Road wagoner and French and Indian War veteran, to lead a fast-moving "Flying Army" composed of upcountry sharpshooters called the Overmountain Men, turning traditional battlefield warfare into a game of deadly chess.

Cornwallis's first step toward invading North Carolina came earlier in September when his troops attempted to take possession of the small crossroad village of Charlotte. There, they were twice repulsed by a pesky partisan militia and cavalry led by Princeton graduate and Salisbury resident William Davie, who placed twenty of his finest sharpshooters—armed with rifles rather than muskets—under the Mecklenburg County Courthouse (today site of the city's Bank of America tower), protected by a high stone wall, with two other companies of men posted behind houses and the garden gates of the village.

On the third attempt, Davie's men withdrew north to Salisbury and Cornwallis was able to briefly occupy Charlotte at a heavy cost of a dozen dead and forty-seven wounded. The incident gave the proud British general notice that taking North Carolina would not be as easy as some predicted, especially with Davie and his partisans constantly harassing British couriers and foraging parties. "Let's get out of here; this place is a damned hornet's nest," Cornwallis famously remarked following another major setback on his unprotected western flank.

A month later, on October 7, at Kings Mountain, nine hundred South Carolina militia (including one John Crockett, father of Davy) were joined by mounted elements of the Overmountain Men under the command of

William Campbell, and approached 1,100 loyalist troops under the command of highly competent Scottish officer Patrick Ferguson, who'd set up a strong defensive position on the narrow summit of the mountain. Firing from behind rocks and trees as they advanced, the Americans forced a desperate Ferguson to mount a disastrous bayonet counter charge in which most of his command, including the Scotsman himself, was killed (157) or wounded (163) or taken prisoner. Patriot losses amounted to just 28 killed and 68 wounded.

"Kings Mountain was a disaster for Cornwallis's invasion plan," writes Waters, "if not the British cause in North America." Wild rumors suddenly flew across the backcountry that the Overmountain Men were planning to march on a key outpost at Ninety Six and perhaps Camden itself, galvanizing South Carolina patriots as they went.

Instead, the Americans quickly retreated over the Broad River and melted back into the hills of the Carolina backcountry with many prisoners in tow.

In his official orders from Nathanael Greene on December 16, Daniel Morgan's "Flying Army" of roughly six hundred Delaware infantrymen, Virginia riflemen, and Continental dragoons under William Washington began harassing the movements of British troops across northern South Carolina, culminating in a devastating encounter on a western Piedmont plain where farmers traditionally tended and traded their cattle. It was called Cowpens. The date: January 17, 1781.

With the Broad River at his opponent's back, "Bloody Ban" Tarleton believed he'd finally cornered Morgan and his elusive "Flying Army," all but guaranteeing its destruction. The confident British officer mounted a full-frontal assault on Morgan's three defensive lines where sharpshooters were arranged behind forest trees, able to pick off the cream of Tarleton's officers. Following a misread command to retreat, Morgan ordered his men to halt, turn, and fire in unison, taking a further heavy toll on the charging British troops. The resurgent militia and simultaneous cavalry charge by William Washington's dragoons pulled off a rare "double envelopment" that prompted the British infantry to begin surrendering en masse. Though he fought valiantly, Tarleton and a handful of his officers reportedly fled the scene, leaving Cornwallis's own "mobile, light army" in ruins. The battle lasted barely an hour with British losses totaling about a hundred dead, two hundred wounded, and five hundred taken prisoner. Morgan lost only twelve and suffered sixty wounded. "The history of the American Revolution must pause at Cowpens," writes Waters, "for there a turning point was achieved."

Following the news of the dramatic patriot victory, Nathanael Greene began moving the remnants of his divided army north, the beginning of the famous Race to the Dan up the Great Wagon Road in which he hoped to get his inferior army safely across the Dan River into Virginia. An enraged Cornwallis ordered his own supply wagons burned and troops stripped of their heavy packs to improve his army's mobility in hopes of catching the brilliant architect who foiled his plan to conquer the South and win the war.

According to the colorful mythology sprung from Greene's brief encounter with Elizabeth Maxwell Steele at her tavern in Salisbury, the American general survived several close calls before he and his ragtag troops crossed rain-swollen rivers to safety in the nick of time.

With the end of my Great Road journey in sight, my boyhood adventure nearly complete, purely for sentimental reasons, I veer due west and spend a rainy morning and afternoon hiking the narrative trails at both Kings Mountain National Military Park and Cowpens Battlefield one last time, which lie just thirty-two miles apart off Interstate 85. Rangers at both parks inform me that visitor numbers are slightly up for the year, which they attribute to America's upcoming 250th anniversary within shouting distance. "What I also hear is that there is still a great deal of pent-up eagerness from Covid to get outside and see the country," a young Cowpens female ranger cheerfully shares. "We're starting to get a lot of family groups. I like to tell them this is one of the places where America won its freedom."

She isn't wrong. I hope the families keep coming.

My next stop is the Great Wagon Road Distilling Company on the east side of Charlotte, not far from the original path of the road through the frontier village where Colonel Davie's "Hornets" gave Lord Cornwallis such a bloody fit.

Two hundred and forty-six years later, I find my friend Ollie Mulligan about to open up for the evening.

Ollie's once-red beard has turned Santa Claus gray since we'd last met just weeks before I set off for Philadelphia in August 2017.

I'd dropped by to write about his award-winning distillery for the state's leading business magazine. Since opening in 2013, Mulligan's Rúa American Whiskey—the name in Gaelic means "red"—has claimed top honors at whiskey competitions from Los Angeles to London, including a recent "Best of the South" honor in the whiskey category of *Garden & Gun* magazine's annual competition. But personally, I was eager to find out what inspired Ollie to name his company the Great Wagon Road Distilling Company.

"When I was planning it, I did a lot of reading about this area and was inspired to learn about the Great Wagon Road that brought many thousands of European settlers through Charlotte and the region at large, including thousands of Scots-Irish settlers," he told me that day over one of the best old-fashioneds I've ever tasted. "Given my own position as an Irish immigrant who settled here, the name was perfect—especially when you consider that it was the Great Wagon Road that brought whiskey to America thanks to Scottish and Irish immigrants who'd been making it for centuries."

During that first meeting, Mulligan (naturally, I was very partial to his name) was intrigued to learn that I was preparing to set off along the road from Philadelphia to Georgia in a matter of days. "Oh, wonderful," he said with his booming Irish laugh. "Do me a favor. When you finish the trip, drop by for another old-fashioned and tell me what the adventure was like."

So here we sit, nearly six years later, an hour before the scheduled opening of his popular distillery's expanded new home in east Charlotte. The old-fashioned he makes me is as delicious as I remember, and I am happy to tell him a few of my favorite adventures along the Road That Made America. But as I soon learn, we've both been changed by our separate journeys down the road.

"Sometimes," he tells me, "I feel like those settlers you read about in Great Wagon Road lore who went through incredible hardship just to endure and survive."

He ticks off half a dozen ways his life has dramatically shifted since we last met. Following impressive opening years of success, the lease on his building ran out and his original partners bailed. "For a while, we were homeless and partnerless, and then Covid hit. Our sales went from three million before Covid to thirty-seven grand almost overnight. We eventually went from twenty-eight employees to two, then down to one—me."

Plans to open a new branch of the distillery in Waxhaws, the birthplace of Andrew Jackson, where Ollie and wife Lorraine purchased land and hoped to build a home, had to be put on hold.

To survive, he rented a warehouse in nearby Concord and began making hand sanitizer, donating 50 percent of it to local hospitals, law enforcement, and other public agencies. The rest he sold through a drive-up window that developed into a brisk business that "at least kept the lights on."

"In true American fashion, slowly but surely, we began lifting ourselves up by the bootstraps and rebuilding the company," he explains. When Covid finally eased its grip, there was no shortage of interested investors eager to be part of the Great Wagon Road distillery comeback story. He leased and later purchased a former brewery in east Charlotte and finished building his house. He also added several new lines of spirits, and even began planning a Wagon Road–themed bar called the Broken Spoke in a concourse at the Charlotte Airport. Business is once again booming.

"They say that anyone who ever makes it in America goes through hard times to get there," he sums up. "Like the settlers of the Great Wagon Road, we've been through a hell of a lot. But we've endured and survived and come back stronger. I think our name says it all."

We make an updated toast to the spirit of the Wagon Road, Ollie Mulligan's brilliant comeback, and the end of a very long journey for us both.

"Would you care for another old-fashioned?" asks his female bartender.

"Sure would," I say. "But I have to go to church."

Out of the blue a couple weeks before, a woman named Cathey Barringer got in touch to say she has a wonderful Great Wagon story to tell me, hoping I might meet her and two friends with similar stories at historic St. John's Church in Mount Pleasant.

In truth, I had not planned to stop there until I googled the church during my hike around Kings Mountain and discovered that it was founded by German Wagon Road settlers in 1745 and is believed to be the oldest Lutheran church in North Carolina, home to a large cemetery full of Wagon Road pioneers, Revolutionary War patriots, and Confederate soldiers.

By my rough count, I've filled up my smartphone's tape recorder function with more than 150 different voices and their stories along America's immigrant highway. So, what's one more for the road, I decide.

As I pull into the church's empty parking lot, I realize that I've been here before. It was on a steamy summer evening in August 1975 when I was twenty-two, the head groomsman at my college roommate Hugh Kluttz's wedding to Mary Goins, the daughter of St. John's head minister. It was a lavish dusk ceremony filled with flowers and lighted candles—the evening heat was so intense, the diminutive bridesmaid standing with me nearly buckled during the exchange of vows, hanging on to my arm for dear life.

"You'll be pleased to know we fully air conditioned the sanctuary several decades ago." Cathey Barringer greets me with a hug and hearty laugh after I reveal my déjà vu experience. She gestures for me to join the round table where she and her two companions, introduced as Deane Casper Moorehead and Ben Callahan, are sitting with various historic documents and open books.

"We all know Hugh Kluttz," Ben says. "He was a couple years ahead of us at Mount Pleasant High. There's lots of Kluttzes in these parts. That's because St. John's is the mother church of Lutheranism in the state. Just about every Wagon Road German name you can think of has roots right here."

"Here in the South, and especially in Cabarrus County," provides Cathey, "there are two things that are most important—your name and dirt."

By "dirt" she means the soil in which one's family roots and relatives are planted. "Growing up here it was always emphasized how important family history is, as much a part of me as my own skin and hair," she continues. "The older ones called this the 'Line' and said the Line must always be honored and protected and passed along to the next generation, something we all lived and breathed as life itself."

I learn that all three have plenty of local "dirt" in common.

Cathey Barringer is the eighth generation of Barringers, seven of which are buried in the St. John's cemetery, including John Paul Barringer—"Pioneer Paul," as she and the others call him—her fifth-great-grandfather, who helped found and fund the creation of St. John's Church not long after he arrived in the mid-1700s.

Deane Casper Moorehead, co-chair of the highly regarded St. John's Heritage Center, also grew up in the church and is rich in family dirt, a direct descendant of Caleb Phifer, a Swiss friend of Pioneer Paul who hailed from the same Palatine region and helped establish the church. A former public-school teacher for thirty-eight years, upon retirement Moorehead took on the monumental task of identifying thirty-five thousand graves across Cabarrus and neighboring Mecklenburg County. She is literally a walking expert on the historical dead and buried of the region.

Ben Callahan's ancestor John Callahan was a Scots-Irishman who came down the Wagon Road in the mid-1700s and settled in neighboring Rowan County, producing eleven children from two wives. Many of his Callahan ancestors continued the road to Tennessee and Mississippi. Ben grew up in Mount Pleasant, and earned a master's degree in history from the University of North Carolina at Chapel Hill before spending his public career serving as police chief of the town of Carrboro. Upon retirement, he came home to Mount Pleasant to research and write history books. His latest work is a comprehensive history of the first Lutheran college in the state, a few miles away in Mount Pleasant.

With all this sacred dirt, I wonder if the Great Wagon Road was known to them as children.

"Oh, *absolutely*," Cathey is first to answer. "As a young child I was told that the only reason I'm here was because Pioneer Paul and others like him were brave enough to cross an ocean as indentured servants, work off their debt, and follow the Wagon Road through the wilderness to North Carolina. That's how everyone got here, always part of any discussion with the older ones. I was told that I was simply part of the legacy of that road."

"No question about it," agrees Ben, who turns out to be an expert on the various colonial-era trading roads that crisscross this part of North Carolina. St. John's, he explains, happens to sit on a well-traveled spur off the Great Wagon Road that passes half a dozen miles to the west through the town of Concord. The spur that ran through Mount Pleasant, he explains, was an early colonial road that went to Charleston, along which both German and Scots-Irish farmers sent wagons loaded with produce to

Charleston's markets. A nearby road, in fact, is named Irish Potato Road, a direct link to its colonial provenance.

"If St. John's was the mother church of Lutheranism in this state," Ben says, "the Great Wagon Road was the mother of those old roads. Some will tell you it really built early America."

Which reminds him of a funny saying direct from colonial times.

"Do you know how America was created? The English built the houses, the Germans built the barns, and the Scots-Irish built the stills."

"You've perfectly summarized the Great Wagon Road," I say, complimenting him, writing it down for future reference.

"Of course," says Deane Moorehead. "Everyone here is essentially related to everyone else in some way or another, including Pioneer Paul."

She spins a fascinating story about how Cabarrus County got its unusual name, after being created out of neighboring Mecklenburg County in the 1790s. With the decision in the state legislature deadlocked between German Lutherans in the northeast and Scots-Irish Presbyterians in the southwest, her ancestors Caleb Phifer and John Paul Barringer privately offered to name the new county after the speaker of the North Carolina Assembly if he would break the tie and cast his vote their way.

"The speaker was named Stephen Cabarrus, a Frenchman who lived way down east in Eden. I don't know if he'd ever been this far west. But that's how Cabarrus County got its name. Pure politicking."

Finally, I ask to hear about Pioneer Paul, who sounds like the poster boy of Wagon Road settlers.

Johan Paulus Beringer—anglicized to John Paul Barringer—was one of eleven children who grew up on a family farm in Schwaigern, Germany, and set off from his native Rhineland for America to seek his fortune at age twenty-two in 1743, arriving at Philadelphia on the ship *Phoenix* on September 30 of that same year.

As was commonplace for many young German farmers fleeing their war-ravaged homeland, Barringer paid for his passage by becoming an indentured servant to a Bucks County family named Eisman. A year later, John Paul married Anna Eliza Eisman, "a strong, handsome pioneer woman—a good shot—who came to America at age 9 or 10," according to the family history. Sometime before joining the great migration down the Wagon Road, the Barringers produced two children and sent money home for his parents and younger brother and sister to join them for the move in North Carolina. His parents died at sea, but two of his brothers eventually joined the family in Carolina, as did three sisters, all settling in the area around Mount Pleasant.

Barringer, it turns out, was one of the first German pioneers to settle in a region dominated by the Scots-Irish, wealthy enough by that point to acquire hundreds of acres of land and welcome fellow German immigrants to join him. He also proposed and funded a Lutheran church to be built near Dutch Buffalo Creek. After his first wife died, he remarried a woman named Catherine Blackwelder who was half his age (fifty-two). They had ten more children.

Early in the Revolutionary War, being too old for active service, he turned down an officer's commission with the British Army and chose instead to stay home and quietly look after the affairs of his close-knit community as a captain of the Colonial militia. Near the end of the conflict, he and twenty other prominent citizens of the area, including his father-in-law, Caleb Blackwelder, were captured by loyalists and sent to a prison in Camden. Upon his release, Barringer rode home afflicted with smallpox but survived for many years thereafter and held several influential posts in newly established Cabarrus County. He died on January 1, 1807, and was buried in the cemetery of the church he helped establish.

As I'm leaving, Cathey quietly pulls me aside. "I read your book about taking your dad back to England when he was dying. I was so sad to read about your girlfriend Kristin Cress being murdered. What a terrible thing for two young people and their families."

I thank her for saying this and ask what made her think to say it. She hands me an old book that looks to be handmade. It turns out to be a vintage St. John's cookbook called the *Grange Range*. She points to the name of the cookbook's chairman: Jane Cress.

"I thought you might like this. The Cress family has a long history in this church. I wonder if Kristin's people originated here."

For a moment, I don't know what to say.

"I think you may be right. Her father's people were from Salisbury."

She smiles and gives me a hug. "Well, take that home to your wife. It's got some wonderful old German recipes in it."

After two hours with these lovely spiritual caretakers, who may be as close to their Wagon Road ancestors as anyone I've met on this odyssey, I drive home to Greensboro through the winter darkness, crossing the Trading Ford at Salisbury and passing Valentine Leonard's Pilgrim Church near Abbotts Creek, veering off to take a spur road of the original Wagon Road that Lord Cornwallis reportedly took to Old Salem to try and catch wily Nat Greene.

Under a nearly full moon that illuminates the rural contours of the winding road, I think about how a true pilgrimage is said to be one in which the traveler ultimately learns more about himself than the passing landscape.

Perhaps this is true. But for the time being, it's enough to think about some of the inspiring people and stories that give me hope for a nation where democracy is said to be hanging by a thread: an old Ben Franklin and a young Daniel Boone, the Susquehanna Muse, real Yorkers, the candlelight of Antietam, a Gettysburg living legend, an awakening at Belle Grove Plantation, Liberty Man, the passion of Adeela Al-Khalili, good old Cousin Steve, a Lost Confederate found, a snowy birthday in Staunton, and final road trips with Mully.

Without question, my life and appreciation of my country have both been enriched by the people and stories of the Great Wagon Road.

And then there is Kristin, my long-lost love, who has never been far from my thoughts over the years and decades. Somewhere in a historic graveyard on my journey, I wrote down an epitaph from a patriot's weathered gravestone that grabbed my heart. The line was from Exodus. "I am sending an angel ahead of you to guard you along the way and to bring you to the place I have prepared for you."

Perhaps because it's a beautiful winter night and the end of my pilgrimage is finally here, the thought occurs that maybe Kristin Cress has been the angel leading me down this long and winding road of my ancestors.

Crazy, I know. But she used to say that someday I would *have* to go find that old Wagon Road we heard about together on a freezing Easter night.

The older I get, the more I believe we're all following an angel somewhere.

EPITAPH

ON A CLEAR, CRISP EARLY SPRING MORNING, I PARK MY CAR NEAR MY brother's house in British Woods and walk the mile or so to the Guilford Courthouse National Military Park, following the route Cornwallis's troops took through a forest of beech and white oaks to the battlefield where the army of Nathanael Greene was lying in wait on March 15, 1781.

The last time I attended the annual reenactment that attracts hundreds of Rev War buffs from across the nation, I was a rookie reporter for the *Greensboro Daily News-Record*. The year was 1977, America's post-bicentennial year. I wrote a story about a family from Maryland that participated in the weekend reenactment, encamped with the 2nd Maryland Continental Regiment.

Not long afterward, unable to shake my sadness over Kristin's death, I quit my reporter's job and took off for France and Britain with my golf bag in tow, eager to roam till my money ran out, hoping to make it to St. Andrews where I could finally play the most famous golf course in the world.

Things did not go as planned. My golf bag got stolen on a train from France to England and I wound up in rainy St. Andrews out of money. After walking the Old Course in the rain, I called my dad, who sent me five hundred bucks to cover a hotel room and the flight home. I arrived home to find a surprise job offer waiting from the *Atlanta Journal-Constitution Sunday Magazine*. A few weeks later, I packed up my modest belongings, kissed my folks goodbye, and took off for Atlanta, eager to shake the dust of my hometown forever.

Funny how life works. Forty years later, those same feet and a plucky Yankee wife brought me home to Greensboro.

Which may explain why some voice in my head told me I needed to attend this year's reenactment, in part because it marks the resumption of the reenactment in the wake of Covid shutdowns. It also will serve as the final chapter of my Great Wagon Road adventure.

Before everything begins, I take a pleasant walk through both the British and American encampments at each end of the city lake, chatting with folks who live and breathe this sort of historical playacting. The most interesting fellows I meet are a father and son who alternate annually between performing as members of Britain's formidable Brigade of Guards and Virginia militia sharpshooters. Today they are both dressed in fringed buckskins. "Every year," says the father, a banker from Portsmouth, Virginia, "the Battle of Guilford Courthouse reminds me of how important our freedom is. It's also a lot of fun to see old friends who live for this sort of thing."

His son jokes that he prefers playing a British officer because he prefers the uniform. "The chicks love it," he quips. "Also, we won the battle."

I happen to know the reenactment's narrator of more than two decades, a dedicated participant of almost half a century named Jay Callaham, a retired communications executive and former army major who served as an adviser on the movie *The Patriot*. Today, as in recent years, Jay is performing the role of Lord Cornwallis.

"No one knows exactly how many troops were involved in the Battle of Guilford Courthouse, but the accepted number includes more than four thousand patriots and nineteen hundred men fighting for the Crown," Callaham tells me moments before the action begins. "Without question, they were the best troops of both armies, the most elite troops with the finest leaders. That's why the stakes and casualties were so high. This really was the Super Bowl of the Revolutionary War."

The battle lasted just over an hour.

Despite a nearly two-to-one advantage for the Americans, both sides fought gallantly. "I never saw such fighting since God made me," Cornwallis later wrote in his memoirs. "The Americans fought like demons."

The British, however, won the battle when Greene tactically gave up the field, providing a Pyrrhic victory to his rival Cornwallis, who lost nearly a quarter of his army and thirty of his officers. Greene's losses totaled 78 killed and 183 wounded.

Cornwallis marched his damaged army to Wilmington to await reinforcements via the British Navy, setting his sights on taking control of Virginia. When help arrived, swelling his army to better than seven thousand troops, he spent the following summer fighting skirmishes against Continental forces under the command of the Marquis de Lafayette before establishing a base on the Williamsburg Neck at Yorktown.

Skillfully trapped by a massive, combined force of better than sixteen thousand American and French troops on the Chesapeake Peninsula, with the British Navy stymied by the French fleet, Lord Cornwallis surrendered on October 17, 1781. The war for American independence was finally over.

With its ably choreographed pageantry, firing cannon, charging cavalries, and coordinated fife and drum movement of troops, the reenactment proves to be a true crowd-pleaser for several hundred spectators young and old who line the field of battle in folding chairs, creating the festive air of a hometown football game.

I even bump into some old high school buddies and an elderly gentleman who used to play golf with my late father. He's wearing a goofy tricornered hat and is eager to know if I "ever finished traveling the Old Wagon Trail."

"Yes, sir. I finished it before it finished me."

He finds this funny. "Anything surprise you on the trail, Jimmy?"

I could give him a lengthy exegesis on the surprising stories and wonderful people I met in my travels, a diverse collection of Americans who share a love affair with our ever-evolving national story.

Instead, I simply reply, "Yessir. All history is personal to someone."

"I like that," he says. "You sound like your daddy. You know, I was the youngest fella in his men's Sunday school class at First Lutheran for years. He was a great moderator, quite the wise character."

I nod and smile, thanking him. Opti was indeed a wise character.

As the reenactment ends and the large crowds begin to surge for the park's main exit road, I decide to take a shortcut to my car through an open gate that borders on a private lane of sprawling Forest Lawn Cemetery.

As I step into the lane, thinking how my Wagon Road pilgrimage was far more personal to me than I could ever have expected, I happen to look straight ahead and see something that makes my breath catch.

A large family stone monument that reads: "Cress."

Fifty feet into the cemetery, I find four Cress headstones nestled in the turf.

The fourth one belongs to Kristin Elizabeth, framed by a pair of peace symbols with an inscription that reads: "She gave to us and showed us how to give."

The epitaph is a line from a letter I wrote Kristin's mom, Alice, shortly after her daughter's funeral service, to explain why I failed to show up for the gravesite service that October day in 1973. I never even learned where she was buried.

Maybe the biggest surprise of all, I suddenly realize, is that the Great Wagon Road finally brought me here.

After a few minutes, I turn around and recross the lane to join the boisterous crowds and Rev War soldiers heading for the battleground exits. I pass a scarlet-coated British officer and a Continental soldier in blue sharing cold beers and a laugh as they stride down the hill together.

As I pass them, I hear familiar words in my head.

This world is not your home, child. There's a much better place waitin' for us all.

I think how good it is that, for the moment at least, we're both finally home.

And with that come the tears.

AFTER THE ROAD

THE STONE IN THE ROAD

AFTER TRAVELING THE GREAT WAGON ROAD FOR ALMOST SIX YEARS, THE LONE souvenir I brought home was a smooth granite rock about the size of my late Grandmother Taylor's biscuits. I found it in the middle of a long-abandoned sunken road running through a patch of woods behind a busy shopping center in suburban Winston-Salem. I spotted it as my companion Kyle Stimson described how the old road disappeared under generations of unchecked urban growth, but was still *here*, he insisted, if you knew exactly where to look.

Ironically, these were almost the identical words my dad used by the Haw River in 1966 when he told me about the Great Wagon Road of our ancestors.

With the journey almost over, that simple granite stone lying in the middle of the long-abandoned road struck me as the perfect souvenir from my travels.

So, I took it home and placed it on my writing desk.

It sits there today.

When I set out for Philadelphia in late summer 2017—the five hundredth anniversary of the Protestant Reformation—I had no clue what to expect from a journey I'd dreamed of making since age thirteen.

The old road, however, placed me in the company of more than a dozen of America's distinguished historians and more than eighty ordinary Americans whose love affairs with our national story and the Great Wagon Road were as rock-solid and enduring as that granite stone. Though only about a third of their voices wound up in my account of the journey, those who didn't make it onto the page will live forever in the memory and field notes of this grateful traveler.

Thanks to them, what began simply as the fulfilment of a boyhood ambition became something far more personal in nature: a pilgrimage in a quest of historical memory and identity that deepened my own understanding of how the past still shapes our lives today.

This book does not purport to be a definitive history of the Great Wagon Road, rather a portrait of the old road as seen through the eyes of the remarkable people keeping its rich legacy and stories alive. I call them the Flame-keepers of the Road That Made America.

I am forever indebted to many individuals and organizations who helped me tell their stories:

Walter Staib, City Tavern, Philadelphia
The Museum of Early Southern Decorative Arts
Robert Leath, former director of exhibits, Museum of Early Southern
   Decorative Arts
Tom Sears Jr., Old Salem architectural historian
Nick Powers, Museum of the Shenandoah Valley
Alexandra Kirtley, Philadelphia Museum of Art
Neil Ronk, historian, Christ Church, Philadelphia
Rick Bravo, Ben Franklin interpreter
Page Talbott, Franklin historian
Charles Rodenbough, Southern historian
Johanna Brown, chief curator and director of Collections, Research,
   and Archeology, Old Salem
Jeff and Beverley Evans, auctioneers and decorative arts experts
Rev. David Cox, historian and history professor
Gabor Boritt, Gettysburg historian and author
Thomas Ryan of LancasterHistory
Heritage Center Museum of Lancaster (PA)
Dr. Gary Freeze, Southern historian
Historic Salisbury Foundation
Dr. Francis Amos, Virginia historian

Rocktown History, Dayton (VA)

Jim Christ, Paoli Battlefield Preservation Fund

The Conestoga Historical Museum

Jack Brubaker, Lancaster (PA) historian

Mitch Sommers, Lancaster writer

Daniel Levitsky, Daniel Boone guide, colonial reenactor

Rick Gray, former Lancaster mayor

Mervin and Kathryn Lapp

Jim High, Lapp neighbor

James Campbell, National Watch and Clock Museum

Columbia (PA) Historic Preservation Society

Jim McClure, author and York County (PA) historian

York County (PA) History Center

Kessell Family Geneaology, Jeannie Harner Roswell

Linda Stanley, Franklin (VA) Historical Society

Keith Rocco, historical artist

Kristen Laise, Belle Grove Plantation

Wayne Sulfridge, Belle Grove docent

Adeela Al-Khalili, Josephine School Community Museum

Dee-Dee Liggins, Josephine School Community Museum

Ed Markel, Inn at Narrow Passage

Carol McBride Fuller, Piedmont Trails/Great Wagon Road Project

Sharon Murray, Antietam battlefield ambassador

Sarah Lee Barnes, Thomas Jefferson descendant

Andrew Phillips, Woodrow Wilson Presidential Library and Museum

Augusta County Historical Society

Cathryn Hankla, Hollins University professor emeritus, poet

Vernie Bolden, pastor, Fifth Avenue Presbyterian Church, Roanoke

Doug Orr, early American music historian

Dowell Lester, Road Scholar

Kyle Stimson, Road Scholar

Haw River Historical Museum

Greensboro (NC) History Museum

Rip Bernhardt, Greensboro history buff

Davie County Historical and Genealogical Society

Randell Jones, historian, Boone expert

Glenn McCorkle, Thyatira Presbyterian Church

Dan Morrill, Charlotte historian

Charlotte Museum of History

Jim and Mary Apple

Eric Elliott, Moravian Archives, Winston-Salem

Sid and Camilla Teague

Chris Garton, writer, Davidson County historian

Jim and Ann Williams, Mecklenburg Historical Association

Gladys Kerr, Museum of the Waxhaws

Thomas Hall, president, Museum of the Waxhaws

David Ward, Fort Mill, South Carolina Wagon Road historian

Bettis Rainsford, South Carolina historian

Craig Wagoner, friend and colonial artifact hunter

Steve Lynch, cousin and collector

Jay Callahan, historical reenactor

Cathey Barringer, St. John's Lutheran Church

Ben Callahan, St. John's Church

Deane Casper Moorehead, co-chair of the highly regarded St. John's
   Heritage Center

Ollie Mulligan, Great Wagon Road Distilling Company

Steve Lynch, George Washington Tate Museum

Roger Dodson, family historian

Earnest Shealy, Newberry Historical Museum

John Rhodes, Beech Island member

Jim and Mary Apple, collectors and Moravian experts

Bill Sherrill, brewer and GWR fellow traveler

Sandy Shelton/Ashely Angel, first readers

Joe Kelleher, first reader

Patrick McDaid, first reader

David Woronoff, newspaper publisher and advisor

Nancy Oakley, *O.Henry* magazine colleague

The editorial staffs of *O.Henry* magazine and *PineStraw Magazine*

Wendy Dodson, my wonderful wife, who lived every mile of the GWR
   with me

BIBLIOGRAPHY AND FURTHER READING

Alexander, Ted. *The Battle of Antietam: The Bloodiest Day* (Charleston, SC: The History Press, 2011).

The Articles of Confederation (Bedford, MA: Applewood Books, 2006).

Babits, Lawrence E. *The Southern Campaigns of the American Revolution*. American History Series (Fort Washington, PA: Eastern National Publisher, 2002).

Babits, Lawrence E., and Joshua B. Howard. *Long, Obstinate, and Bloody: The Battle of Guilford Courthouse* (Chapel Hill: University of North Carolina Press, 2009).

Baker, Jean. *James Buchanan* (New York: Times Books, 2004).

Bartenstein, Fred, ed. *Roots Music in America: Collected Writings of Joe Wilson* (Knoxville: University of Tennessee Press, 2017).

Bearss, Edwin C. *Fields of Honor: Pivotal Battles of the Civil War* (Washington, DC: National Geographic, 2006).

Berg, A. Scott. *Wilson* (New York: Random House, 2013).

Billington, Ray Allen. *Westward Expansion: A History of the American Frontier* (New York: Macmillan Publishing, 1974).

Birkner, Michael J., Randall M. Miller, and John W. Quist. *The Worlds of James Buchanan and Thaddeus Stevens* (Baton Rouge: LSU Press, 2019).

Blight, David W. *Race and Reunion: The Civil War in American Memory* (Cambridge, MA: Belknap Press, 2001).

Boritt, Gabor. *The Gettysburg Gospel: The Lincoln Speech That Nobody Knows* (New York: Simon & Schuster/Lincoln Library, 2006).

Borneman, Walter R. *The French and Indian War: Deciding the Fate of North America* (New York: HarperCollins, 2006).

Boulard, Garry. *The Worst President: The Story of James Buchanan* (Bloomington, IN: iUniverse, 2015).

Brands, H. W. *Andrew Jackson: His Life and Times* (New York: Anchor Books, 2006).

———. *Woodrow Wilson* (New York: Times Books, 2003).

Brubaker, Jack. *Massacre of the Conestogas: On the Trail of the Paxton Boys in Lancaster County* (Charleston, SC: The History Press, 2010).

Byrd, William, and William K. Boyd. *William Byrd's Histories of the Dividing Line betwixt Virginia and North Carolina* (New York: Dover Publications, Inc., 1967).

Cheever, Susan. *Drinking in America: Our Secret History* (New York: Hachette Book Group, 2015).

Cooper, John Milton, Jr. *Woodrow Wilson: A Biography* (New York: Alfred Knopf, 2009).

Cox, R. David, Rev. *Lee Chapel at 150: A History* (Buena Vista, CA: Mariner Publishing, 2018).

———. *The Religious Life of Robert E. Lee* (Grand Rapids, MI: Wm. B. Eerdmans Publishing Co., 2017).

Cozzens, Peter. *Shenandoah 1862: Stonewall Jackson's Valley Campaign* (Chapel Hill: University of North Carolina Press, 2008).

Crews, C. Daniel. *My Name Shall Be There: The Founding of Salem* (Winston-Salem, NC: Moravian Archives, 1995).

Dabney, Virginius. *Virginia: The New Dominion; A History from 1607 to the Present* (New York: Doubleday & Company, 1971).

Diffenderffer, Frank. *The German Immigration into Pennsylvania Through the Port of Philadelphia, 1700 to 1775.* Reprint (London, England: Forgotten Books, 2015).

Dotson, Rand. *Roanoke, Virginia 1882–1912: Magic City of the New South* (Knoxville: University of Tennessee Press, 2017).

Edgar, Walter. *South Carolina: A History* (Columbia: University of South Carolina, 1998).

Elli, Joseph J. *American Sphinx: The Character of Thomas Jefferson* (New York: Vintage Books, 1998).

———. *Founding Brothers: The Revolutionary Generation* (New York: Alfred A. Knopf, 2001).

———. *His Excellency George Washington* (New York: Random House, 2004).

Fischer, David Hackett. *Albion's Seed* (New York: Oxford University Press, 1989).

Fogleman, Aaron Spencer. *Hopeful Journeys: German Immigration, Settlement, and Political Culture in Colonial America 1717–1775* (Philadelphia: University of Pennsylvania Press, 1996).

Foster, Genevieve. *The World of William Penn* (Atascadero, CA: Beautiful Feet Books, 1973).

Goodheart, Adam. *1861: The Civil War Awakening* (New York: Alfred A. Knopf, 2011).

Gordon, John W. *South Carolina and the American Revolution: A Battlefield History* (Columbia: University of South Carolina, 2003).

Greenberg, Amy S. *Lady First: The World of First Lady Sarah Polk* (New York: Alfred A. Knopf, 2019).

Hamel, Beverly. *Bethania: The Village by the Black Walnut Bottom* (Charleston, SC: The History Press, 2009).

Hampton, Bob, and George Schember, eds. *Walking in the Footsteps of General Daniel Morgan* (Winchester, VA: Winchester-Frederick County Historical Society, 2016).

Hannah-Jones, Nikole, Caitlin Roper, Ilena Silverman, and Jake Silverman, eds. *The 1619 Project: A New Origin Story* (New York: The New York Times, 2021).

Hoefling, Larry J. *Scots and Scotch Irish: Frontier Life in North Carolina, Virginia, and Kentucky* (Riverside, CA: Inlandia Press, 2009).

Hofstra, Warren R. *The Planting of New Virginia: Settlement and Landscape in the Shenandoah Valley* (Baltimore, MD: The Johns Hopkins University Press, 2004).

Hofstra, Warren R., ed. *Sweet Dreams: The World of Patsy Cline* (Champagne: University of Illinois Press, 2013).

Hofstra, Warren R., and Karl Raitz, eds. *The Great Valley Road of Virginia* (Charlottesville: University of Virginia Press, 2010).

Holsworth, Jerry. *Civil War Winchester* (Charleston, SC: The History Press, 2011).

Isaacson, Walter. *Benjamin Franklin: An American Life* (New York: Simon & Schuster, 2003).

Jonas, W. Glenn, Jr., ed. *Religious Traditions of North Carolina: History, Tenets and Leaders* (Jefferson, NC: McFarland & Company/The North Caroliniana Society, 2018).

Jones, Randell. *Before They Were Heroes at King's Mountain* (Winston-Salem, NC: Daniel Boone Footsteps, 2011).

Kanefield, Teri. *The Extraordinary Suzy Wright: A Colonial Woman on the Frontier* (New York: Abrams Books for Young Readers, 2016).

Katcher, Philip. *The Civil War: Day by Day* (New York: Chartwell Books, 2017).

Kenny, Kevin. *Peaceable Kingdom Lost: The Paxton Boys and the Destruction of William Penn's Holy Experiment* (New York: Oxford University Press, 2009).

Kidd, Thomas S. *The Great Awakening: The Roots of Evangelical Christianity in Colonial America* (New Haven, CT: Yale University Press, 2007).

Klein, Phillip S., and Ari Hoogenboom. *A History of Pennsylvania* (New York: McGraw Hill, 1973).

Leonard, Jacob Calvin, DD, Rev. *Centennial History of Davidson County, North Carolina* (Morgantown, PA: Higginson Book Company, 1927).

Lepore, Jill. *The Story of America: Essays on Origins* (Princeton: Princeton University Press, 2012).

Lester, Darrell. *Season in Stokes: A Proud Look Back* (Madison, NC: Twin Rivers Publishing Company, 1984).

Leyburn, James G. *The Scotch-Irish: A Social History* (Chapel Hill: University of North Carolina Press, 1962).

Lindsay, Debra J. *Maria Martin's World: Art and Science, Faith and Family in Audubon's America* (Tuscaloosa: University of Alabama Press, 2018).

McClure, James. *Nine Months in York Town: American Revolutionaries Labor on Pennsylvania's Frontier* (York, PA: York Daily Record, 2001).

McCrary, John Raymond, Sr. *Thoughts About Things I Love* (Cleveland: Central Publishing House, 1941).

McGuire, Thomas J. *Battle of Paoli* (Mechanicsburg, PA: Stackpole Books, 2000).

McPherson, James M. *Antietam: Crossroads of Freedom; The Battle That Changed the Course of the Civil War* (Oxford, UK: Oxford University Press, 2002).

———. *Hallowed Ground: A Walk at Gettysburg* (San Francisco: Crestline Books, 2017).

Meacham, Jon. *American Gospel: God, the Founding Fathers, and the Making of a Nation* (New York: Random House, 2006).

———. *American Lion: Andrew Jackson in the White House* (New York: Random House, 2008).

Merry, Robert W. *A Country of Vast Designs: James K. Polk, the Mexican War, and the Conquest of the American Continent* (New York: Simon & Schuster, 2009).

Meyer, Duane. *The Highland Scots of North Carolina, 1732–1776* (Chapel Hill: University of North Carolina Press, 1961).

Mingus, Scott L., Sr., and James McClure. *Civil War Stories from York County, Pa.* (York, PA: Scott Mingus Enterprises, 2020).

Mitchell, Sarah E. *Men's Clothing 1760–1785* (Chatham, VA: Mitchells Publications, 2012).

Mobley, Joe A., ed. *The Way We Lived in North Carolina* (Chapel Hill: University of North Carolina Press, 2003).

Morgan, Robert. *Boone: A Biography* (Chapel Hill, NC: Algonquin Books of Chapel Hill, 2007).

Murphy, Andrew R. *William Penn: A Life* (New York: Oxford University Press, 2019).

Neese, James Everette, Rev. *The Dutch Settlement on Abbotts Creek: A History of Pilgrim Reformed United Church of Christ* (Booneville, NC: Heritage Press, 1979).

Niven, Penelope, and Cornelia Wright. *Old Salem: The Official Guidebook* (Winston-Salem, NC: Old Salem Museums & Gardens, 2000).

Noyalas, Jonathan A. *The Battle of Cedar Creek: Victory from the Jaws of Defeat* (Charleston, SC: The History Press, 2009).

Osborn, William M. *The Wild Frontier* (New York: Random House, 2000).

Pawlak, Kevin R. *Shepherdstown in the Civil War: One Vast Confederate Hospital* (Charleston, SC: The History Press, 2015).

Piedmont, Donlan. *Peanut Soup and Spoonbread: An Informal History of the Hotel Roanoke* (Blacksburg: Virginia Tech Real Estate Foundation, 1994).

Quarles, Garland R. *George Washington and Winchester, Virginia, 1748–1758* (Winchester, VA: Winchester-Frederick County Historical Society, 2016).

Ritchie, Fiona, and Doug Orr, eds. *Wayfaring Strangers* (Chapel Hill: University of North Carolina Press, 2014).

Roeber, A. G. *Palatines, Liberty, and Property: German Lutherans in Colonial British America* (Baltimore, MD: Johns Hopkins University Press, 1993).

Rouse, Parke, Jr. *Planters and Pioneers: Life in Colonial Virginia* (New York: Hastings House Publishers, 1968).

———. *The Great Wagon Road: From Philadelphia to the South* (Petersburg, VA: Dietz Press, 1995).

Schaefer, Elizabeth Meg. *Wright's Ferry Mansion: The House* (Columbia, PA: The Von Hess Foundation, 2005).

Schlesinger, Arthur M., Jr. *The Age of Jackson* (New York: New American Library, 1945).

Schuyler, David. *A City Transformed: Redevelopment, Race, and Suburbanization in Lancaster, Pennsylvania, 1940–1980* (University Park: Pennsylvania State University Press, 2002).

Stimson, R. Kyle. *The Great Philadelphia Wagon Road in Forsyth County, N.C.: 1750–1770* (Forsyth County, NC: R.K. Stimson, 1999).

Sutton, J. E. *A History of the Moravian Church* (Charleston, SC: BiblioBazaar, 2006).

Trussell, John B. B., Jr. *William Penn: Architect of a Nation* (Harrisburg: Pennsylvania Historical and Museum Commission, 1990).

Turner, Frederick Jackson. *The Frontier in American History* (Tucson: University of Arizona Press, 1986).

Turner, Herbert Snipes, DD. *Church in the Old Fields: Hawfields Presbyterian Church and Community in North Carolina, 1738–1960* (Chapel Hill: University of North Carolina Press, 1962).

Vanderburg, Timothy W. *Cannon Mills and Kannapolis: Persistent Paternalism in a Textile Town* (Knoxville: University of Tennessee Press, 2013).

Walbert, David. *Garden Spot: Lancaster County, the Old Order Amish, and the Selling of Rural America* (Oxford, UK: Oxford University Press, 2002).

Warren, Robert Penn. *John Brown: The Making of a Martyr* (Nashville, TN: J. S. Sanders Books, 1993).

Waters, Andrew. *The Quaker and the Gamecock* (Havertown, PA: Casemate, 2019).

———. *To the End of the World: Nathanael Greene, Charles Cornwallis, and the Race to the Dan* (Yardley, PA: Westholme Publishing, 2023).

Waugh, John C. *The Class of 1846: From West Point to Appomattox* (New York: Warner Books, 1994).

Webb, Jim. *Born Fighting: How the Scots-Irish Shaped America* (New York: Broadway Books, 2004).

Weidensaul, Scott. *The First Frontier: The Forgotten History of Struggle, Savagery, and Endurance in Early America* (Boston, MA: Houghton Mifflin Harcourt, 2012).

Wilentz, Sean. *Andrew Jackson* (New York: Times Books, 2005).

Wineapple, Brenda. *The Impeachers: The Trial of Andrew Johnson and the Dream of a Just Nation* (New York: Random House, 2019).

Wittenberg, Eric J., and Scott L. Mingus Sr. *The Second Battle of Winchester: The Confederate Victory That Opened the Door to Gettysburg* (El Dorado Hills, CA: Savis Beatie LLC, 2016).

Woodmansee, Lee. *You Can Tell You're a Yorker If . . .* (Manasquan, NJ: Winemiller Press, 1997).

ABOUT THE AUTHOR

JAMES DODSON is the author of sixteen books, including *Final Rounds*, *A Golfer's Life* (with Arnold Palmer), *Ben Hogan: An American Life*, *American Triumvirate*, and *The Range Bucket List*. His work has appeared in more than fifty magazines and newspapers worldwide. He is a two-time winner of the United States Golf Association's Herbert Warren Wind Award for best golf book of the year. In 2011, Dodson was selected for membership in the Order of the Long Leaf Pine by the governor of North Carolina, a prestigious award for exemplary service to the state. He is the founding editor of *O.Henry* magazine. He lives with his wife in North Carolina.